Complete Canadian Curriculum

MATH

ENGLISH

SOCIAL STUDIES

SCIENCE

Grade 4

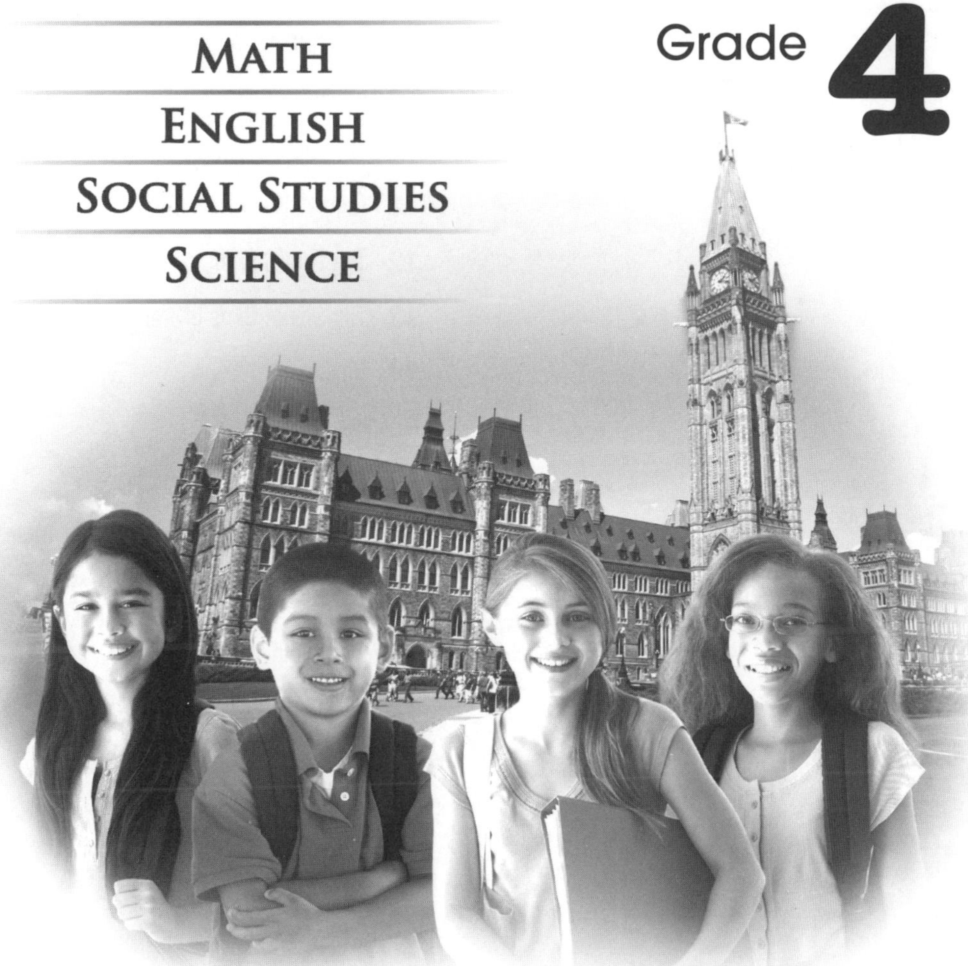

Printed in China

ISBN: 978-1-897164-32-7

Contents Grade 4

Mathematics

English

ISBN: 978-1-897164-32-7

Social Studies

Science

Answers

ISBN: 978-1-897164-32-7

ISBN: 978-1-897164-32-7

ISBN: 978-1-897164-32-7

1

Numbers to 10 000

- Write, compare, and order whole numbers to 10 000.
- Identify the value of a digit in a 4-digit number.
- Round 4-digit numbers.

Count and write the numbers. Then write the 4-digit number on the sign.

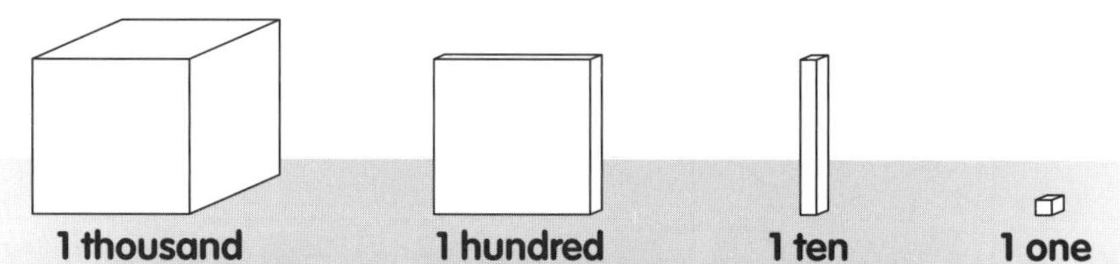

①

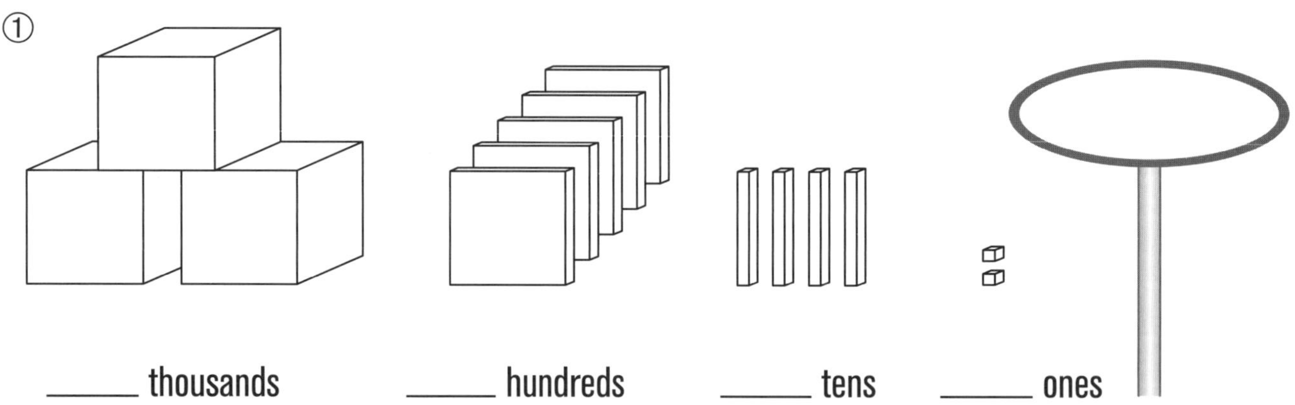

_____ thousands _____ hundreds _____ tens _____ ones

②

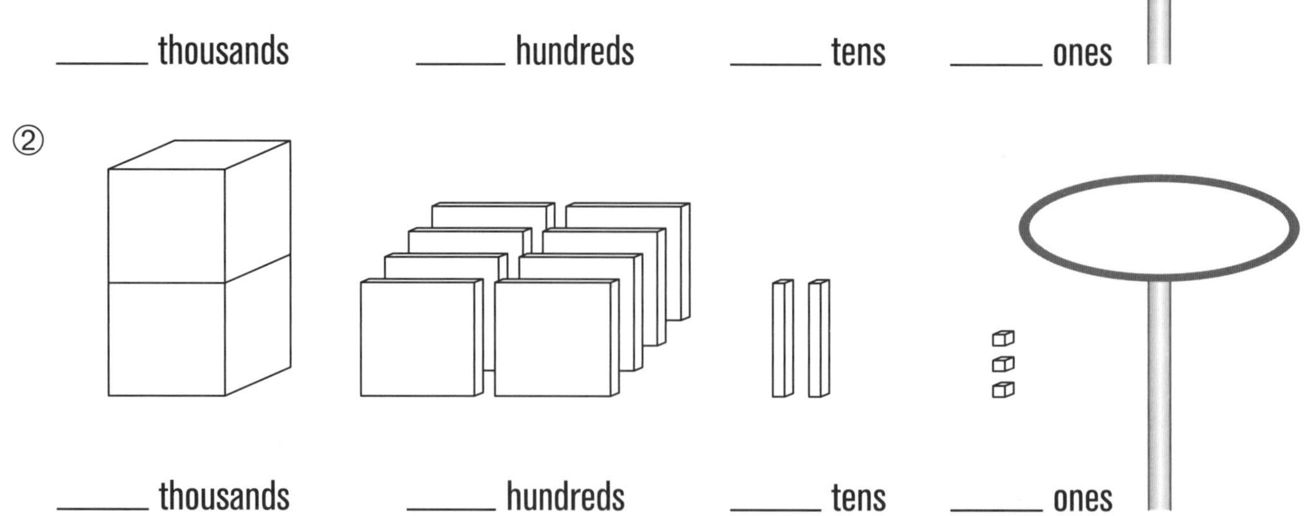

_____ thousands _____ hundreds _____ tens _____ ones

ISBN: 978-1-897164-32-7

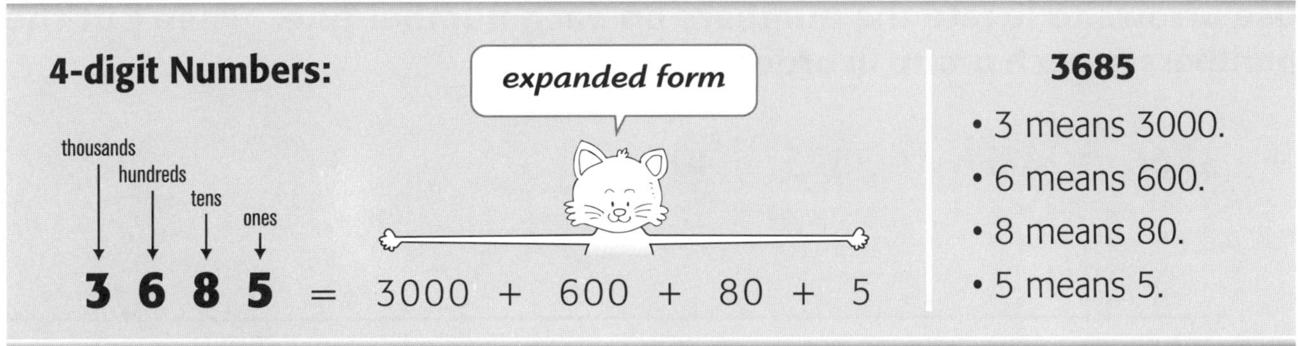

4-digit Numbers:
expanded form
thousands
hundreds
tens
ones
3 6 8 5 = 3000 + 600 + 80 + 5
3685
• 3 means 3000.
• 6 means 600.
• 8 means 80.
• 5 means 5.

Fill in the missing numbers.

③ 3257 = 3 thousands _____ hundreds _____ tens _____ ones

④ 9064 = _____ thousands _____ tens _____ ones

⑤ _________ = 7 thousands 2 hundreds 6 tens

⑥ _________ = 6 thousands 8 tens 4 ones

⑦ 5816 = 5000 + _____ + 10 + _____

⑧ 3649 = _____ + 600 + _____ + 9

Use the given digits in each group to form the greatest 4-digit number, the least 4-digit number, and one 4-digit number that is in between.

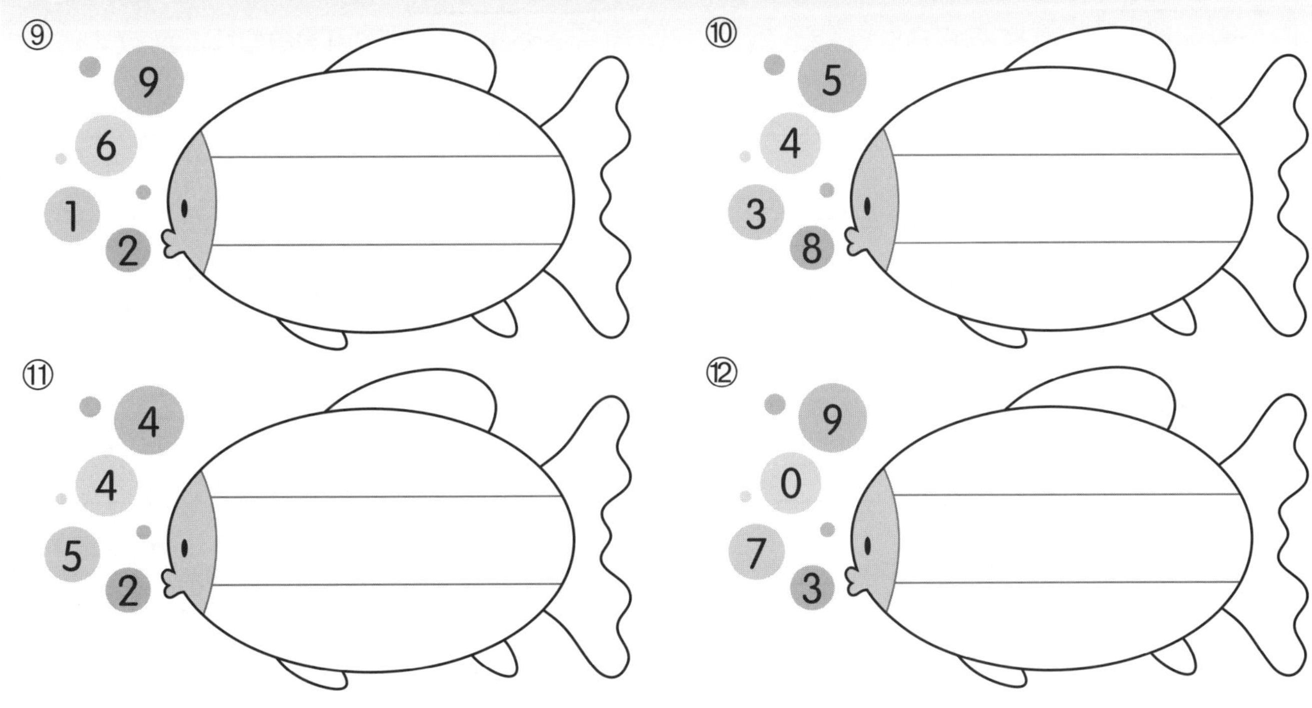

ISBN: 978-1-897164-32-7

Use arrows to locate the numbers on each number line. Then put the numbers in each group in order.

⑬ **3766 4276 3825 4063**

3766

3000 4000 5000

From greatest to least: ______________________

⑭ **5161 5611 5116 6511 6151**

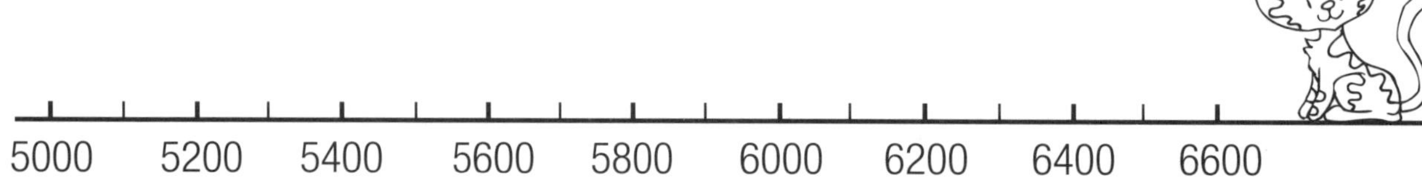

From least to greatest: ______________________

Write the meaning of each digit.

⑮ **7563**

7 means ________ .

5 means ________ .

6 means ________ .

3 means ________ .

⑯ **6914**

6 means ________ .

9 means ________ .

1 means ________ .

4 means ________ .

⑰ **2485**

2 means ________ .

4 means ________ .

8 means ________ .

5 means ________ .

⑱ **3879**

3 means ________ .

8 means ________ .

7 means ________ .

9 means ________ .

ISBN: 978-1-897164-32-7

Round 3547 to the nearest

ten.	hundred.	thousand.
3547 ← 7 > 5, round up	3547 ← 4 < 5, round down	3547 ← 5, round up
3550	**3500**	**4000**

Round the numbers.

Round to the nearest

		ten	hundred	thousand
⑲	6527	______	______	______
⑳	3865	______	______	______
㉑	4129	______	______	______
㉒	9476	______	______	______
㉓	5031	______	______	______
㉔	7750	______	______	______

Write the numbers.

㉕ 

Four hundred sixty-five dollars

$ ______

㉖ 

Seven hundred ninety dollars

$ ______

㉗

Six hundred fifty pieces

______ pieces

㉘

My score is ______ .

Ted

Ted's score:
2000 more than 3267

ISBN: 978-1-897164-32-7

Addition and Subtraction of 3-Digit Numbers

- Add or subtract 3-digit numbers.
- Estimate and check the answers.
- Solve word problems.

Mom, I'll buy this outfit for you once I've saved up $204.

Do the addition.

① $\begin{array}{r} 384 \\ +\ 165 \\ \hline \end{array}$

② $\begin{array}{r} 279 \\ +\ \ 62 \\ \hline \end{array}$

③ $\begin{array}{r} 147 \\ +\ 258 \\ \hline \end{array}$

④ $\begin{array}{r} 324 \\ +\ 181 \\ \hline \end{array}$

⑤ $\begin{array}{r} 504 \\ +\ 176 \\ \hline \end{array}$

⑥ 79 + 254 = ____________

⑦ 317 + 317 = ____________

⑧ 243 + 188 = ____________

⑨ 555 + 46 = ____________

Round each number to the nearest hundred. Do the estimate. Then find the exact answer.

⑩ $\begin{array}{r} 305 \\ +\ 286 \\ \hline \end{array}$

Estimate

⑪ 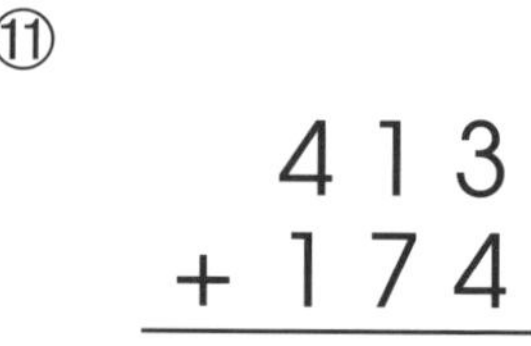

$\begin{array}{r} 413 \\ +\ 174 \\ \hline \end{array}$

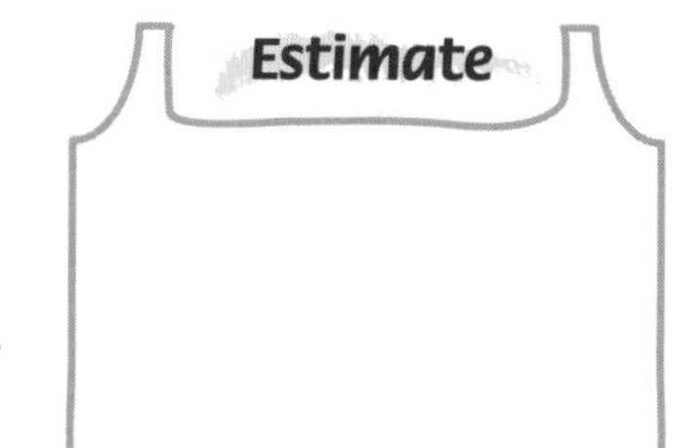

⑫ 225 + 166 = ____________ **Estimate** ____________

⑬ 568 + 125 = ____________ **Estimate** ____________

ISBN: 978-1-897164-32-7

Do the subtraction. The answers shows the popsicle sticks the children have collected for the Art class. Then answer the questions.

⑭

Tim

$$\begin{array}{r} 273 \\ -\ 109 \\ \hline \end{array}$$

Elaine

$$\begin{array}{r} 345 \\ -\ 216 \\ \hline \end{array}$$

Adam

$$\begin{array}{r} 410 \\ -\ 277 \\ \hline \end{array}$$

Tiffany

$$\begin{array}{r} 600 \\ -\ 371 \\ \hline \end{array}$$

Gary

$$\begin{array}{r} 405 \\ -\ 135 \\ \hline \end{array}$$

David

$$\begin{array}{r} 764 \\ -\ 298 \\ \hline \end{array}$$

Louis

514 – 333 = ______

Nancy

653 – 446 = ______

Gloria

822 – 567 = ______

Sam

914 – 481 = ______

⑮ Who collected the most? ______

⑯ Who collected the fewest? ______

⑰ Who collected 100 more sticks than Elaine? ______

⑱ Who collected 300 fewer sticks than Sam? ______

⑲ What is the difference between the number of sticks collected by David and Gary? ______ sticks

ISBN: 978-1-897164-32-7

Round each number to the nearest ten to do the estimate. Then find the exact answer.

⑳

365
− 134

Estimate

㉑

437
− 254

Estimate

㉒

147
+ 362

Estimate

㉓

314
+ 289

Estimate

Check the answer to each question. Put a check mark in the space provided if the answer is correct; otherwise, put a cross and find the correct answer.

㉔

A 452 − 183 = 269

B 713 − 467 = 256

C 804 − 379 = 525

D 685 − 296 = 289

E 300 − 166 = 143

F 584 − 376 = 208

Check

A

269
+ 183

B

C

D

E

F

ISBN: 978-1-897164-32-7

Mr. Rice works in a fitness centre. He recorded the number of people attending the yoga classes in the past three months. Help him complete the table and answer the questions.

㉕

Month	January	February	March
No. of Men	389	225	
No. of Women	463		486
Total		673	704

㉖ How many men attended the yoga classes from January to March?

____________ = ______ ______ men

㉗ How many women attended the yoga classes in January and February?

____________ = ______ ______ women

㉘ How many more women attended the classes in January than in February?

____________ = ______ ______ more

㉙ How many fewer men attended the classes in February than in January?

____________ = ______

______ fewer

㉚ *Mom, the regular price of this yoga outfit is $204. It is on sale now. The price cut is $29. Do you know how much it costs now?*

____________ = ______

$ ______

ISBN: 978-1-897164-32-7

3

Addition of 4-Digit Numbers

- Add 4-digit numbers with or without grouping.
- Use different methods to find answers in a faster way.
- Solve word problems.

There are 2462 spectators watching me.

Do the addition.

① $2561 + 4108$

② $3793 + 204$

③ $4412 + 3074$

④ $1859 + 2016$

⑤ $475 + 3141$

⑥ $3881 + 4914$

⑦ 3474 + 1135 = ________

⑧ 2463 + 4185 = ________

⑨ 749 + 1320 = ________

⑩ 3668 + 331 = ________

Find the total number of jellybeans in each pair.

⑪ 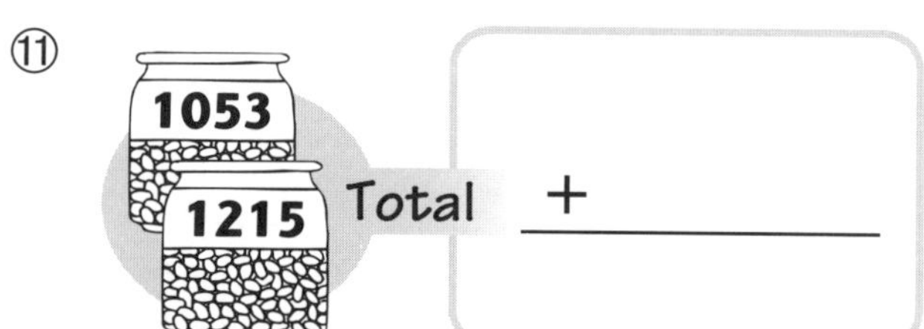

+ ________

⑫ 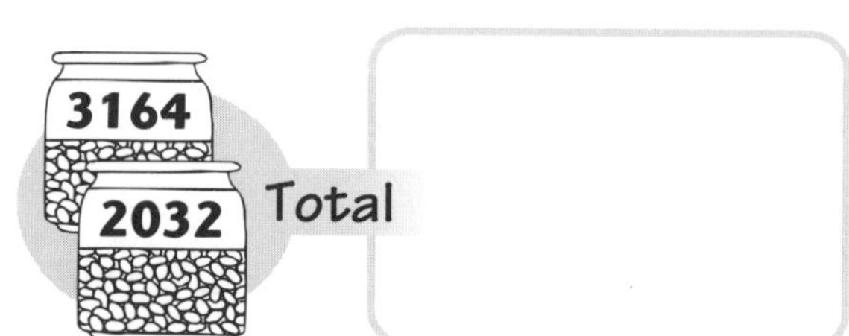

⑬ 

⑭ 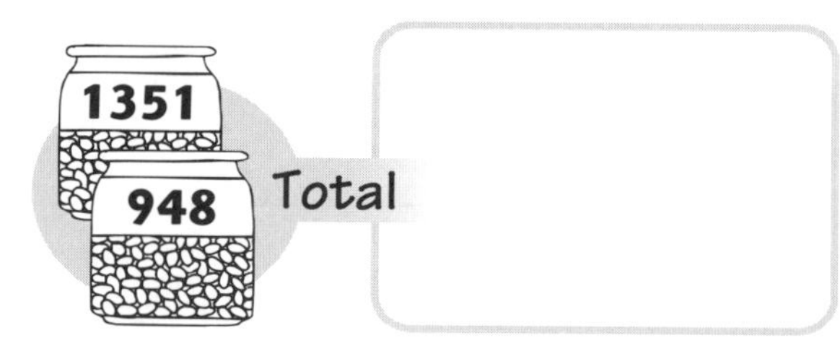

ISBN: 978-1-897164-32-7

Do the addition. The answers show the clothing produced by a factory last year. Then answer the questions.

⑮

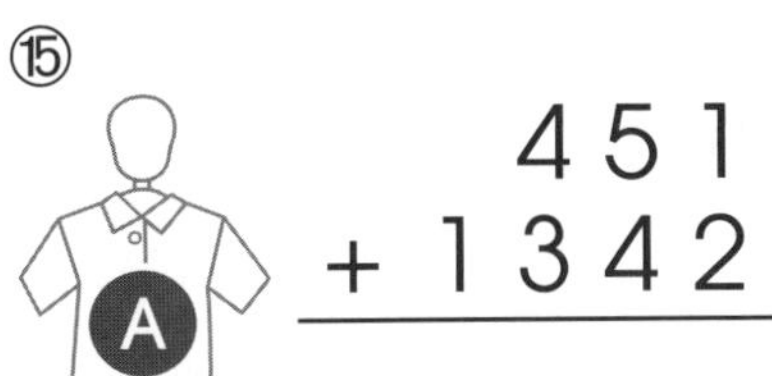

A: 451 + 1342 = ______

B: 1016 + 147 = ______

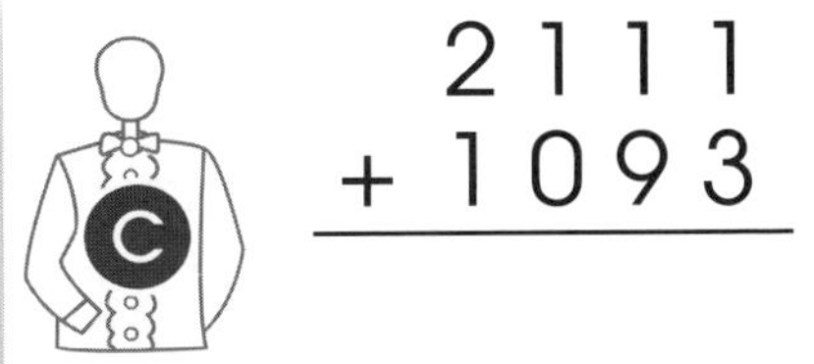

C: 2111 + 1093 = ______

D: 866 + 213 = ______

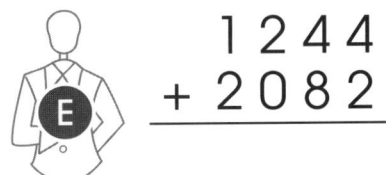

E: 1244 + 2082 = ______

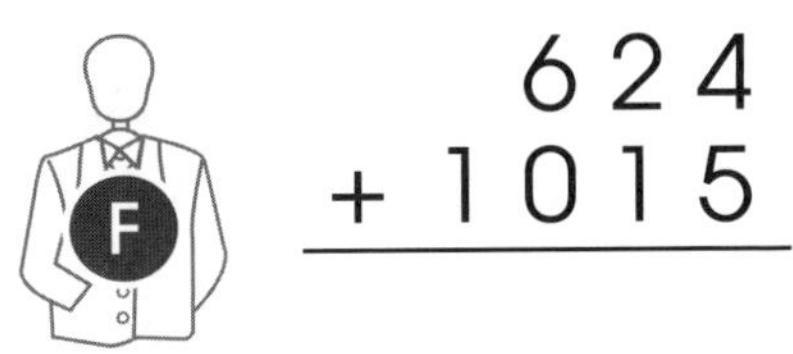

F: 624 + 1015 = ______

G: 1142 + 2364 = ______

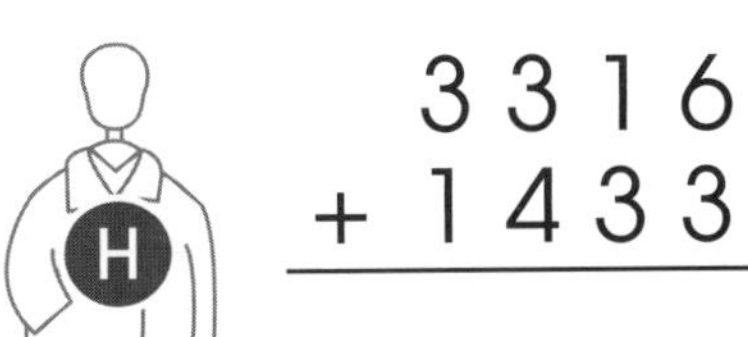

H: 3316 + 1433 = ______

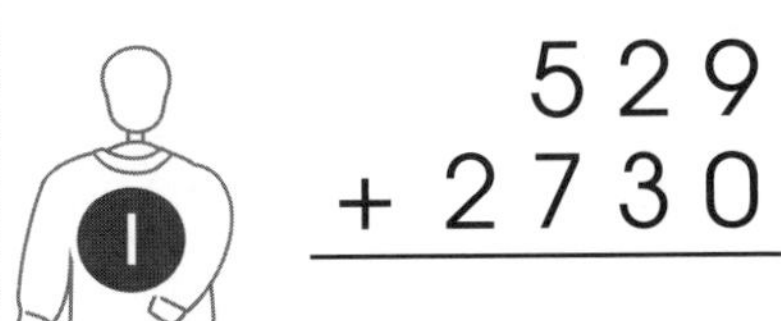

I: 529 + 2730 = ______

⑯ How many pieces of A and B were produced in all?

______ pieces

⑰ If the number of leather jackets produced was 402 more than that of D, how many leather jackets were produced?

______ leather jackets

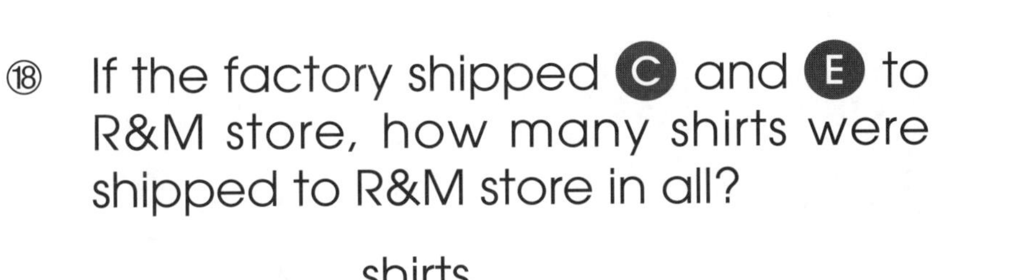

⑱ If the factory shipped C and E to R&M store, how many shirts were shipped to R&M store in all?

______ shirts

ISBN: 978-1-897164-32-7

e.g. 4217 + 1914 = 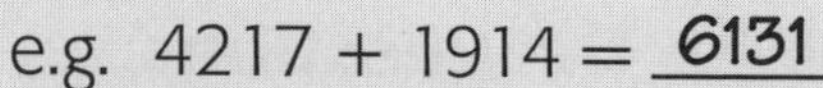 6131

1st Add the digits in each place separately.

5000 + 1100 + 20 + 11

2nd Regroup.

6000 + 100 + 30 + 1

Use the above method to do the addition. Then use vertical addition to find the answer again.

⑲ 3529 + 1346 = ______

1st 4000 + ______________________

2nd ______________________

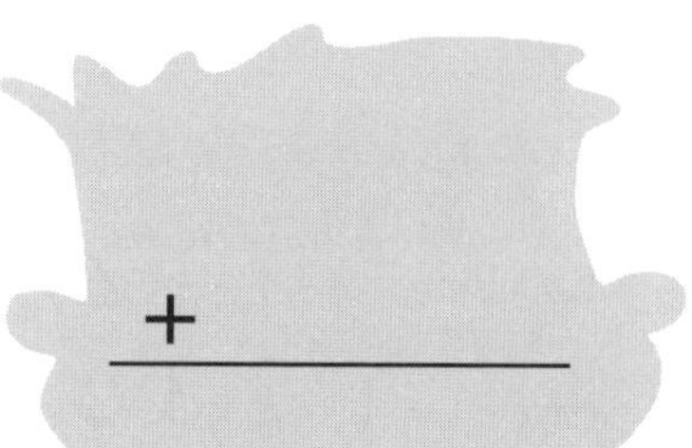

⑳ 4714 + 1637 = ______

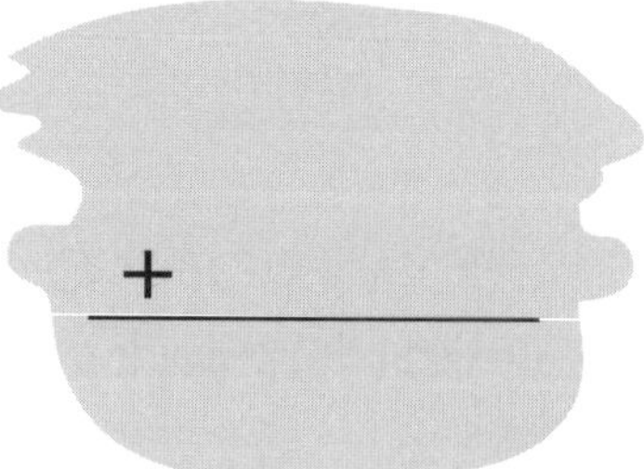

㉑ 3588 + 4091 = ______

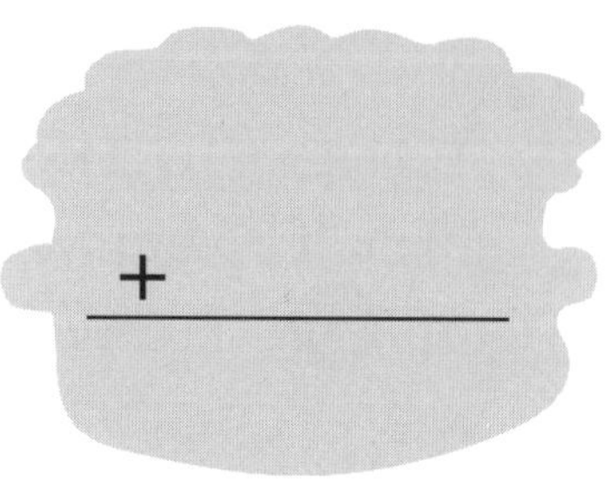

Find the missing numbers.

㉒
```
    3 _ 6 _
  + _ 5 8 2
  ---------
    6 0 4 7
```

㉓
```
    _ 3 3 _
  + 1 7 _ 4
  ---------
    4 0 5 0
```

㉔
```
    1 _ 7 3
  + _ 5 _ 9
  ---------
    4 1 9 2
```


ISBN: 978-1-897164-32-7

Sometimes we can write a number in a different way which helps us find the answer faster.

e.g. 3992 + 1629 = 5621

Rewrite: 1629 = 8 + 1621

3992 + 8 + 1621
= 4000 + 1621
= 5621

Use the above method to rewrite one of the numbers. Then find the answer.

㉕ 1995 + 1628 = ________

Rewrite 1628 = ____ + 1623

㉖ 4998 + 3774 = ________

Rewrite

㉗ 3996 + 2577 = ________

Rewrite

㉘ 1425 + 1994 = ________

Rewrite

㉙ 4836 + 2995 = ________

Rewrite

㉚ 7058 + 993 = ________

Rewrite

Solve the problems.

㉛ Shawn puts his baseball cards into two boxes. If each box holds 1586 baseball cards, how many baseball cards does Shawn have in all?

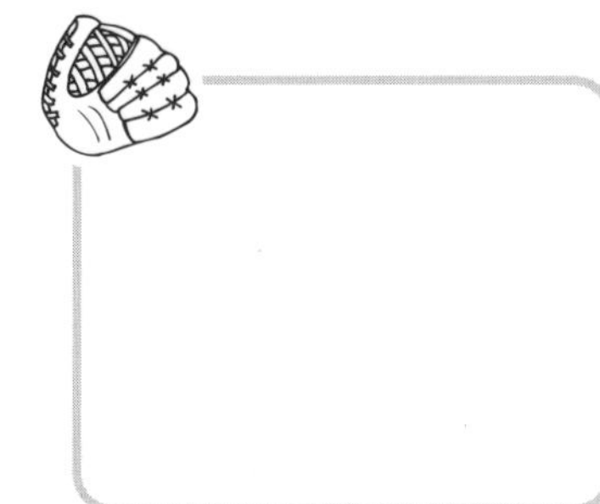

________ baseball cards

㉜ *I spent 1008 h practising baseball last year and 1116 h this year. How many hours in all have I spent practising baseball?*

________ hours

ISBN: 978-1-897164-32-7

4

Subtraction of 4-Digit Numbers

- Subtract 4-digit numbers with or without borrowing.
- Use different methods to find answers in a faster way.
- Solve word problems.

Do the subtraction.

① $\begin{array}{r} 3965 \\ -\ 1824 \\ \hline \end{array}$

② $\begin{array}{r} 8763 \\ -\ 4621 \\ \hline \end{array}$

③ $\begin{array}{r} 3642 \\ -\ 1535 \\ \hline \end{array}$

④ $\begin{array}{r} 2984 \\ -\ 192 \\ \hline \end{array}$

⑤ $\begin{array}{r} 3068 \\ -\ 1952 \\ \hline \end{array}$

⑥ 9683 – 2265 = ________

⑦ 5032 – 1710 = ________

⑧ 4522 – 486 = ________

⑨ 6274 – 1065 = ________

Find the number of screws left in each box.

⑩ 

Used: 1066

Left: ________

⑪ 

Used: 844

Left: ________

⑫ 

Used: 1065

Left: ________

ISBN: 978-1-897164-32-7

All the furniture is on sale now. Find the sale price of each item. Then answer the questions.

⑬

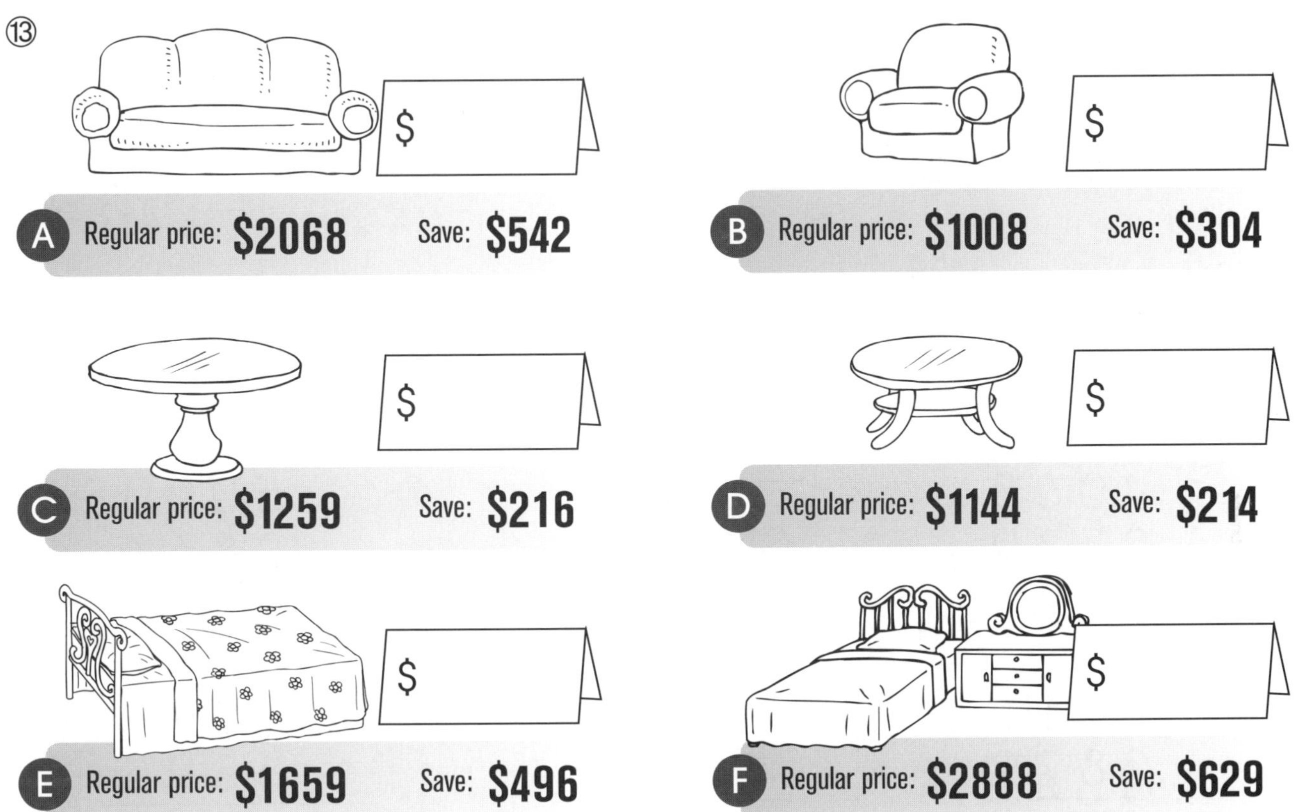

⑭ What is the price difference between the armchair and the couch?

__________ = __________ __________

⑮ What is the price difference between the tables?

__________ = __________ __________

⑯ Susan wants to buy E, but she has $322 only. How much more money does she need?

__________ = __________ __________

⑰ If F is further reduced by $425, what will the new price be?

__________ = __________ __________

ISBN: 978-1-897164-32-7

e.g. 4245 – 2816 = ______

Align the numbers.	Subtract the ones.	Subtract the tens.	Subtract the hundreds.	Subtract the thousands.
4245 − 2816	3 15 / 4245 − 2816 = 9	3 15 / 4245 − 2816 = 29	3 12 3 15 / 4245 − 2816 = 429	3 12 3 15 / 4245 − 2816 = 1429

4245 – 2816 = **1429**

If you can't take away, borrow 1 from the column on the left.

Do the subtraction.

⑱ 4068 − 2779

⑲ 5493 − 3897

⑳ 5000 − 2864

㉑ 3116 − 2879

㉒ 7235 − 5868

㉓ 6294 − 3395

㉔

A 4651 – 2688 = ______

B 9682 – 3794 = ______

C 2586 – 787 = ______

D 6103 – 4594 = ______

E 7337 – 6586 = ______

F 8064 – 2585 = ______

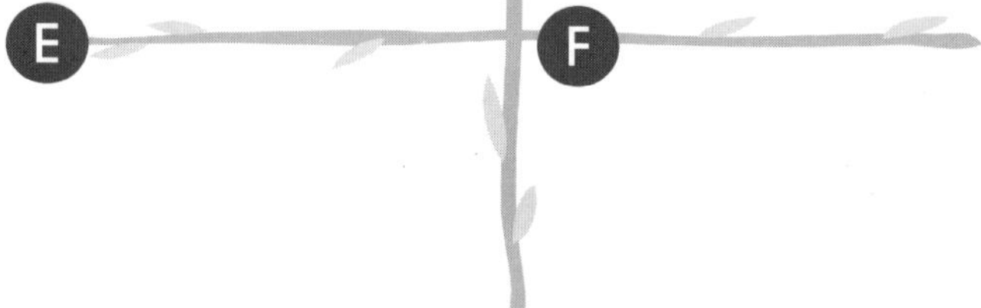

ISBN: 978-1-897164-32-7

e.g. 6819 – 3998 = 2821

- Add 2 to 3998, it is 4000.
- 6819 – 4000 = 2819
- Since 6819 has subtracted a number which is 2 more than the actual number, we need to add 2 back to 2819 to get the final answer.
- 2819 + 2 = **2821**

This method helps me find the answer in a faster way.

Use the above method to do subtraction. Then use vertical subtraction to find the answer again.

㉕ 4763 – 2997 = ________

- Add ________ to 2997, it is ________ .
- 4763 – ________ = ________
- ________ + ________ = ________

㉖ 6287 – 4996 = ________

Solve the problems.

㉗ *A big box holds 1682 dog biscuits. If my dog eats 372 biscuits, how many will be left?*

________________ = ________ ________

㉘ *Tim walks me every day. Trail A is 2885 m long. If trail B is 394 m shorter, how long is trail B?*

________________ = ________ ________

ISBN: 978-1-897164-32-7

5

Addition and Subtraction of 4-Digit Numbers

- Add or subtract 4-digit numbers.
- Check and estimate the answers.
- Solve word problems.

Find the answers.

① $\begin{array}{r} 1257 \\ +\ 2684 \\ \hline \end{array}$

② $\begin{array}{r} 3239 \\ -\ 1088 \\ \hline \end{array}$

③ $\begin{array}{r} 5234 \\ -\ 2766 \\ \hline \end{array}$

④ 8462 – 7593 = ________

⑤ 1423 + 6811 = ________

⑥ 3527 + 1732 = ________

⑦ 5024 – 4666 = ________

⑧ 547 + 8365 = ________

⑨ 3009 – 1148 = ________

⑩ 2465 + 1838 = ________

⑪ 2101 – 598 = ________

⑫ 4173 – 2368 = ________

⑬ 4207 + 1188 = ________

Put "+" or "–" in the circles.

⑭ $\begin{array}{r} 3275 \\ \bigcirc\ 1823 \\ \hline 5098 \end{array}$

⑮ $\begin{array}{r} 3465 \\ \bigcirc\ \ \ 869 \\ \hline 2596 \end{array}$

⑯ $\begin{array}{r} 4067 \\ \bigcirc\ 1538 \\ \hline 5605 \end{array}$

⑰ 3287 ◯ 1652 = 4939

⑱ 3817 ◯ 1386 = 5203

ISBN: 978-1-897164-32-7

Find the sum and difference for each pair of numbers.

⑲ 2083 1689

\+ ______ | − ______

⑳ 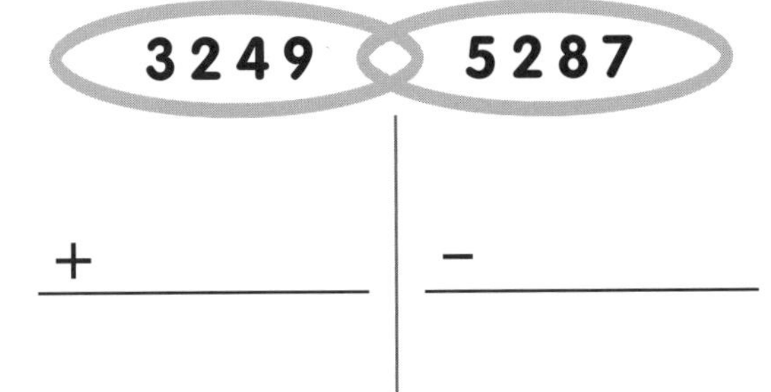

See how many people went on the rides last week. Round each number to the nearest hundred. Then estimate the total and answer the questions.

㉑ A

No. of Adults: 1364 (about)
No. of Children: 2876 (about)
Total: about ______ people

B

No. of Adults: 4065 (about)
No. of Children: 1759 (about)
Total: about ______ people

C

No. of Adults: 2411 (about)
No. of Children: 2035 (about)
Total: about ______ people

㉒ About how many more people went on B than C? about ______ more

㉓ About how many more people went on C than A? about ______ more

ISBN: 978-1-897164-32-7

Use addition or subtraction to check the answers. Put a check mark in the spaces provided; otherwise, put a cross and write the correct answers.

㉔ Tom's Questions

A 3657 + 1898 = *5555*

B 4101 – 2583 = *1418*

C 7056 – 3849 = *3217*

D 5244 + 858 = *6102*

E 6183 – 4795 = *1388*

A
```
  5555
- 1898
```

㉕ Linda's Questions

A 4250 – 2783 = *1467*

B 1864 + 3918 = *5882*

C 6274 – 5996 = *268*

D 3201 + 1899 = *5100*

E 4283 – 2888 = *1295*

ISBN: 978-1-897164-32-7

Solve the problems.

㉖

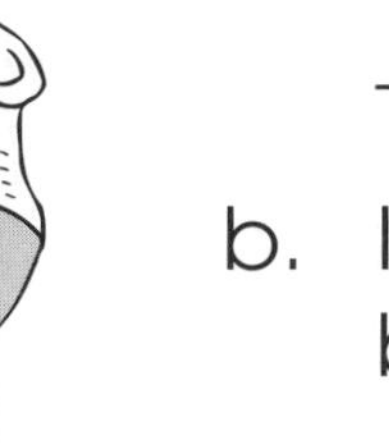

a. Calvin the Clown has a bag of stickers. If he gives 1692 stickers to the girls and the rest to the boys, how many stickers do the boys get?

________________ = ________

____

b. If a box can hold 480 more stickers than a bag, how many stickers can it hold?

________________ = ________

____

㉗

No. of Hamburgers Sold
last week: **4765**
this week: **3688**

a. How many hamburgers were sold in the past two weeks?

________________ = ________

____

b. How many fewer hamburgers were sold this week than last week?

________________ = ________

____

㉘

Tim, I had 145 candies at first. I took some from your bag and put them into my bowl. Now I have 1000 candies. Do you know how many candies I took from you?

________________ = ________

____

ISBN: 978-1-897164-32-7

6

Multiplication (1)

- Multiply to 9 x 9.
- Multiply 2-digit numbers by 1-digit numbers without carrying.
- Solve problems involving multiplication.

There are 48 chocolates.

Do the multiplication.

① 9×3 ② 6×6 ③ 4×5 ④ 2×9

⑤ 7×8 ⑥ 5×3 ⑦ 4×9 ⑧ 6×7

⑨ 3 x 3 = ______ ⑩ 6 x 5 = ______

⑪ 4 x 8 = ______ ⑫ 7 x 7 = ______

⑬ 6 x 9 = ______ ⑭ 9 x 7 = ______

⑮ 8 x 2 = ______ ⑯ 5 x 0 = ______

⑰ 3 x 7 = ______ ⑱ 8 x 6 = ______

Find the missing numbers.

⑲ 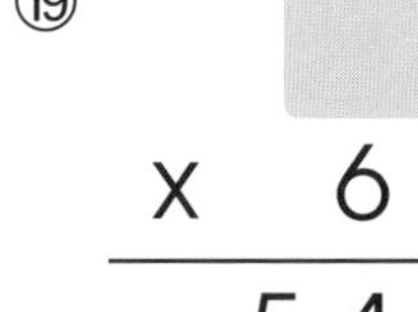 x 6 = 54

⑳ ☐ x 5 = 25

㉑ 8 x ☐ = 24

㉒ 7 x ☐ = 63

ISBN: 978-1-897164-32-7

Solve the problems.

㉓ How many days are there in 4 weeks?

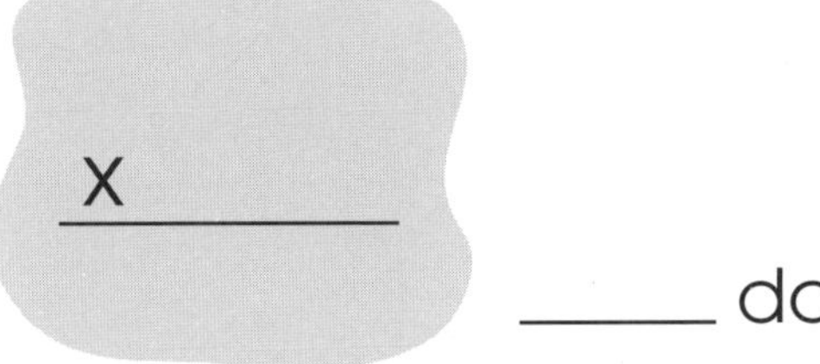

_____ days

㉔ A mug costs $3. How much do 8 mugs cost?

㉕ How many balls are there in 6 boxes?

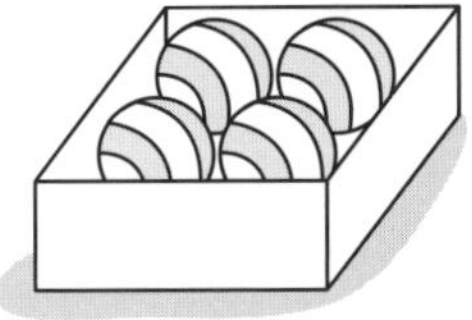

㉖ How many boxes of juice are there in 9 packs?

㉗ Tim buys 5 robots. How much does he need to pay?

$8

㉘ What is the total weight of 9 bags of potatoes?

㉙ What is the total thickness of 5 books?

㉚ What is the total value of 8 nickels?

Multiply 2-digit numbers by 1-digit numbers:

1st Multiply the ones.

2nd Multiply the tens.

e.g. 43 x 3 = **129**

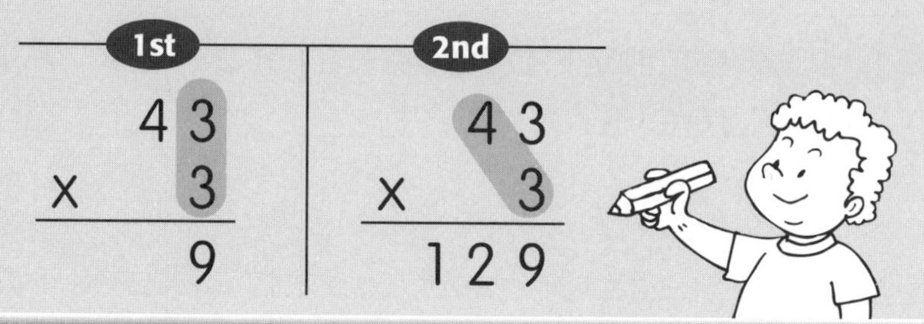

Do the multiplication.

㉛ 12 x 3 =

㉜ 24 x 2 =

㉝ 31 x 7 =

㉞ 32 x 4 =

㉟ 51 x 6 =

㊱ 82 x 3 =

㊲ 60 x 9 = ______

㊳ 74 x 2 = ______

㊴ 41 x 5 = ______

㊵ 63 x 3 = ______

Find the totals.

㊶

3 cans: ______ beads

4 cans: ______ beads

㊷

6 ribbons: ______ cm

9 ribbons: ______ cm

㊸

4 bags: ______ candies

7 bags: ______ candies

㊹

2 boxes: ______ straws

3 boxes: ______ straws

ISBN: 978-1-897164-32-7

Solve the problems.

㊺ 

a. How many party hats are there in 4 packs?

__________ = _____ ________

b. How much do 20 packs of party hats cost?

__________ = _____ ________

㊻ 

a. How much do 11 dozen roses cost?

__________ = _____ ________

b. How many roses are there in 3 dozen?

__________ = _____ ________

㊼ 

a. The number of cows on Joe's farm is 2 times as many as Sam's. How many cows are there on Joe's farm?

__________ = _____ ________

b. The number of chickens on Sam's farm is 3 times the number of pigs. How many chickens does Sam have?

__________ = _____ ________

㊽ *If I eat 32 chocolates every day, how many chocolates do I eat in 4 days?*

__________ = _____ ________

ISBN: 978-1-897164-32-7

7

Multiplication (2)

- Multiply 2-digit numbers by 1-digit numbers with carrying.
- Solve problems involving multiplication.

Do the multiplication.

① $\begin{array}{r} \bigcirc \\ 37 \\ \times \quad 8 \\ \hline \end{array}$

② $\begin{array}{r} \bigcirc \\ 52 \\ \times \quad 7 \\ \hline \end{array}$

③ $\begin{array}{r} \bigcirc \\ 45 \\ \times \quad 9 \\ \hline \end{array}$

④ $\begin{array}{r} \bigcirc \\ 73 \\ \times \quad 4 \\ \hline \end{array}$

⑤ $\begin{array}{r} \bigcirc \\ 64 \\ \times \quad 5 \\ \hline \end{array}$

⑥ $\begin{array}{r} \bigcirc \\ 28 \\ \times \quad 6 \\ \hline \end{array}$

⑦ 49 x 7 = ________

⑧ 63 x 8 = ________

⑨ 55 x 3 = ________

⑩ 38 x 2 = ________

⑪ 17 x 6 = ________

⑫ 44 x 9 = ________

Find the total weights.

⑬ 

8 bags:

________ g

⑭ 

4 cans:

________ g

⑮ 

9 packs:

________ pieces

ISBN: 978-1-897164-32-7

Find the total costs.

⑯

	Total Cost
4 cars	$
5 cars	$
7 cars	$

⑰

	Total Cost
3 dolls	
7 dolls	
8 dolls	

⑱

$54

	Total Cost
3 robots	
6 robots	
8 robots	

⑲

	Total Cost
2 pigs	
5 pigs	
9 pigs	

Round each number to the nearest ten. Then fill in the blanks.

⑳ about _____ cookies

There are about _______ cookies in 7 cans.

㉑ about _____ ¢

6 corn cobs cost about _______ ¢.

㉒ about _____ flowers

There are about _______ flowers in 9 bunches of flowers.

ISBN: 978-1-897164-32-7

Fill in the missing numbers.

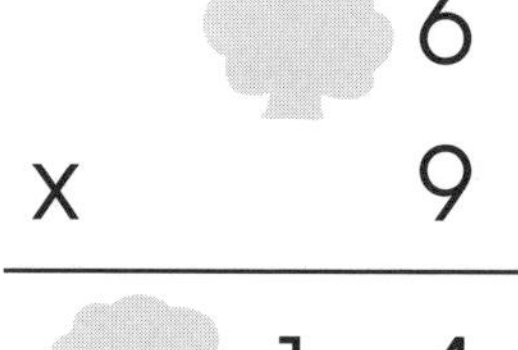

㉓ ☐6 × 9 = ☐14

㉔ 36 × ☐ = 2☐8

㉕ ☐9 × 6 = 3☐4

㉖ ☐2 × ☐ = 504

㉗ 7☐ × 9 = 67☐

㉘ 6☐ × 5 = ☐15

Solve the problems.

㉙ 

How many baseball cards are there in 9 packs?

______ baseball cards

㉚ 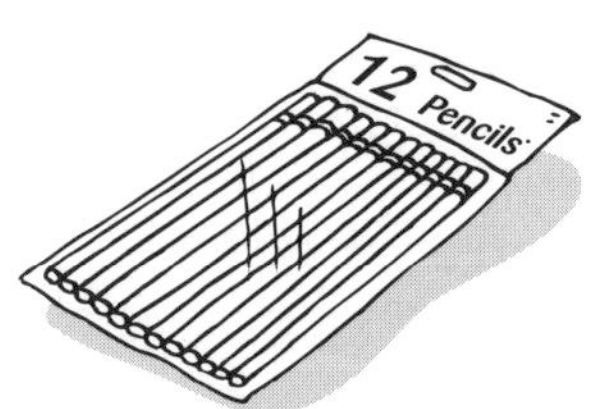

Mrs. Green buys 8 packs of pencils for her students. How many pencils does Mrs. Green buy in all?

______ pencils

㉛ 

Uncle Sam buys 5 boxes of pop. How many cans of pop does Uncle Sam buy in all?

______ cans

㉜ 

Baby Bob uses one bag of diapers each month. How many diapers does Baby Bob need in half a year?

______ diapers

ISBN: 978-1-897164-32-7

e.g. There are 12 red marbles and 15 blue marbles in a box. How many marbles are there in 4 boxes?

Sometimes we need to do some calculation in our mind first.

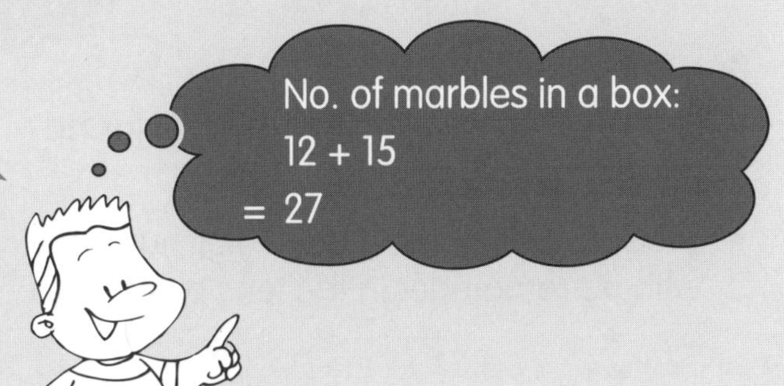

4 x 27 = **108**

There are 108 marbles in 4 boxes.

Solve the problems.

㉝ Joe has 8 yellow stickers and 34 green stickers. The number of stickers that Peter has is 4 times of Joe's. How many stickers does Peter have?

__________ = ______ __________

㉞ A bottle of perfume costs $82, but you can save $15 if you buy it this week. How much do 8 bottles cost if Mrs. White buys them while they are on sale?

__________ = ______ __________

㉟ Janet uses 3 yellow ribbons and 6 red ribbons to make a bow. How many ribbons does she need to make 54 bows?

__________ = ______ __________

㊱ *A box has 16 cans of cat food. If my mom bought 3 boxes last week and 4 boxes this week, how many cans of cat food did she buy in all?*

__________ = ______

____

ISBN: 978-1-897164-32-7

8

Division (1)

- Divide to 81 ÷ 9.
- Understand division terms – dividend, divisor, quotient, and remainder.
- Divide 2-digit numbers by 1-digit numbers with no remainder in the tens place.

You can make 5 strings of 6 beads with 2 beads left.

Do the division.

① $5\overline{)\,20}$

② $5\overline{)\,42}$ R ___

③ $7\overline{)\,64}$ R ___

④ 63 ÷ 9 = ________

⑤ 39 ÷ 6 = ________

⑥ 36 ÷ 4 = ________

⑦ 38 ÷ 7 = ________

⑧ 32 ÷ 8 = ________

⑨ 41 ÷ 5 = ________

⑩ 55 ÷ 9 = ________

⑪ 68 ÷ 8 = ________

⑫ 47 ÷ 6 = ________

⑬ 53 ÷ 8 = ________

Fill in the missing numbers.

⑭ 9) 3 ☐ → ☐ R ☐; 3 6; 3

⑮ 8) ☐ 4 → 5 R ☐; ☐ ☐; 4

⑯ 6) ☐ 5 → 7 R 3; ☐ ☐; 3

ISBN: 978-1-897164-32-7

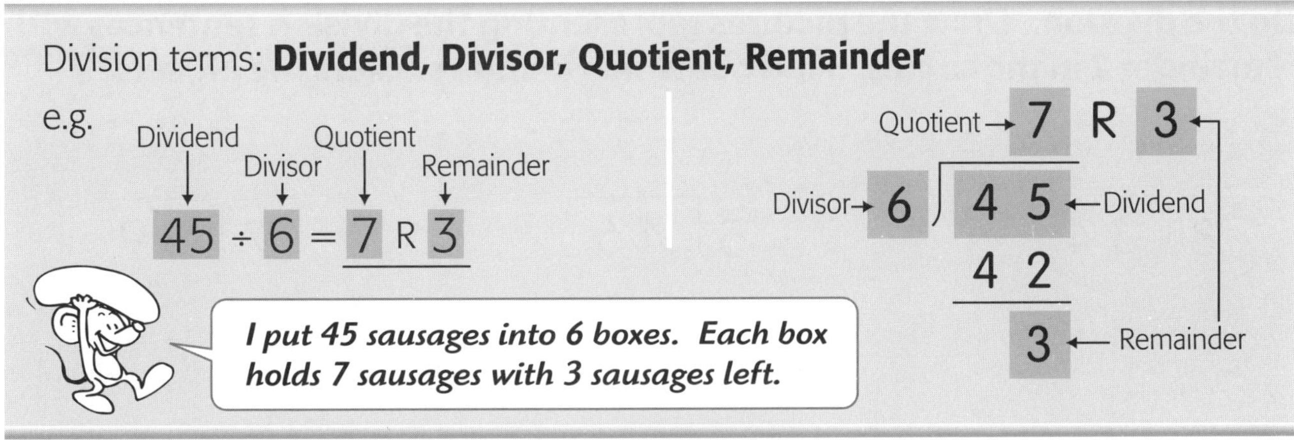

Division terms: **Dividend, Divisor, Quotient, Remainder**
e.g.
Dividend
Divisor
Quotient
Remainder
45 ÷ 6 = 7 R 3
I put 45 sausages into 6 boxes. Each box holds 7 sausages with 3 sausages left.
Quotient → 7 R 3
Divisor → 6) 45 ← Dividend
42
3 ← Remainder

Do the division. Then colour the numbers.

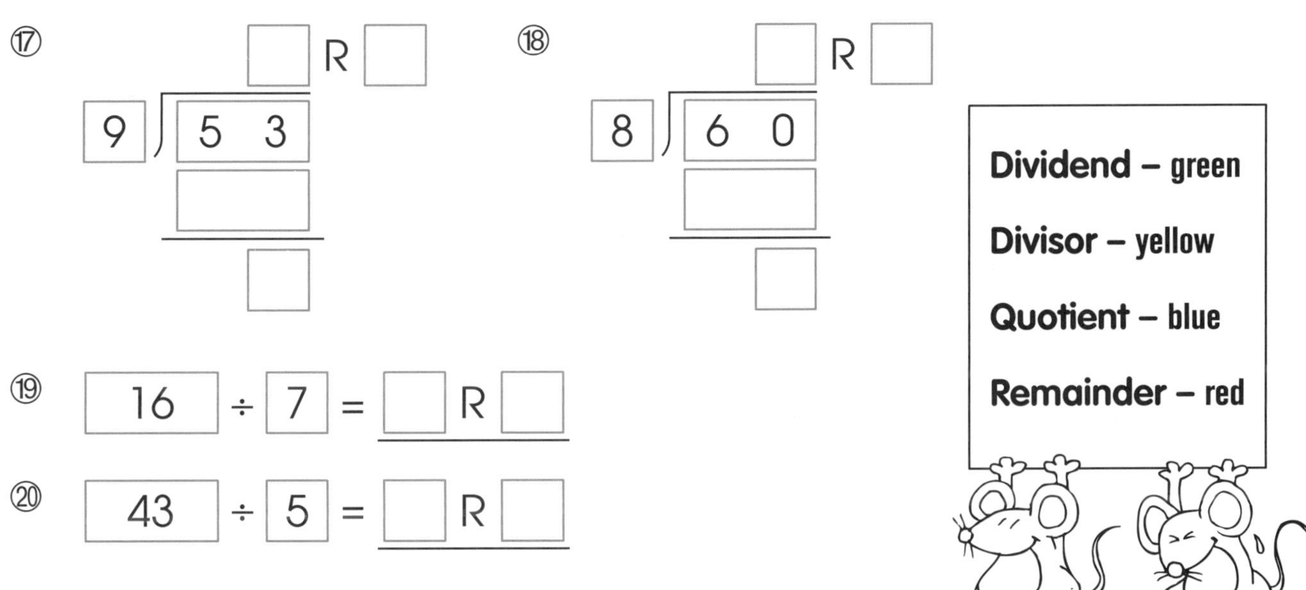

Complete the table.

㉑

Division Sentence	Dividend	Divisor	Quotient	Remainder
a. 39 ÷ 6 = ___ R ___			6	3
b.	28	5	5	
c. 43 ÷ 7 =				
d.	50	8		2
e. 67 ÷ 9 =				

ISBN: 978-1-897164-32-7

Do the division. Draw the pictures representing the division sentences with remainder 2 in the circles. Find out which animal stickers the pig has.

㉒

㉓

㉔

㉕

㉖

㉗

㉘ 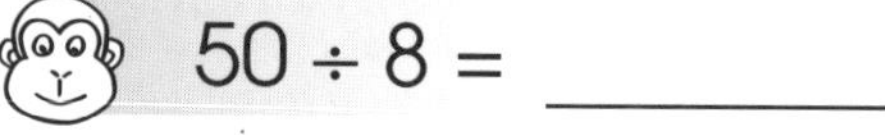 50 ÷ 8 = ________

㉙  62 ÷ 7 = ________

㉚  47 ÷ 5 = ________

㉛  31 ÷ 4 = ________

㉜  28 ÷ 9 = ________

㉝  42 ÷ 8 = ________

㉞  65 ÷ 7 = ________

ISBN: 978-1-897164-32-7

2-digit number ÷ 1-digit number:

1st Divide the tens.

2nd Divide the ones.

e.g. 62 ÷ 3 = **20R2**

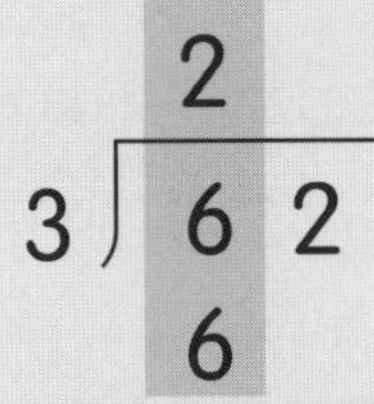

Divide the tens.

$$\begin{array}{r} 2 \\ 3\overline{)62} \\ \underline{6} \end{array}$$

Divide the ones.

$$\begin{array}{r} 20 \text{ R2} \\ 3\overline{)62} \\ \underline{6} \\ 2 \end{array}$$

Sometimes we need to add "0" in the quotient.

Do the division.

35. $2\overline{)49}$

36. $4\overline{)86}$

37. $3\overline{)98}$

38. $6\overline{)67}$

39. $5\overline{)54}$

40. $2\overline{)65}$

41. 47 ÷ 4 = ________

42. 73 ÷ 7 = ________

43. 62 ÷ 6 = ________

44. 85 ÷ 4 = ________

45. 59 ÷ 5 = ________

46. 89 ÷ 8 = ________

47. *We want to make 3 necklaces. How many beads are there on each necklace? How many beads are left?*

________________ = ________

____

ISBN: 978-1-897164-32-7

9 Division (2)

- Divide 2-digit numbers by 1-digit numbers.
- Solve problems involving division.

If we share the chocolates, each of us gets 13 chocolates with 1 chocolate left.

Do the long division.

① $3\overline{)46}$ = ☐☐ R ☐

② $2\overline{)57}$ = ☐☐ R ☐

③ $4\overline{)65}$ = ☐☐ R ☐

④ $5\overline{)86}$

⑤ $3\overline{)74}$

⑥ $6\overline{)90}$

⑦ $8\overline{)92}$

⑧ $4\overline{)72}$

⑨ $6\overline{)85}$

ISBN: 978-1-897164-32-7

Find the answers.

⑩ 49 ÷ 3 = ________

⑪ 52 ÷ 4 = ________

⑫ 92 ÷ 8 = ________

⑬ 77 ÷ 6 = ________

⑭ 81 ÷ 7 = ________

⑮ 66 ÷ 5 = ________

Find the answers. Do long division in the spaces provided.

⑯ Katie divides 60 candies equally into 5 boxes. How many candies are there in each box?

_____ candies

⑰ A mug costs $3. How many mugs can be bought with $50? How much is left?

_____ mugs; $ _____ left

⑱ Mr. Green gives 46 stickers to 3 children. How many stickers does each child get? How many stickers are left?

_____ stickers; _____ sticker(s) left

⑲ Mrs. Winter divides 62 children into 4 groups. How many children are there in each group? How many children are left?

_____ children; _____ children left

ISBN: 978-1-897164-32-7

Fill in the missing numbers.

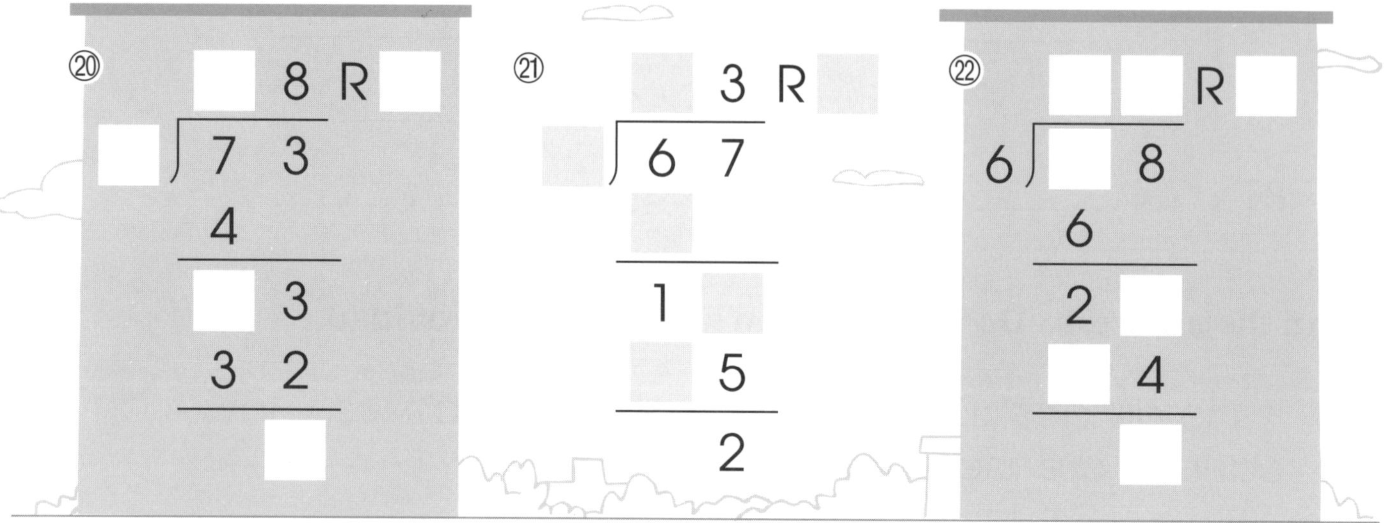

Look at the pictures. Answer the questions.

㉓

Jimmy puts a bag of marshmallows equally on 5 plates. How many marshmallows are there on each plate?

____________ = ________

_____ marshmallows

㉔

If Mrs. Smith puts all 92 crayons into boxes, how many boxes of crayons will she get? How many crayons will be left?

____________ = ________

_____ boxes; _____ crayons left

㉕

Uncle Sam pays $75 for the bear key chains. How many bear key chains will he get? How much will he have left?

____________ = ________

_____ bear key chains; $ _____ left

ISBN: 978-1-897164-32-7

Solve the problems.

㉖ Tim earned $85 in 5 weeks from delivering newspapers and George earned $72 in 4 weeks.

a. How much did each person earn in one week?

$ ______

$ ______

b. Who has a better pay? ____________

㉗ There are two box sizes available for Kevin to hold his 68 cupcakes.

a. How many of each box are needed to hold all the cupcakes? How many cupcakes are left?

______ boxes;

______ cupcakes left

______ boxes;

______ cupcakes left

b. *If I put all the cupcakes into the bigger boxes and give the remaining ones to my friend, how many cupcakes will my friend get?*

____

ISBN: 978-1-897164-32-7

10

More about Multiplication and Division

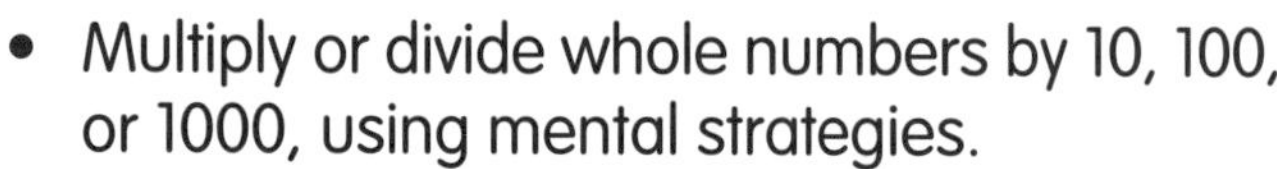

- Multiply or divide whole numbers by 10, 100, or 1000, using mental strategies.
- Use multiplication and addition to check the answers of division problems.

Read what Raymond says.
Then find the answers mentally.

When you multiply a number by 10, add 1 zero to the number. Add 2 zeros when you multiply by 100 and 3 zeros when you multiply by 1000.

① 6 x 100 = ________ ② 7 x 1000 = ________

③ 35 x 10 = ________ ④ 9 x 1000 = ________

⑤ 27 x 100 = ________ ⑥ 42 x 10 = ________

⑦ 81 x 1000 = ________ ⑧ 320 x 10 = ________

⑨ 94 x 10 = ________ ⑩ 5 x 1000 = ________

Write 10, 100, or 1000 to complete the multiplication sentences.

⑪ 5 x ______ = 5000 ⑫ 16 x ______ = 16 000

⑬ 32 x ______ = 320 ⑭ 430 x ______ = 4300

⑮ 60 x ______ = 6000 ⑯ 504 x ______ = 50 400

⑰ 100 x ______ = 1000 ⑱ 75 x ______ = 75 000

ISBN: 978-1-897164-32-7

Read what Susan says. Then find the answers mentally.

When you divide a number by 10, remove 1 zero from the number. Remove 2 zeros when it is divided by 100 and 3 zeros when it is divided by 1000.

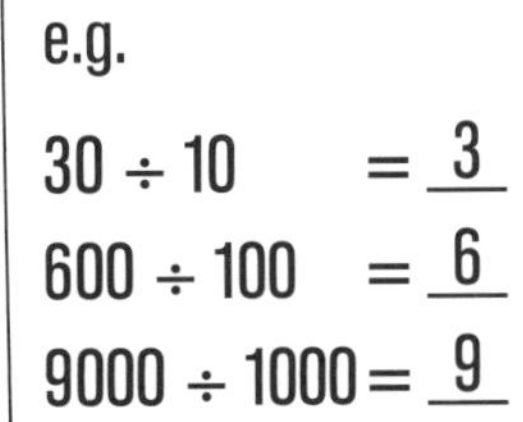

e.g.

30 ÷ 10 = 3

600 ÷ 100 = 6

9000 ÷ 1000 = 9

⑲ 40 ÷ 10 = ______

⑳ 8000 ÷ 100 = ______

㉑ 600 ÷ 10 = ______

㉒ 7000 ÷ 1000 = ______

㉓ 500 ÷ 100 = ______

㉔ 180 ÷ 10 = ______

㉕ 2050 ÷ 10 = ______

㉖ 4000 ÷ 1000 = ______

Write 10, 100, or 1000 to complete the division sentences.

㉗ 4500 ÷ ____ = 45

㉘ 3690 ÷ ____ = 369

㉙ 1200 ÷ ____ = 12

㉚ 4000 ÷ ____ = 400

㉛ 3020 ÷ ____ = 302

㉜ 5000 ÷ ____ = 5

㉝ 4830 ÷ ____ = 483

㉞ 9000 ÷ ____ = 90

Put "x" or "÷" in the circles.

㉟ 4800 ◯ 100 = 48

㊱ 950 ◯ 10 = 9500

㊲ 3 ◯ 1000 = 3000

㊳ 4000 ◯ 100 = 40

㊴ 100 ◯ 100 = 1

㊵ 3600 ◯ 10 = 360

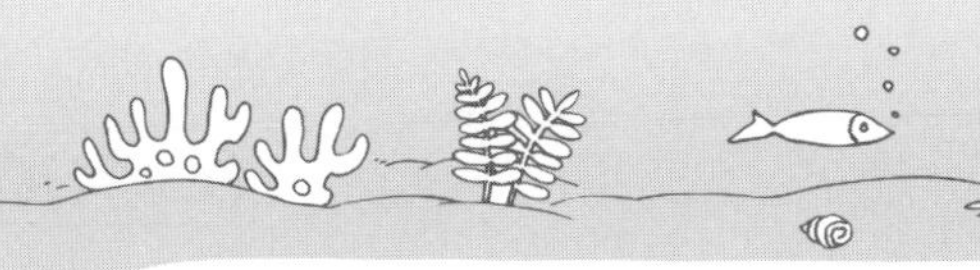

ISBN: 978-1-897164-32-7

Steps to check the answer of a division problem:

1st Quotient x Divisor

2nd Answer from **1st** + Remainder

If the answer from **2nd** is the same as the dividend, the answer of the division problem is correct.

e.g. Is 64 ÷ 5 = 12R4 correct?

1st 12 x 5 = 60

2nd 60 + 4 = 64 ← same as the dividend

The answer **12R4** *is correct.*

Check the answer of each division sentence. Put a check mark in the space provided if it is correct; otherwise, put a cross and write the correct answer.

41. 76 ÷ 3 = 25R1

Check
1st ______ x ______ = ______
2nd ______ + ______ = ______

42. 45 ÷ 2 = 22R1

Check
1st
2nd

43. 89 ÷ 7 = 12R4

Check
1st
2nd

44. 95 ÷ 6 = 15R5

Check
1st
2nd

Do the division. Then check the answers.

45. 69 ÷ 4 = ______

46. 75 ÷ 6 = ______

47. 81 ÷ 7 = ______

ISBN: 978-1-897164-32-7

Fill in the boxes with numbers to complete the division. Then check the answers.

```
      □ 5 R □
   □ ) 4 □
       3
       □ □
       1 5
         2
```

⑲

```
      □ 2 R □
   □ ) □ 7
       7
       1 □
       □ □
         3
```

Solve the problems.

⑩ Tim has $5. Sue has 10 times Tim's amount. How much does Sue have?

____

⑪ Mr. Smith has 4600 hockey cards. If he puts all the hockey cards equally into 10 boxes, how many hockey cards will there be in each box?

____

⑫ Each ribbon is 16 cm long. What is the total length of 1000 ribbons?

____

I have put 1300 jellybeans in my trophy. If I share my jellybeans with 9 friends, how many jellybeans will each of us get?

____

ISBN: 978-1-897164-32-7

Length and Distance

- Estimate, measure, and record length, height, and distance, using mm, cm, dm, m, or km.
- Describe the relationships between various units of length.
- Solve problems related to lengths or distances.

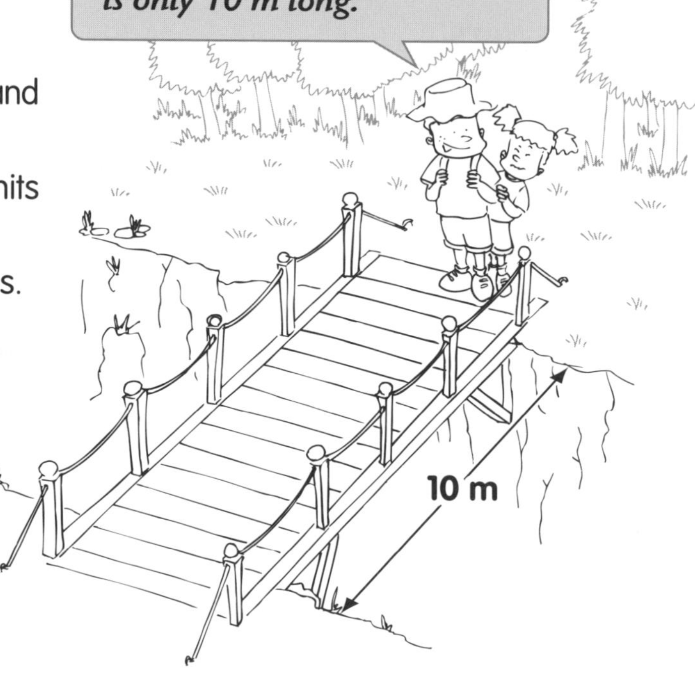
Don't be scared. The bridge is only 10 m long.
10 m

Fill in the blanks with the given units to complete the sentences.

mm cm m km

① The length of a highway is about 60 _____ .

② The length of a pencil is about 15 _____ .

③ The height of the CN Tower is about 600 _____ .

④ A quarter is about 2 _____ thick.

⑤ 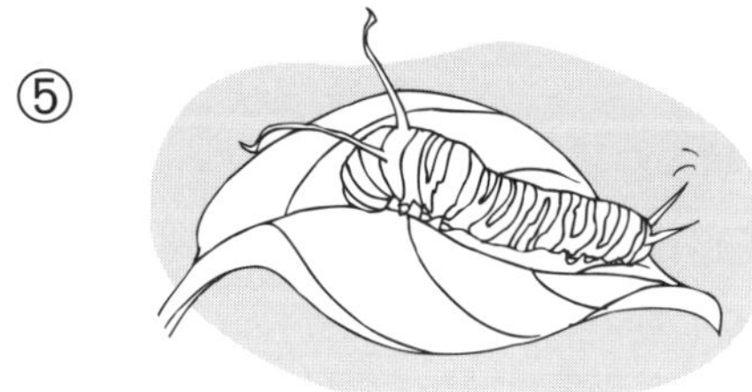

a. The leaf is about 6 _____ long.

b. The worm is about 45 _____ long.

⑥ a. The height of the mountain is about 3 _____ .

b. Aunt Mary is about 162 _____ tall.

c. The distance between Aunt Mary and the mountain is about 980 _____ .

d. Aunt Mary's stick is about 1 _____ long.

ISBN: 978-1-897164-32-7

The relationships between the units:

1 km = 1000 m

1 m = 10 dm = 100 cm

1 dm = 10 cm

1 cm = 10 mm

e.g.

Fill in the blanks.

⑦ 6 m = ________ cm

⑧ 8 km = ________ m

⑨ 5 cm = ________ mm

⑩ 7 m = ________ dm

⑪ 8 dm = ________ cm

⑫ 600 cm = ________ m

⑬ 3000 m = ________ km

⑭ 90 cm = ________ dm

⑮ 40 mm = ________ cm

⑯ 100 dm = ________ m

Compare the measures in each pair. Fill in the blanks.

⑰

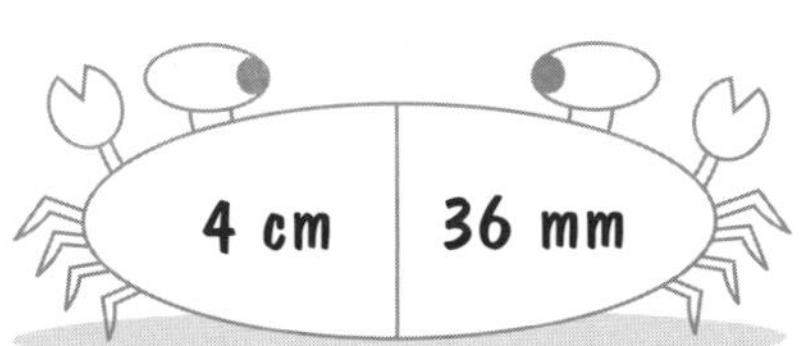

Since 4 cm = ________ mm,

________ is greater.

⑱

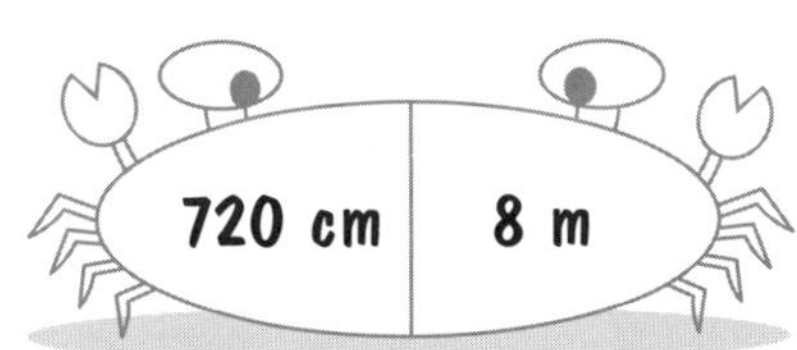

Since 8 m = ________ cm,

________ is greater.

⑲

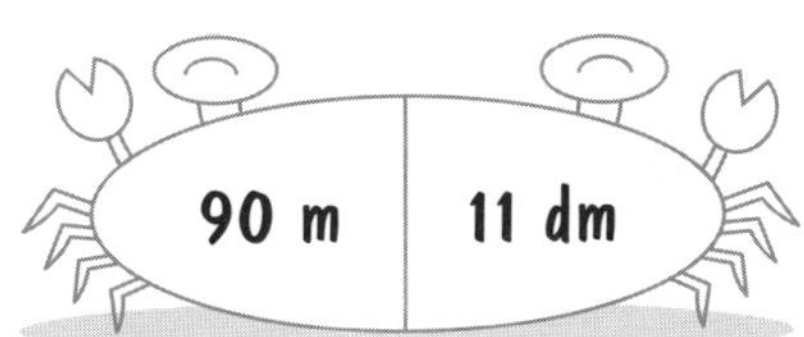

Since 90 m = ________ dm,

________ is smaller.

⑳

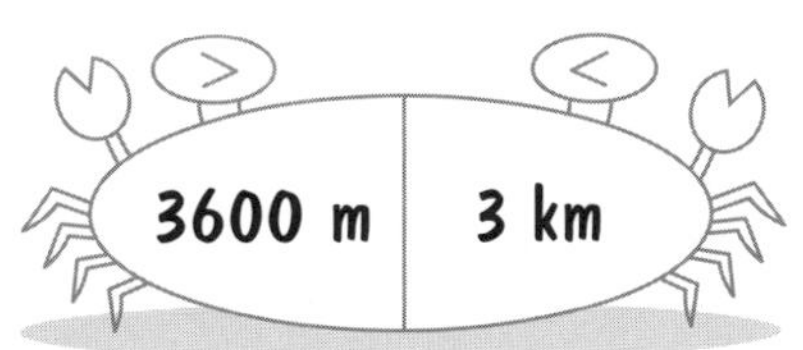

Since 3 km = ________ m,

________ is smaller.

ISBN: 978-1-897164-32-7

Do the measurement. Then draw the picture and fill in the blanks.

㉑ Measure and record the length of Ⓐ and Ⓑ. Draw a string Ⓒ 6 mm shorter than Ⓑ and record its length.

Ⓐ ______ mm

Ⓑ ______ mm

Ⓒ ______ mm

㉒ Ⓒ is ______ cm long.

㉓ Ⓒ is ______ mm longer than Ⓐ.

㉔ *If Ⓒ is cut into 2 equal pieces, how long is each piece?*

______ mm

Look at the picture. Estimate the heights or distances. Then draw lines to complete the grid to find the actual measurements.

㉕

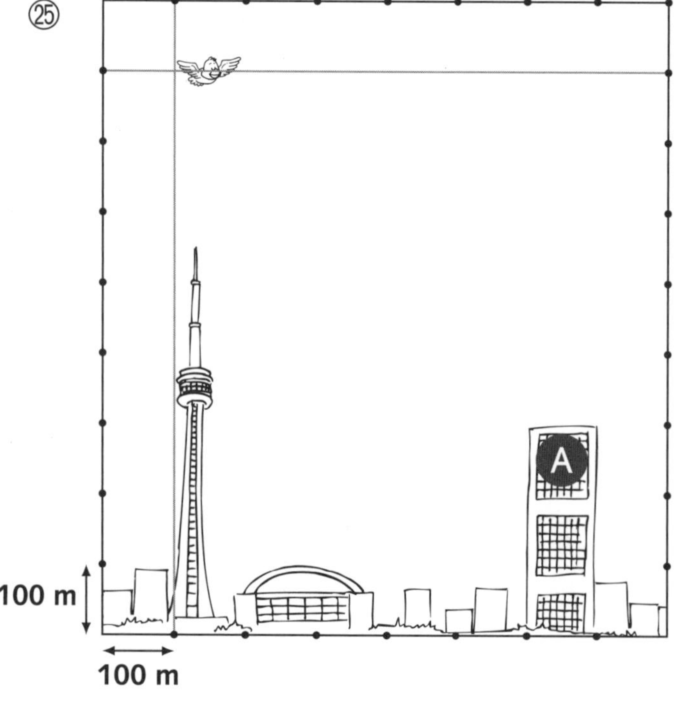

	Estimate	Actual
Height		
CN Tower:	______	______
Rogers Centre:	______	______
Building Ⓐ:	______	______
Distance between CN Tower and		
the bird:	______	______
Building Ⓐ:	______	______

ISBN: 978-1-897164-32-7

Read the clue. Draw the pictures and label the distances to complete the map. Then answer the questions.

- From Deadly Swamp to Spooky Jungle: **half a kilometre**
- From Spinky Crocodiles to Spooky Jungle passing through Venus Flytrap, which is halfway between them: **3000 m**
- From Spooky Jungle to Spinky Crocodiles: **3 km 500 m**
- From Spinky Crocodiles to Treasure Box: **1 km 800 m**

26.

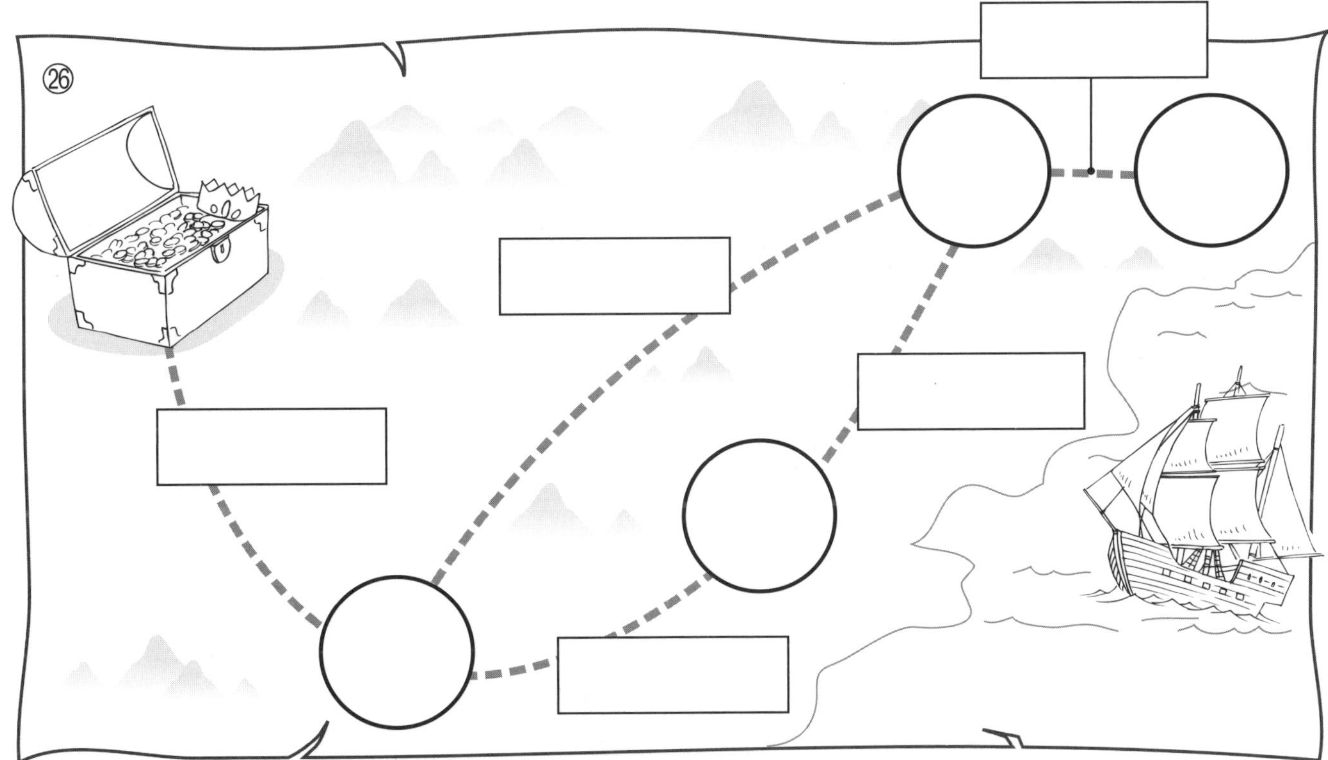

27. *What's the distance between Venus Flytrap and Spinky Crocodiles?*

____

28. *What's the shortest distance from Deadly Swamp to Treasure Box?*

____

ISBN: 978-1-897164-32-7

12

Perimeter and Area

- Estimate, measure, and record the perimeters and areas of polygons.
- Choose the most appropriate units to measure the side lengths and perimeters of various polygons.
- Find the relationship between the side lengths of a rectangle and its perimeter and area.

The perimeter of the fireplace is 162 cm.

Measure and record the side lengths of each polygon to the nearest mm. Then find the perimeter.

①

Side length: ____________

Perimeter: ____________

Length: ____________

Width: ____________

Perimeter: ____________

Side length: ____________

Perimeter: ____________

Side length: ____________

Perimeter: ____________

Side length:

____

Perimeter:

____

Side length: ____________

Perimeter: ____________

ISBN: 978-1-897164-32-7

Find the perimeters of the shapes.

②

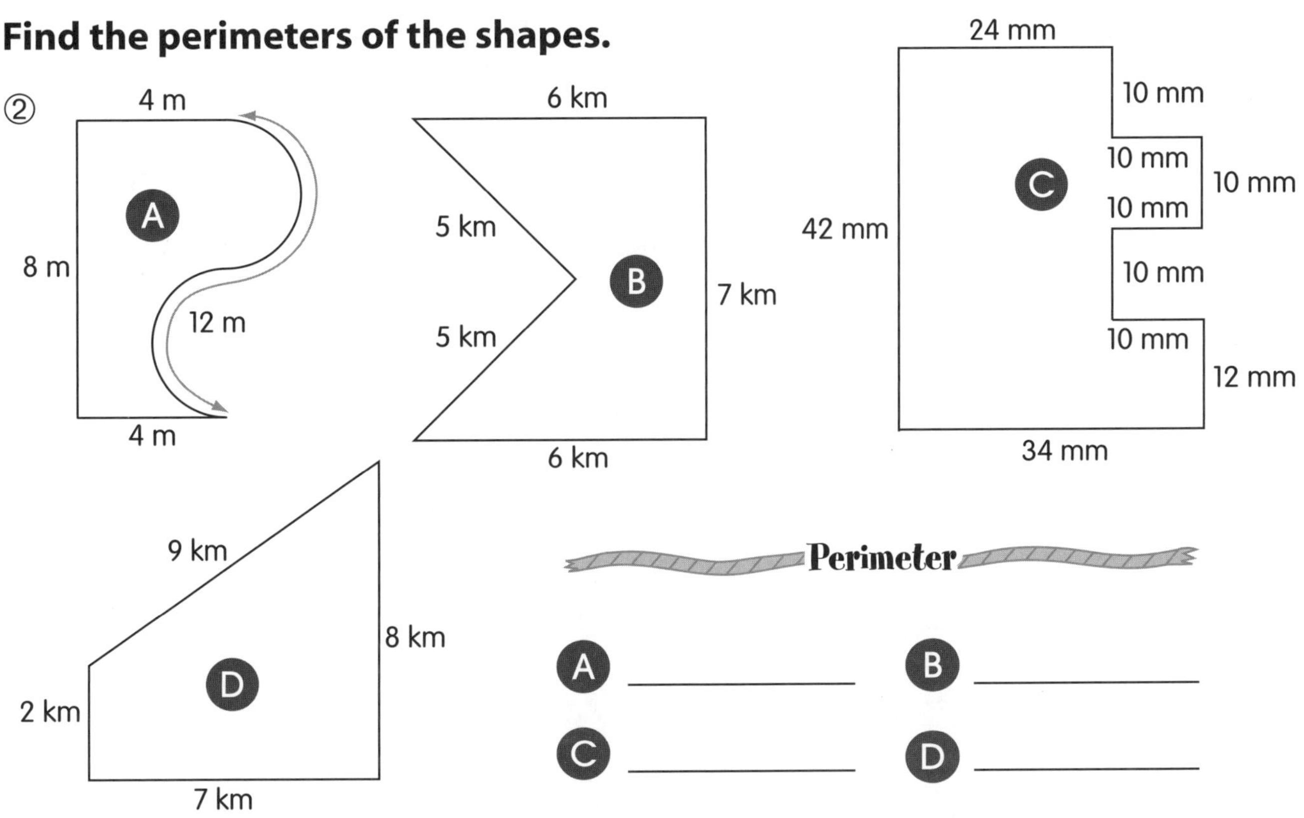

Perimeter

A ____________ B ____________

C ____________ D ____________

Write the most appropriate unit you would use to find the perimeter of each thing.

mm cm dm m km

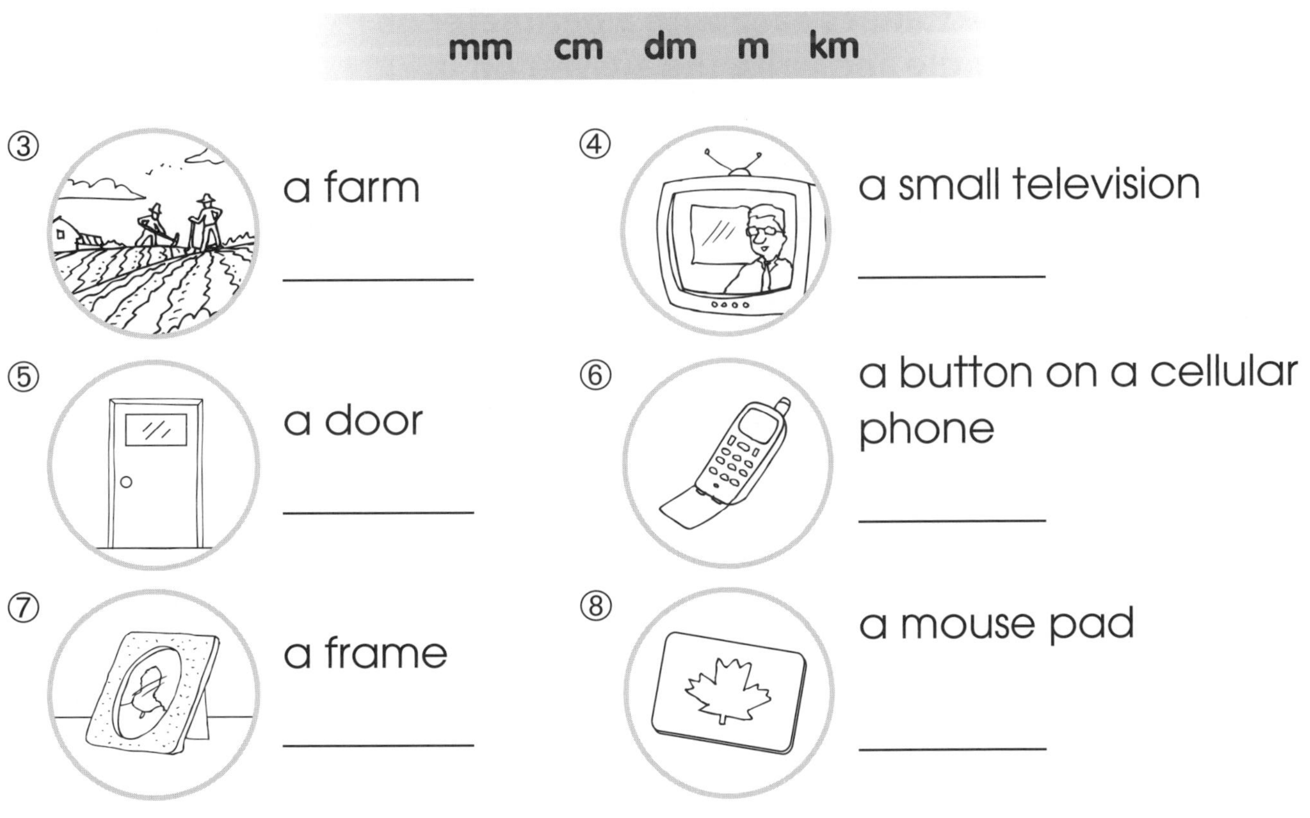

③ a farm ____________

④ a small television ____________

⑤ a door ____________

⑥ a button on a cellular phone ____________

⑦ a frame ____________

⑧ a mouse pad ____________

ISBN: 978-1-897164-32-7

Check the correct circle to tell what you would consider: perimeter or area.

⑨ *My mom wants to buy a carpet for covering the floor of her bedroom.*

◯ Perimeter
◯ Area

⑩ *I want to frame a poster.*

◯ Perimeter
◯ Area

⑪ *I want to buy a bed sheet for my bed.*

◯ Perimeter
◯ Area

⑫ *I want to fence my backyard.*

◯ Perimeter
◯ Area

Draw 3 different rectangles each with a perimeter of 14 cm. Then find the area of each rectangle and write the answer on it.

⑬

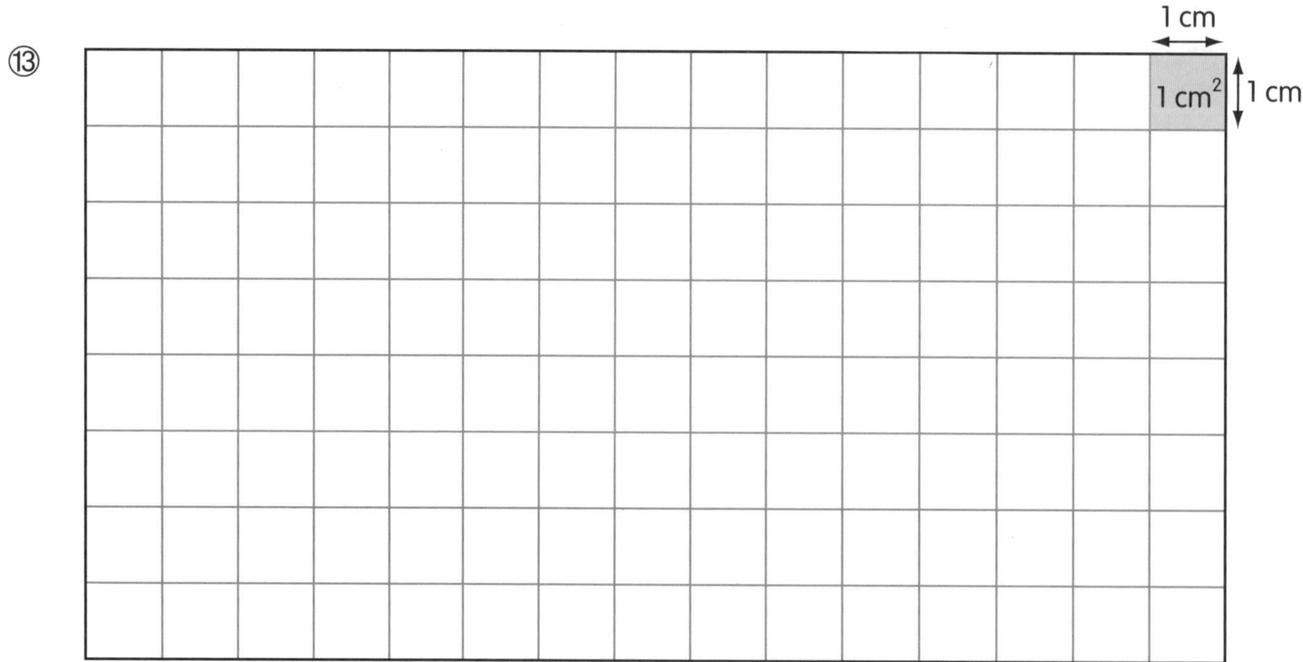

ISBN: 978-1-897164-32-7

Find the lengths, widths, perimeters, and areas of the rectangles. Then answer the questions.

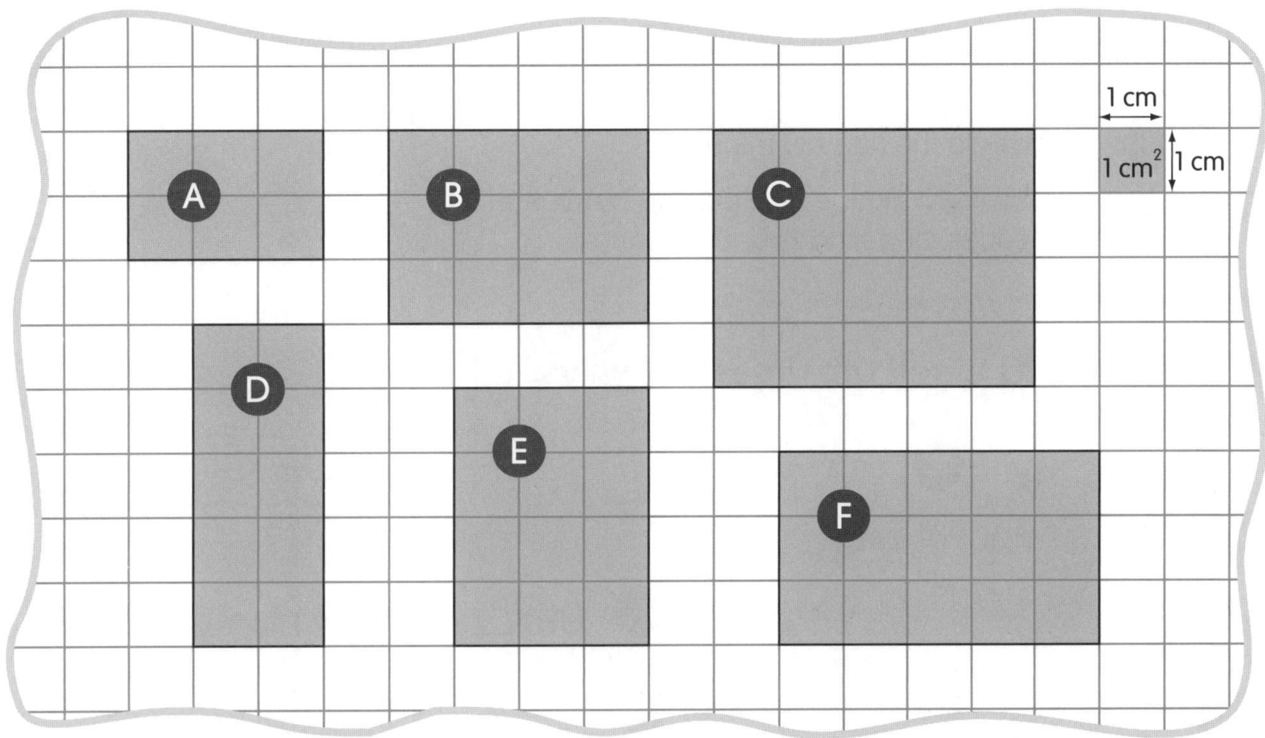

⑭

	A	B	C	D	E	F
Length	3 cm					
Width	2 cm					
Perimeter						
Area						

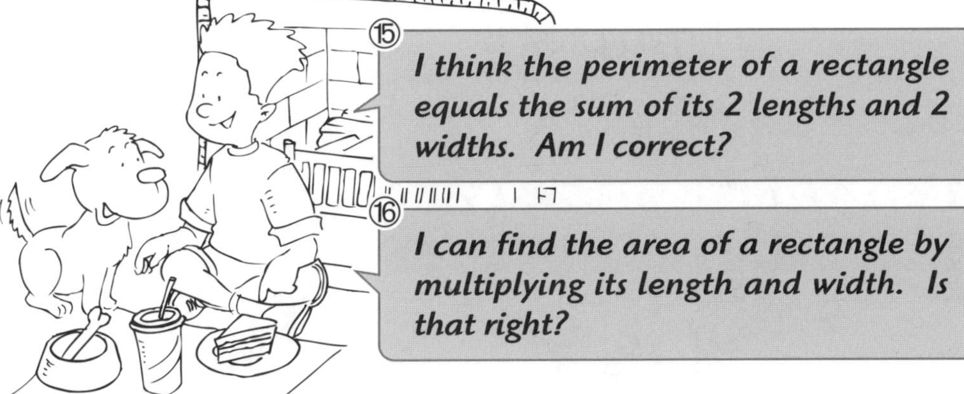

⑮ *I think the perimeter of a rectangle equals the sum of its 2 lengths and 2 widths. Am I correct?* ____________

⑯ *I can find the area of a rectangle by multiplying its length and width. Is that right?* ____________

ISBN: 978-1-897164-32-7

Time

- Read and write time in 12-hour notation.
- Determine elapsed time.
- Find the intervals to the nearest minute.
- Solve problems involving the relationship between years and decades, or decades and centuries.

Starts at 10:55
1 min
3 min
5 min
It took me 9 min from washing to finishing an apple. I finished the apple at 11:04.

Fill in the blanks to tell the times in 2 ways.

① 

A 05: ______ ; 17 min past ______

B ______ :58 ; 2 min to ______

C ______ ; ______

D ______ ; ______

E ______ ; ______

F ______ ; ______

Draw the clock hands to show the times.

② 20 min to 10

③ 21 min past 8

④ 26 min to 5

ISBN: 978-1-897164-32-7

Look at the pictures and the schedules of the children. Answer the questions.

⑤

Brush teeth – 5 min
Eat breakfast – 10 min
Wash and get dressed – 10 min
Get backpack ready – 5 min
Get to school – 15 min

a. How long does it take Jason from getting up to reaching his school? ______________

b. Will Jason be at school by 8:30 in the morning? ______________

c. If Jason spends the same amount of time on his morning routine and arrives at school at 8:10, at what time should he get up? ______________

⑥

Make cookies – 30 min
Clean up the kitchen – 20 min
Set table – 5 min
Have afternoon tea – 15 min

a. How long does it take Maria from making cookies to finishing afternoon tea? ______________

b. Will Maria finish her afternoon tea at 3:00 in the afternoon? ______________

c. If Maria does not need to clean up the kitchen, at what time will she have her afternoon tea? ______________

ISBN: 978-1-897164-32-7

We can use subtraction to find time intervals. Sometimes we need to change 1 hour to 60 minutes to find the time intervals.

e.g. From 6:38 to 8:15

```
  7  75
  8̸ : 1̸5   ← 15 < 38, change
                1 h to 60 min.
- 6 : 38       60 + 15 = 75
---------
  1 : 37
```

The time interval is 1 h 37 min.

Find the time intervals. Show your work.

⑦ From 5:48 to 9:25

```
  8    85
  9̸ : 2̸5
- 5 : 48
---------
```

Time interval: ____________

⑧ From 1:52 to 4:33

Time interval: ____________

⑨ From 10:35 to 12:13

Time interval: ____________

⑩ From 3:42 to 6:18

Time interval: ____________

Solve the problems.

⑪ Andy starts building his robot at 3:52 in the afternoon and finishes at 6:27. How long does it take him to build his robot? ____________

⑫ Ted starts his project at 4:18 and it takes him 1 hour and 25 minutes to finish it. At what time does Ted finish his project? ____________

ISBN: 978-1-897164-32-7

Relationships between units of time:

1 decade = 10 years

1 century = 10 decades
= 100 years

My family has had this farm for 10 decades, or 1 century. I have been working here for 30 years, or 3 decades.

Fill in the blanks.

⑬ 30 years
= ______ decades

⑭ 4 centuries
= ______ decades

⑮ 60 decades
= ______ centuries

⑯ 5 decades
= ______ years

⑰ 800 years
= ______ centuries

⑱ 3 centuries
= ______ years

⑲ 9 centuries
= ______ decades

⑳ 60 years
= ______ decades

Read what the children say. Solve the problems.

㉑ *It is 2012. My grandfather's house was built 2 centuries ago. What year was that?* ______

㉒ *I'm 1 decade old. My uncle is 2 decades older than I am. How old is he?* ______

㉓ *If I plant an apple tree in my backyard in 2015, how old will it be in 2615?*

_____ centuries old or _____ decades old

ISBN: 978-1-897164-32-7

14

Mass, Capacity, and Volume

- Record and compare objects, using standard units of mass (e.g. g or kg) or capacity (e.g. mL or L).
- Understand the relationships between g and kg or mL and L.
- Measure and record the volumes of objects.

Choose the appropriate unit for the mass of each object. Write "g" or "kg".

① 

② 

③ 

1 kg = 1000 g

Fill in the blanks.

④ 2 kg = ________ g

⑤ 3000 g = ________ kg

⑥ 5 kg = ________ g

⑦ 9000 g = ________ kg

⑧ 1 kg 200 g = ________ g

⑨ 1 kg 60 g = ________ g

⑩ 5 kg 4 g = ________ g

⑪ 4 kg 800 g = ________ g

Put the things in order from the heaviest to the lightest. Write the letters.

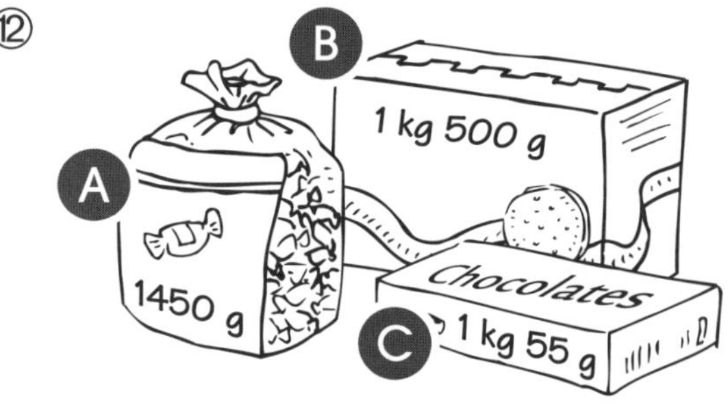

______ , ______ , ______

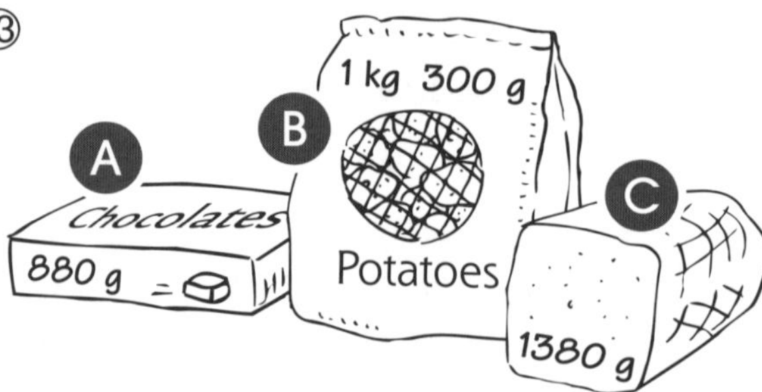

______ , ______ , ______

ISBN: 978-1-897164-32-7

1 L = 1000 mL

Litre – measures larger capacities
e.g. a bathtub

Millilitre – measures smaller capacities
e.g. a juice box

8 L 650 mL = 8000 mL + 650 mL
= 8650 mL

Choose the appropriate unit for the capacity of each container. Write "mL" or "L"

⑭ a mug ______

⑮ a big toy box ______

⑯ a small water bottle ______

⑰ a pail ______

Write the capacity of each container in mL. Then put each group of containers in order from the one with the greatest capacity to the one with the least.

⑱

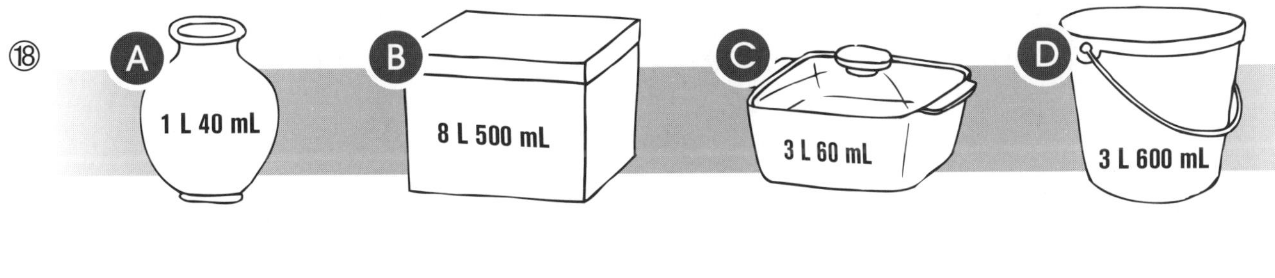

________ ________ ________ ________

In order: ____________________

⑲

________ ________ ________ ________

In order: ____________________

ISBN: 978-1-897164-32-7

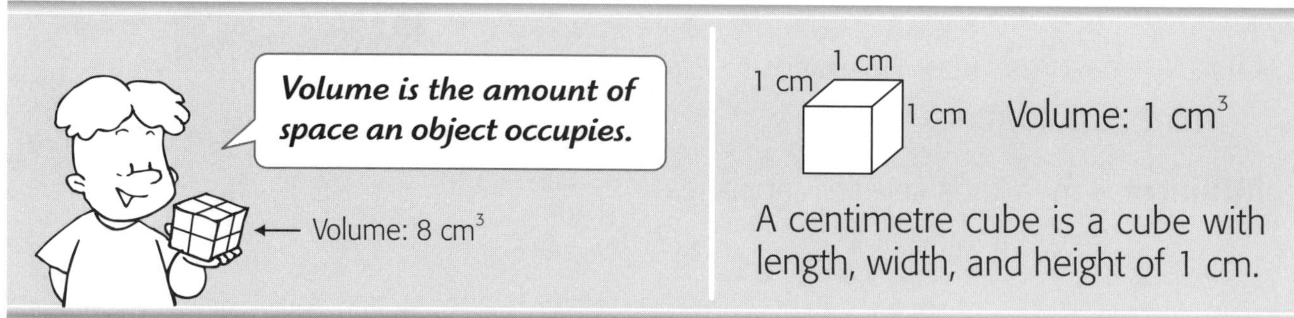

Volume is the amount of space an object occupies.
Volume: 8 cm³
1 cm
1 cm
1 cm
Volume: 1 cm³
A centimetre cube is a cube with length, width, and height of 1 cm.

Complete the table to tell which models are built with the given number of centimetre cubes. Write the letters.

⑳

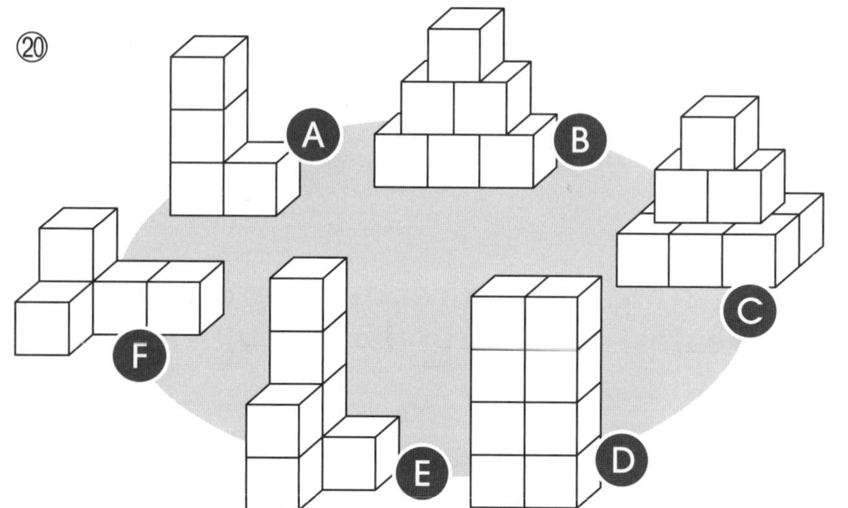

Built by	Model
4	
5	
6	
7	
8	
9	

Count and write the number of centimetre cubes in each model.

㉑

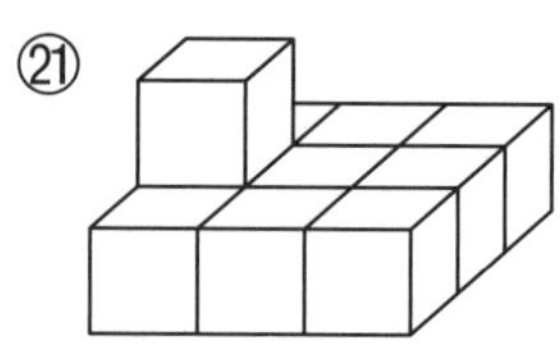

_____ cm^3

㉒

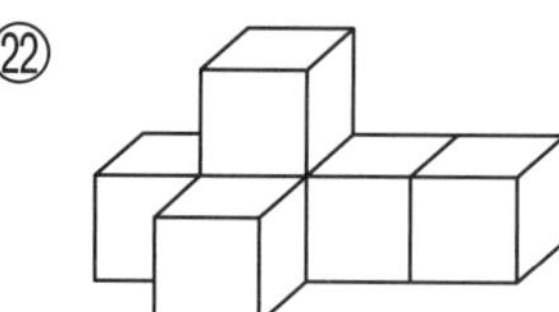

_____ cm^3

㉓

_____ cm^3

㉔

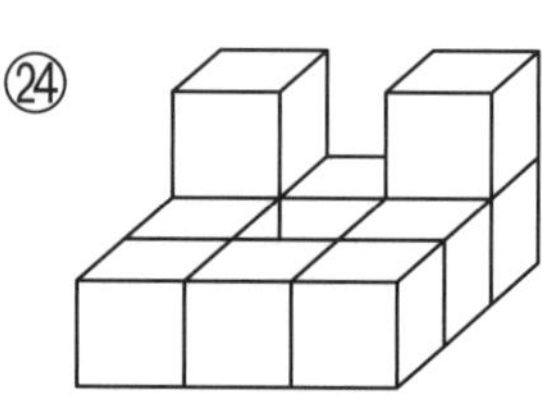

_____ cm^3

㉕

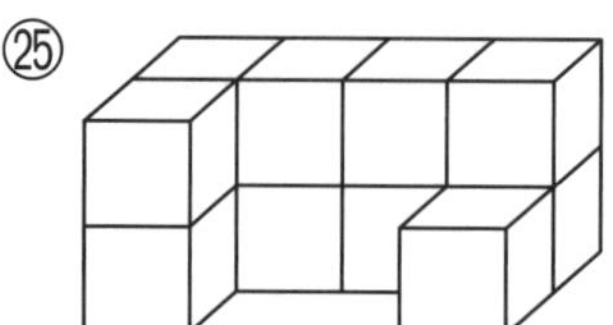

_____ cm^3

ISBN: 978-1-897164-32-7

Count and write the number of centimetre cubes in each rectangular prism. Tell how many more cubes are needed to fill each prism and find the volume. Then answer the questions.

26.

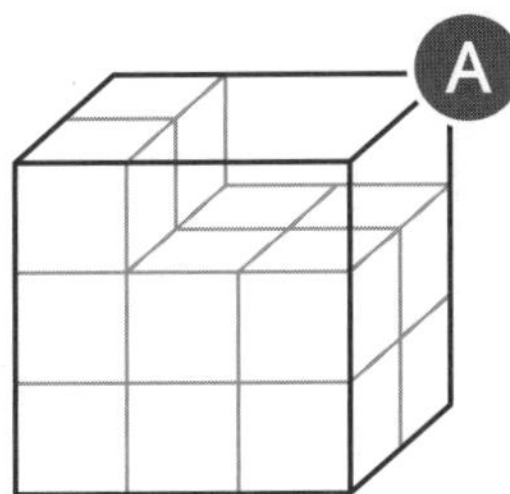

- ______ centimetre cubes are used.
- ______ more centimetre cubes are needed.

Volume of A = ______ cm^3

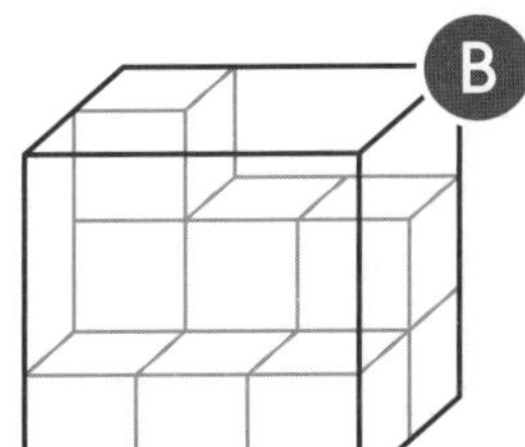

- ______ centimetre cubes are used.
- ______ more centimetre cubes are needed.

Volume of B = ______ cm^3

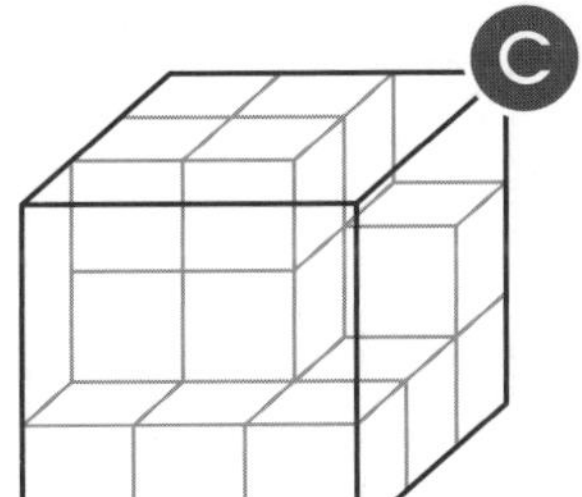

- ______ centimetre cubes are used.
- ______ more centimetre cubes are needed.

Volume of C = ______ cm^3

27. *Which prism has the greatest volume?*

______

28. *If I use the cubes in A and B to build a new prism, which prism do I build?*

P

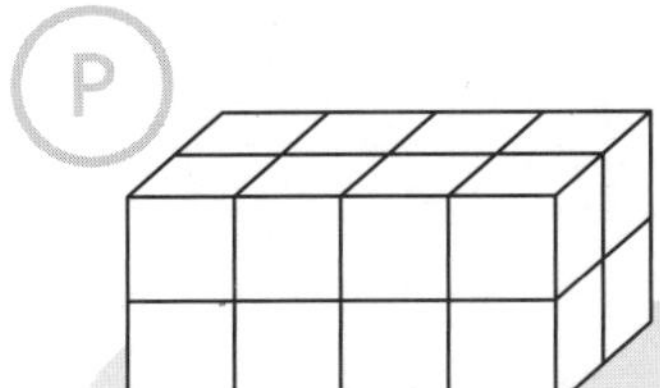

Q

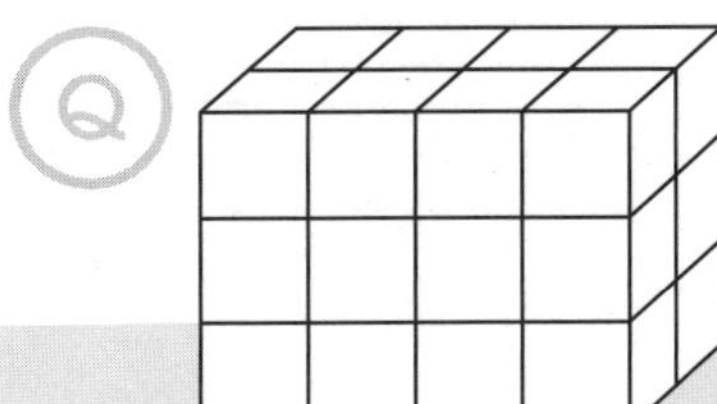

R

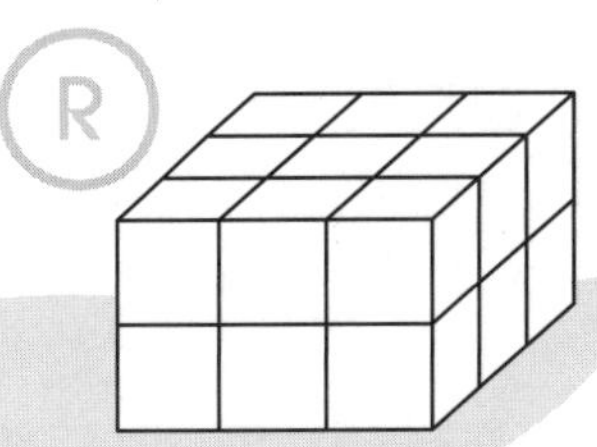

ISBN: 978-1-897164-32-7

Review 1

Fill in the missing numbers.

① 4563 = ____ thousands ____ hundreds ____ tens ____ ones

② 7905 = ____ thousands ____ hundreds ____ ones

③ 6058 = ________ + 50 + ________

④ ________ = 9000 + 100 + 60 + 7

Write the meaning of each digit. Then round the number.

⑤ 5629

a. 5 means ________ ; 6 means ________ ;

2 means ________ ; 9 means ________

b. Round to the nearest hundred: ________

⑥ 

a. 3 means ________ ; 7 means ________ ;

5 means ________ ; 1 means ________

b. Round to the nearest thousand: ________

Check the answer of each question. Put a check mark in the space provided if the answer is correct; otherwise, put a cross and find the correct answer.

⑦ 395 – 209 = *196* Check

⑧ 731 – 287 = *443* Check

⑨ 948 – 879 = *69* Check

⑩ 503 – 165 = *338* Check

ISBN: 978-1-897164-32-7

Find the sum and difference for each pair of numbers.

⑪

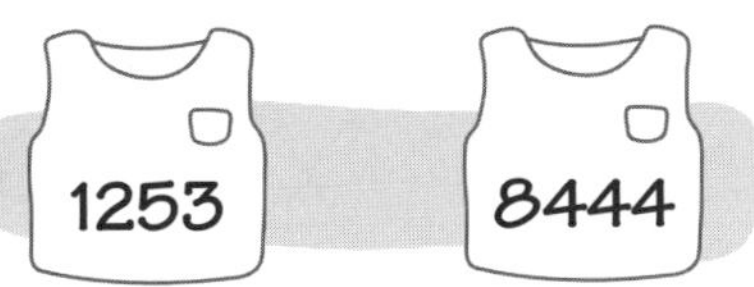

SUM ______________

DIFF. ______________

⑫

SUM ______________

DIFF. ______________

⑬

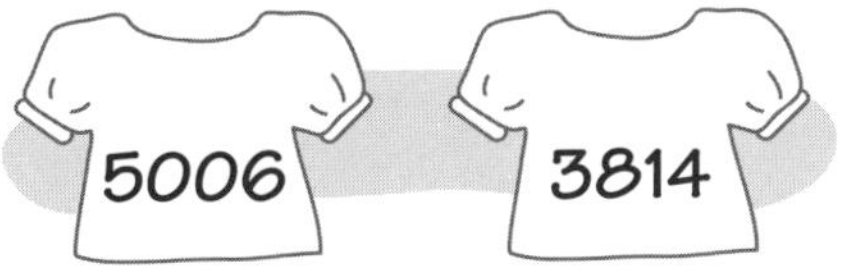

SUM ______________

DIFF. ______________

⑭

SUM ______________

DIFF. ______________

Complete the table. Then answer the questions.

⑮

No. of Visitors	1st Half of the Year	2nd Half of the Year	Whole Year
Men	4653	3750	
Women	3815		8317

⑯ *How many visitors were there in the 1st half of the year?*

______________ = ________ ______________

⑰ *How many visitors were there in the 2nd half of the year?*

______________ = ________ ______________

⑱ *How many more men than women visited the museum this year?*

______________ = ________ ______________

ISBN: 978-1-897164-32-7

Find the answers.

⑲ 7×9

⑳ 39×6

㉑ 45×8

㉒ $7 \overline{)65}$

㉓ $6 \overline{)92}$

㉔ $5 \overline{)85}$

㉕ 74 x 4 = ________

㉖ 86 x 3 = ________

㉗ 46 ÷ 2 = ________

㉘ 57 ÷ 5 = ________

㉙ 51 x 6 = ________

㉚ 27 x 9 = ________

㉛ 83 ÷ 8 = ________

㉜ 68 ÷ 3 = ________

Solve the problems.

㉝ How many cookies are there in 8 boxes?

____________ = ________ ____________

㉞ If there are 2 cookies in a pack, how many packs of cookies are there in a box?

____________ = ________ ____________

㉟ If Uncle Sam needs 54 sausages, how many packs of sausages does he need to buy?

____________ = ________ ____________

ISBN: 978-1-897164-32-7

Check the answer of each division sentence. Put a check mark in the space provided if it is correct; otherwise, put a cross and write the correct answer.

36 69 ÷ 4 = *17 R 1*

Check

37 82 ÷ 7 = *12 R 2*

Check

38 94 ÷ 6 = *16 R 2*

Check

39 53 ÷ 5 = *10 R 3*

Check

Measure and record the distances between the pictures. Then answer the questions.

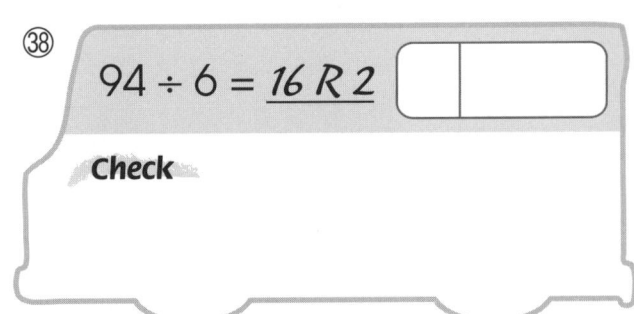

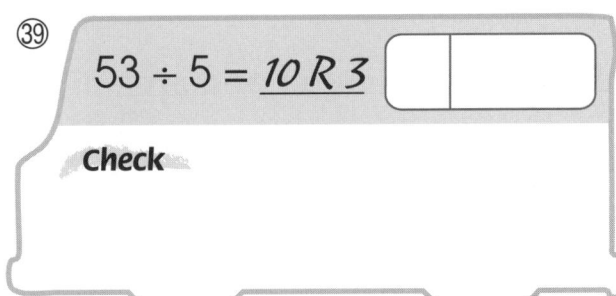

40

Distance between

the hearts: __________

the stars: __________

the moons: __________

41 What is the shortest distance between

a. a star and a moon? __________

b. a heart and a moon? __________

ISBN: 978-1-897164-32-7

Write the most appropriate unit for finding the perimeter of each of the following things.

mm cm dm m km

㊷ a construction site ______ ㊸ a locker mirror ______

㊹ a desk ______ ㊺ a wall ______

㊻ a tablet ______ ㊼ a serving tray ______

Find the perimeter and area of each shape.

㊽

	Perimeter	Area
A		
B		
C		
D		

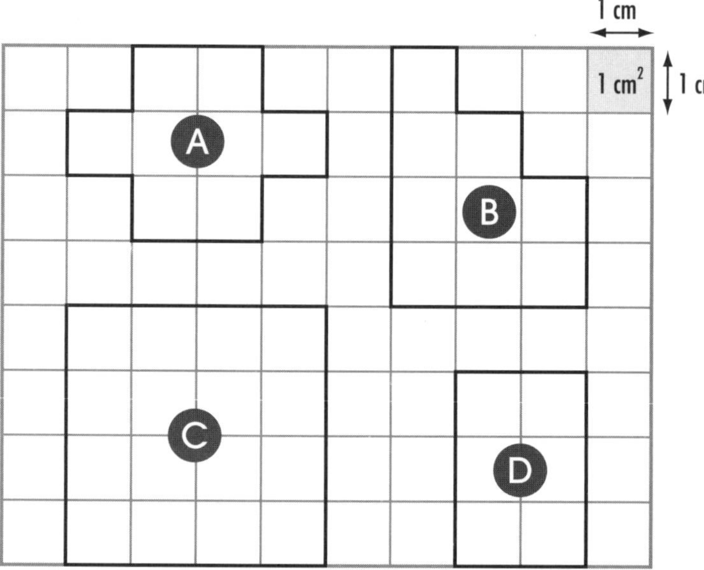

Draw the clock hands to show the time. Then tell the time in a different way.

㊾ 14 min past 7

___ : ___

㊿ 9:38

______

51 2:53

______

ISBN: 978-1-897164-32-7

Look at the picture and Susan's schedule. Answer the questions.

I started my work at 3:45.

52

Check e-mail	5 min
Reply e-mail	15 min
Do research for Science project	30 min
Print saved images	10 min

a. How long did it take Susan to do all her work on the computer? ________

b. Did Susan finish all her work before 5:00? ________

c. If it only took Susan 20 min to do research for the Science project, at what time would Susan finish her work? ________

Each centimetre cube weighs 100 g. Count and write the number of centimetre cubes in each model. Then find the weight of the model.

53

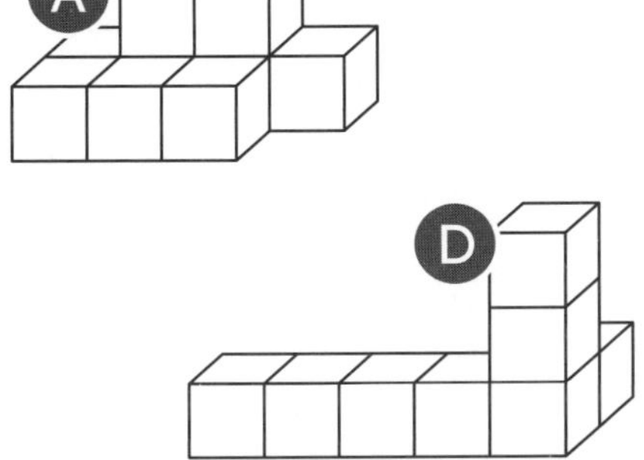
A
D

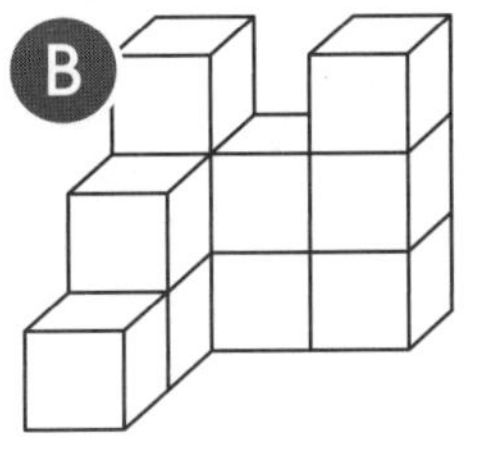
B

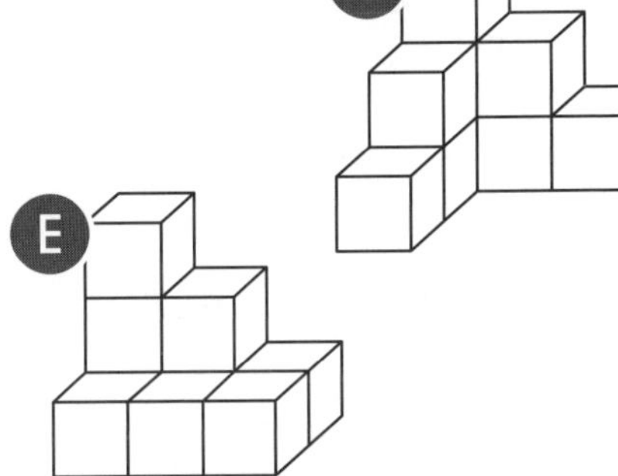
C
E

	A	B	C	D	E
No. of Centimetre Cubes	cm^3				
Weight	g				

ISBN: 978-1-897164-32 7

15

Fractions

- Use standard fractional notation to tell the shaded parts of a whole.
- Understand the meanings of the denominator, numerator, and equivalent fractions.
- Compare and order fractions.

6 equal parts,
1 part shaded
Each of us has $\frac{1}{6}$ of a pizza.

Look at each figure. Trace the dotted lines. Then fill in the boxes with numbers to show the shaded parts in each figure.

①

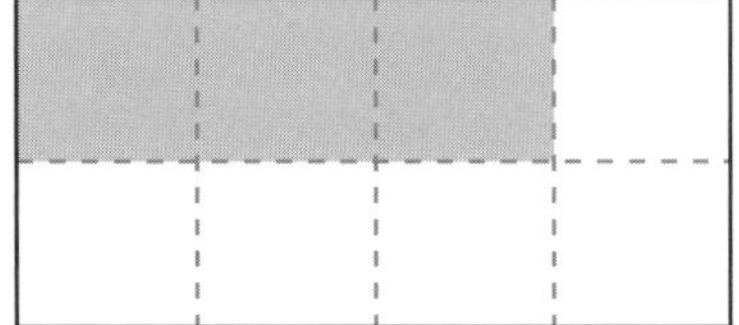

← no. of parts shaded

← no. of equal parts

②

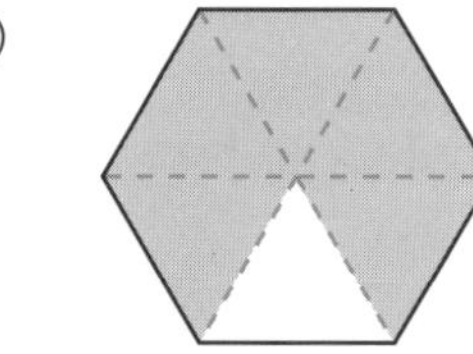

← no. of parts shaded

← no. of equal parts

Colour 2 parts and write a fraction to show the coloured parts in each figure.

③

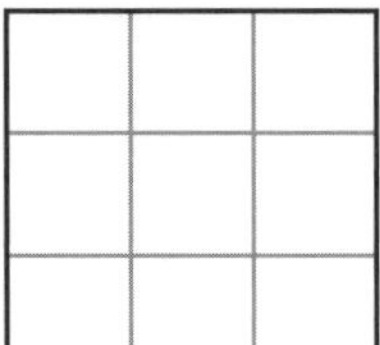

_____ is coloured.

④

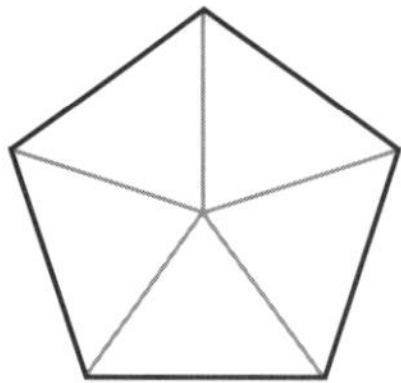

_____ is coloured.

⑤

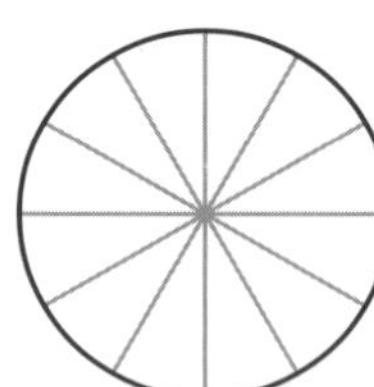

_____ is coloured.

⑥

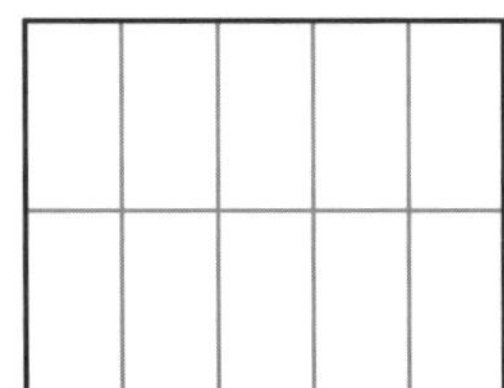

_____ is coloured.

⑦

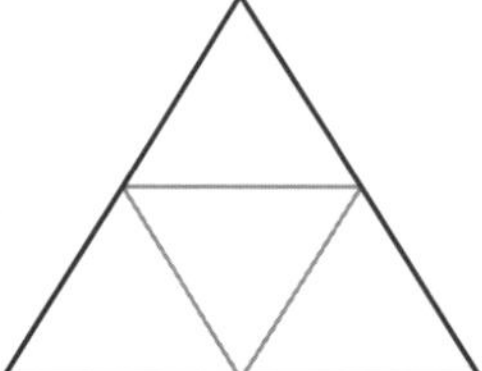

_____ is coloured.

⑧

ISBN: 978-1-897164-32-7

Numerator: the number above the line in a fraction

Denominator: the number below the line in a fraction

e.g. $\frac{3}{4}$ — 3 ← numerator (no. of parts shaded); 4 ← denominator (no. of equal parts in a whole)

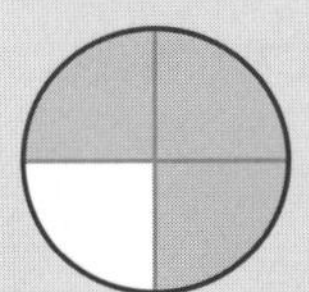

Circle the fractions that have a numerator greater than 4.

⑨ $\frac{3}{7}$ $\frac{5}{6}$ $\frac{1}{5}$ $\frac{7}{10}$ $\frac{3}{4}$ $\frac{2}{6}$ $\frac{2}{3}$ $\frac{9}{10}$ $\frac{7}{12}$

Colour the fractions that have a denominator smaller than 6.

⑩

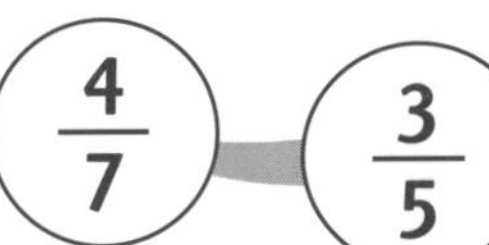

$\frac{2}{3}$

$\frac{3}{9}$ $\frac{1}{4}$ $\frac{5}{8}$

Draw lines to cut each figure and colour the correct number of parts to show the fraction given.

⑪ $\frac{4}{9}$

⑫ $\frac{7}{8}$

⑬ $\frac{1}{2}$

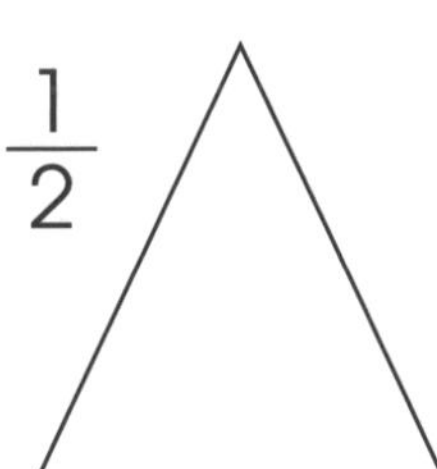

⑭

⑮

⑯

ISBN: 978-1-897164-32-7

Equivalent fractions: fractions that represent the same part of a whole

e.g.

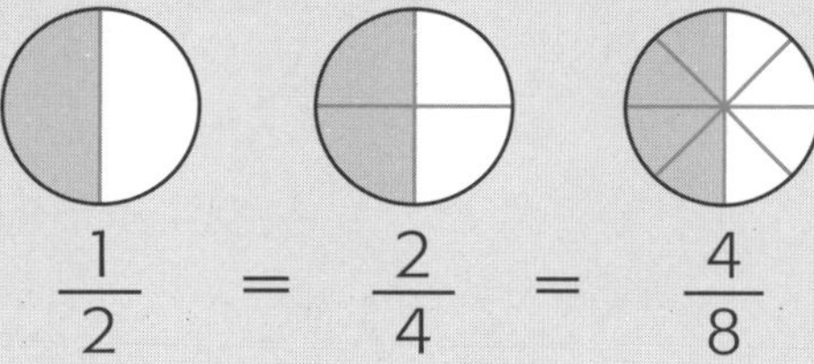

$\frac{1}{2} = \frac{2}{4} = \frac{4}{8}$

$\frac{1}{2}$, $\frac{2}{4}$, and $\frac{4}{8}$ are equivalent fractions.

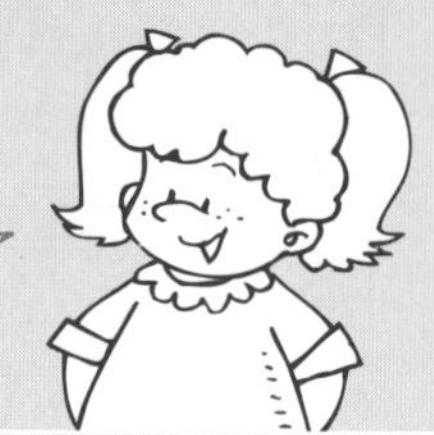

Write a fraction to show the shaded parts in each figure. Then fill in the blanks with fractions to complete the sentences.

⑰ A 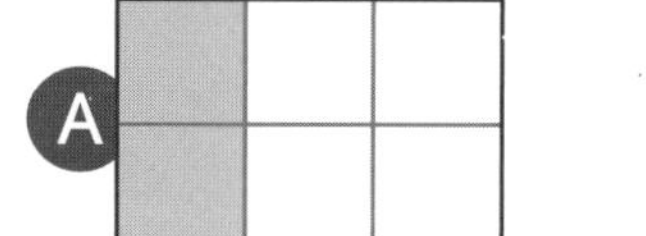 ______ B ______ C 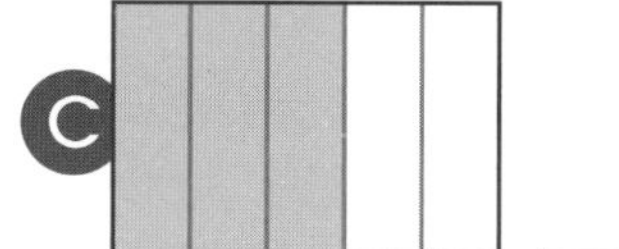 ______

______ and ______ are equivalent fractions.

⑱ A 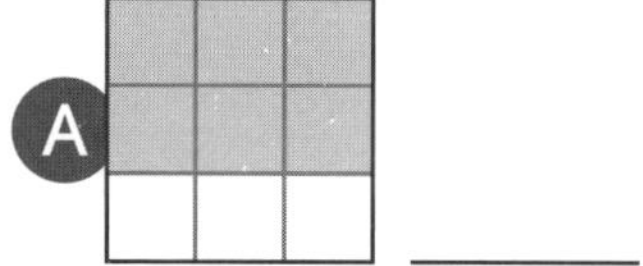 ______ B 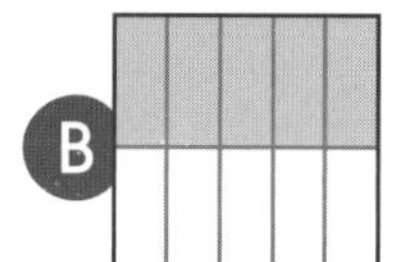 ______ C 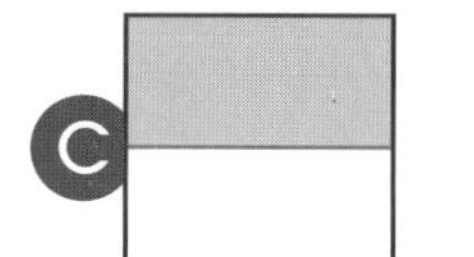 ______

______ and ______ are equivalent fractions.

Draw figures to show that the fractions in each pair are equivalent.

⑲ 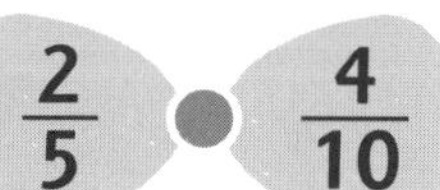

⑳ 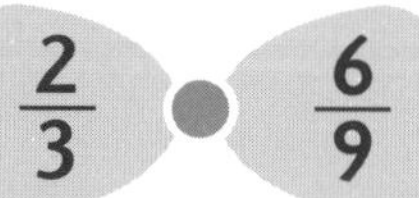

㉑ $\frac{1}{4}$ ● $\frac{2}{8}$

ISBN: 978-1-897164-32-7

Write a fraction to show the shaded parts in each figure. Then put ">" or "<" in the circle.

㉒ 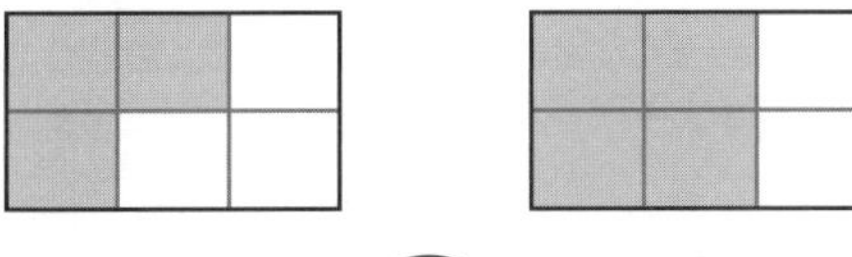

$\frac{}{6}$ ◯ ______

㉓ 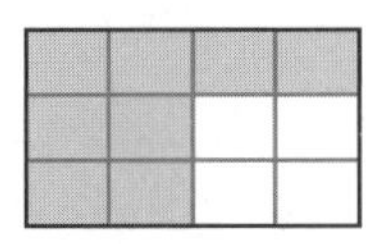

______ ◯ ______

㉔ 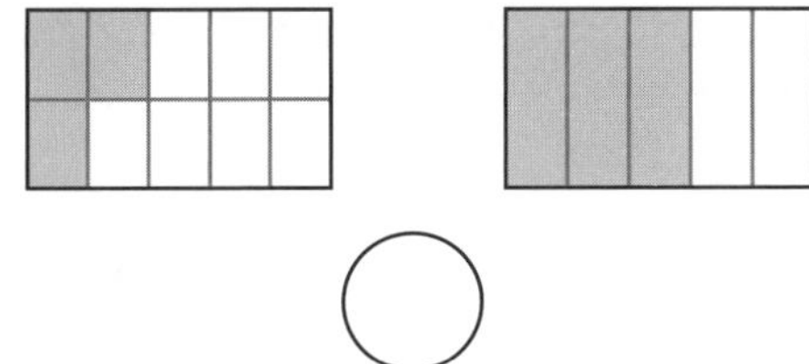

____ ◯ ______

㉕ 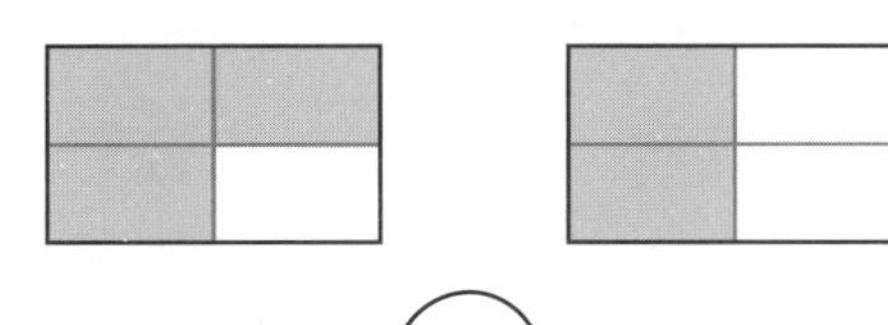

______ ◯ ______

Circle the greater fraction.

㉖ $\frac{7}{8}$ $\frac{6}{8}$

㉗ $\frac{9}{10}$ $\frac{5}{10}$

㉘ $\frac{1}{7}$ $\frac{1}{3}$

㉙ $\frac{4}{9}$ $\frac{4}{5}$

㉚ $\frac{2}{6}$ $\frac{6}{7}$

㉛ $\frac{8}{9}$ $\frac{2}{4}$

Put the fractions in order. Then answer the question.

㉜ $\frac{1}{3}$ $\frac{9}{10}$ $\frac{3}{5}$

< <

㉝ $\frac{3}{4}$ $\frac{1}{5}$ $\frac{3}{8}$

< <

㉞ $\frac{5}{9}$ $\frac{3}{10}$ $\frac{1}{4}$

< <

㉟ *I have $\frac{2}{5}$ of a pizza, Sam has $\frac{2}{10}$, Joe has $\frac{7}{8}$, and Tim has $\frac{1}{4}$. Who has the most pizza?*

______ has the most pizza.

ISBN: 978-1-897164-32-7

16

Decimals

- Write, compare, and order decimal numbers to tenths.
- Understand the place value in decimal numbers and the relationship between fractions and decimals to tenths.
- Use number lines to locate decimal numbers.

0.3 of my balloons have stripes.

Put a decimal point in the correct place to show how much of each diagram is shaded. Then write the decimal in words.

①

In numeral: **0 9**

In words: ______ tenths

②

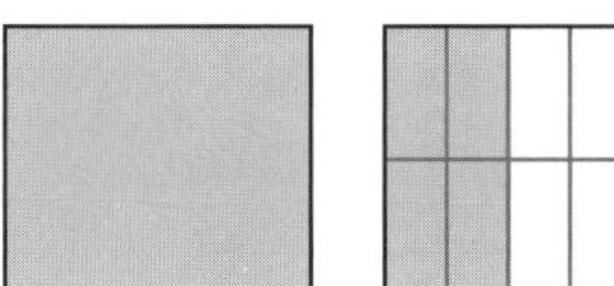

In numeral: **1 4**

In words: ______ and ______ tenths

③

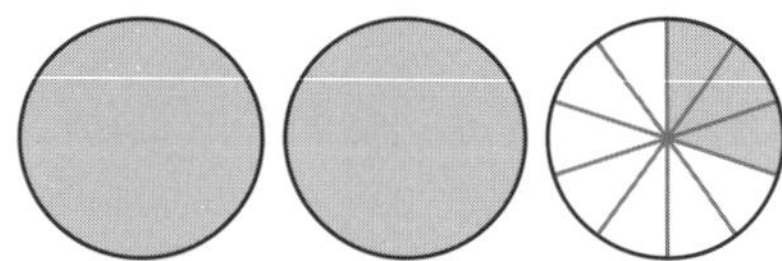

In numeral: **2 3**

In words: ____________________

④

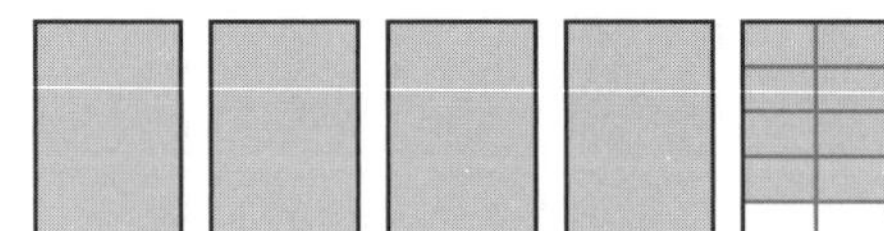

In numeral: **4 8**

In words: ____________________

Colour the diagrams to match each decimal given. Then write the decimal in words.

⑤ **2.7**

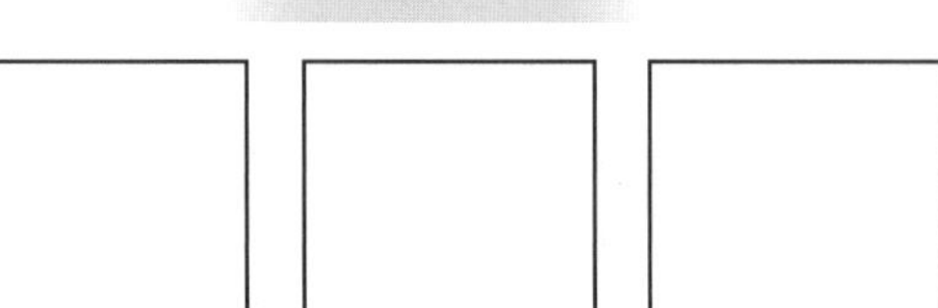

In words: ____________________

⑥ **3.5**

In words: ____________________

ISBN: 978-1-897164-32-7

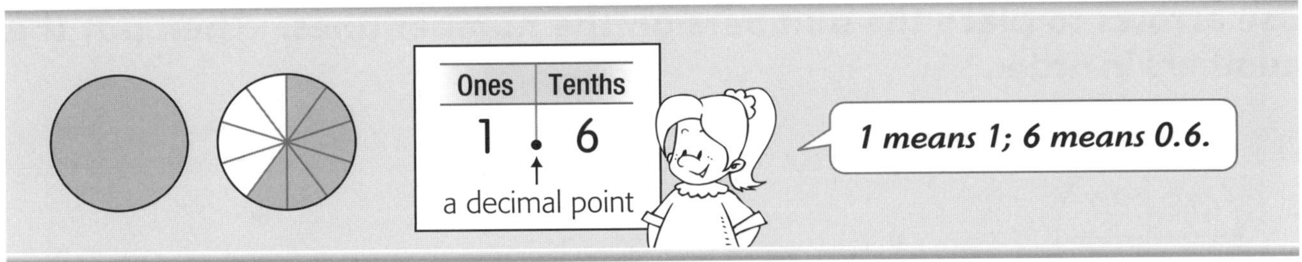

Write the meaning of each highlighted digit.

⑦ 5.**6** ________ ⑧ 1**7**.5 ________ ⑨ **3**2.4 ________

⑩ 10.**8** ________ ⑪ 5.**2** ________ ⑫ **9**0.3 ________

⑬ 2**5**.1 ________ ⑭ 6.**4** ________ ⑮ 3**4**.6 ________

Write as decimals. Then colour the greater one in each pair.

⑯ 6 and 2 tenths 

5 and 9 tenths

⑰ 11 and 6 tenths

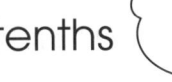

20 and 1 tenth

⑱ 4 and 5 tenths  

5 and 4 tenths 

⑲ 13 and 1 tenth 

1 and 3 tenths 

Write a decimal and a fraction to show how much of each diagram is shaded.

⑳ 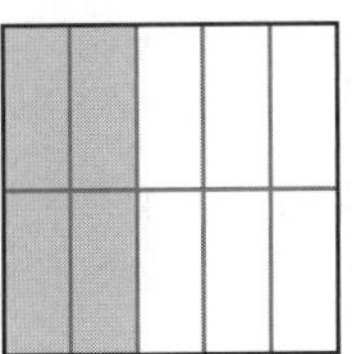

________ = ________
decimal fraction

㉑ 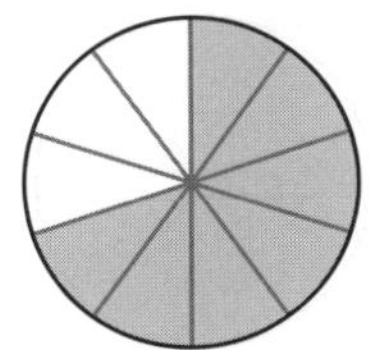

________ = ________
decimal fraction

㉒ 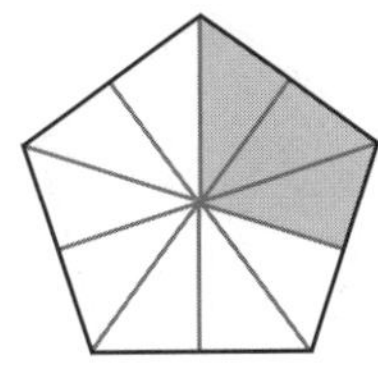

________ = ________
decimal fraction

ISBN: 978-1-897164-32-7

Use arrows to place the numbers on the number lines. Then put the numbers in order.

㉓

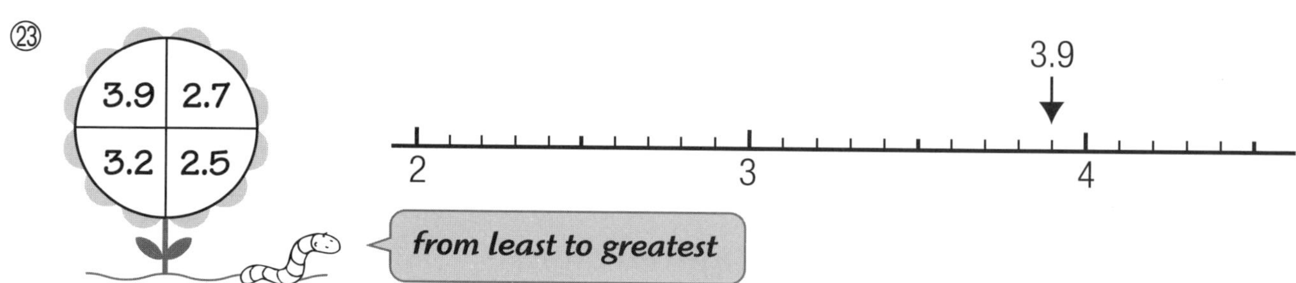

㉔

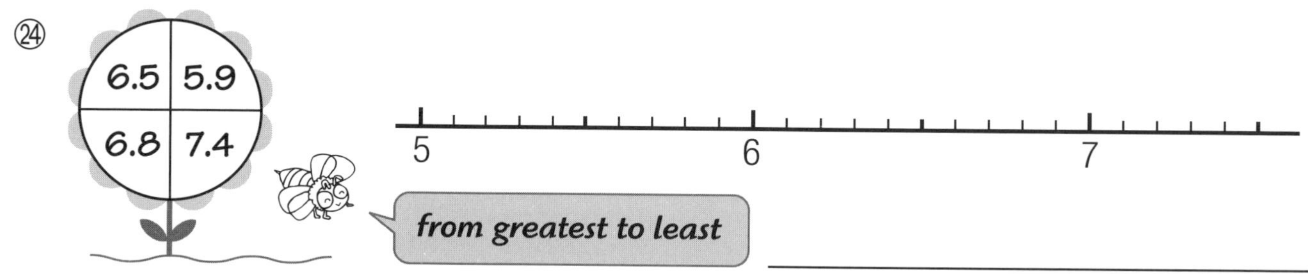

Read what the girl says. Help her draw number lines and show the locations of decimals. Then fill in the blanks.

㉕ *Draw a number line that extends from 3 to 6. Then mark the locations of 4.0, 4.8, and 5.1.*

㉖ *Draw a number line that extends from 8 to 11. Then mark the locations of 8.4, 9.5, 9.8, and 10.3.*

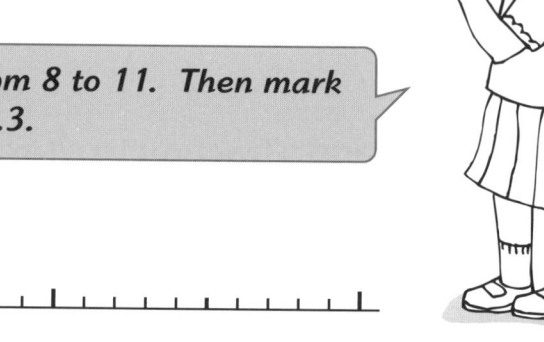

㉗ 5.1 is greater than 4.8 by ______ .

㉘ 9.8 is less than 10.3 by ______ .

ISBN: 978-1-897164-32-7

Write the decimals.

㉙ 2 tenths greater than 9.5 ______

㉚ 3 tenths less than 8.4 ______

㉛ 5 tenths greater than 7.6 ______

㉜ 2 tenths less than 5.1 ______

Fill in the missing decimals.

㉝ 6.2 6.4 6.6 ______ ______ 7.2 7.4 ______ 7.8

㉞ 9.4 9.3 9.2 ______ 9.0 ______ ______ 8.7 8.6

㉟ 4.5 5.0 5.5 ______ ______ 7.0 ______ 8.0 8.5

㊱ 8.9 9.9 ______ ______ ______ 13.9 14.9 15.9

Write the distances between Ann and the gift boxes in the spaces provided. Then answer the questions.

㊲

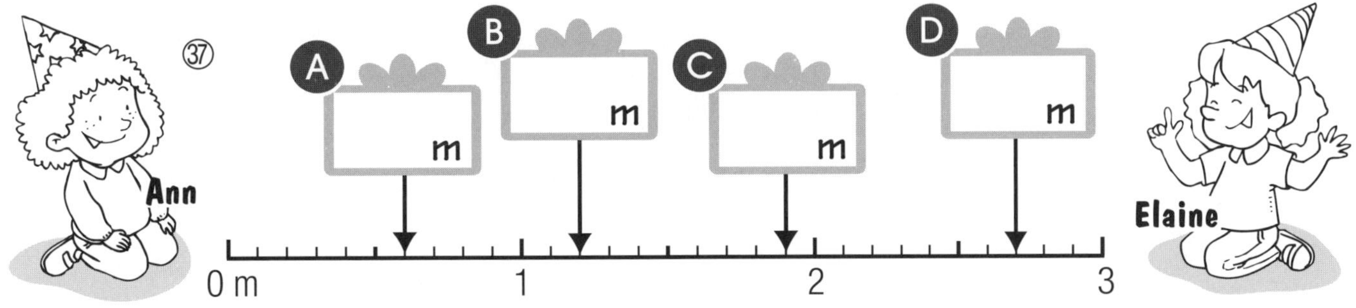

㊳ Which gift box is closest to Elaine? ______

㊴ What is the distance between Elaine and the closest gift box? ______

㊵ What is the distance between Ⓐ and Ⓑ? ______

㊶ What is the distance between Ⓒ and Ⓓ? ______

ISBN: 978-1-897164-32-7

17

Addition and Subtraction of Decimals

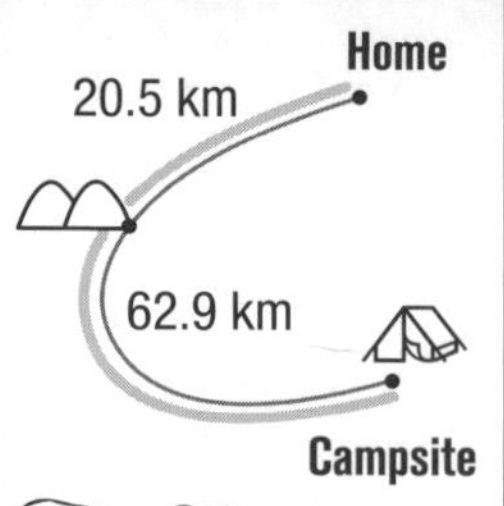

- Add or subtract decimal numbers to tenths.
- Solve problems involving addition or subtraction of decimal numbers.

We have to travel 83.4 km from our home to the campsite.

Put a decimal point in the answer to complete each vertical addition.

① $\begin{array}{r} 4.5 \\ +\ 3.6 \\ \hline 8\ 1 \end{array}$

② $\begin{array}{r} 8.2 \\ +\ 3.6 \\ \hline 1\ 1\ 8 \end{array}$

③ $\begin{array}{r} 9.4 \\ +\ 4.6 \\ \hline 1\ 4\ 0 \end{array}$

Do the addition.

④ $\begin{array}{r} 8.5 \\ +\ 4.9 \\ \hline \end{array}$

⑤ $\begin{array}{r} 7.5 \\ +\ 9.2 \\ \hline \end{array}$

⑥ $\begin{array}{r} 4.6 \\ +\ 4.6 \\ \hline \end{array}$

⑦ $\begin{array}{r} 12.7 \\ +\ 9.4 \\ \hline \end{array}$

⑧ $\begin{array}{r} 14.4 \\ +\ 8.8 \\ \hline \end{array}$

⑨ $\begin{array}{r} 5.3 \\ +\ 18.8 \\ \hline \end{array}$

⑩ 16.8 + 6.2 = ________

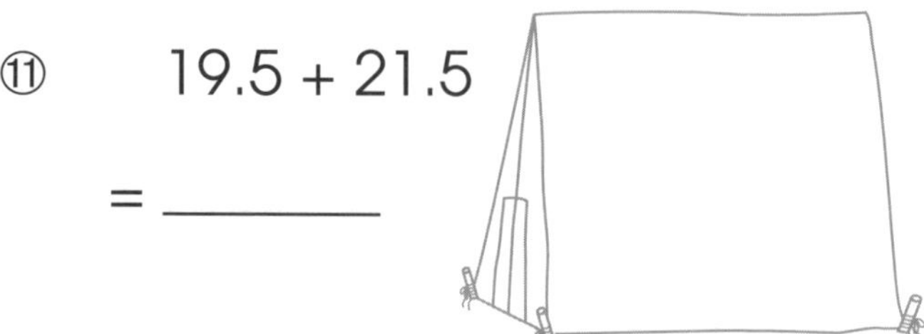

⑪ 19.5 + 21.5 = ________

⑫ 3.9 + 12.7 = ________

⑬ 9.4 + 7.8 = ________

⑭ 5.6 + 5.8 = ________

⑮ 9.2 + 17.8 = ________

ISBN: 978-1-897164-32-7

The children are playing games. Help them find their total scores. Then answer the questions.

Record

	1st Round	2nd Round		1st Round	2nd Round
Tim	9.6	5.8	Lucy	7.6	6.6
Ray	8.1	11.9	Sue	10.7	3.3
Mark	12.5	6.3	Lily	8.2	4.4

⑯

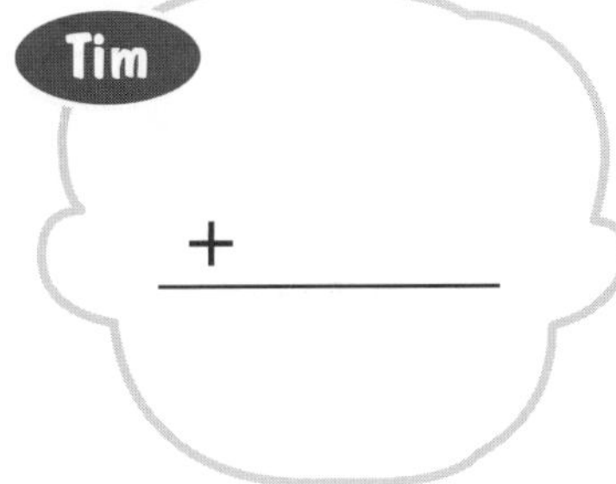

⑰ Who has the highest score? ____________

⑱ Who has the lowest score? ____________

⑲ What is the total score of the boys' team?

____________________________ = ________ ____________

⑳ What is the total score of the girls' team?

____________________________ = ________ ____________

㉑ Which team has a higher score? ____________

ISBN: 978-1-897164-32-7

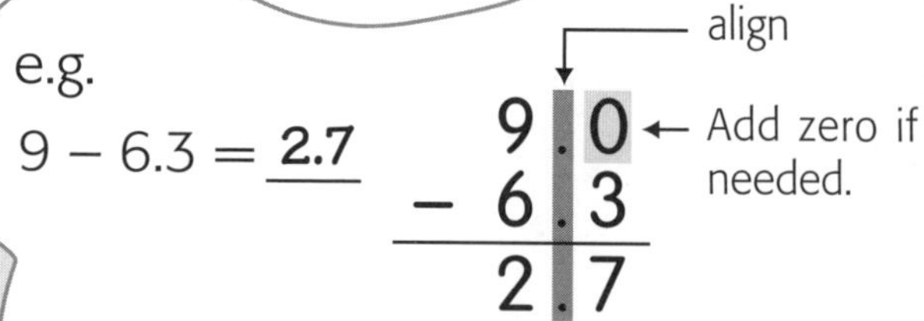

Subtracting decimals:

1st Align the decimal points.

2nd Subtract the same way we subtract whole number.

3rd Put the decimal point in the answer.

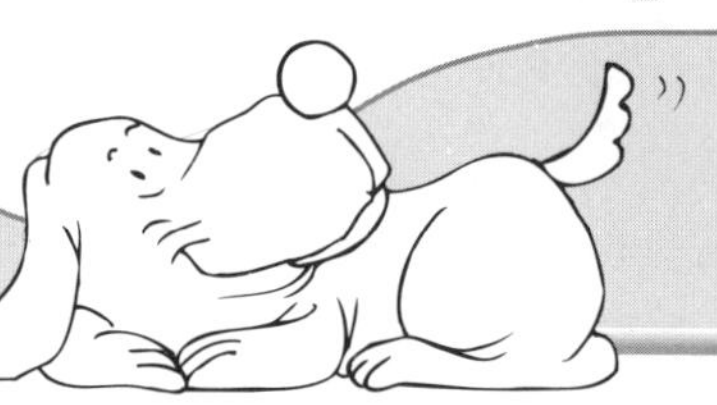

Do the subtraction.

㉒ 14.7 – 5.8 = ______

㉓ 10.2 – 4.6 = ______

㉔ 8.5 – 2.7 = ______

㉕ 8 – 3.4 = ______

㉖ 14 – 6.9 = ______

㉗ 20 – 13.2 = ______

㉘ 7.7 – 5.9 = ______

㉙ 8.5 – 4.8 = ______

㉚ 13.6 – 6.7 = ______

㉛ 15 – 9.8 = ______

Fill in the missing numbers.

㉜
```
  1 □ . □
–   6 . 8
---------
    9 . 1
```

㉝
```
  2 □ . 3
–   8 . □
---------
  1 1 . 6
```

㉞
```
  □ 5 . □
– 1 □ . 6
---------
  2 3 . 8
```


ISBN: 978-1-897164-32-7

Find the answers.

35. 9.5 + 2.7 = ________
36. 18.7 – 6.9 = ________
37. 13.4 – 8.9 = ________
38. 20 – 18.4 = ________
39. 7.6 + 8.6 = ________
40. 2.5 + 19.8 = ________

Solve the problems.

41. 
Juice
1.3 L

Aunt Linda has a box of juice. If she drinks 0.8 L of juice, how much juice will be left?

____________________ = ________ __________

42. 
0.8 kg

Nicholas has two bags of candies. How many kilograms of candies does he have in all?

____________________ = ________ __________

43. 
Ann
I'm 1.3 m tall.

Uncle Jason is 0.4 m taller than Ann. How tall is Uncle Jason?

____________________ = ________ __________

44. 
38.2 m

Mr. Shaw cuts the rope into two pieces. If one piece is 16.4 m long, how long is the other piece?

____________________ = ________ __________

45. 
My husband, my two sons, and I each drink 1 big bottle of water every day. How much water do we drink in all each day?

1.4 L

____________________ = ________

____

ISBN: 978-1-897164-32-7

18

Money

- Read and write money amounts to $100.
- Add and subtract money amounts to make purchases and changes up to $10.

I can save $15.66 if I buy it today.

$98.65
– $82.99
$15.66

~~$98.65~~ $82.99

Estimate and find the exact amount of money in each group.

① A

B

C

D

Group	Estimate		Actual	
A	dollars	cents	dollars	cents or $
B				
C				
D				

ISBN: 978-1-897164-32-7

Draw the fewest bills and coins to show the cost of each item. Then find the total costs and price differences.

②

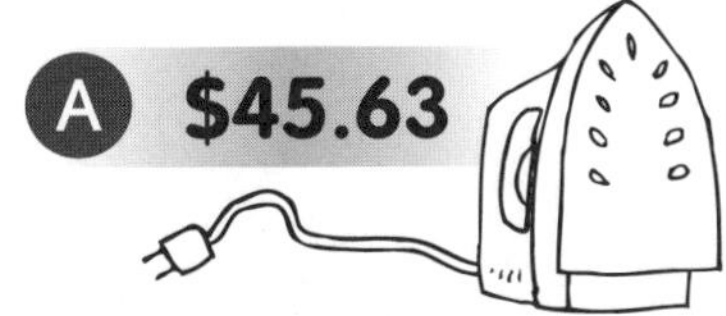

Ⓐ $45.63

Ⓑ $53.17

Ⓒ $97.55

Ⓓ $32.82

Key

$50

$20

$10

$5

$2

$1

25¢

10¢

5¢

1¢

③ **Total Cost**

Ⓐ and Ⓓ

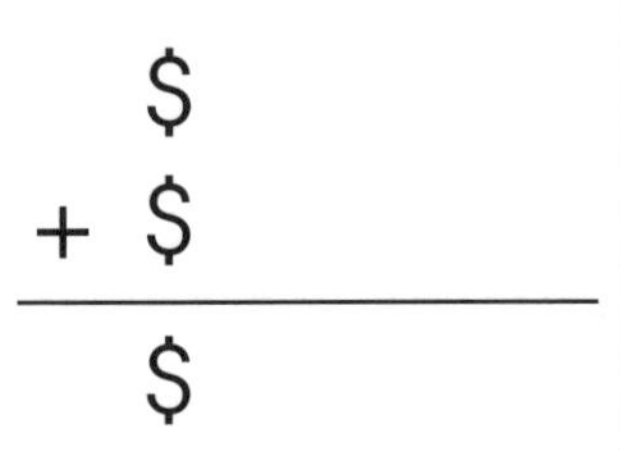

$
+ $
$

Ⓑ and Ⓓ

④ **Price Difference**

Ⓑ and Ⓒ

$
− $
$

Ⓐ and Ⓒ

ISBN: 978-1-897164-32-7

Look at the cost of each item. Fill in the missing information on each receipt. Then answer the questions.

⑤

Uncle Ben's Toyland

Item	Cost
Mr. Frog	
Mr. Frog	
Robot	
Total	
Cash	$50.00
Change	

⑥

Uncle Ben's Toyland

Item	Cost
Tricycle	
Doll	
Puzzle	
Total	
Cash	$70.01
Change	

⑦

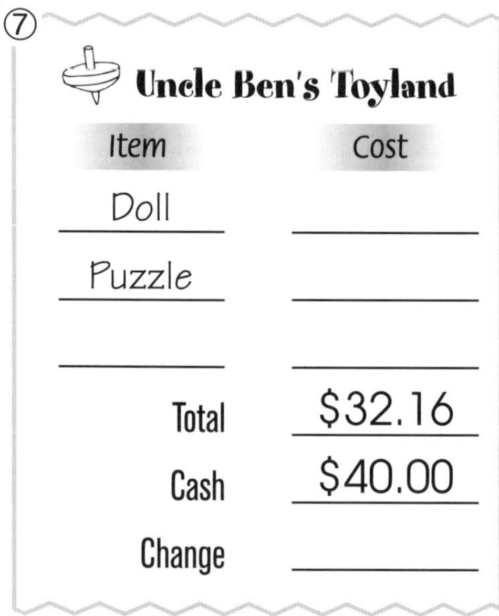

Uncle Ben's Toyland

Item	Cost
Doll	
Puzzle	
Total	$32.16
Cash	$40.00
Change	

⑧

Uncle Ben's Toyland

Item	Cost
Mr. Frog	
Tricycle	
Total	
Cash	$51.00
Change	$ 0.48

⑨ Jimmy buys a robot and a toy car for $45.64. How much is the toy car?

____________ = ______ ______

⑩ If the sale price of the tricycle is $28.66, how much is saved?

____________ = ______ ______

ISBN: 978-1-897164-32-7

Solve the problems.

⑪ a. How much do two cakes cost?

b. If Mrs. Smith pays $40 for a cake, what is her change?

$32.65

⑫ a. Jack has $28. If he wants to buy a calculator, how much more does he need?

b. If a storybook costs $7.65 more than a calculator, how much does the storybook cost?

$40.89

⑬ a. *I've bargained with the salesman for a better price. If I pay only $42.98 now, how much do I save?*

b. *If I want to buy two bags at this bargain price, how much do I need to pay?*

ISBN: 978-1-897164-32-7

19

2-D Shapes (1)

square
rectangle
Sam, don't you know that they are all quadrilaterals?

- Draw the lines of symmetry of 2-D shapes.
- Identify and compare different types of quadrilaterals.

Trace the dotted lines to show the lines of symmetry of each shape. Then write the numbers.

①

A
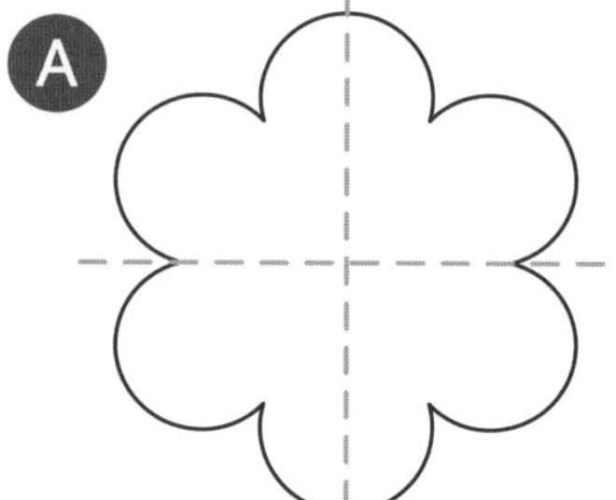

B
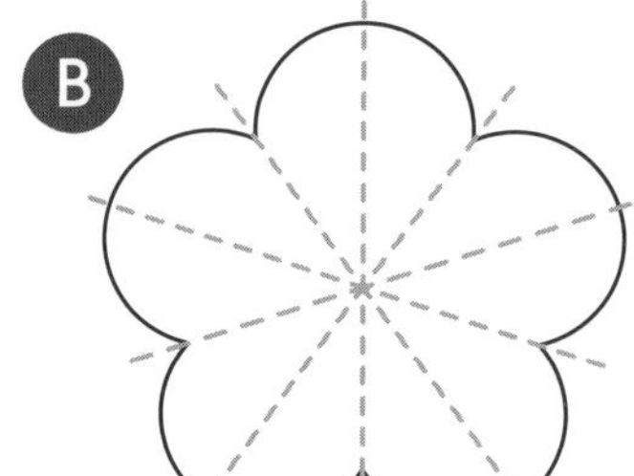

C
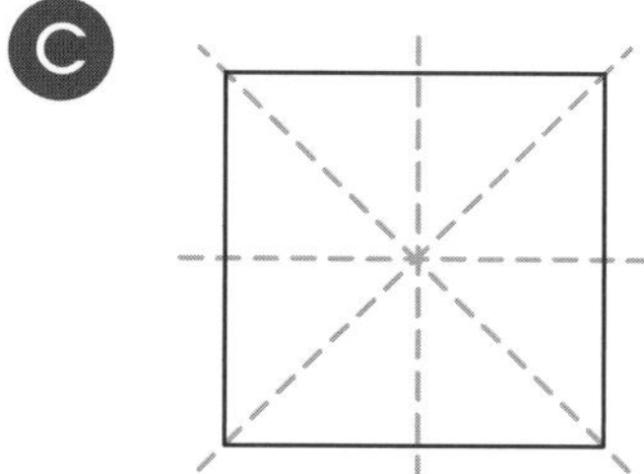

D
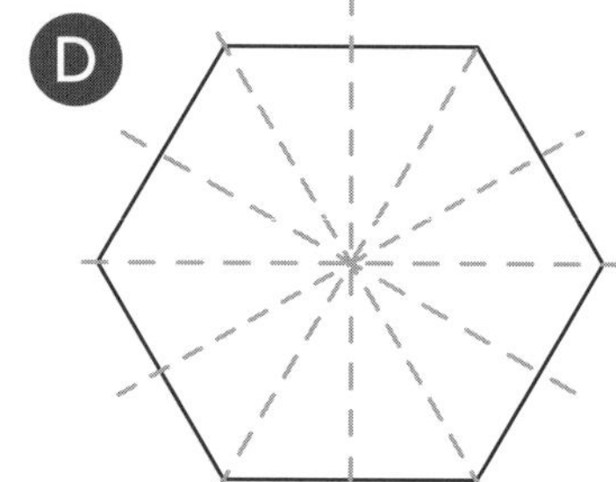

E
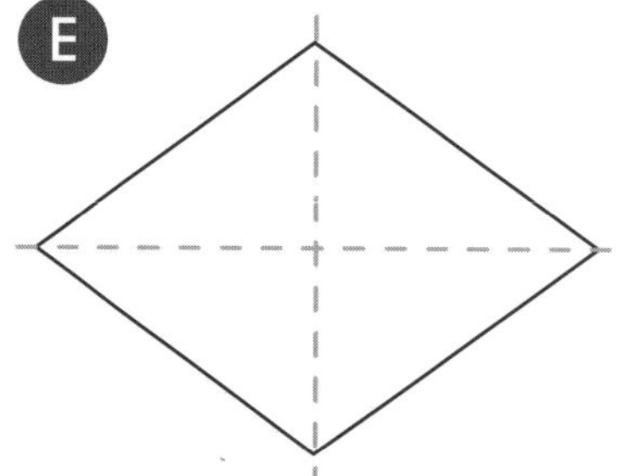

F
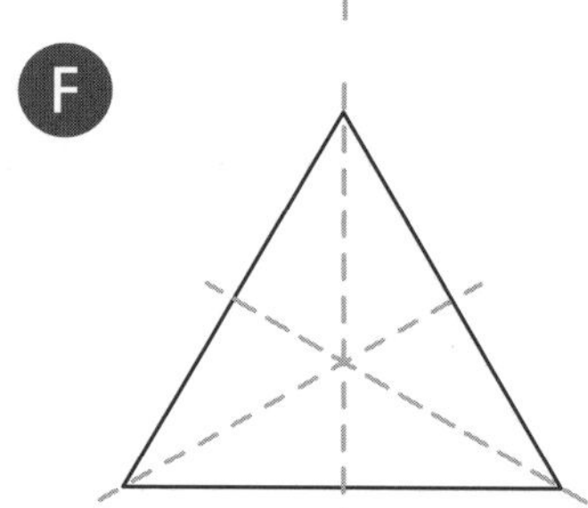

G
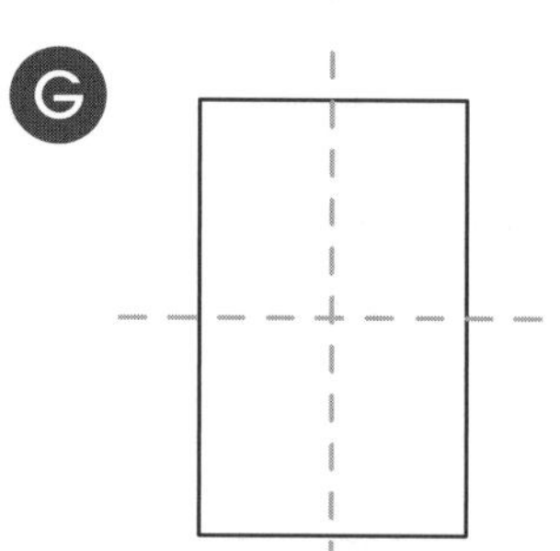

H
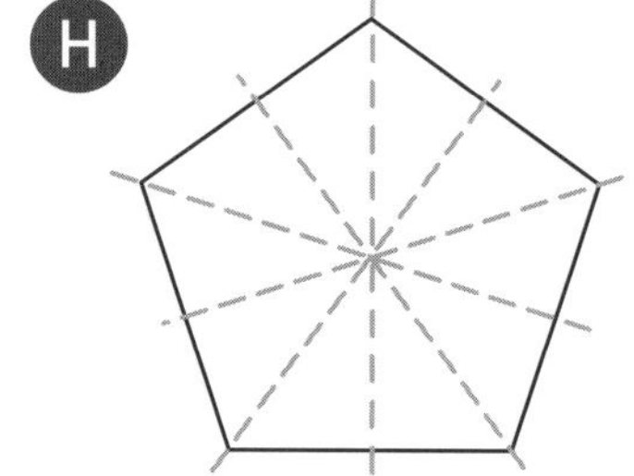

I
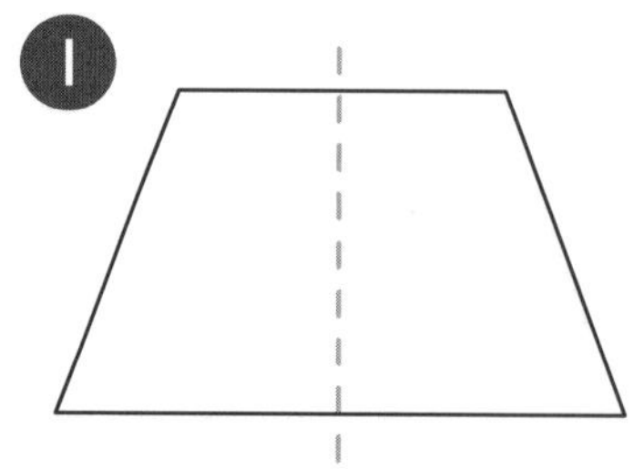

Shape	No. of Line(s) of Symmetry
A	
B	
C	
D	
E	
F	
G	
H	
I	

ISBN: 978-1-897164-32-7

Put a check mark in the circle if the sentence is correct; otherwise, put a cross.

② A rectangle has 2 lines of symmetry.

③ A regular pentagon has 5 lines of symmetry.

④ A parallelogram has 1 line of symmetry.

⑤ *The bigger the square, the more the lines of symmetry it has.*

The dotted line is the line of symmetry of each shape. Draw the missing side(s) to complete the shape. Then name the two small shapes that you can see in the big shape.

⑥

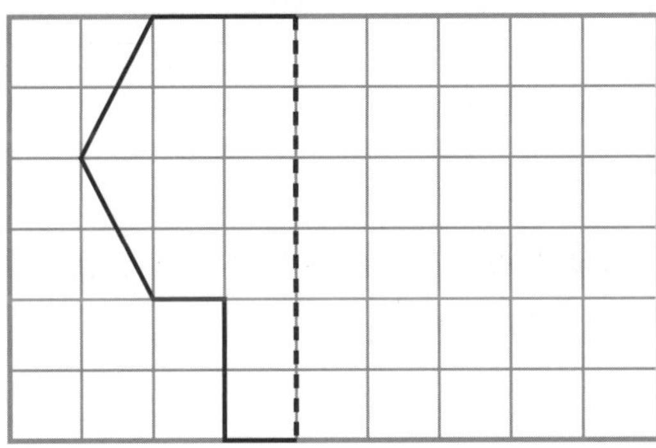

______ ; ______

⑦

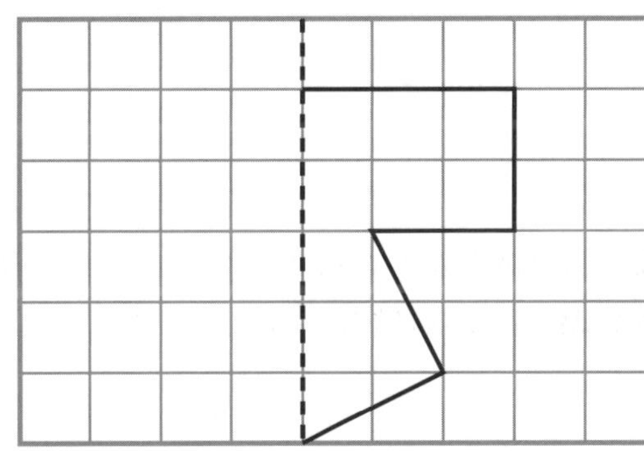

______ ; ______

⑧

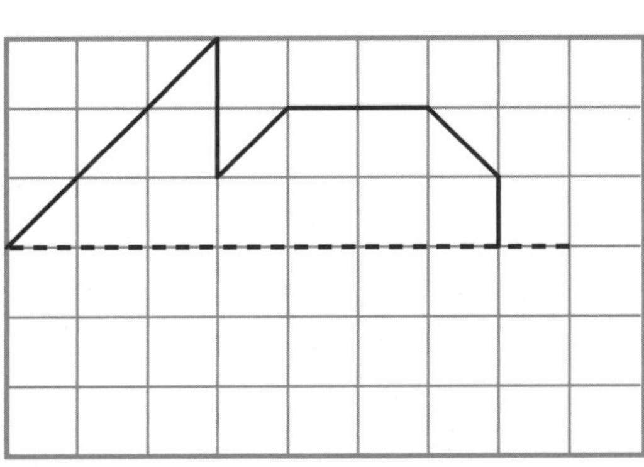

______ ; ______

⑨

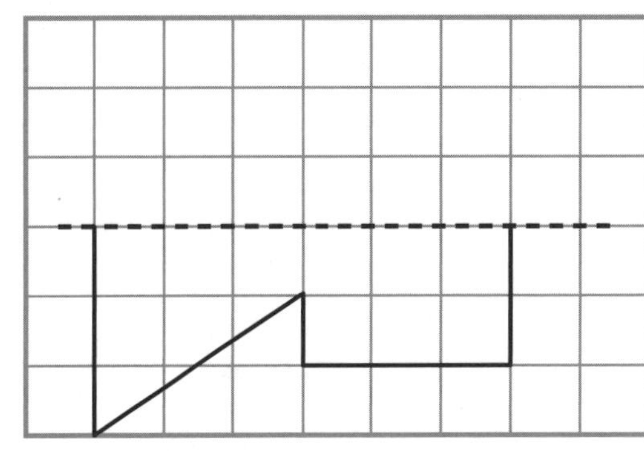

______ ; ______

ISBN: 978-1-897164-32-7

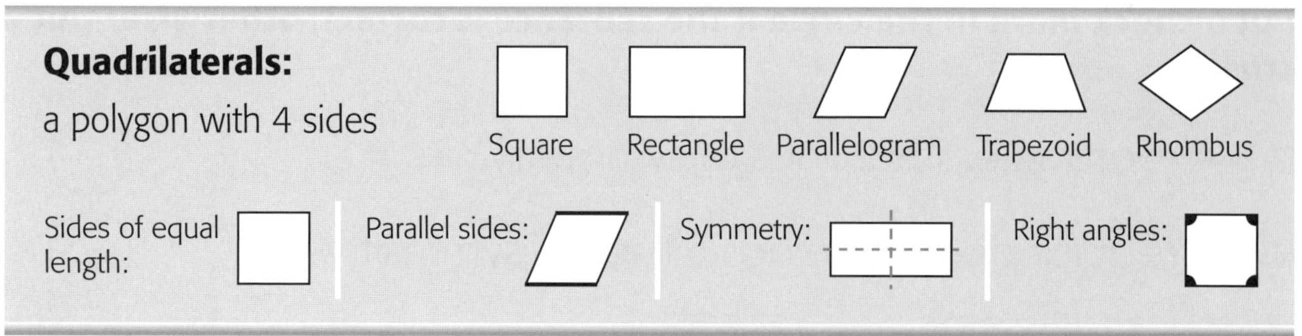

Draw the missing side of each quadrilateral. Then name it.

⑩

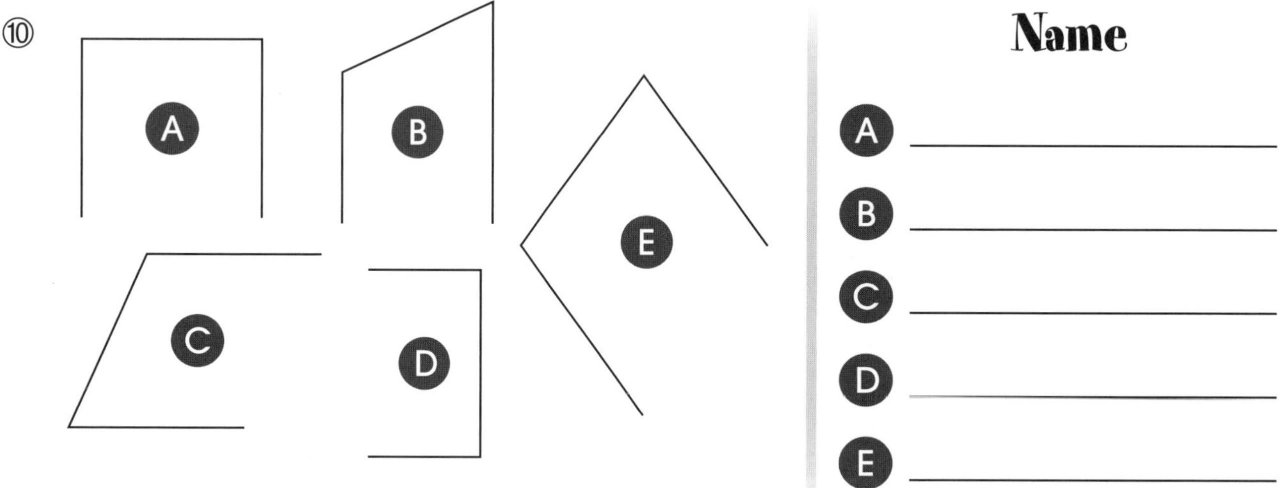

Measure and record the side lengths of each quadrilateral in cm. Then colour the quadrilateral if its sides have equal length.

⑪

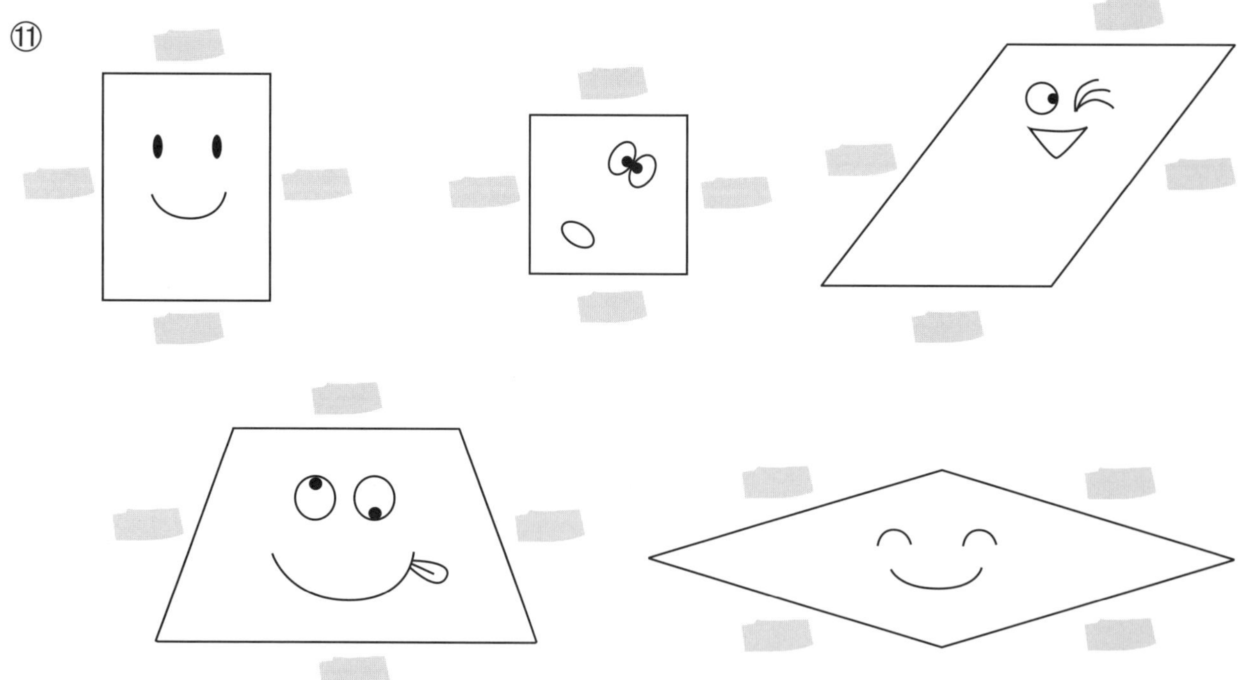

ISBN: 978-1-897164-32-7

Colour each pair of parallel sides of each quadrilateral in different colours. Then answer the questions.

⑫

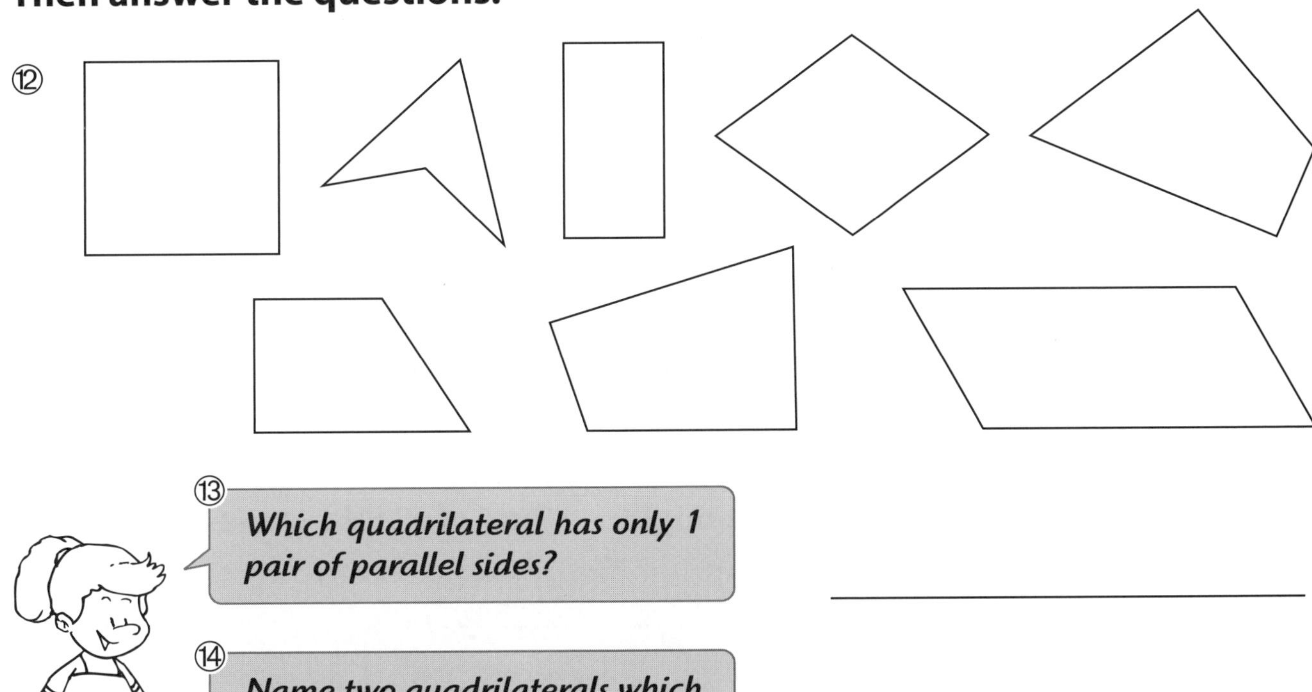

⑬ *Which quadrilateral has only 1 pair of parallel sides?* ____________________

⑭ *Name two quadrilaterals which have 2 pairs of parallel sides.* ____________________

Draw a quadrilateral to match the descriptions.

⑮
- 2 lines of symmetry
- 4 right angles

⑯
- 4 sides with the same length
- no right angle

⑰
- 1 pair of parallel sides
- 2 right angles

⑱ *It has 2 pairs of parallel sides, but it has no right angle.*

ISBN: 978-1-897164-32-7

20

2-D Shapes (2)

- Identify and describe angles.
- Relate the names of the angles to their measures in degrees.
- Draw symmetrical designs.

right angle
I've chewed off a piece with a right angle.

See how the paper is folded and opened. Use the given words to describe the angles that are formed.

straight angle **right angle** **half of a right angle**

① fold open ____________

② fold open ____________

③ fold fold open ____________

④ fold open ____________

⑤ fold open ____________

ISBN: 978-1-897164-32-7

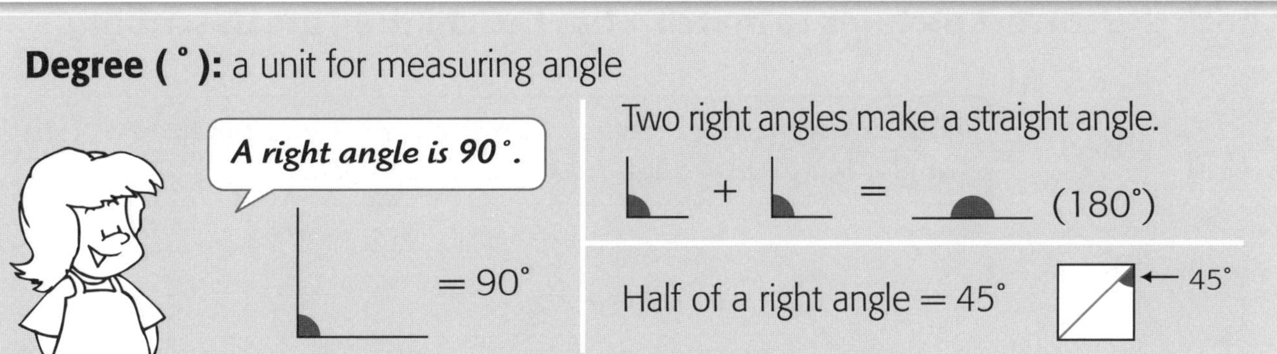

Degree (°): a unit for measuring angle
A right angle is 90°.
= 90°
Two right angles make a straight angle.
+
=
(180°)
Half of a right angle = 45°
45°

Find the measure in degrees for each marked angle.

⑥ ⑦

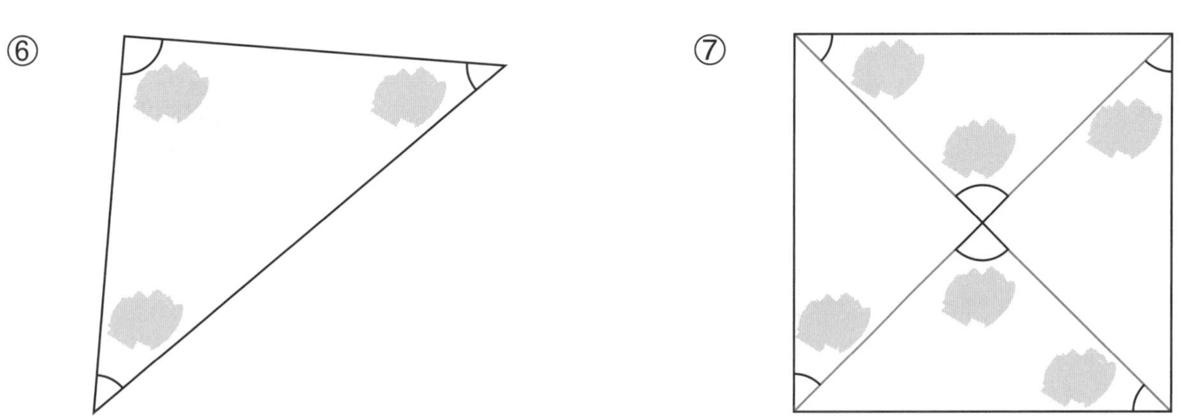

See how the paper is cut. Find the measure in degrees for each angle formed by the cut vertices.

⑧ ⑨ ⑩

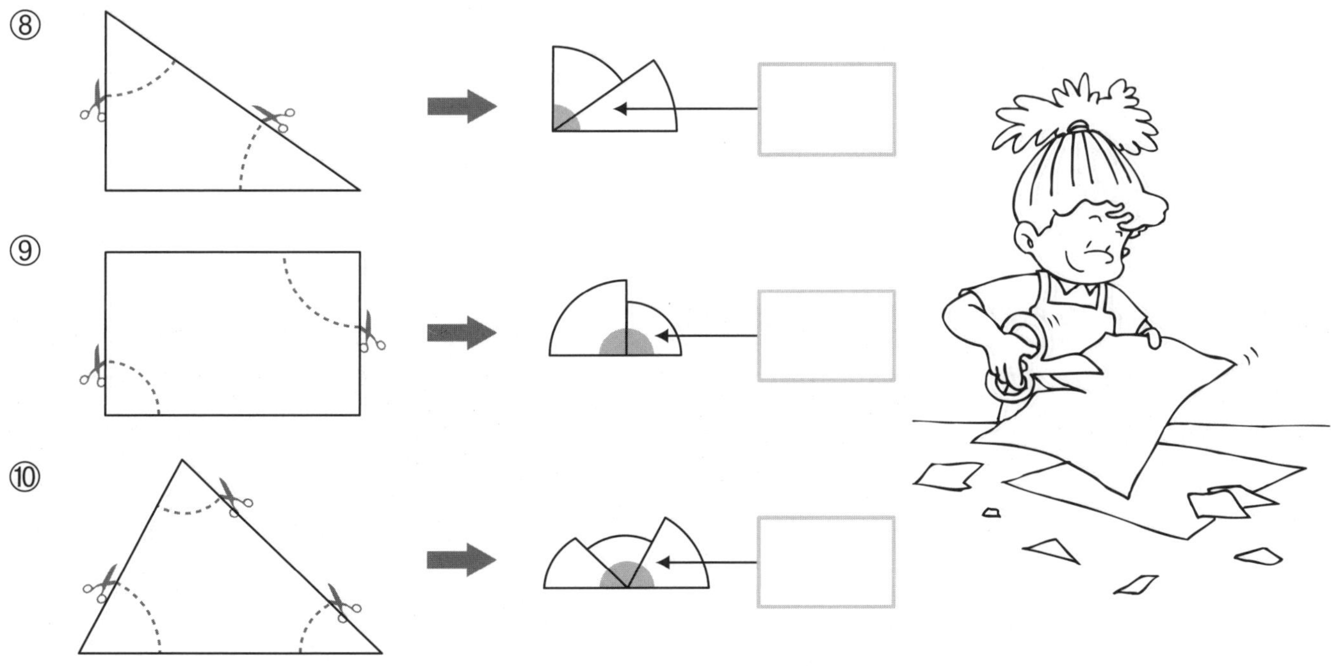

ISBN: 978-1-897164-32-7

Check the correct pictures to match what the children are describing.

⑪ *The angle the door makes with the wall is smaller than a right angle, but greater than half of a right angle.*

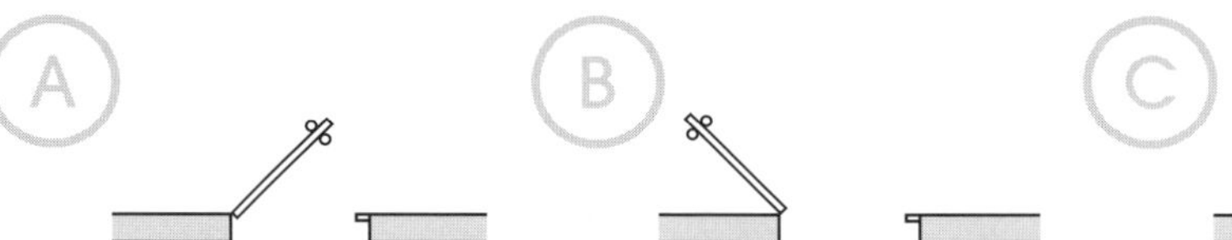

A B C

⑫ 

The angle that I can make with my legs is smaller than a straight angle, but greater than a right angle.

A  B  C 

⑬ 

I can make an angle of 180° with my pencils.

A 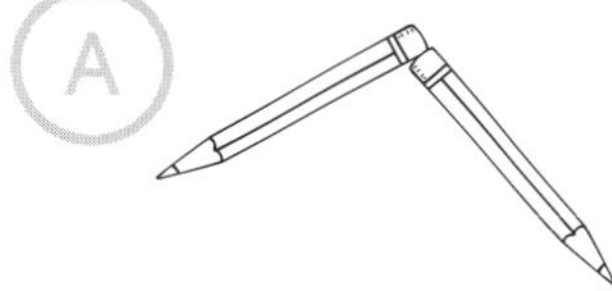 B  C 

⑭ 

I can make an angle which is smaller than 180° but greater than 90° with my scissors.

A 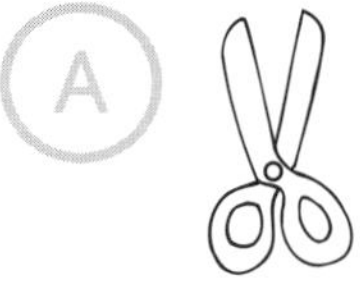 B  C 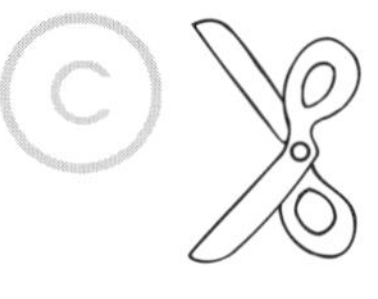

Draw a line to construct each angle.

⑮ an angle that is greater than 90° but smaller than 180°

⑯ an angle smaller than 90° but greater than 45°

ISBN: 978-1-897164-32-7

Describe the angles formed by the clock hands.

⑰ ______________________________

____

⑱ ______________________________

____

Draw the missing parts of each symmetrical picture.

⑲

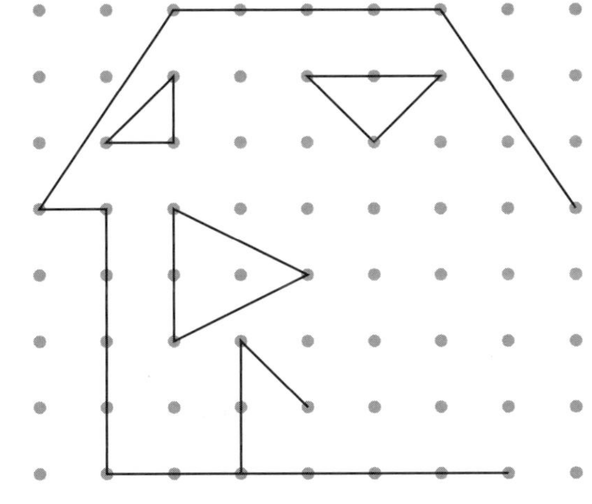

⑳

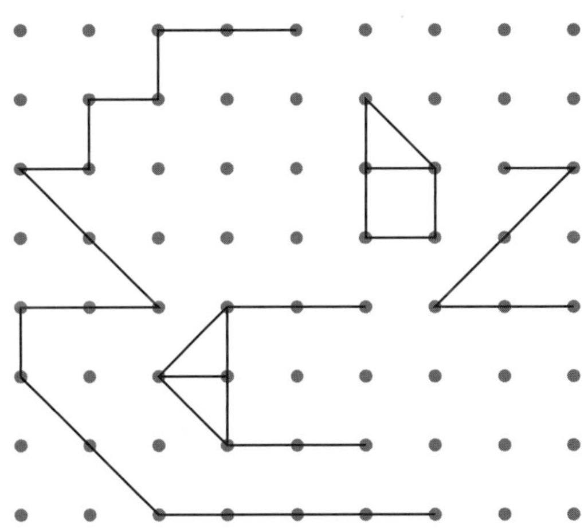

㉑

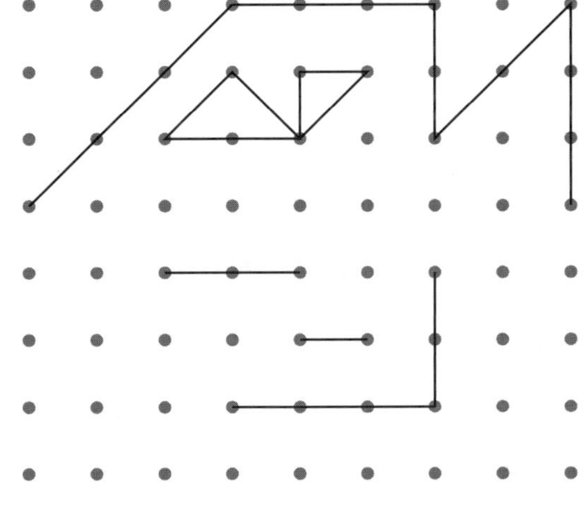

㉒

ISBN: 978-1-897164-32-7

21

3-D Figures (1)

- Identify, describe, and clarify different prisms and pyramids.
- Construct and sketch the skeletons of 3-D figures.

Name each 3-D figure. Then count and write the number of triangular faces that each figure has.

①

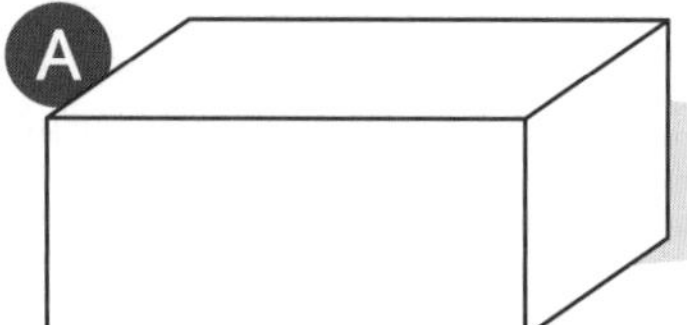

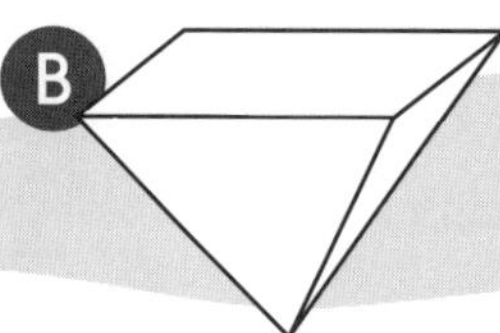

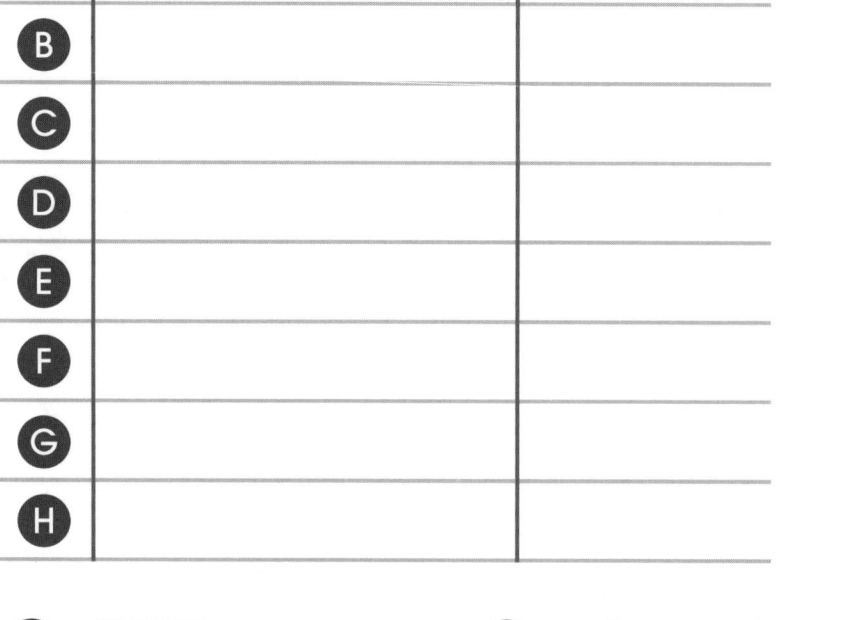

	Name	No. of Triangular Faces
A		
B		
C		
D		
E		
F		
G		
H		

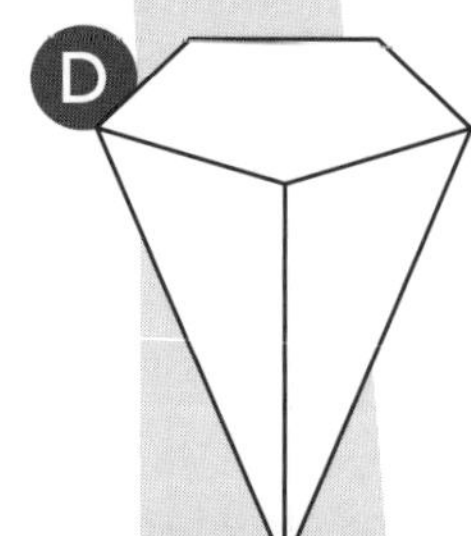

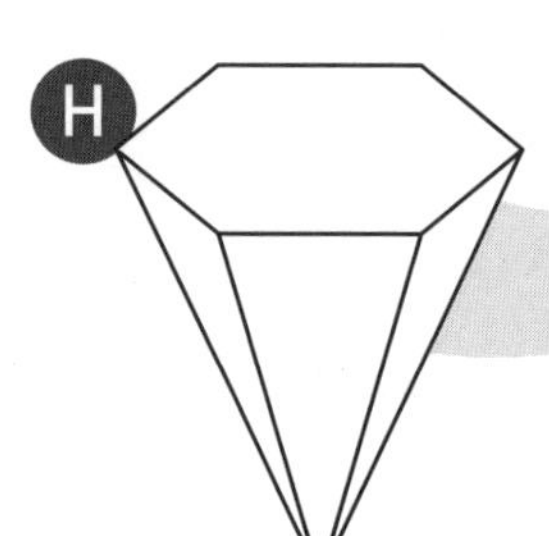

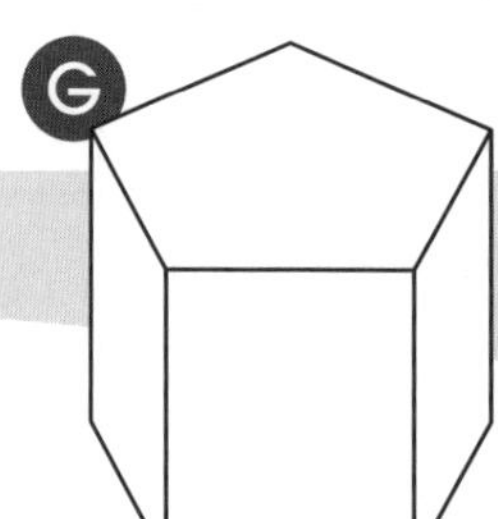

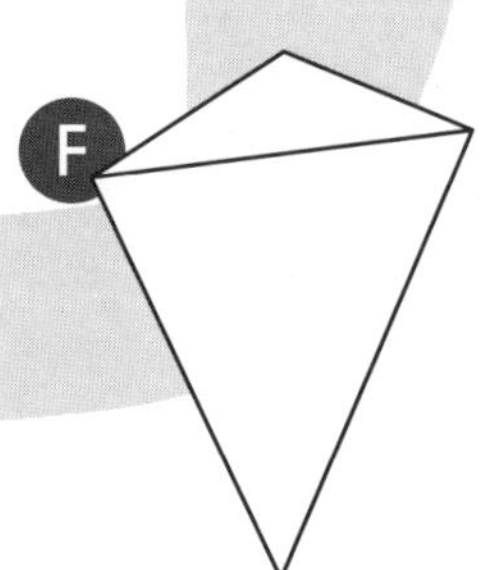

ISBN: 978-1-897164-32-7

The children are describing their 3-D figures. Fill in the blanks with the correct words or numbers to complete the descriptions.

② *It is a ______________________ . It has _____ triangular face(s) and _____ rectangular face(s). It has _____ vertices and _____ edges.*

③ *It is a ______________________ . It has _____ faces, _____ vertices, and _____ edges. All the faces are in the shape of a ______________ .*

See how the children above described their 3-D figures again. Use the same ways to describe these 3-D figures.

④

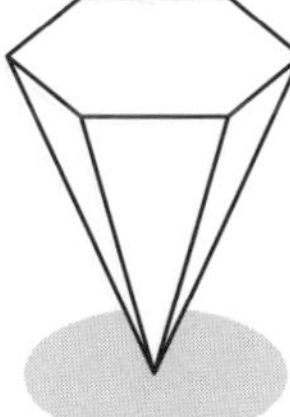

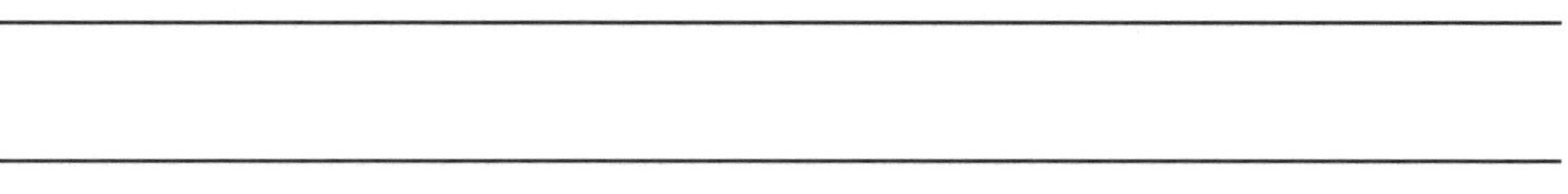

____

____

____

⑤

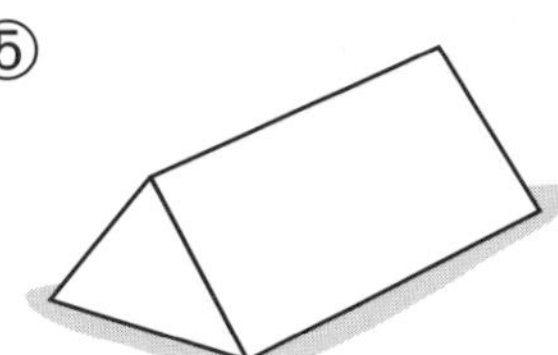

____

____

____

⑥

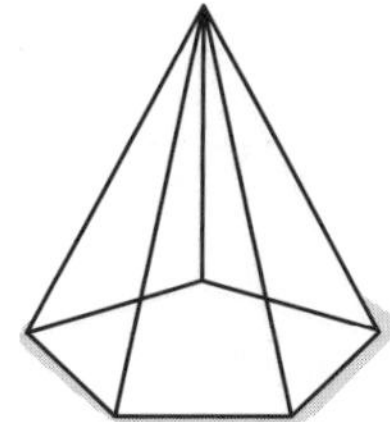

____

____

____

ISBN: 978-1-897164-32-7

Draw the missing edges to complete the skeleton of each 3-D figure. Then name the figure and fill in the blanks.

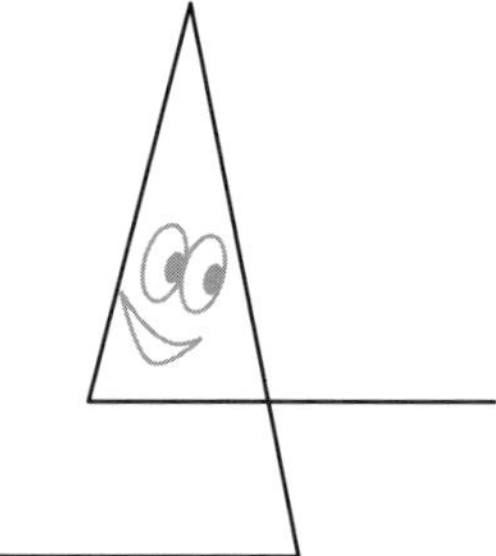

Name: ____________________

Things needed to build it:

- _____ sticks
- _____ marshmallows

Name: ____________________

Things needed to build it:

- _____ sticks
- _____ marshmallows

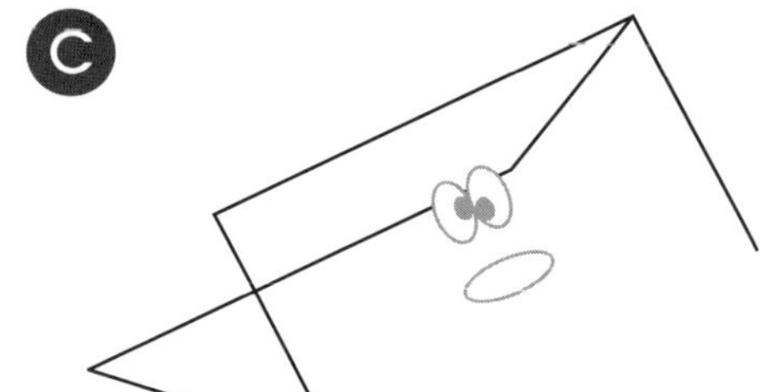

Name: ____________________

Things needed to build it:

- _____ sticks
- _____ marshmallows

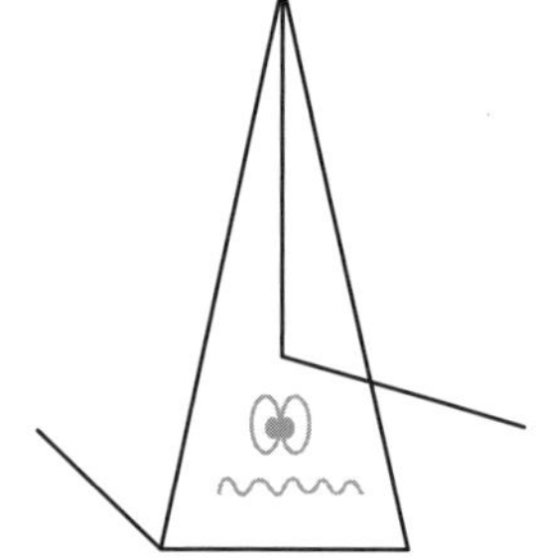

Name: ____________________

Things needed to build it:

- _____ sticks
- _____ marshmallows

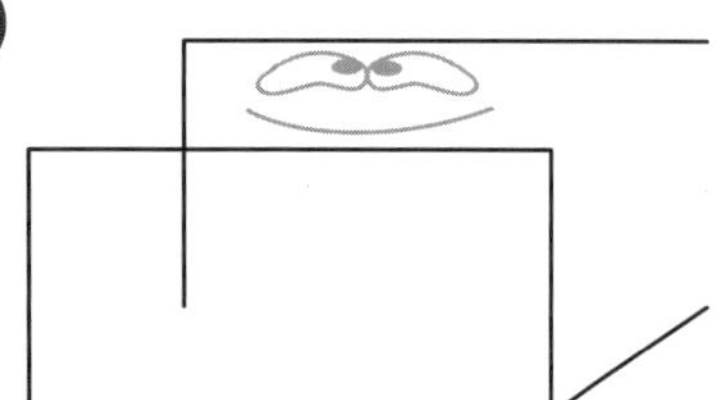

Name: ____________________

Things needed to build it:

- _____ sticks
- _____ marshmallows

ISBN: 978-1-897164-32-7

Complete the tables. Then answer the questions.

⑧ **Prisms**

	No. of Vertices	No. of Edges	No. of Faces
Triangular prism			
Rectangular prism			
Pentagonal prism			
Hexagonal prism			

⑨ **Pyramid**

	No. of Vertices	No. of Edges	No. of Faces
Triangular pyramid			
Rectangular pyramid			
Pentagonal pyramid			
Hexagonal pyramid			

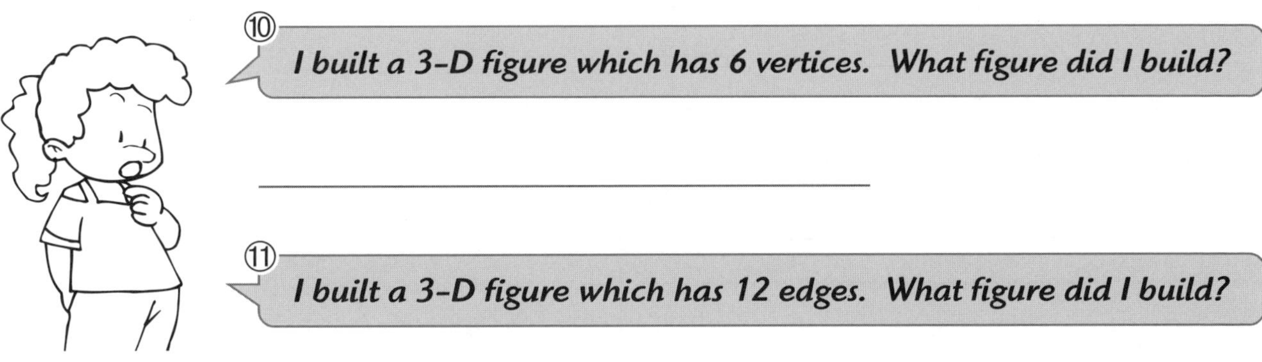

⑩ *I built a 3-D figure which has 6 vertices. What figure did I build?*

____

⑪ *I built a 3-D figure which has 12 edges. What figure did I build?*

____

⑫ *I used 12 sticks with the same length to build a 3-D figure. What figure did I build?*

____

ISBN: 978-1-897164-32-7

3-D Figures (2)

- Identify nets of prisms and pyramids.
- Draw and describe nets of rectangular and triangular prisms.
- Construct 3-D figures using only congruent shapes.

Check the correct net for each 3-D figure.

① Rectangular pyramid

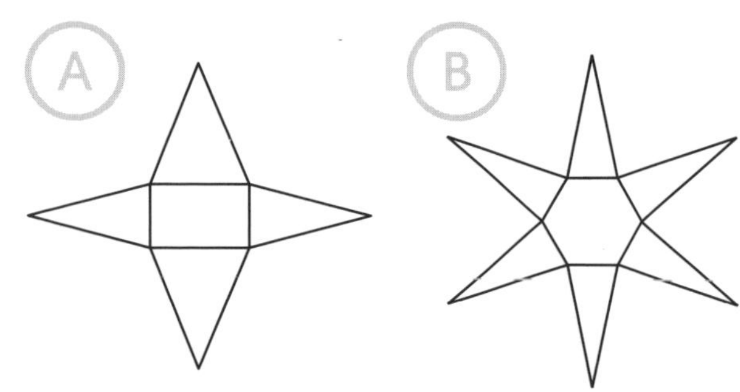

② Hexagonal prism

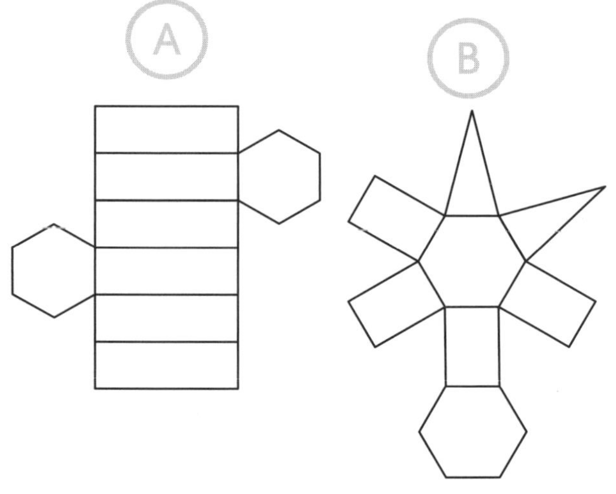

③ Triangular prism

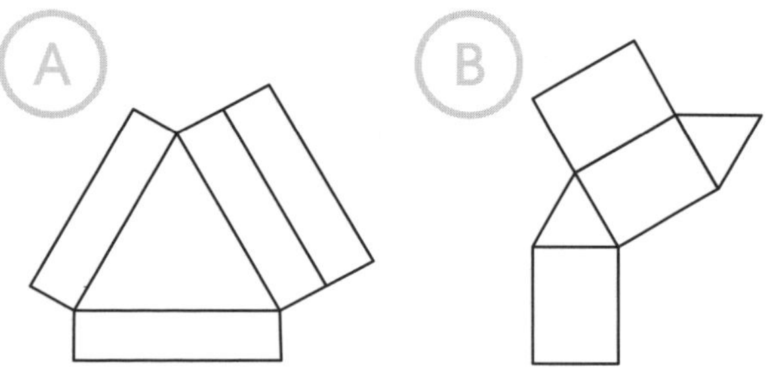

④ Pentagonal pyramid

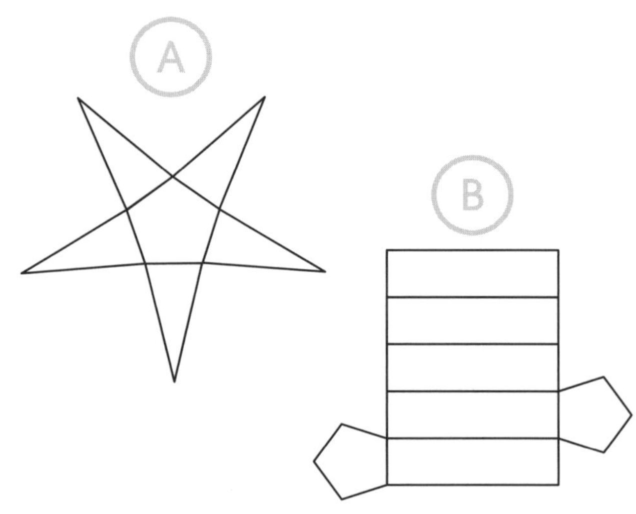

⑤ Cube

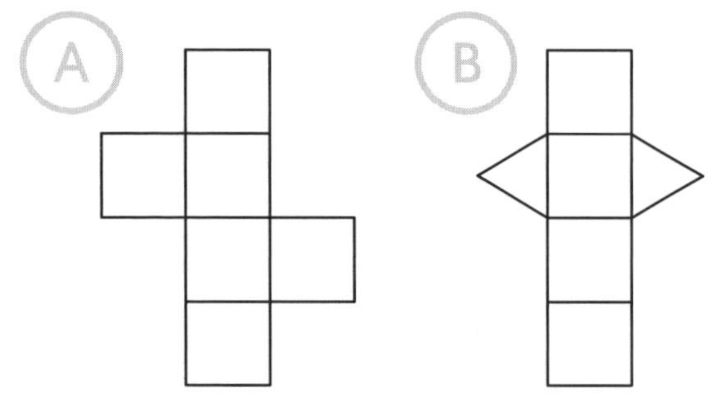

ISBN: 978-1-897164-32-7

Draw the missing parts of each net.

⑥

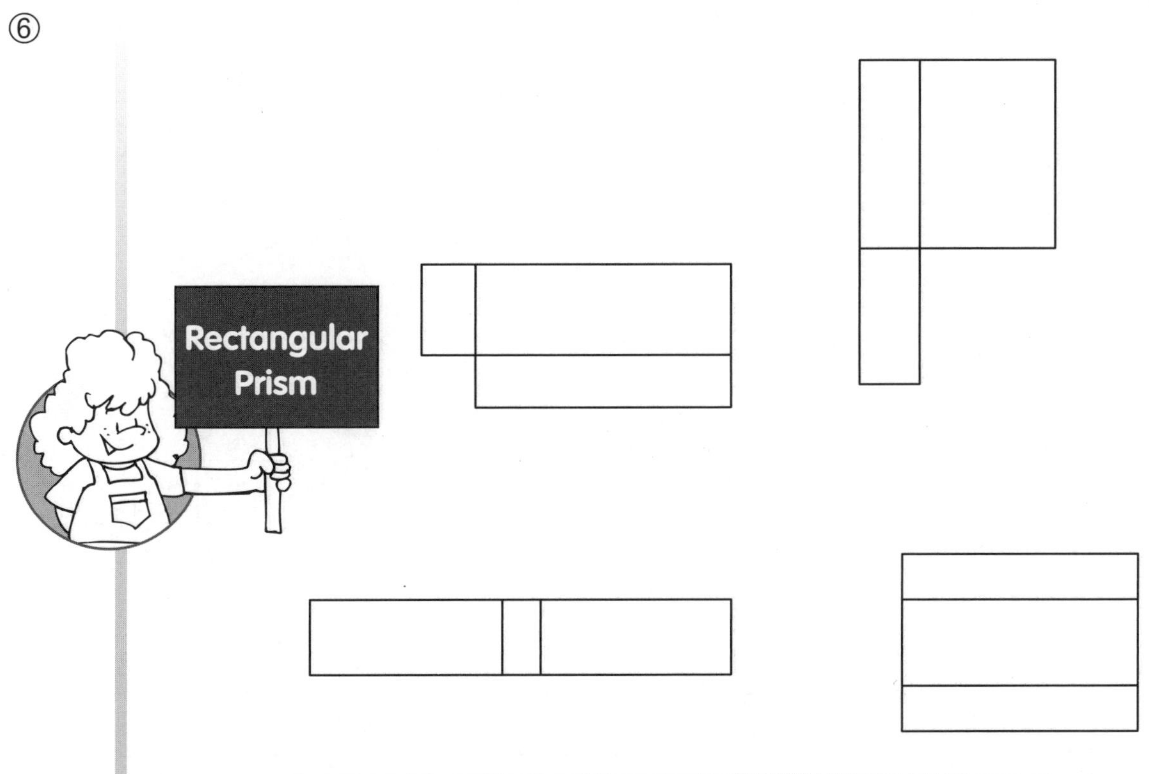

⑦

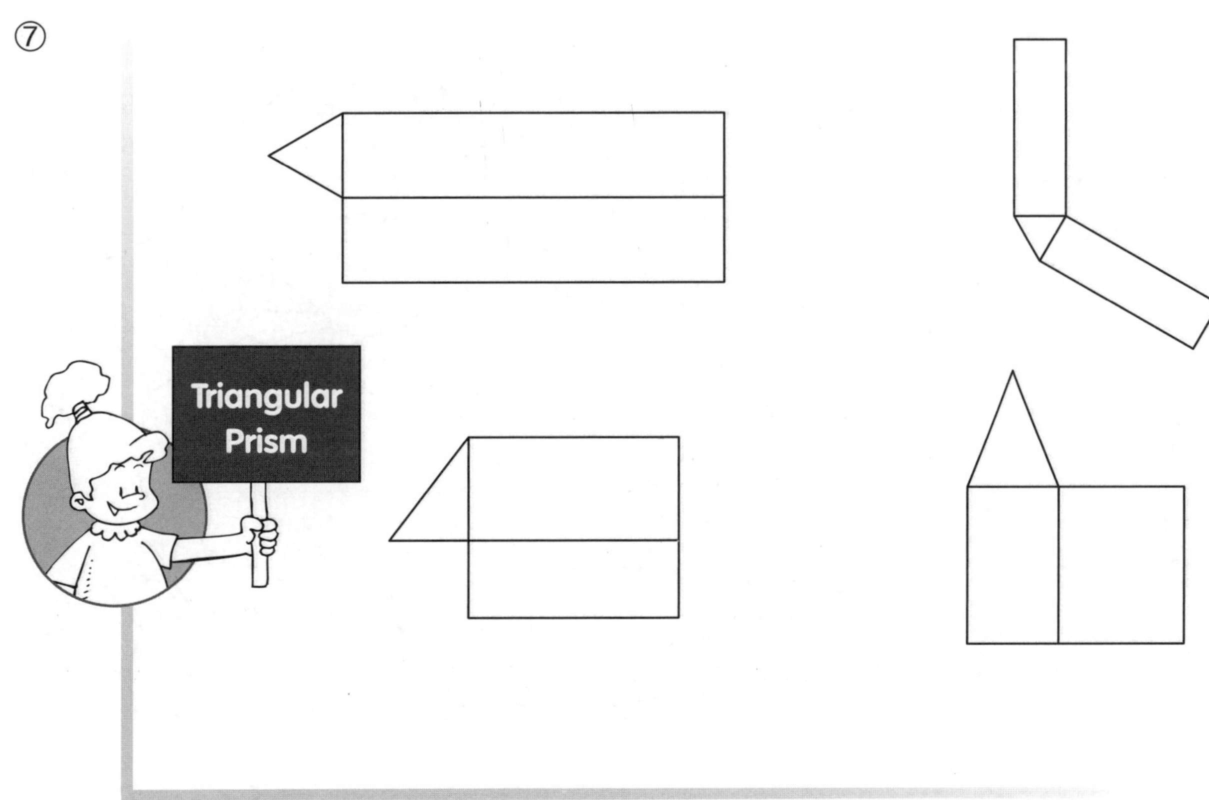

ISBN: 978-1-897164-32-7

Colour the nets that can form cubes. Then draw 3 more nets that are different from the coloured ones.

⑧ A B C D E F G H I J

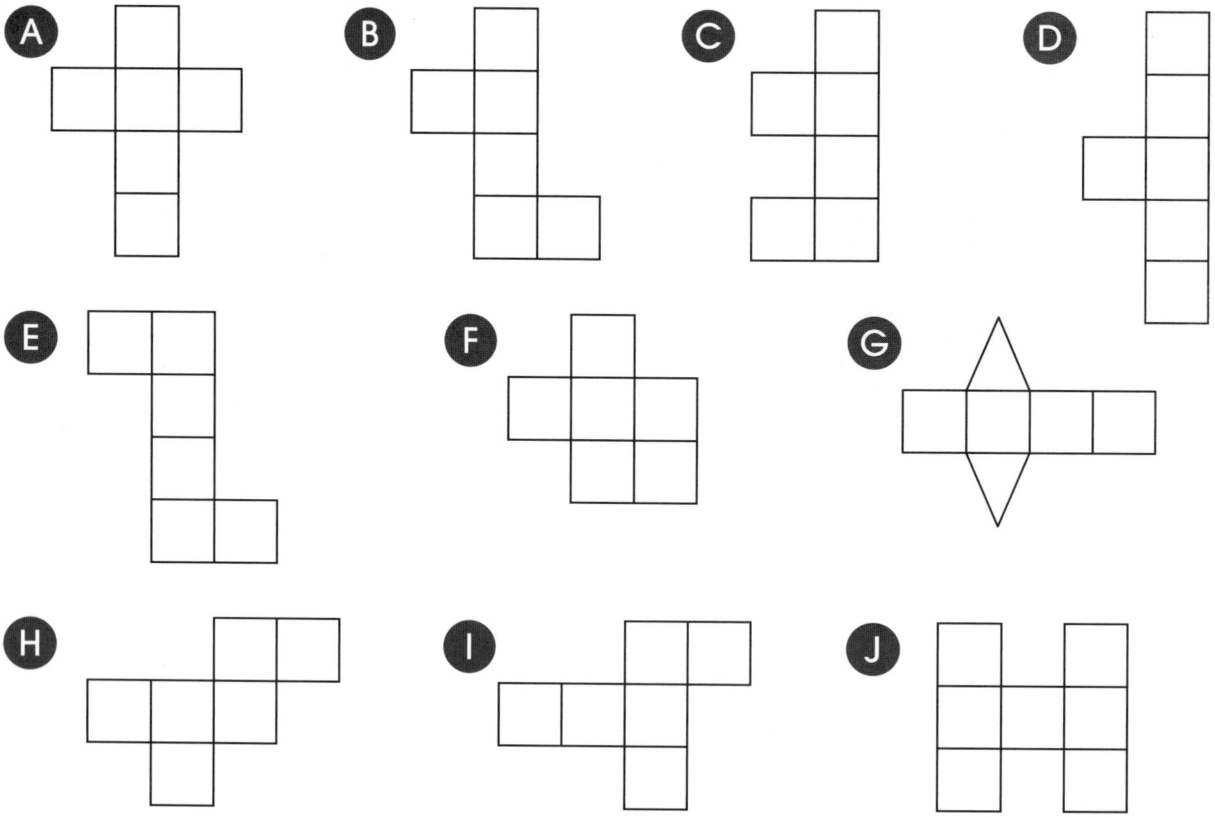

⑨

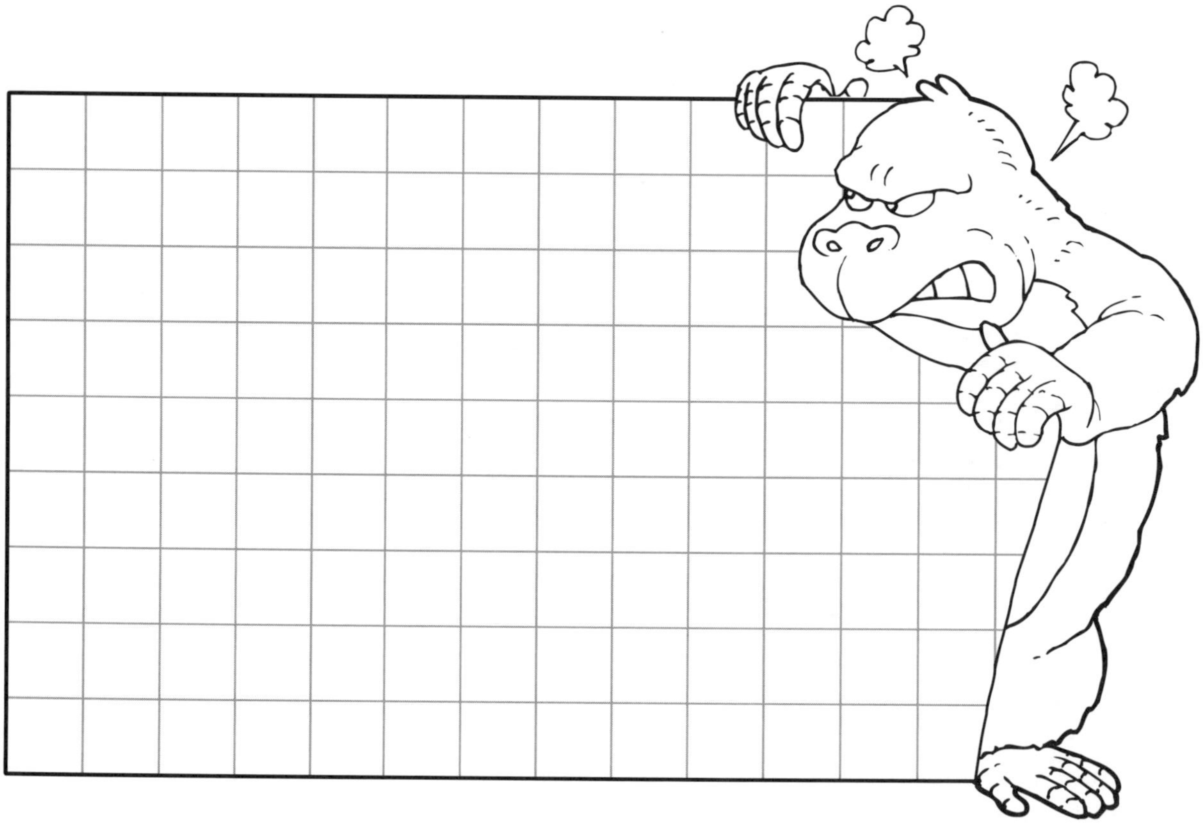

ISBN: 978-1-897164-32-7

Tetrahedron:

a 3-D figure with 4 faces; each face is an equilateral triangle

Do you like my tetrahedron?

Check the net that can form a tetrahedron.

⑩

A 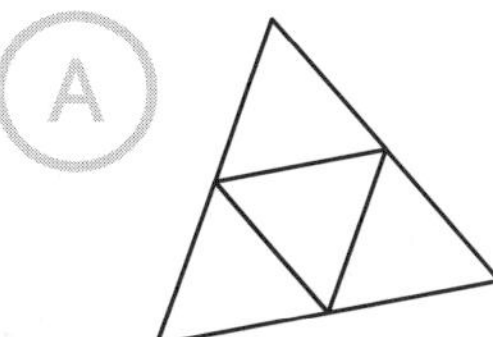

B 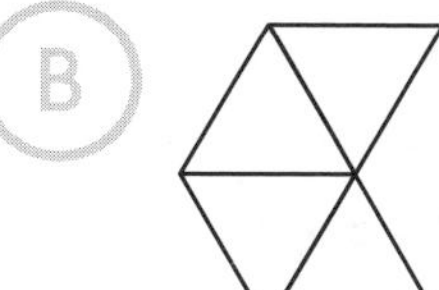

C 

D 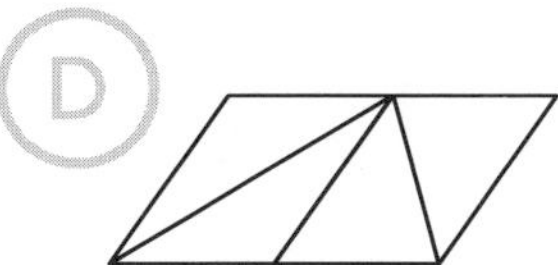

E 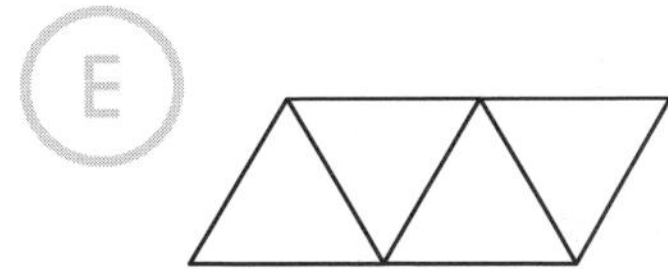

F 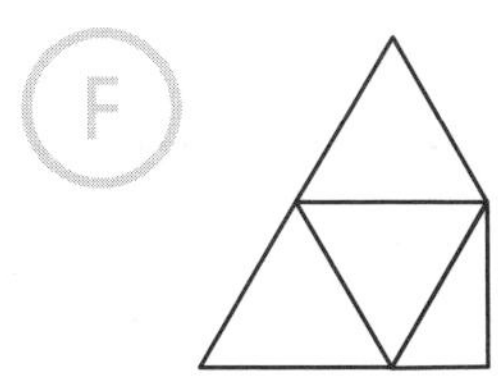

Trace the triangle in the circle with tracing paper. Then cut it out and use it to draw the missing face(s) of each net for a tetrahedron.

⑪

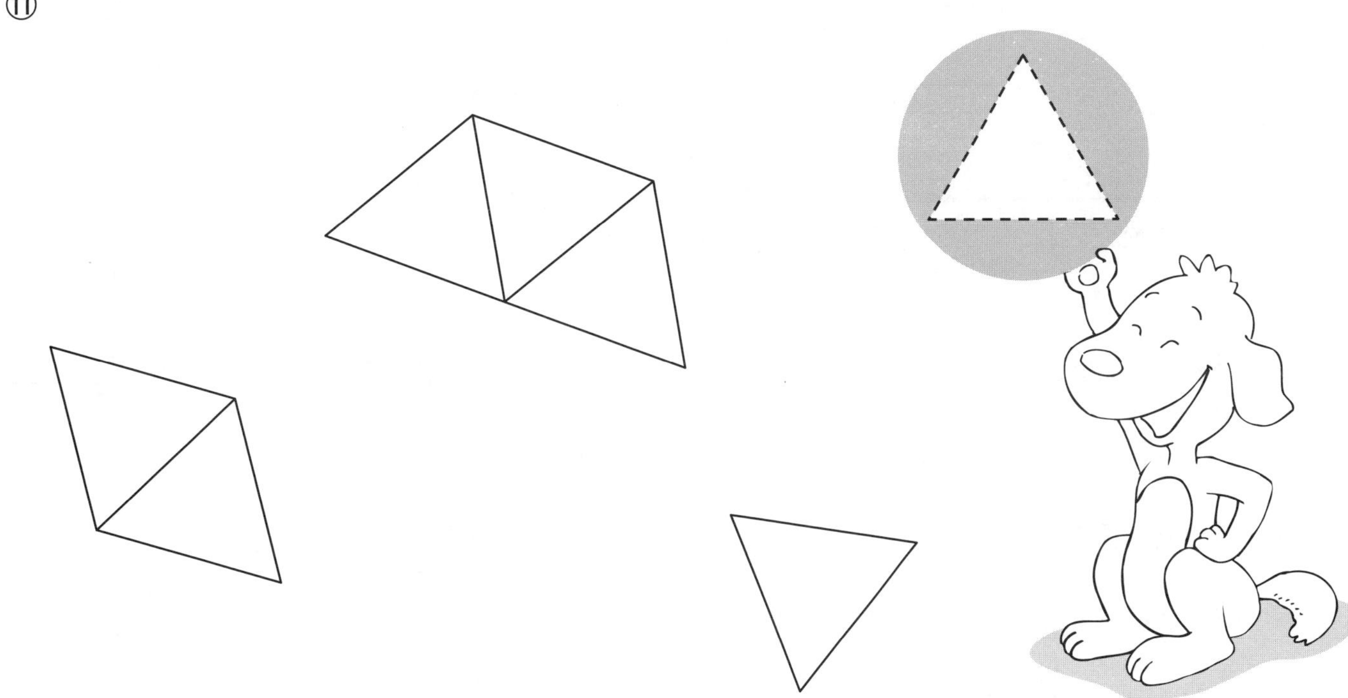

23

Grids

- Identify and describe the location of an object using a grid system.
- Describe movement from one location to another.

We have to go 2 squares up and 3 squares left to get to our new home.

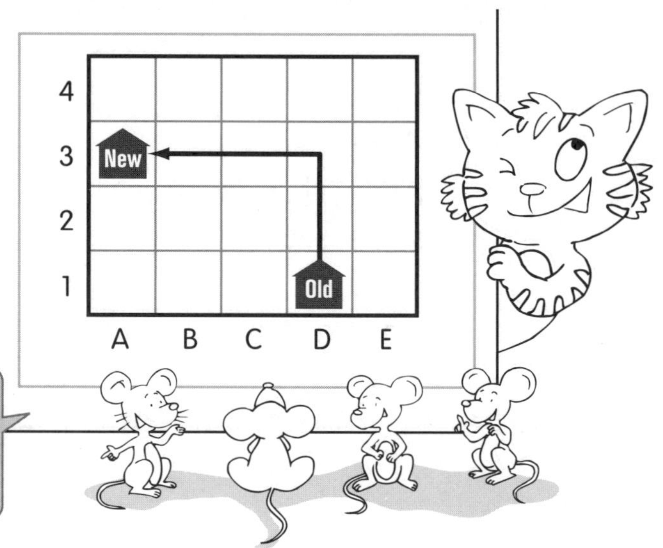

Look at the grid. Write the locations of the toys. Then answer the questions.

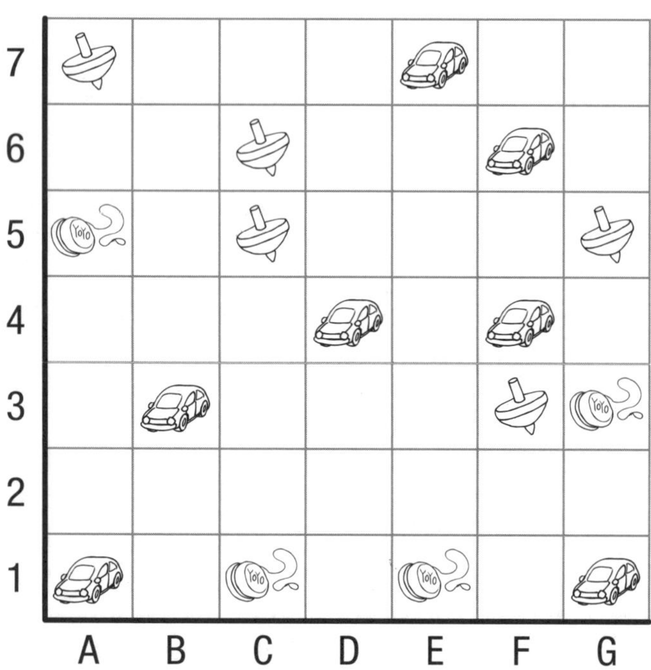

① Locations of the Toys

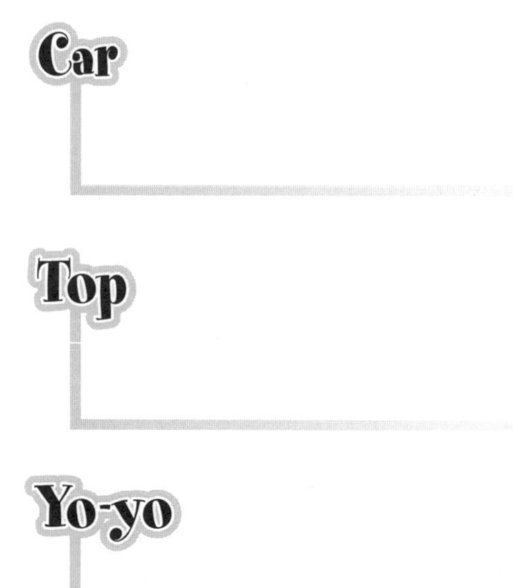

② How many columns are there on the grid? ________

③ How many rows are there on the grid? ________

④ How many toys are there in column F? ________

⑤ How many toys are there in row 4? ________

⑥ Which row has the most toys? ________

ISBN: 978-1-897164-32-7

Look at the grid. Answer the questions.

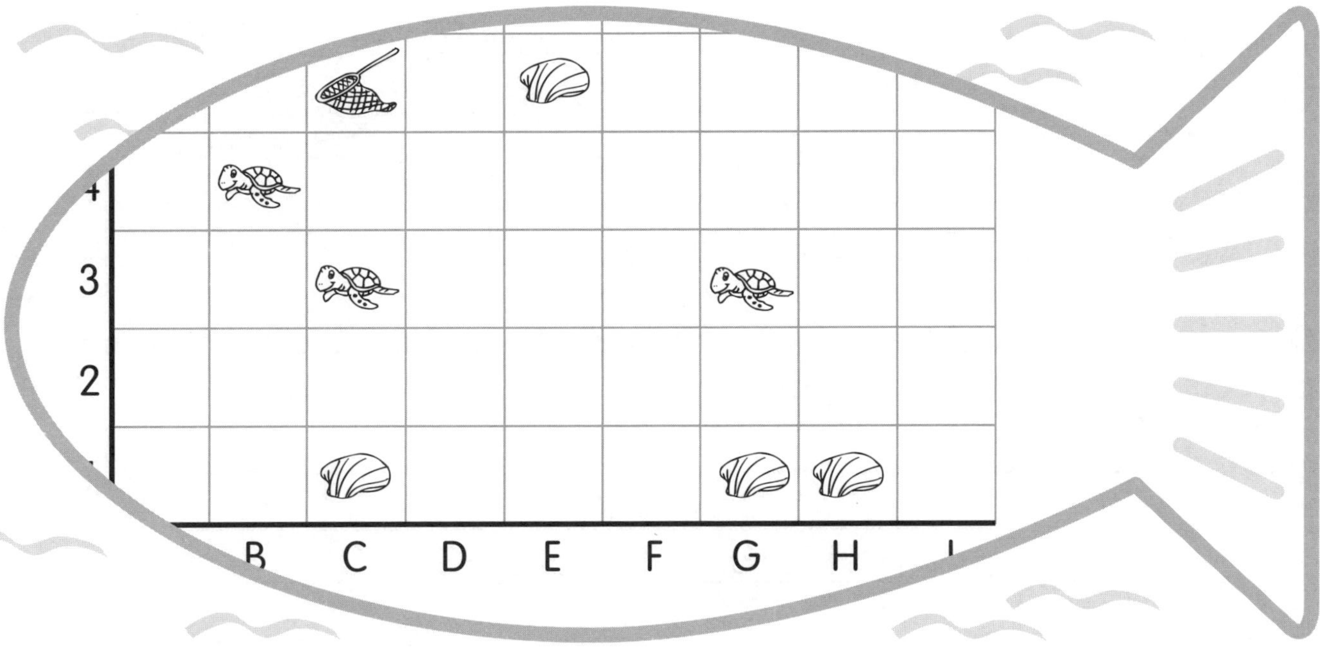

⑦ a. Locations of the shells: ____________________

b. Locations of the turtles: ____________________

⑧ Draw 1 big fish at H5 and 3 small fish at B2, D1, and F5.

⑨ If the shell at E5 sinks to the bottom, what is its new location? Describe the path that it takes.

____

⑩ If the big fish wants to eat the closest small fish, which one should it eat? Describe the path that it takes.

____

⑪ The turtle at G3 wants to find its friend at B4. What is the shortest path that it should take?

____

ISBN: 978-1-897164-32-7

Movement of objects:

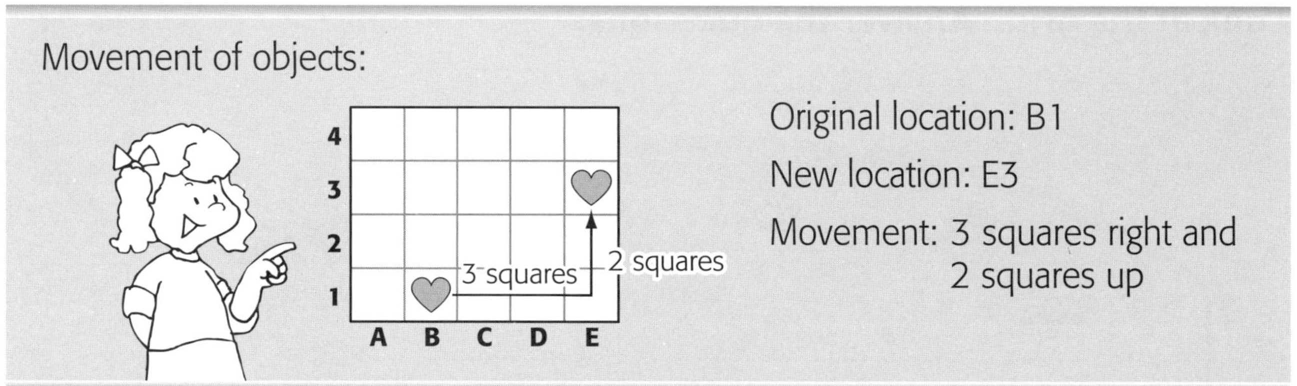

Original location: B1

New location: E3

Movement: 3 squares right and 2 squares up

Draw lines and label the axes of the grid. Then draw the paths and the objects and find their new locations.

⑫

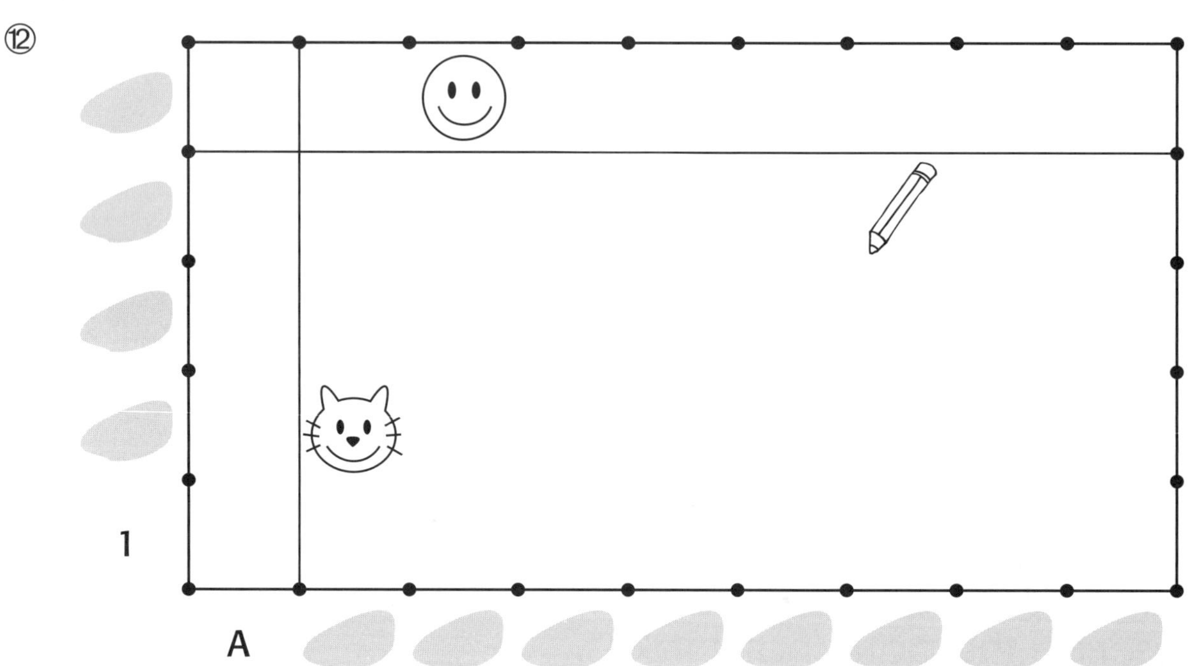

⑬ 

Move the pencil 2 squares left and 3 squares down. What is its new location? ______

⑭ 

Move the cat 6 squares right and 3 squares up. What is its new location? ______

⑮ 

Move the happy face 3 squares right, 2 squares down, and then 4 squares left. What is its new location? ______

ISBN: 978-1-897164-32-7

Complete the grid. Then draw the pictures and answer the questions.

⑯

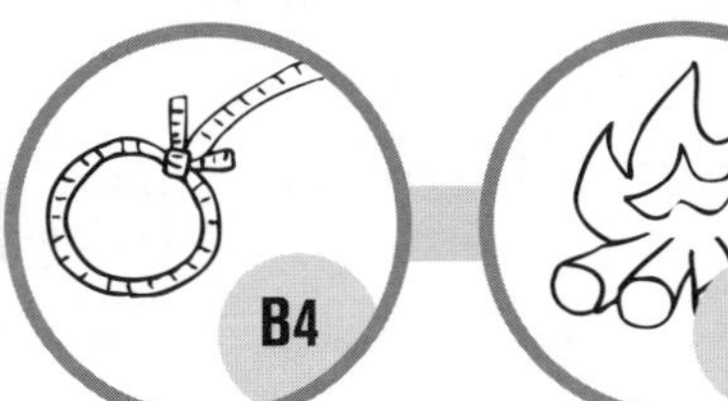

F3
E3

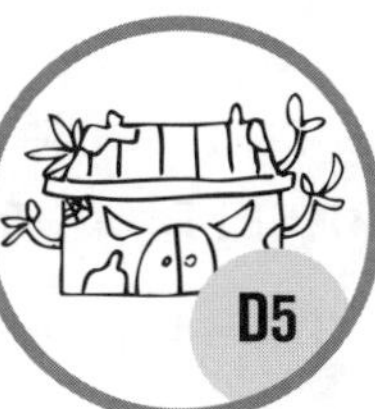

D2 D3 C2 C3

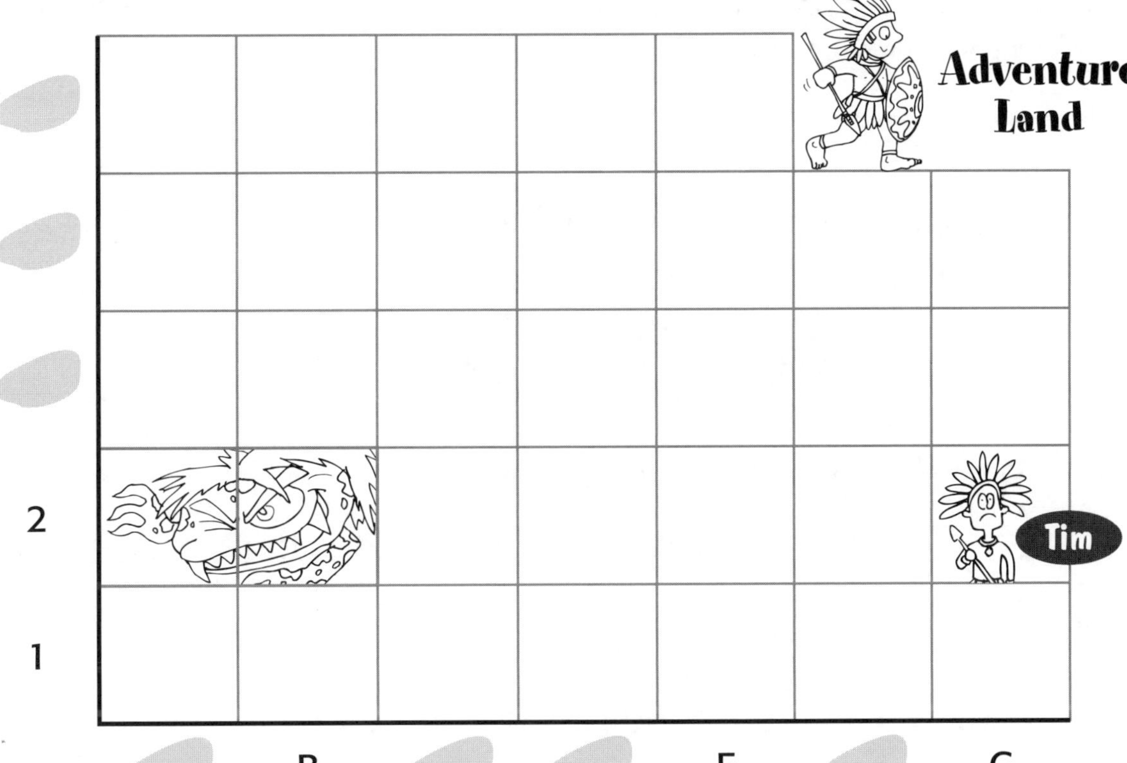

⑰ What is the location of Tim? ________

⑱ What is the location of the monster? ________

⑲ How many squares are covered by the swamp? ________

⑳ How many squares are covered by the poisonous thorn? ________

㉑ ***What is the safest way Tim should take to get to the monster?***

____

____

ISBN: 978-1-897164-32-7

24

Patterning (1)

- Extend, describe, and create repeating, growing, or shrinking number patterns.
- Connect each term in a pattern with its term number.
- Create a number pattern involving addition, subtraction, or multiplication.

One, two, four, eight, growing.
Nine, seven, five, three, shrinking.
One, two, one, two, repeating.
I love number patterning.

Describe each number pattern with the given words. Then write the next two numbers.

growing repeating shrinking

① **5 6 8 9 11 12 14**

It is a ______________ pattern. The next two numbers are _____ and _____ .

② **90 80 70 60 50 40**

It is a ______________ pattern. The next two numbers are _____ and _____ .

③ **5 11 11 5 11 11 5 11**

It is a ______________ pattern. The next two numbers are _____ and _____ .

④ **81 80 78 77 75 74 72**

It is a ______________ pattern. The next two numbers are ________ and ________ .

ISBN: 978-1-897164-32-7

Follow each pattern rule to create a number pattern. Then describe the pattern.

⑤ 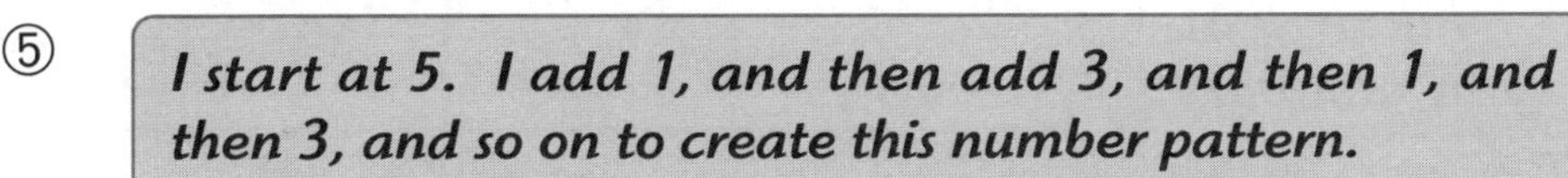
I start at 5. I add 1, and then add 3, and then 1, and then 3, and so on to create this number pattern.

5 ____ ____ ____ ____ ____ a ________ pattern

⑥ Start at 10. Multiply each number by 2 to get the next number.

____ ____ ____ ____ ____ ____ a ________ pattern

⑦ Start at 95. Subtract 1, and then subtract 2, and then 1, and then 2, and so on.

____ ____ ____ ____ ____ ____ a ________ pattern

⑧ 

I start at 45. I subtract 3, and then add 1, and then subtract 3, and then add 1, and so on to create this number pattern.

____ ____ ____ ____ ____ ____ a ________ pattern

Find out the pattern rule for each number pattern. Circle the correct answer.

⑨ 8 16 15 30 29 58

- 2 x 1   - 1 x 2   x 2 - 1

⑩ 72 70 67 65 62 60

- 3 - 2   - 2 - 3   - 2 + 3

⑪ 24 26 27 29 30 32

x 1 + 2   + 1 + 2   + 2 + 1

⑫ 2 6 7 21 22 66

x 3 + 1   x 1 + 3   + 4 + 1

ISBN: 978-1-897164-32-7

We can record the patterns in a table of values that shows the term numbers and the terms.

e.g. 1, 4, 7, 10, ...

Term Number	1	2	3	4
Term	1	4	7	10

The 4th term is **10**.

Record each number sequence in a table of values. Then fill in the blanks.

⑬ 9, 13, 17, 21, 25, 29, 33, ...

a.

Term Number							
Term							

b. The 3rd term is ______ and the 6th term is ______ .

⑭ 86, 85, 83, 82, 80, 79, 77, ...

a.

Term Number							
Term							

b. The 2nd term is ______ and the 5th term is ______ .

⑮ 7, 14, 13, 26, 25, ...

a.

Term Number	Term

b. *The 7th term is ______ .*

⑯ 8, 12, 10, 14, 12, ...

a.

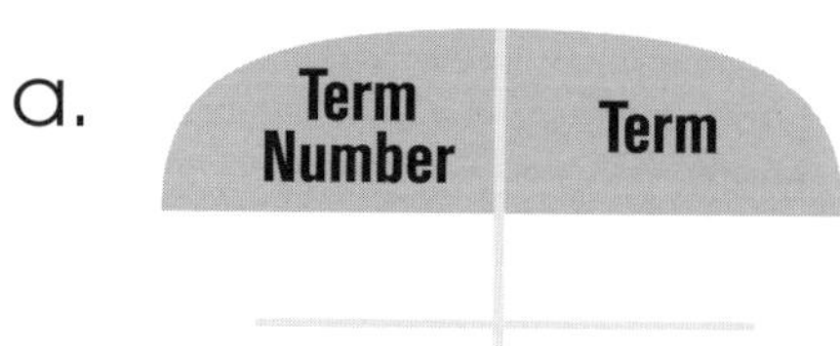
Term Number
Term

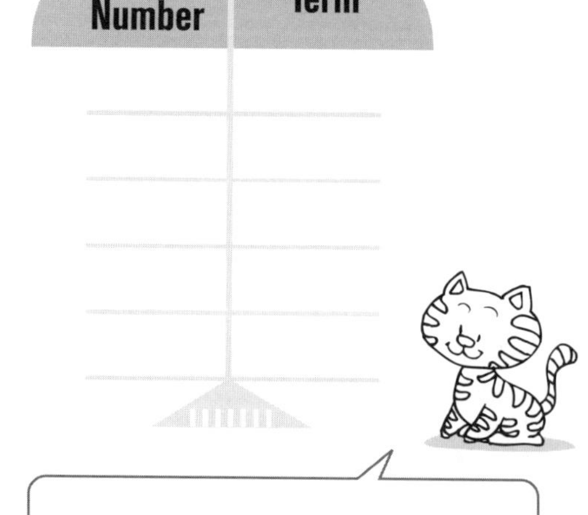

b. *The 8th term is ______ .*

ISBN: 978-1-897164-32-7

Follow each pattern rule to write the first 6 terms of a number sequence .

⑰ Start at 2 and multiply each term by 3 to get the next term.

____

⑱ Start at 10 and add 2 to each term to get the next term.

____

Use a table to show the first week's savings of each girl. Then answer the questions.

⑲ **Ann**

She saves 20¢ on the first day. Then each day after that she saves 4¢ more than the day before.

Term Number	Term

⑳ **Sue**

She saves 48¢ on the first day. Then each day after that she saves 3¢ less than the day before.

Term Number	Term

㉑ *On which day do the girls save the same amount? How much does each save?*

____

ISBN: 978-1-897164-32-7

Patterning (2)

- Make predictions related to repeating geometric and numeric patterns.
- Extend and create repeating patterns that result from reflections.
- Determine the inverse relationship between multiplication and division and find the missing numbers in equations.

I know there are 5 squares and 10 circles in 5 groups.

Follow the pattern to draw the next two groups of shapes. Then complete the table and fill in the blanks.

① a.

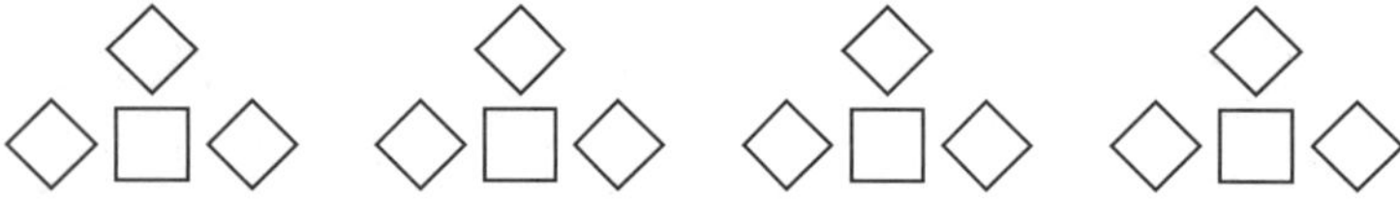

b.

No. of Groups	1	2	3	4	5	6
No. of Squares						

c. *There are ______ squares in 8 groups.*

② a.

b.

No. of Groups	1	2	3	4	5	6
No. of Rectangles						
No. of Parallelograms						

c. *There are ______ rectangles and ______ parallelograms in 9 groups.*

ISBN: 978-1-897164-32-7

The line in bold is the line of reflection. Complete each reflection image. Then follow the pattern that is created by using the shape itself and its reflection image to fill the spaces.

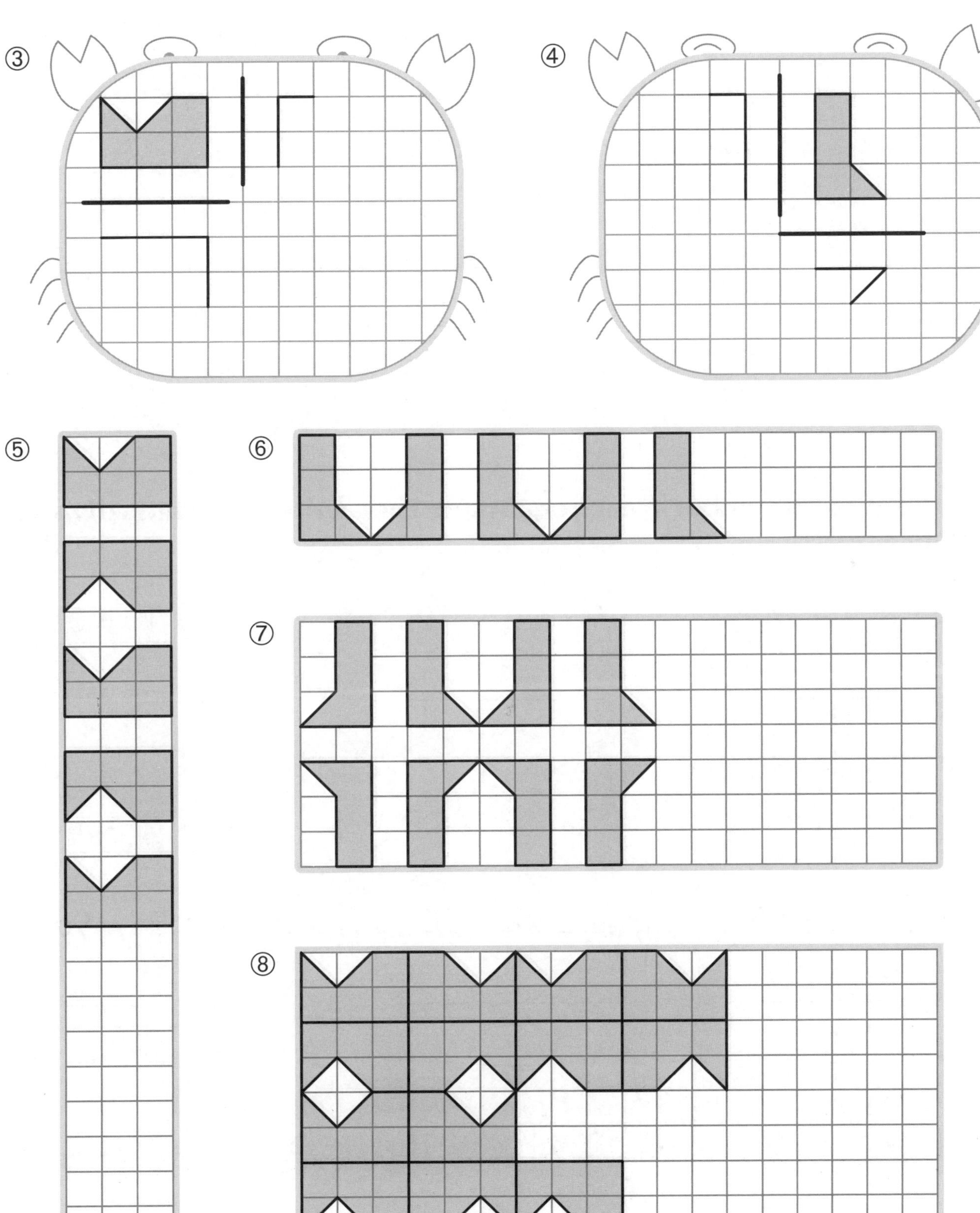

ISBN: 978-1-897164-32-7

Look at each given number sentence. Find the missing number.

⑨ 4 x 5 = 20

   ÷ 4 = 5

⑩ 27 ÷ 9 = 3

3 x   = 27

⑪ 14 x 2 = 28

28 ÷   = 14

⑫ 64 ÷ 4 = 16

   x 16 = 64

⑬ 91 ÷ 7 = 13

7 x   = 91

⑭ 24 x 3 = 72

   ÷ 3 = 24

Find the missing number in each equation. Then write a matching division sentence.

⑮ 4 x ____ = 24

____

⑯ 9 x ____ = 72

____

⑰ ____ x 10 = 30

____

㉑ 11 x ____ = 99

____

㉒ 25 x ____ = 75

____

㉓ ____ x 16 = 32

____

ISBN: 978-1-897164-32-7

Use the "guess-and-test" method to find answers.

e.g.  x 19 = 95

Guess	Test
2	**2** x 19 = 38 (not 95) ✘
3	**3** x 19 = 57 (not 95) ✘
5	**5** x 19 = 95 ✔

Use the "guess-and-test" method to find the missing numbers.

㉔ 18 x ★ = 72

Guess	Test

★ =

㉕ ☀ x 17 = 85

Guess	Test

☀ =

㉖ 78 ÷ ☽ = 26

Guess	Test

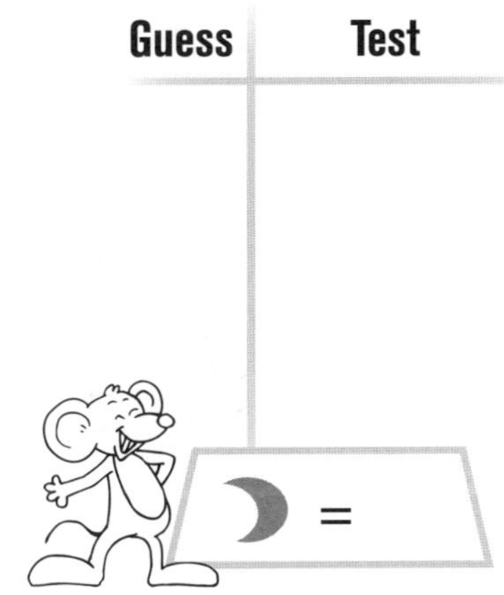

Find the missing numbers.

㉗ 7 x _____ = 119

㉘ 9 x _____ = 45

㉙ 50 ÷ _____ = 5

㉚ _____ x 12 = 96

㉛ _____ ÷ 7 = 6

㉜ 48 ÷ _____ = 24

㉝ 6 x 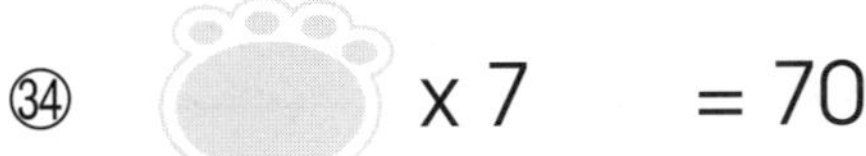 = 6000

㉞  x 7 = 70

㉟  x 100 = 500

㊱ 1000 x  = 4000

Do you remember when a whole number is multiplied by 10, 100, or 1000, you can just add 1 zero, 2 zeros, or 3 zeros to the number to get the answer?

ISBN: 978-1-897164-32-7

26

Graphs (1)

- Read and describe data presented in stem-and-leaf plots and double bar graphs.
- Understand and identify the median and mode in a set of data.

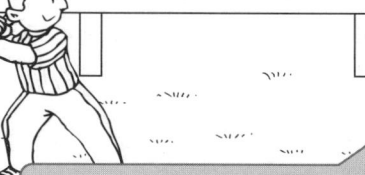

No. of Hours of Practice Last Month

Stem	Leaves
2	0 0 3 5 9
3	0 1 1
4	(2) 3 4 4
5	1 4 7 7 7

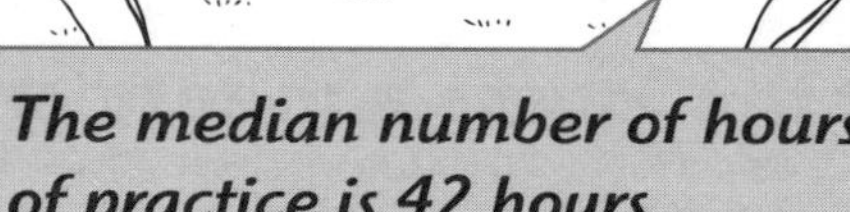

The median number of hours of practice is 42 hours.

Look at the stem-and-leaf plot. Answer the questions.

Number of Bounces in One Minute

Stem	Leaves
2	0 1 1 3 4 8 9
3	1 1 2 2 2 3 3 3 3
4	0 0 1 6
5	4 5 5

① *How many children were surveyed in all?* ________

② What is the highest record? ________

③ What is the lowest record? ________

④ How many children got the highest record? ________

⑤ How many children had 32 bounces? ________

⑥ How many children had more than 45 bounces? ________

⑦ *I'm good at basketball. There were only two children with more bounces than I. Do you know how many bounces I had?*

____

ISBN: 978-1-897164-32-7

Read the graph showing the favourite storybooks of the children. Then answer the questions.

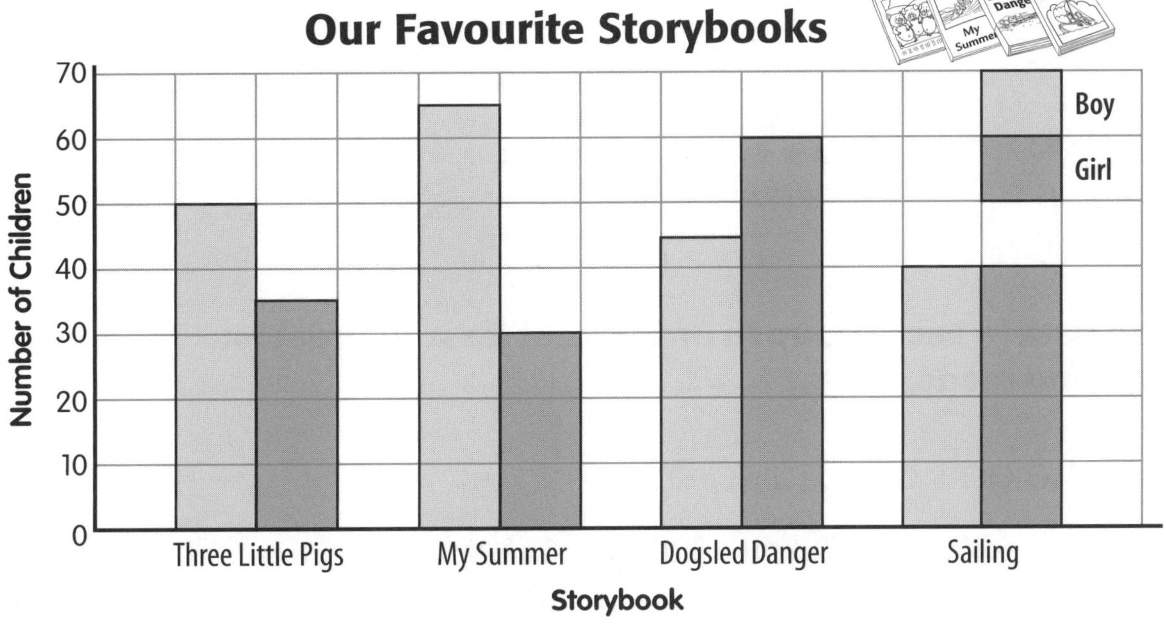

⑧ Title of the graph: ______________________

⑨ Label of the vertical axis: ______________________

⑩ Label of the horizontal axis: ______________________

⑪ How many boys like "Three Little Pigs"? ____________

⑫ How many girls were surveyed in all? ____________

⑬ How many children were surveyed in all? ____________

⑭ Which storybook is liked by the same number of boys and girls? How many boys and girls in all like this book? ____________

⑮ *239 of the surveyed children are members of the Reading Club. How many children are not the members of the Reading Club?*

____

ISBN: 978-1-897164-32-7

Median is the middle value in a set of values arranged in order. If there is an even number of numbers, the median is the average of the two middle numbers.

e.g. 3, 10, 12, 28 Median = average of 10 and 12
= 11

There are 4 numbers. 10 and 12 are the middle numbers.

The median is **11** .

Put the data in each group in order from least to greatest. Then find the median and mode.

⑯ The heights of 15 children:

130 cm	145 cm	128 cm	130 cm	144 cm
130 cm	132 cm	142 cm	141 cm	136 cm
135 cm	135 cm	129 cm	130 cm	141 cm

In order: 128, 129, ______________________

____

Median

Mode

⑰ The savings of 20 children:

$3 $2 $4 $5 $5 $2 $3 $4 $7 $9
$10 $4 $5 $7 $8 $10 $5 $6 $2 $9

In order: ______________________

____

Median

Mode

⑱ The number of marbles that 17 children have:

45 66 29 58 27 54 66 23 40
26 54 58 70 66 25 66 66

In order: ______________________

____

Median

Mode

ISBN: 978-1-897164-32-7

Stem-and-leaf plot:

e.g.

Stem	Leaves
1	9 9
2	3 6 6 7
4	8 9 9 9
5	0 4 4

Since these 13 numbers are put in the correct order, the number in the middle is the median.

The median of this set of data is **48**.

Look at each stem-and-leaf plot. Find the median.

⑲ **Number of Hours Spent on Watching TV Each Week**

Stem	Leaves
1	0 0 1 4 5 8
2	1 3 3 3 3 4 9
3	0 4

Median: ________

⑳ **Number of Hours Spent on Practising the Guitar Each Month**

Stem	Leaves
1	5 5 6 6 8
2	3 3 7 7 7 7
3	0 1 1
4	2 3 5 5

Median: ________

㉑ **Ages of a Group of People**

Stem	Leaves
0	6 7 7 8 9 9
1	4 5
2	2 2 3 6 7 8
3	0 0 1 6 9

Median: ________

㉒ **Weights of Bags of Potato Chips (in g)**

Stem	Leaves
5	3 3 6 6 8 8
6	5 5 5
7	0 0 8 9
9	0 0 5 5 9
10	0 5 7 7 8

Median: ________

㉓ **Lengths of Games (in min)**

Stem	Leaves
9	8 8
10	0 2 5 5 6 8 8
11	6 6 9 9
12	0 0 1

The median is ________.

ISBN: 978-1-897164-32-7

27

Graphs (2)

- Complete or make stem-and-leaf plots or double bar graphs to show the data.
- Draw conclusions or describe the shape of a set of data across its range of values, presented in tables or graphs.

Number of Flowers We Visited

Stem	Leaves
3	3 5 5
5	4 4 6 (6) 7 7 8
6	2 2
9	0

This set of data bunches up around the median.

Uncle Jim recorded the number of pizzas sold each day in April. Help him complete the stem-and-leaf plot to show the data. Then answer the questions.

75	29	63	62	75	44	60	65	44	46	29	30	34	62	63
35	34	48	44	68	70	44	65	63	75	44	35	60	44	60

①

Stem	Leaves

② On how many days in April were more than 68 pizzas sold?

③ Check the correct sentences to describe the data.

(A) The mode number of pizzas sold is 44.

(B) This set of data spreads out evenly.

(C) The median number of pizzas sold is 54.

ISBN: 978-1-897164-32-7

See how many marbles the children have. Help them answer the questions and make a double bar graph with a title and a key to show the data.

	Ann	Jill	Bob	Tony	Sue
Green Marbles	85	75	65	50	35
Red Marbles	45	75	80	85	30

④ What is the range of the data? ______

⑤ In multiples of what number will be the appropriate scale of the graph? ______

⑥

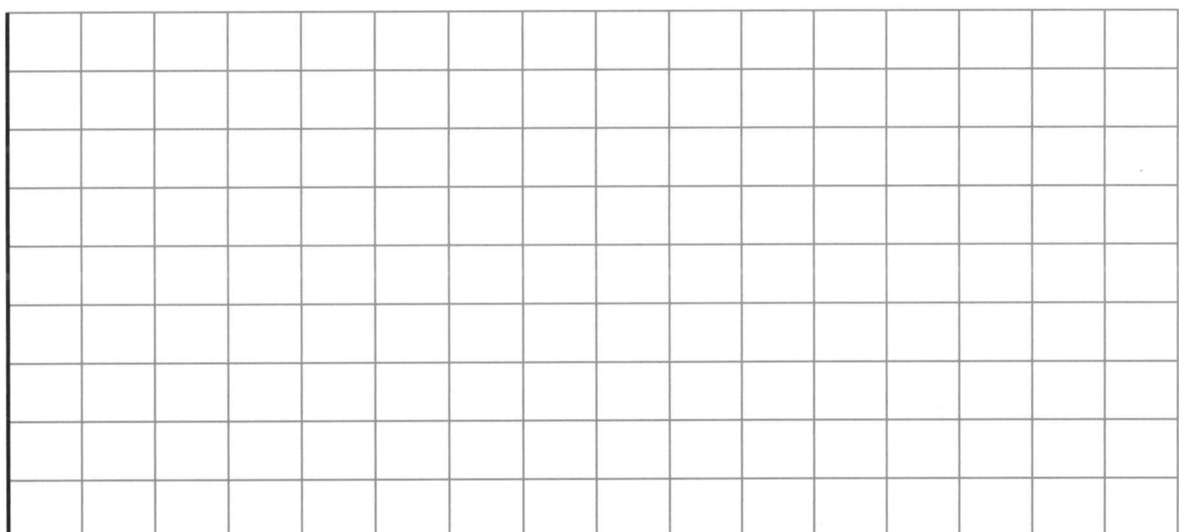

⑦ Who has the most marbles? ______

⑧ How many green marbles do the children have in all? ______

⑨ Write a sentence to describe the graph.

____

ISBN: 978-1-897164-32-7

Judy asked a group of people about the number of apples they picked on a farm yesterday. Help her make a stem-and-leaf plot to show the data. Then answer the questions.

⑩

Stem	Leaves

⑪ What is the median number of apples? ______

⑫ What is the mode number of apples? ______

⑬ What is the range of the number of apples? ______

⑭ How many people were asked in all? ______

⑮ How many people picked more than 60 apples? ______

⑯ *I love apples. I picked the second most apples. Do you know how many apples I picked?*

______

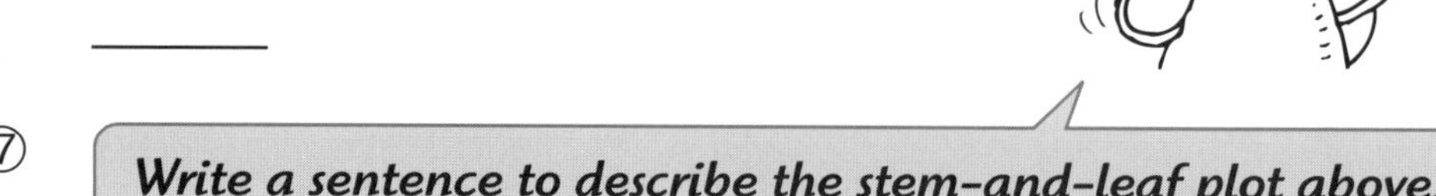

⑰ *Write a sentence to describe the stem-and-leaf plot above.*

______

______

ISBN: 978-1-897164-32-7

See how many pails of honey were collected each month. Make a double bar graph to show the data. Then answer the questions.

	Apr	May	Jun	Jul	Aug	Sep
No. of Small Pails	4	6	12	15	22	10
No. of Big Pails	3	7	10	20	25	3

⑱

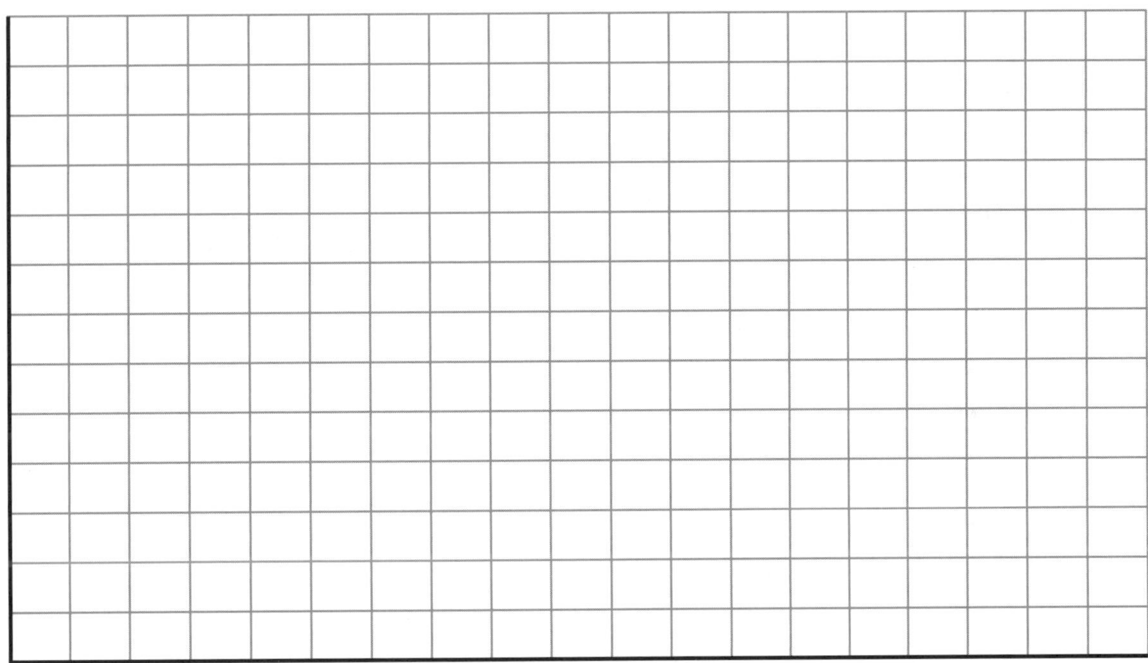

⑲ Write a sentence to describe the graph.

____

____

⑳ *If a big pail holds 1 L of honey, how much honey did we collect with big pails from April to September?*

____

ISBN: 978-1-897164-32-7

28

Probability

- Predict the frequency of an outcome in a probability experiment.
- Determine how the number of repetitions of a probability experiment can affect the conclusion drawn.

Amy tosses two number cubes and calculates the sum. Help her complete the addition chart and list the possible outcomes. Then put a check mark in the circle if the sentence is correct; otherwise, put a cross.

①

1st Cube / 2nd Cube	1	2	3	4	5	6
1		3	4	5		
2			5			8
3	4				8	
4		6				10
5			8	9		
6			9	10		

Possible outcomes:

____

____

②

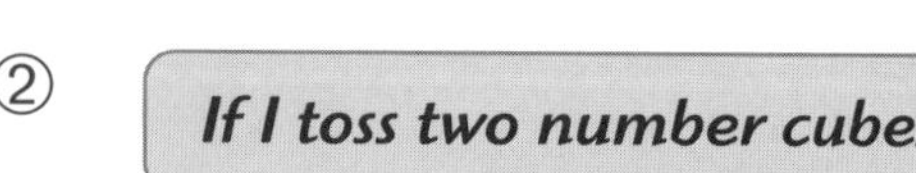

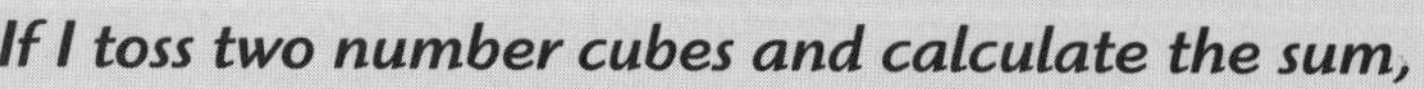
If I toss two number cubes and calculate the sum,

a. 1 is one of the possible outcomes. ◯

b. it is possible to get a sum greater than 10. ◯

c. there are 12 possible outcomes in all. ◯

d. there will be the greatest chance of getting 7. ◯

e. it is unlikely to get either 2 or 12. ◯

ISBN: 978-1-897164-32-7

The children are going to toss two number cubes 40 times and calculate the sum for each toss. Check the children that have a reasonable prediction and explain.

③

Outcome / No. of Times	Amy	George	Celine	Brian
2	1	8	1	4
3	2	7	1	6
4	3	6	4	1
5	4	5	4	1
6	6	4	5	3
7	8	3	7	7
8	6	2	5	7
9	4	1	5	2
10	3	2	4	0
11	2	1	2	5
12	1	1	2	4

④ Explain: ____________________

____

Read what Brenda says. Help her predict the result.

⑤ *If you toss a pair of number cubes 100 times and calculate the sum for each toss, how many times would you expect to get each outcome?*

Outcome	No. of Times
2	
3	
4	
5	
6	
7	
8	
9	
10	
11	
12	

ISBN: 978-1-897164-32-7

Look at the spinners and read the sentences. Check the best predictions and explain.

⑥ *Spin me 50 times. Predict how many times the pointer will land on each section.*

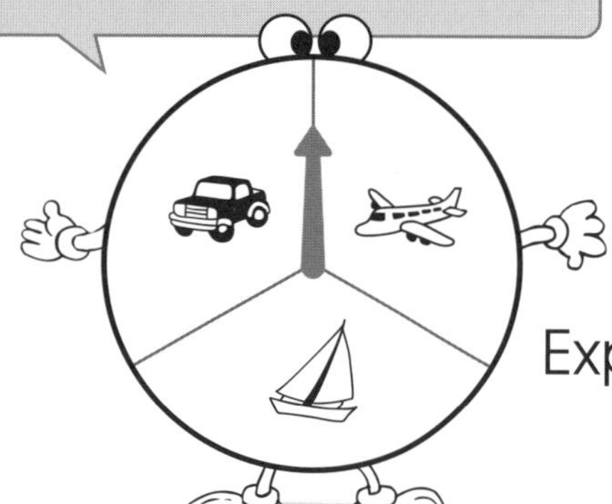

Prediction	Car	Plane	Boat
A	17 times	16 times	17 times
B	20 times	15 times	15 times
C	18 times	9 times	23 times

Explain: ______________________________

____

⑦ *Spin me 40 times. Predict how many times the pointer will land on each section.*

Prediction	Star	Heart	Diamond
A	18 times	6 times	16 times
B	11 times	17 times	12 times
C	25 times	9 times	6 times

Explain: ______________________________

____

Judy predicts how many times the pointer will land on each section in 100 spins. Draw lines and colour the spinner to match her prediction.

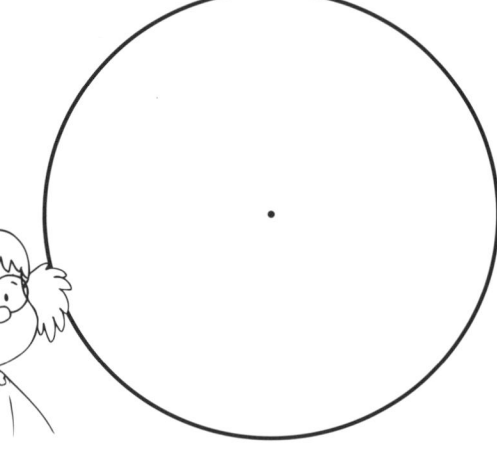

⑧ *It will land on yellow about 12 times, green about 26 times, red about 26 times, and blue about 36 times.*

ISBN: 978-1-897164-32-7

Each child tossed a coin 10 times and recorded how many times tails came up. Help the children complete the table and combine their individual results to determine a group result. Then answer the questions.

⑨ 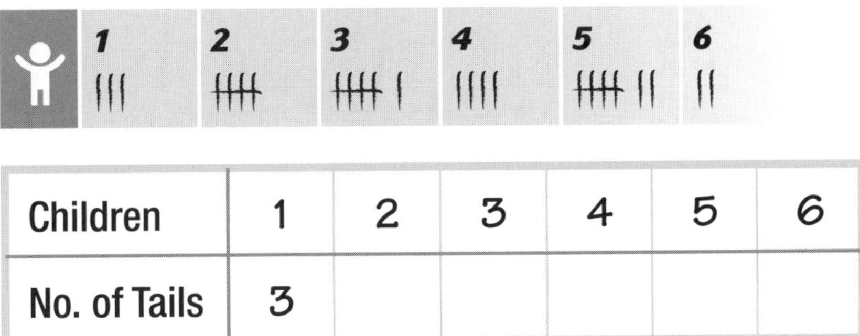

Children	1	2	3	4	5	6
No. of Tails	3					

b. **Group Result**

Total number of tosses: ________

Total number of tails: ________

⑩ 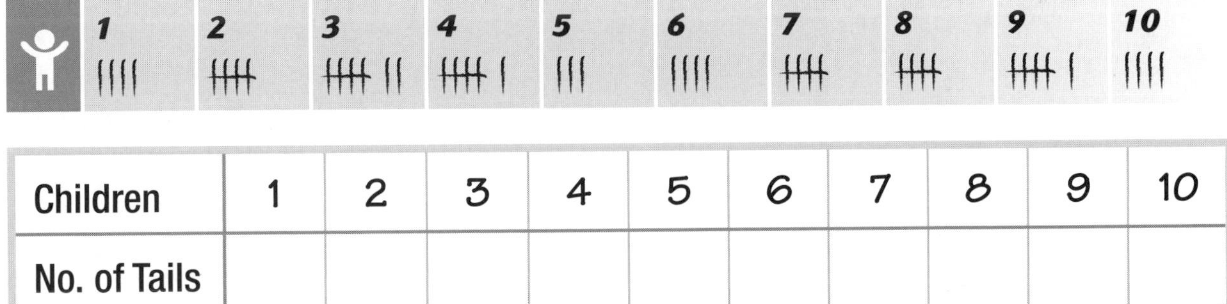

Children	1	2	3	4	5	6	7	8	9	10
No. of Tails										

b. **Group Result**

Total number of tosses: ________

Total number of tails: ________

⑪ *I think that the more probability experiments we have, the better the result will be. Am I correct?*

____

Review 2

Write as decimals. Colour the diagrams to match the decimals given. Then use arrows to place the decimals on the number line and put them in order.

① a. 4 and 6 tenths = ______

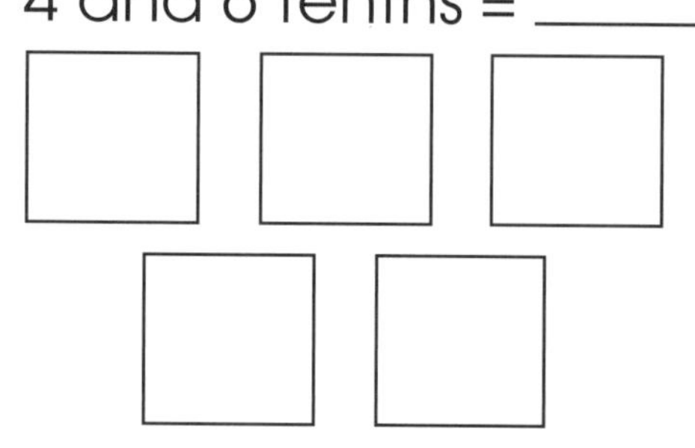

b. 3 and 2 tenths = ______

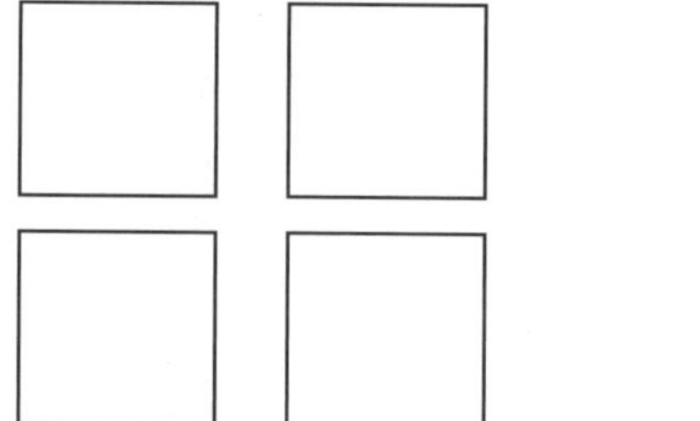

c. 3 and 5 tenths = ______

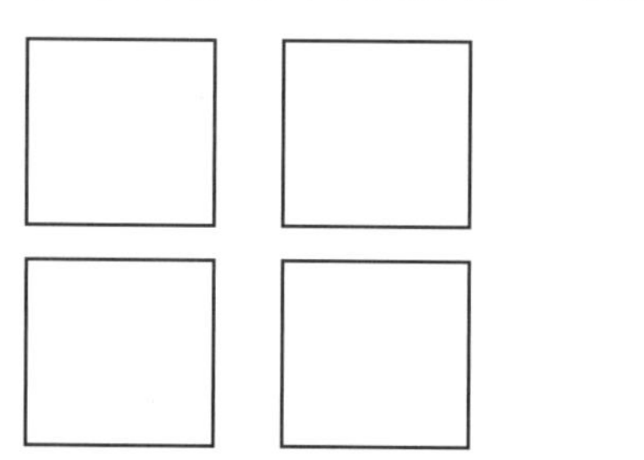

d. 4 and 3 tenths = ______

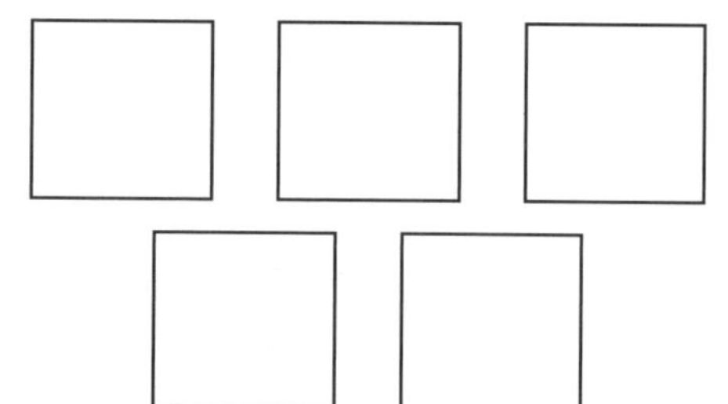

②

③ From least to greatest: ________________________

Draw lines to cut each figure and colour the correct number of parts to show the fraction given. Then circle the correct fraction.

④ $\frac{5}{6}$  $\frac{1}{2}$ 

$\frac{5}{6}$ $\frac{1}{2}$ is greater.

⑤ $\frac{1}{3}$ 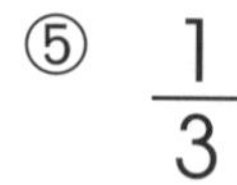  $\frac{4}{9}$ 

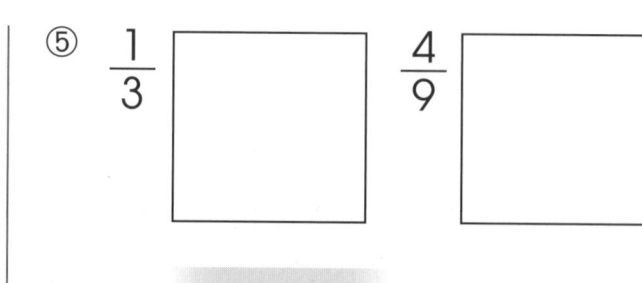

$\frac{1}{3}$ $\frac{4}{9}$ is smaller.

ISBN: 978-1-897164-32-7

The answers are the numbers representing the stickers. Do the addition and subtraction to help the children find their stickers.

⑥

$14.7 + 6.5$	$68.3 - 29.7$	$37.7 + 18.5$
(cat) ______	(octopus) ______	(seal) ______
$32.8 + 5.9$	$50.0 - 11.6$	$65.4 - 17.8$
(fish) ______	(crab) ______	(cow) ______
$75.2 - 59.6$	$40.8 - 36.9$	$59.6 + 15.7$
(snake) ______	(turtle) ______	(pig) ______

(mouse) $11.7 + 25.3 =$ ______ (rabbit) $61 - 41.6 =$ ______

(lion) $9.4 + 17.9 =$ ______ (elephant) $25 - 18.8 =$ ______

⑦ 

My sticker has a number that has a 9 in its tenth column. Which sticker is mine? ______

⑧ 

The number on the sticker that I like is the second greatest. Do you know which sticker I like? ______

⑨ *Which sticker is 0.1 greater than the octopus?* ______

ISBN: 978-1-897164-32-7

Find the cost of each item. Then find the total cost or price difference.

⑩

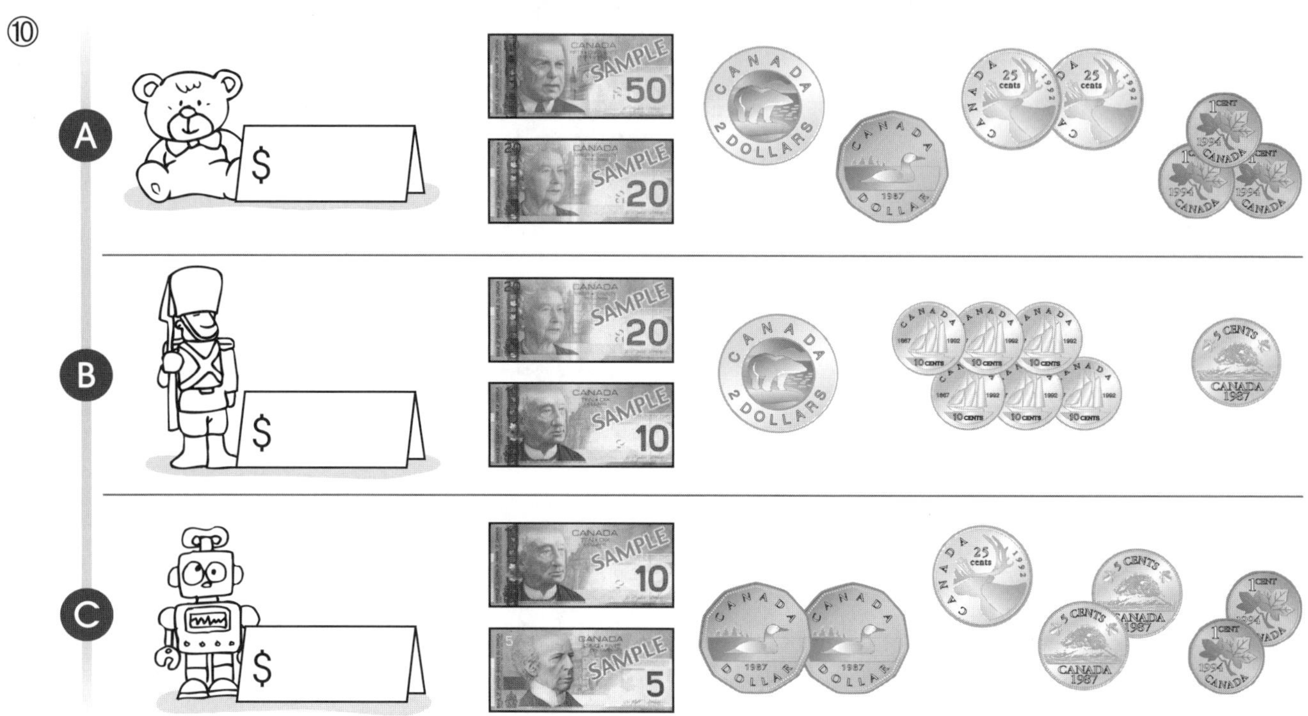

A $

B $

C $

⑪ Total cost of A and C :

______

______

⑫ Total cost of B and C :

______

______

⑬ Price difference of B and C :

______

______

⑭ Price difference of A and C :

______

______

ISBN: 978-1-897164-32-7

Name the quadrilaterals. Draw lines and find the measures of the angles. Then answer the questions.

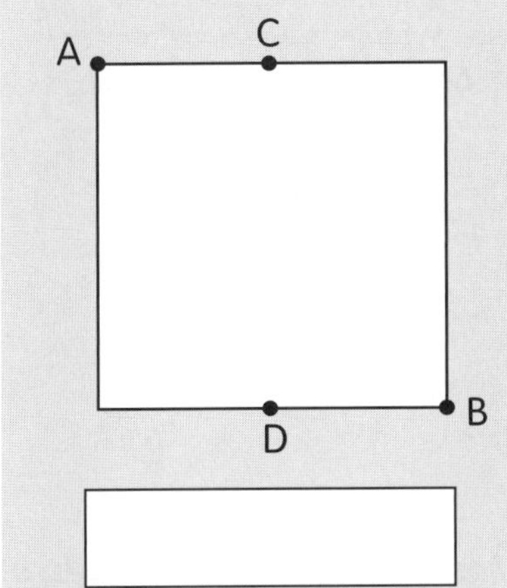

Draw a line from A to B and a line from C to D. What is the measure of each small angle formed by the lines AB and CD?

______

Is the line CD the line of symmetry of this shape? ______

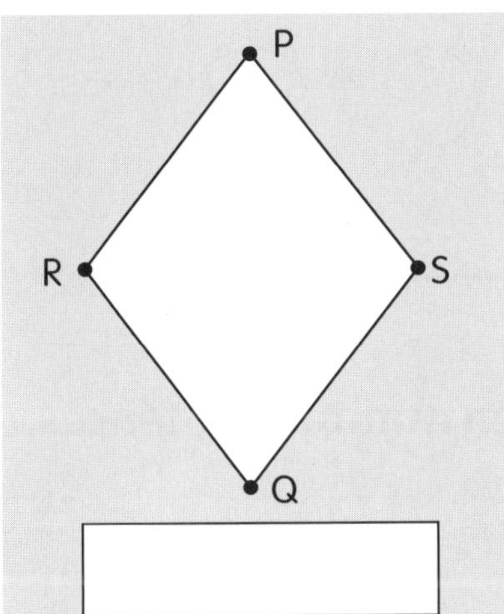

Draw a line from P to Q and a line from R to S. What is the measure of each angle formed by the lines PQ and RS?

______

How many pairs of parallel sides does this shape have? ______

Check the correct net for each 3-D figure. Then fill in the blanks with the correct numbers.

⑰ Triangular prism

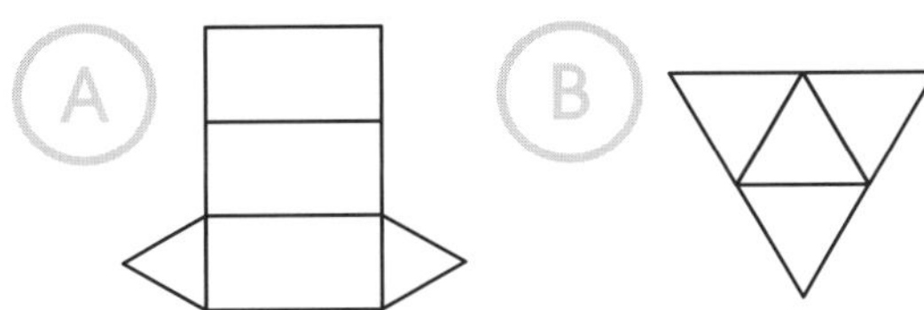

- ______ rectangular face(s)
- ______ triangular face(s)
- ______ vertices
- ______ edges

⑱ Rectangular pyramid

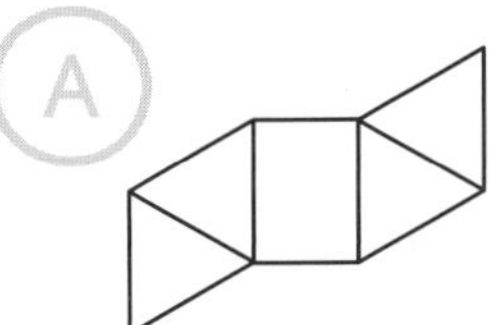

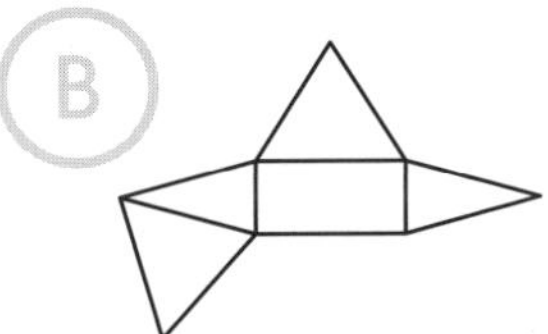

- ______ rectangular face(s)
- ______ triangular face(s)
- ______ vertices
- ______ edges

ISBN: 978-1-897164-32-7

Read what each animal says. Create a number sequence with 6 terms for each pattern rule. Then answer the questions.

⑲ 

Start at 7 and multiply each term by 2 to get the next term.

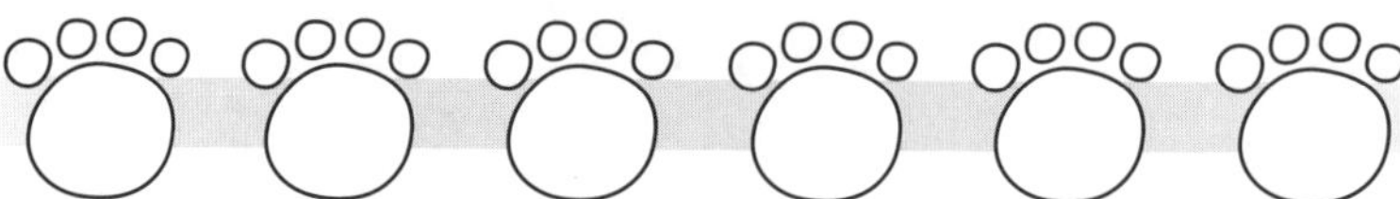

What is the 8th term? ______

⑳ 

Start at 96 and subtract 3 from each term to get the next term.

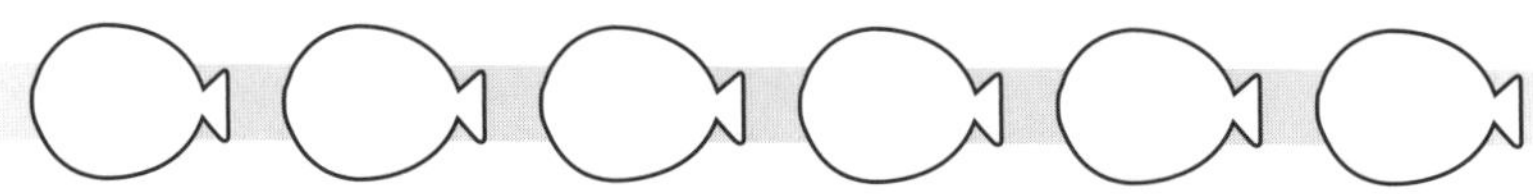

What is the 9th term? ______

Find the missing numbers with the help of the given number sentences.

㉑ ____ ÷ 5 = 25

㉒ ____ x 9 = 126

㉓ 126 ÷ ____ = 18

㉔ 5 x ____ = 155

㉕ 9 x ____ = 225

㉖ 18 x ____ = 90

㉗ 90 ÷ ____ = 10

- 155 ÷ 5 = 31
- 18 x 7 = 126
- 126 ÷ 9 = 14
- 90 ÷ 5 = 18
- 10 x 9 = 90
- 225 ÷ 25 = 9
- 25 x 5 = 125

Find the missing numbers.

㉘ ____ x 32 = 96

㉙ 108 ÷ ____ = 36

㉚ 7 x ____ = 700

㉛ 49 ÷ ____ = 7

㉜ ____ ÷ 4 = 12

㉝ ____ x 16 = 64

ISBN: 978-1-897164-32-7

Read the stem-and-leaf plot showing the lengths of ribbon that Mrs. Shaw has. Then answer the questions.

I can use a piece of 65-cm ribbon to make a ribbon flower.

Lengths of Ribbon

Stem	Leaves
1	8 8 9
3	0 1 1 3 5 5 5 5
4	1 2 2 4 4
6	3 7 7 8 8 8
9	0 0 6

34. How many pieces of ribbon does Mrs. Shaw have? ____________

35. How long is the longest ribbon? ____________

36. What is the median length of the ribbon? ____________

37. What is the mode length of the ribbon? ____________

Look at the spinner and read the sentence. Check the best prediction and explain.

Spin me 60 times. Predict how many times the pointer will land on each section.

38.

Prediction	Pencil	Crayon	Ruler
A	16 times	18 times	26 times
B	16 times	32 times	12 times
C	22 times	9 times	29 times

Explain: ______________________________

____

____

ISBN: 978-1-897164-32-7

ISBN: 978-1-897164-32-7

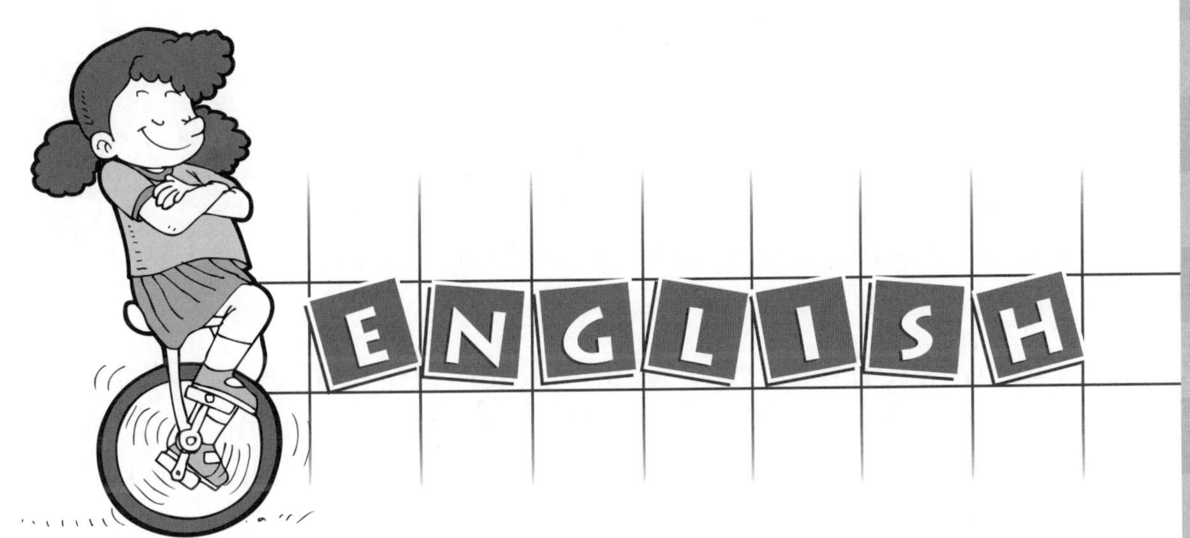

ISBN: 978-1-897164-32-7

1

Tim *Horton*

Canada has more doughnut shops per person than any other countries in the world! Why do we love doughnuts so much? It could be because of a man named Tim Horton.

Tim Horton's real name was Miles Gilbert Horton. He was born in Cochrane, Ontario in 1930. He loved to play hockey. When he was 19 years old, he joined the Toronto Maple Leafs and played with them for 17 years, helping the team to win the Stanley Cup four times.

In 1963, Tim decided to open a doughnut shop in Hamilton, Ontario. One year later, Tim invited a talented businessman, who used to be a police officer, to take over the running of the doughnut shop. Soon many cities in Canada had "Tim Hortons" shops. Why did Tim let another person take over his company? Well, Tim was very busy playing hockey still!

Soon after, Tim began to play for the New York Rangers, and later the Pittsburgh Penguins, and the Buffalo Sabres. Meanwhile, his doughnut business was getting bigger and more Canadians were eating doughnuts!

Sadly, Tim Horton died in a car accident in 1974. "Tim Hortons" is now the largest coffee and doughnut chain in Canada. There are more than 2500 shops all across Canada, as well as some in the United States, the United Kingdom, Ireland, and even Afghanistan.

ISBN: 978-1-897164-32-7

A. Check the meanings of the underlined words as they are used in the passage.

1. joined: ____ fastened one thing to another
   ____ took part in
2. open: ____ start a business
   ____ unfold
3. running: ____ moving faster than walking
   ____ operation
4. chain: ____ connected metal links or rings
   ____ group of shops owned by the same company

B. Write numbers to put the events in order.

____ Tim played for the New York Rangers.

____ Tim died in a car accident.

____ Tim joined the Toronto Maple Leafs.

____ Tim opened his first doughnut shop.

____ Tim invited a partner to run the doughnut shop.

C. Do you think Tim Hortons would be as popular as it is without Tim's partner? Explain.

____

____

____

ISBN: 978-1-897164-32-7

Nouns

A **common noun** names any person, place, thing, or animal.

Examples: officer city coffee deer

A **proper noun** is the name for a specific person, place, thing, or animal. It always begins with a capital letter.

Examples: Gilbert Hamilton Internet Bambi

D. Write the nouns in the correct groups. Write two more nouns in each group.

hockey

Tim Hortons

Stanley Cup

doughnut

E. Rewrite the sentences by correcting the common and proper nouns.

1. Mr. and mrs. Schwimmer like chatting in a Coffee Shop.

____

2. The Calgary flames is a very strong Hockey team.

____

3. My Brother wants to be a Firefighter.

____

ISBN: 978-1-897164-32-7

Adjectives

A **comparative adjective** compares two things. It is formed by adding "er" to or "more" before the base form.

Example: This skirt is cheaper and more beautiful than that one.

A **superlative adjective** compares three or more things. It is formed by adding "est" to or "most" before the base form.

Example: Liz is the smartest and most popular student in class.

Some comparative and superlative adjectives are irregular.

F. Complete the table of adjectives.

Base Form	Comparative	Superlative
1. great		
2. talented		
3. famous		
4. sweet		

G. Fill in the blanks with the correct form of the given adjectives.

1. Dad is drinking (much) ____________ coffee than before.
2. The (late) ____________ score is surprising.
3. Sam is the (new) ____________ player on the team.
4. The store at the corner is (near) ____________ than the one on Beehive Road.
5. He is the (reliable) ____________ member in the club.

ISBN: 978-1-897164-32-7

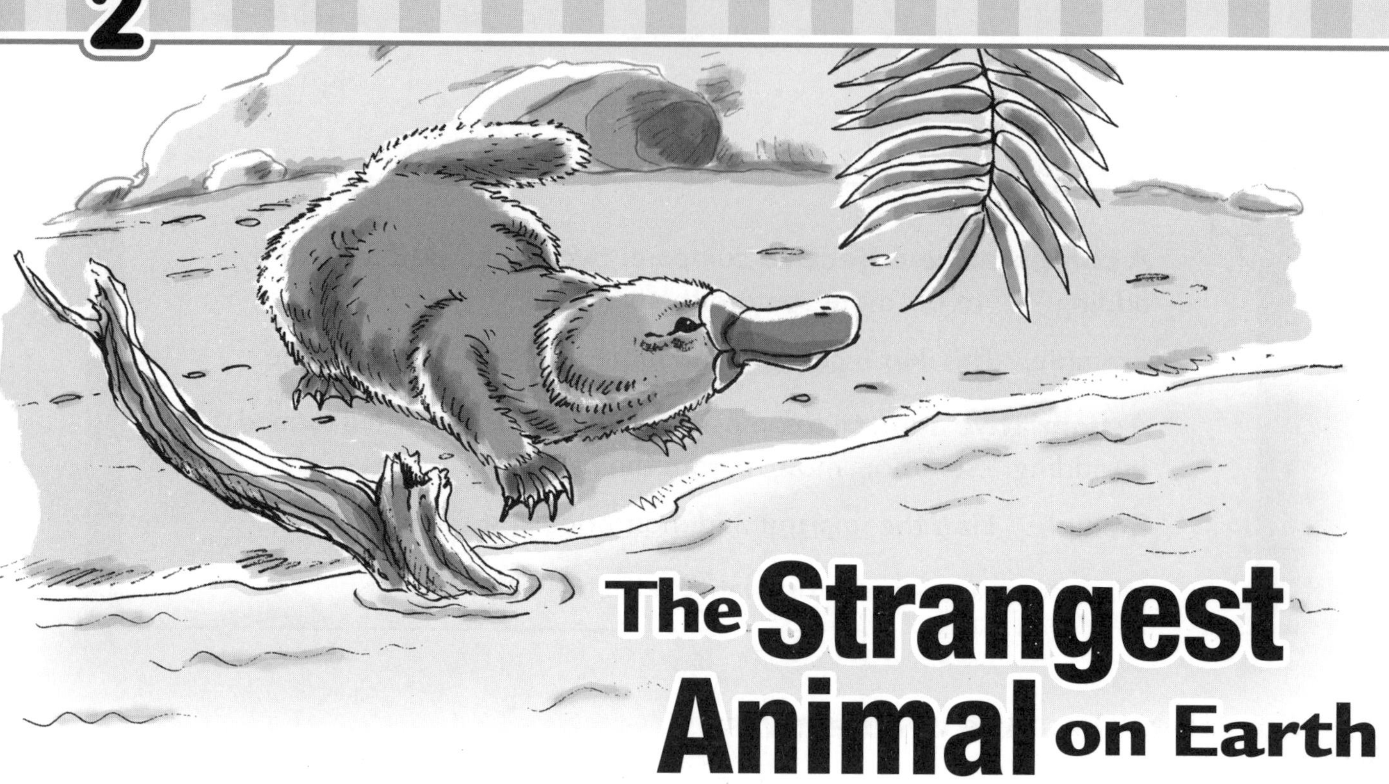

The Strangest Animal on Earth

What animal has fur and gives milk to its young like a mammal, but lays eggs like a bird or a reptile? What animal has webbed feet and a bill like a duck, but has a tail that looks much like a beaver's?

It's the duck-billed platypus, one of the strangest animals on Earth! Duck-billed platypi (the plural form of platypus) like to live in burrows near freshwater streams and ponds, and can be found only in eastern Australia and Papua New Guinea. They are about the size of a cat and weigh about three kilograms. They are good swimmers, but because their legs stick out at their sides, they walk like a lizard on land.

Duck-billed platypi like to eat meat, especially crayfish, worms, snails, shrimp, and other small animals from the water. They also eat small land rodents. Male platypi have a poisonous spike on their ankles which can be used to protect themselves from other animals, or to kill small animals for food. They have a lifespan of between 10 and 17 years.

This kind of animal, a warm-blooded mammal that lays eggs, is very rare. We call them monotremes. There used to be many kinds of monotremes, but they died out a long time ago. We can only see their fossils now. Today, there are only three living monotremes: the duck-billed platypus and two kinds of echidnas, or "spiny anteaters".

ISBN: 978-1-897164-32-7

A. Complete the information about the duck-billed platypus.

1. Habitat ______________________________

2. Size ______________________________

3. Weight ______________________________

4. Diet ______________________________

____

5. Lifespan ______________________________

B. Answer these questions.

1. In what way does a duck-billed platypus resemble each of the following animals?

   a. a bird

   ____

   b. a duck

   ____

   c. a beaver

   ____

2. What is the poisonous spike on the ankle of the male platypus for?

   ____

   ____

ISBN: 978-1-897164-32-7

Verbs

A **transitive verb** requires an object (the receiver of the action of the verb) to complete its meaning. An **intransitive verb** does not require an object to complete its meaning. Some verbs can be transitive or intransitive.

Examples: We sang the birthday song. (transitive)
("The birthday song" is an object in this sentence.)
We sang loudly together. (intransitive)
(There is no object in this sentence.)

C. Underline the verb in each sentence. Write whether they are transitive (T) or intransitive (I).

1. The duck-billed platypus swims well. ______
2. They have legs sticking out at their sides. ______
3. They love meat. ______
4. Daniel eats a lot of meat. ______
5. He seldom exercises. ______
6. He sleeps ten hours a day. ______

D. Use each verb as a transitive and an intransitive verb to write sentences.

1. **grow**

   Transitive: ______

   Intransitive: ______

2. **change**

   Transitive: ______

   Intransitive: ______

ISBN: 978-1-897164-32-7

Adverbs

An **adverb** describes a verb. Most adverbs are formed by adding "ly" to an adjective.

Example: The picture shows <u>clearly</u> what a duck-billed platypus looks like.

E. Complete the puzzle with adverbs formed from the clue words.

For adjectives ending in "y", drop the "y" and add "ily" to form adverbs.

1.	steady				A					
2.	glad				D					
3.	heavy				V					
4.	special				E					
5.	proud				R					
6.	probable				B					

F. Write a sentence of your own using each of the following adverbs.

1. softly

   ____

2. brightly

   ____

3. terribly

   ____

ISBN: 978-1-897164-32-7

Madagascar
A Strange Zoo

Madagascar is an island country about 480 kilometres east of southern Africa. It is famous for its unique fauna (animal life) and flora (plant life). There are so many things in Madagascar that you cannot find anywhere else on Earth!

Lemurs are the most famous of Madagascar's unique animals. They are a primitive type of monkey, and are related to humans. The fanaloka is a kind of civet cat and the tenrec is a kind of hedgehog unique to the island. Madagascar has hissing cockroaches, flying fox bats, bee-eating birds, and giant tortoises. Almost all of the reptiles and half of the birds on the island are not found anywhere else.

Madagascar has many strange and unusual plants. There are huge palms and many orchids. The national tree of Madagascar is the baobab tree. There are eight different species of baobab trees on the island.

Why does Madagascar have such special plants and animals? Madagascar used to be connected to Africa. About 165 million years ago, it broke off from Africa and began to drift away. The animals and plants back in Africa were changing over time, but those on Madagascar did not change as much. The flora and fauna have been separated from their ancestors for millions of years.

Many of Madagascar's unique plants and animals are extinct. We must make sure that we protect what is left.

ISBN: 978-1-897164-32-7

A. Check the main idea of the passage.

_____ Madagascar was part of Africa millions of years ago.

_____ Lemurs are one of the unique animals in Madagascar.

_____ Madagascar has many species of unique animals and plants.

_____ The fauna and flora in Madagascar have not changed much over the last millions of years.

B. Fill in the blanks with words formed by unscrambling the letters in parentheses.

1. Madagascar has its own (quueni) __________ animals and plants.
2. Many (sseepic) __________ of animals and plants on the island cannot be found anywhere else in the world.
3. The fauna and flora there are different from their (cessanort) __________ .
4. Hissing cockroaches and flying fox bats are some (lanuuus) __________ animals living in Madagascar.
5. Millions of years ago, Madagascar was (notedccen) __________ to Africa.

ISBN: 978-1-897164-32-7

Subjects

The **subject** of a verb is the person or thing that performs the action. It can be a noun or a pronoun.

Example: The <u>habitats</u> of many living things are being destroyed.

C. Underline the subjects in the sentences.

1. Many plants and animals are extinct.
2. World Wildlife Fund is involved in many conservation projects.
3. Dad promised to take me to the zoo this summer.
4. We can see many kinds of animals at the zoo.
5. I want to go on a pony ride.
6. My brother has two tortoises.

D. Write a suitable subject for each sentence.

1. ____________________ is rising in the east.
2. ____________________ waters the plants every day.
3. ____________________ has a new pet dog.
4. ____________________ like climbing up the fence.
5. ____________________ have not been to Africa.
6. ____________________ loves reading books about nature.

ISBN: 978-1-897164-32-7

Objects

The **object** of a verb is the person or thing that receives the action. It is made up of the bare object and its modifiers. It can be a noun or a pronoun.

Example: Mrs. Franklin has donated <u>money</u> to WWF.

E. Check if the underlined words in the sentences are objects. Put a cross if they are not.

1. <u>Our cat</u> gave birth to three kittens.
2. Grandpa bought a new cage <u>last Friday</u>.
3. He has grown <u>some cherry trees</u> in his backyard.
4. The beaver builds <u>its lodge</u> with tree branches.
5. The cat has scared <u>the birds</u> away.

F. Use each word as an object to write a sentence of your own.

1. monkey

   ____

2. reptiles

   ____

3. Africa

   ____

4. environment

   ____

ISBN: 978-1-897164-32-7

Velcro

An Amazing Invention

One day, a Swiss inventor named George de Mestral was walking in the woods. Later, he saw that many burrs had stuck to his wool pants. He wondered why they were hard to pull off. He looked at the burrs under a microscope, and saw that each burr was made up of tiny hooks. These hooks were sticking to the loops in the fabric of his wool pants.

The man decided that this was a good way to make things stick together. He took his idea to a textile designer in France. Together they invented a kind of "locking tape" fabric that fastened together using a system of hooks and loops.

But they did not know what to call it. Hook n' loop? Locking tape? It didn't seem quite right. At last, they decided to call this great invention Velcro. "Vel" comes from the word "velours", the French word for "velvet", and "cro" comes from "crochet", the French word for "hook".

Today Velcro is used everywhere, and many companies make it. But the word "Velcro" is a brand name, and belongs to the company started by George de Mestral.

You probably have a strip of hooks and a strip of loops to fasten your jacket, or your running shoes. But is your clothing made with real Velcro – or someone else's imitation?

ISBN: 978-1-897164-32-7

A. Write "T" for the true sentences and "F" for the false ones.

1. George de Mestral was a Swiss. ____
2. He found many burrs on his wool pants after a walk in the woods. ____
3. He realized that each burr was made up of tiny loops. ____
4. He took his "hooks and loops" idea to a textile designer in France. ____
5. They decided to call the invention "locking tape". ____
6. "Cro" comes from a Greek word meaning hook. ____
7. The word "Velcro" is a brand name. ____
8. Velcro is only used on jackets and running shoes. ____

B. Find words from the passage for the meanings below.

1. copy ____________
2. become attached ____________
3. an instrument for a larger view of things ____________
4. one who designs things as a profession ____________
5. prickly flower head that clings to clothing ____________

ISBN: 978-1-897164-32-7

Subjects and Predicates

A sentence is made up of a **subject** and a **predicate**.

One or more nouns together with their modifiers form the complete subject.

The predicate of a sentence describes what the subject is or what it does.

Example: Jim and his sister (subject) invented a massage device for their parents (predicate).

C. Put a vertical line between the subject and predicate in each sentence.

1. Grandpa invented a device that can trap mice.
2. He had looked at various kinds of mice traps before he made his own.
3. My brother wants to invent something too.
4. He is thinking of inventing a device to replace the remote control for the TV.
5. He and his friend are looking for relevant information.

D. Underline the complete subjects in the sentences.

1. George and a French designer invented Velcro.
2. Hooks and loops are the basic idea of the invention.
3. My running shoes are fastened with Velcro.
4. I wear them to school every day.
5. Marco and Eric think that my shoes are cool.

ISBN: 978-1-897164-32-7

E. Match the subjects with the predicates. Write the letters.

Ⓐ can minimize the risk of injury

Ⓑ toured around the world to show their work

Ⓒ has expanded its business over the years

Ⓓ mean a lot to the designer

Ⓔ have changed the way people live

Ⓕ is on sale this week

1. Many inventions ____ .
2. Her armband ____ .
3. His company ____ .
4. Fastening your seatbelt ____ .
5. The award and the public's recognition ____ .
6. The designer and the producer ____ .

F. Complete the sentences with suitable predicates.

1. Her latest design ______________________________

   ______________________________ .

2. The industry ______________________________

   ______________________________ .

3. A lot of hard work ______________________________

   ______________________________ .

4. Many trials and errors ______________________________

   ______________________________ .

ISBN: 978-1-897164-32-7

The Zzzzipper!

You probably use a zipper every day. We find zippers on our clothes, our boots, our school bags, and our pencil cases. Zippers are everywhere! What would we do without them?

People had to make do with buttons until about 100 years ago. The zipper was invented and patented on August 29, 1893 by an American mechanical engineer named Whitcomb Judson. He called it a "clasp locker". It was made using small hooks and loops. It didn't work very well, though. Although Judson displayed it at the 1893 Chicago World's Fair to a wide audience, not many people were impressed. He did sell 20 of these "clasp lockers" to the United States Postal Service to put on their mailbags, though.

In 1913, a Swedish engineer named Gideon Sundback produced a better version with metal teeth. He called it a "separable fastener" and sold many to the United States Army.

In 1923, B. F. Goodrich (a man famous for making rubber car tires) ordered 150 000 of them for his new product – rubber galoshes. He called the fasteners zippers because that was the sound he heard when the separable fastener was being pulled together.

The zipper invention got even better when it was made using a coil. Metal coils were easily bent out of shape, but in the 1960s, new flexible coils were being made out of synthetic material. The zipper was working better than ever!

ISBN: 978-1-897164-32-7

A. Read the clues. Complete the crossword puzzle with words from the passage.

Across

A. protected from imitation
B. that can be bent easily
C. showed

Down

1. variant form of something
2. excited

B. Complete the table about the development of the zipper.

	Year	Event
1.		Whitcomb Judson invented and patented the clasp locker.
2.	1913	
3.		B. F. Goodrich called the separable fastener "zipper".
4.	1960s	

ISBN: 978-1-897164-32-7

Subject-Verb Agreement

The **verb** must **agree** with the **subject** in a sentence. If the subject is singular, a singular verb should be used. If the subject is plural, a plural verb should be used.

Examples: Maria wants to replace the buttons with a zipper.
We all agree with her.

C. Circle the correct verb for each sentence.

1. Daniel like / likes jackets with a zipper.
2. We need / needs 20 buttons to make the puppets.
3. Each of them have / has a bag of materials.
4. These stuffed geese was / were made by Kitty and Paula.
5. Do / Does they have enough for the show?

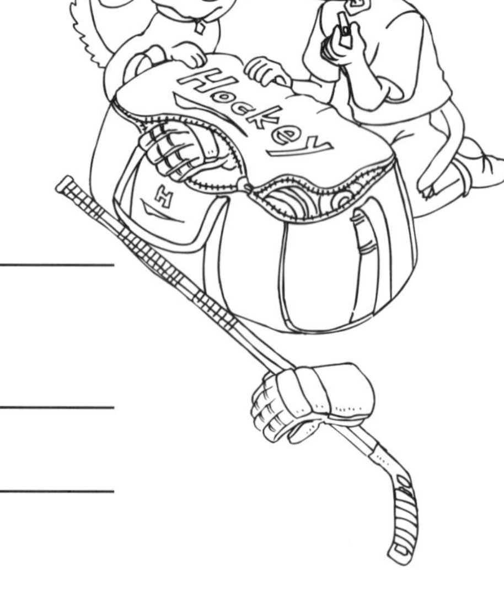

D. Check if the underlined words are correct. If not, write the correct words on the lines.

1. The zipper on my bag is broken. ____________
2. I have to buy a new bag for my hockey gear. ____________
3. It take time to find the right one. ____________
4. Little William always forget to zip his pencil case. ____________
5. I thinks he should get one without a zipper. ____________

ISBN: 978-1-897164-32-7

E. Write a suitable subject for each sentence.

1. ______________ matches the boots.
2. ______________ makes 100 000 zippers a day.
3. ______________ were working on their project.
4. ______________ do not need to work tomorrow.
5. ______________ wants to design a new fastener.

F. Rewrite the following sentences. Change the singular subjects to plural and the plural subjects to singular. Make changes to the verbs and other words too.

1. The teachers are preparing for the Open Day.

   The teacher is preparing for the Open Day.

2. Some grade four students have invented this device.

   ____

3. It is very useful on rainy days.

   ____

4. These invitation cards look cute.

   ____

5. The speaker is going to demonstrate the invention.

   ____

6. That experiment has given us some insights.

   ____

ISBN: 978-1-897164-32-7

6

Third Culture Kids

Emily St. Denny is 15 years old. She was born in Beijing, China, where her mother worked as a French teacher and her father taught English. When she was five years old, Emily and her family moved to Belgrade, Serbia. When she was seven years old, she moved to Nairobi, Kenya, where her little sister was born. Two years later, her family moved to Hong Kong, where she attended a French international school. After five years, the family moved to France.

Emily's mother was born in France. Emily's father is American. Emily says her little sister is very much French, like her mother. But after living in so many different places, Emily does not really know who she is. If pressed, she says she feels American more than anything else, as English is her first language. But she has never lived there! Welcome to the world of a "Third Culture Kid".

This term (shortened to "TCK") was made up in the 1960s by Doctors Ruth and John Useem. They used it to talk about the experience of mainly immigrant children growing up between two cultures: their culture of "origin" (or that of their parents), and the place they are currently living.

Today, TCK also refers to children who have travelled a lot and who are "culturally-blended". These are children who are familiar with many cultures and not as familiar with their parents'.

ISBN: 978-1-897164-32-7

A. Complete the table about Emily.

	Age	Place of Residence
1.	Birth	
2.	5	
3.	7	
4.		Hong Kong
5.	14	

B. Explain the following terms from the passage. Then use Emily's story as examples.

1. culture of origin

____

____

2. culturally-blended

____

____

____

C. Write three things that you think Emily may be different from her classmates in France.

1. ______________________________

2. ______________________________

3. ______________________________

ISBN: 978-1-897164-32-7

Subject and Object Pronouns

A **subject pronoun** replaces a noun as the subject in a sentence. "I", "you", "we", "they", "he", "she", and "it" are subject pronouns.

An **object pronoun** replaces a noun as the object in a sentence. "Me", "you", "us", "them", "him", "her", and "it" are object pronouns.

Example: Sam keeps the cards in a box.
He keeps them in a box.

D. Circle the correct pronouns.

1. Emily was born in China. Now, he / she lives in France.
2. France is a beautiful country. It / He is famous for its wine.
3. Emily's dad loves French wine. It / He visited some vineyards in Burgundy last summer.
4. Her father and my dad want to make their own wine. He / They enrolled in a wine making course.
5. I / You always ask my mom for more orange juice and you / she will say to me, "Okay, but I / you have to finish your cereal first."
6. Mom and I like juice. We / She have fresh orange juice every morning.

ISBN: 978-1-897164-32-7

E. Fill in the blanks with the correct pronouns.

Emily and I are classmates. I have known 1. ________ for almost a year. Emily and her family have lived in many places before. 2. ________ moved here to live with Emily's grandpa last year. 3. ________ owns a cake shop near our school. 4. ________ is about ten minutes away from school. Emily and I walk home together. 5. ________ stop by to say "bonjour" to her grandpa every day. I like 6. ________ very much as 7. ________ always treats 8. ________ cakes and tarts.

F. Rewrite the sentences by replacing the underlined words with pronouns.

1. <u>Emily's mother</u> was born in France.

   ____

2. <u>Emily's father</u> speaks to <u>Emily and Kelly</u> in English.

   ____

3. <u>Emily and Kelly</u> walk <u>their dog</u> to the park every day.

   ____

4. <u>English</u> is not widely spoken in France.

   ____

ISBN: 978-1-897164-32-7

Deborah Ellis:
Writing Books that Help Children

Deborah Ellis loves to write. One day she entered a writing competition held by a Canadian publisher. Her story did not win the competition, but the publishing company decided to publish it anyway. The book was called *Looking for X*. It was a real surprise then, when *Looking for X* won a Governor General's Literary Award the following year!

In 1999, Deborah spent time in Pakistan, working in refugee camps that housed mostly Afghan families. She heard stories of young girls who had to cut their hair off and dress up like boys in order to earn money for their families. At that time, women in Afghanistan were not allowed to leave their homes.

Deborah wrote *The Breadwinner*, a story about a young Afghan girl named Parvana. It became a huge success all around the world. Then Deborah's father said he wanted to know what happened next to Parvana, so Deborah wrote a sequel called *Parvana's Journey*. The series became a trilogy when Deborah wrote *Mud City*, the story of Parvana's friend Shauzia, in a refugee camp. All the money Deborah earns from the sale of these books goes to Women for Women in Afghanistan, Street Kids International, and UNICEF.

Deborah Ellis's books have helped readers better understand the difficult lives that many children have. She has said, "The world's children are a blessing to all of us. They are also our responsibility."

ISBN: 978-1-897164-32-7

A. Match the words with the definitions.

1. publish ____
2. refugee ____
3. sequel ____
4. trilogy ____
5. blessing ____

(A) group of three related works

(B) novel that continues the story of an earlier one

(C) print and distribute to the public

(D) something good that you are thankful for

(E) one forced to leave his or her country and seek protection

B. Write numbers to put the events in order.

____ *Looking for X* won a Governor General's Literary Award.

____ Deborah worked in refugee camps in Pakistan.

____ Deborah wrote *Parvana's Journey*.

____ Deborah wrote *The Breadwinner*.

____ Deborah wrote *Looking for X*.

____ Deborah wrote *Mud City*.

C. Explain what Deborah said in your own words: "The world's children... our responsibility."

____

____

____

ISBN: 978-1-897164-32-7

Possessives

A **possessive pronoun** tells who possesses something or is related to someone.

Possessive pronouns: mine, yours, ours, theirs, his, hers

A **possessive adjective** tells to whom the noun that it describes belongs or is related.

Possessive adjectives: my, your, our, their, his, her, its

Examples: This is my cell phone. (possessive adjective)
This cell phone is mine. (possessive pronoun)

D. Circle the correct words.

1. Rob bought a copy of *Mud City* yesterday. He will lend me his / hers when he finishes reading it.
2. All of us bring my / our own lunch here. Have you brought your / yours ?
3. Do you know when your / yours parents will be back?
4. I can tie my / your own shoelaces but little Candy cannot tie hers / its .
5. My / Mine dog wags it / its tail when I come home.
6. Gena and Kelly clean their / theirs room once a week. We should clean our / ours too.
7. The twin brothers ride their / theirs bikes to school.

ISBN: 978-1-897164-32-7

E. Check if the underlined words are correct. If not, write the correct words in the speech boxes.

1. Sue and <u>her</u> father volunteered to do the car wash.
2. Look! The baby ducks are swimming after <u>theirs</u> mother.
3. Will this dollhouse be <u>my</u>?
4. Do you think we can finish <u>ours</u> in two days?
5. The actress donates <u>hers</u> income to charity.
6. <u>His</u> story is published in today's paper.

F. Rewrite each sentence with a possessive pronoun or a possessive adjective.

1. Is this your kite?

   ____

2. These are their toys.

   ____

3. That hat is hers.

   ____

4. This will be your desk.

   ____

5. Will this hamster be ours?

   ____

ISBN: 978-1-897164-32-7

8

A Letter from the School Nurse

Dear Parents,

There has been a confirmed case of conjunctivitis in your child's class.

Conjunctivitis, also called "pinkeye", is an infection of the membrane on the inside of the eyelid, and also covering the eyeball. It is caused by viruses or bacteria. Conjunctivitis is contagious. It is usually spread by touching the infected eye/eyes, and then touching other surfaces, such as a telephone, doorknobs, etc.

Symptoms include stinging, itching, or reddening of the eye/eyes. There may be a white sticky discharge. When waking, the eye/eyes may have a crust and be difficult to open. Vision may be blurry.

If your child has any of these symptoms, please treat them for conjunctivitis. We suggest warm compresses on the closed eye/eyes for five to ten minutes, at least four times a day. This should be followed by antibiotic eyedrops ordered by your health care provider. Follow the doctor's instructions.

To prevent spreading, tell your children not to share washcloths, towels, pillows, or eye makeup. They should avoid touching their eyes and wash hands frequently.

Thank you for your attention.

Yours sincerely,

Registered Nurse

ISBN: 978-1-897164-32-7

A. Read the clues. Complete the crossword puzzle with words from the passage.

Across

A. prevent
B. often
C. become widely felt

Down

1. proved to be true
2. pads or cloths pressed on something
3. unclear

B. Fill in the blanks with words from the passage.

1. Olivia wrote the letter to the parents because she wanted to have their ________________ .
2. Conjunctivitis is a kind of eye ________________ .
3. Reddening of the eyes is one of the ________________ of conjunctivitis.
4. Pinkeye is caused by ________________ or ________________ .
5. Children should not share their towels or eye makeup because conjunctivitis is ________________ .

ISBN: 978-1-897164-32-7

Some **prepositions** tell the time of an event and the place of something.

Examples: Alex goes skating <u>on</u> Thursdays.
There is some orange juice <u>in</u> the fridge.

C. Circle the correct prepositions.

The school nurse gave us a talk about conjunctivitis. She showed an eye model 1. at / on screen. The talk finished 2. at / on four o'clock. We were asked to submit a slogan for the "Protect Our Eyes" campaign 3. in / by next Friday. Our class will have a brainstorming session 4. on / in Monday morning.

Our class will join a sports camp for children with low vision 5. from / on July 10 to July 14 6. of / at W. Ross Macdonald School. We will act as volunteers to help the visually-impaired children 7. in / on the camp. We will guide them 8. between / to and 9. from / off the field every day. I look forward to the camp because I have not been involved in this kind of voluntary work before.

ISBN: 978-1-897164-32-7

More on Prepositions

Certain **prepositions** are used after particular words or expressions.

Example: Mrs. Grant is very kind <u>to</u> us.

D. Fill in the blanks with the correct prepositions.

1. What's wrong __________ your eyes?
2. Can you stop staring __________ me?
3. We may go sightseeing – it depends __________ the weather.
4. Do not borrow face cloths __________ others.
5. Mom is not ready yet. She is still looking __________ her sunglasses.

E. Check if the underlined prepositions are correct. If not, write the correct words on the lines.

I ran <u>to</u> Ryan at the library this morning. He has been suffering <u>from</u> eye pain for three days. I am really sorry <u>to</u> him because he cannot take part <u>in</u> the swimming practice. His family doctor could not find the reason <u>about</u> the pain and referred him <u>to</u> a specialist. Ryan is very anxious <u>at</u> the swimming gala because the pain may prevent him <u>to</u> joining the competition.

1. __________
2. __________
3. __________
4. __________
5. __________
6. __________
7. __________
8. __________

ISBN: 978-1-897164-32-7

English
A Worldwide Language

Languages change over time. New words are invented (like "mouse pad" or "blogging") based on new inventions. Other new words come from other languages. For example, when you tell your mother you are going to serve her a special Mother's Day breakfast of coffee and croissants with marmalade, and a side order of yogurt, you are using words from at least three other languages ("coffee" and "yogurt" are Turkish words, "croissant" is a French word, and "marmalade" is a Portuguese word)!

Of course, it is easy to know when some words we use come from other languages. For example, most of the names of Australian animals are from that country's aboriginal languages: kangaroo, kookaburra, koala, and wombat. Japanese foods, such as sushi and tempura are familiar to us, and so are their Japanese names. This is the same with many Chinese food words, such as dim sum and chow mein.

But you might be surprised to learn that some words you have been using for a long time are not originally English words. For example, "kindergarten" is a German word, "mosquito" is a Spanish word, "cinema" is a Greek word, "robot" is a Czech word, "orangutan" is a Malay word, and "sauna" is a Finnish word.

Even though these words were not English to begin with, they are now certainly a part of the ever-growing English language.

Words are fascinating things, don't you think?

ISBN: 978-1-897164-32-7

A. Match the words with their language of origin.

1.		yogurt •	• Greek
2.		dim sum •	• German
3.		tempura •	• Spanish
4.		mosquito •	• Chinese
5.		cinema •	• Turkish
6.		kindergarten •	• Japanese

B. Circle the languages spoken in these countries in the word search.

Canada Germany France China
Japan Turkey Greece Czech Republic
Finland Portugal Spain Malaysia

p	F	r	e	C	z	M	a	y	F	i	n	n	T	u	r	G
o	i	S	p	z	J	a	P	o	r	t	u	g	u	e	s	e
r	n	p	G	e	r	l	G	r	e	e	k	F	r	e	C	r
t	n	a	e	c	J	a	p	a	n	e	s	e	k	k	z	m
F	i	n	i	h	e	y	a	n	c	s	C	h	i	n	e	a
e	s	h	S	p	a	n	i	s	h	c	h	e	s	i	o	n
C	h	i	n	e	s	e	E	n	g	l	i	s	h	o	n	h

ISBN: 978-1-897164-32-7

The Simple Present Tense

The **simple present tense** talks about facts, present actions, and habitual actions. Most present tense verbs for third person singular subjects are formed by adding "s/es" to the base form.

Example: Donald speaks Spanish well.

C. Write "P" for sentences in the simple present tense and "O" for sentences in other tenses.

1. *Sesame Street* used to be my favourite TV program.
2. Many people grew up with the show.
3. How many of us learned our "ABC" from the show?
4. Elmo is still my favourite character.
5. I have stuffed toys of all the characters in the show.
6. I put all of them on my bed.
7. My cousin plays with the toys whenever she comes to visit us.
8. She likes Ernie the best.
9. I will show you the toys when you come to visit us next time.

ISBN: 978-1-897164-32-7

D. Circle the correct verbs to complete the story.

I 1. have / has a new classmate. Her name 2. is / are Kim. She 3. will be / is from Korea. She 4. speak / speaks little English because her parents 5. talk / talks in Korean at home. They 6. run / runs a Korean restaurant near our school. It 7. serve / serves Korean food like kimchi and bibim bap. Kim 8. bring / brings her own lunch every day. Her lunch box 9. look / looks different from mine and the food 10. seem / seems to be very tasty.

E. Change the following sentences to the simple present tense.

1. Jack was interested in learning Korean.

____

2. He wanted to buy a dictionary.

____

3. The children are playing word games at home.

____

4. Sandy always won the game.

____

ISBN: 978-1-897164-32-7

Thailand's
Floating Lantern Festival

Thailand has a festival called Loy Krathong. "Loy" means "to float" and "krathong" is a lotus-shaped boat made of banana leaves. This festival usually takes place on the night of the full moon in November.

On this day, people in Thailand make krathongs. They put flowers, incense, and candles on their little boats, and then let them sail away on the water. They believe that the krathongs carry away bad luck.

Not only is Loy Krathong Festival a beautiful sight to see, but it is also a time of joy. Usually, there are firework displays. People do a traditional dance called Ramwong and sing the Loy Krathong Song on this day.

Loy Krathong Song (English translation)

The full moon of the twelfth month,
As water fills the banks,
We, all men and women,
Have really good fun on Loy Krathong Day,
Float, float the krathongs,
Float, float the krathongs,
And after we have floated our krathongs,
I invite you my dear,
To come out and dance,
Ramwong on Loy Krathong Day,
Ramwong on Loy Krathong Day,
Good merit brings us happiness,
Good merit brings us happiness.

ISBN: 978-1-897164-32-7

A. Match the facts. Write the letters.

1. Loy Krathong ____
2. krathong ____
3. Ramwong ____
4. Thailand ____
5. candles ____

(A) a boat made from banana leaves
(B) a traditional dance
(C) light the boats
(D) a festival
(E) a country

B. Answer these questions.

1. When do people celebrate Loy Krathong Festival?

____

2. What is the shape of a krathong?

____

3. What do people put on their krathongs?

____

4. Why do people let krathongs sail away on the water?

____

5. What else do people do apart from sailing krathongs?

____

6. Why is Loy Krathong Festival a beautiful sight to see?

____

ISBN: 978-1-897164-32-7

The Simple Past Tense

The **simple past tense** shows what happened in the past. Most past tense verbs are formed by adding "d/ed" to the base form. Some stay the same or change in spelling.

Example: Uncle Lee toured around Asia last summer.

C. Check the sentences that are in the simple past tense.

1. Mr. Dixie went to Thailand. ____
2. He likes sailing. ____
3. The incense smells good. ____
4. Did you see the pictures? ____
5. We enjoyed the firework displays. ____
6. They were magnificent. ____

D. Circle the correct past form of the words on the left.

1. **celebrate**	celebrated	celebrateed	celebrate
2. **throw**	throwed	threw	thrown
3. **cost**	costed	cast	cost
4. **carry**	carry	carryed	carried
5. **float**	float	floated	floaten

ISBN: 978-1-897164-32-7

E. Fill in the blanks with the past form of the correct words.

be explain teach cut
pick give say roll
bring show

Last week, Mrs. Powers 1.__________ us to make Thai krathongs in the Arts and Crafts lesson. She 2.__________ each of us a plastic bowl and some coloured paper. We 3.__________ our own glue and scissors. She 4.__________ us some samples of krathongs and 5.__________ to us how to make them. All of them 6.__________ beautiful. I 7.__________ some red and yellow paper and 8.__________ the edges in zigzag lines. Then I 9.__________ the tips to make them curl. Mrs. Powers 10.__________ that I had done a good job.

F. Use the past form of each word to write a sentence of your own.

1. see __________
2. fill __________
3. wear __________
4. stop __________

ISBN: 978-1-897164-32-7

Happy "Wet" New Year

These days, Thailand celebrates the calendar New Year on the first day of January. But it wasn't always this way: Thailand used to celebrate their new year in April with the Songkran Festival. This festival starts on April 13 and lasts from three to ten days, depending on which part of Thailand you are in.

Thai people believe that the New Year, or springtime, is a time to "throw out the old and bring in the new". Songkran is "Spring Cleaning Day" across Thailand; it is part of their religious beliefs that useless items will bring bad luck if not thrown away.

The Songkran Festival is celebrated with water. On the afternoon of April 13, people carefully clean their images and statues of Buddha. Young people show respect to their elders and seek their blessings by pouring scented water into the hands of parents and grandparents.

The Songkran Festival is also a time of fun and joy. Everyone throws water on each other on the streets! Why? There were legends about serpents that sprayed water on the land. If these serpents sprayed a lot of water, there would be a lot of rain. Some people believe that throwing water at people is another way of asking for rain and they need the rain for farming. Whether or not this is true does not seem to matter to the people of Thailand on the day of the Songkran Festival – they are having a splash!

ISBN: 978-1-897164-32-7

A. Write "T" for the true sentences and "F" for the false ones.

1. People in different parts of Thailand celebrate the Songkran Festival for different periods of time.
2. People throw away useless items at Songkran.
3. They believe that getting rid of useless items will bring them luck.
4. People clean their Buddha statues at the Songkran Festival.
5. People poured scented waters into the hands of their children to show their care.
6. Some people believe that throwing water at people is another way of asking for wealth.

B. Check the main idea of the passage.

A Thailand celebrates New Year on January 1.

B People in Thailand respect their elders.

C People in Thailand celebrate New Year with water.

C. Imagine it is the Songkran Festival in Thailand. Will you throw water at others? Why or why not?

ISBN: 978-1-897164-32-7

The Future Tense

The **future tense** shows what will happen in the future. The verb is formed by adding "will/shall" before the base form of the verb. "Will" can be used with all subjects while "shall" is used with "I" or "we".

Example: My Thai pen pal <u>will come</u> to Canada at Easter.

D. Underline the future tense verbs in the following sentences.

1. My grandparents will visit Thailand next week.
2. We shall see them off at the airport.
3. They will stay at a resort near the beach.
4. Grandpa will take many photos with his digital camera.
5. Grandma will enjoy a quiet time there.
6. They will send us postcards.
7. They will be back for Christmas.

E. Circle the correct words to complete the paragraph.

Katherine 1. will / shall visit us in New Year. She will 2. spend / spent a week here. Dad will 3. takes / take us on a ski trip in Barrie. We 4. will / are join a beginner's program there. Dad will 5. be / being there to watch us. He 6. will / shall take his new video camera with him and 7. record / recording the trip.

ISBN: 978-1-897164-32-7

F. Look at Andrew's New Year's resolutions. Write them in complete sentences.

1. make my bed
2. eat fewer candies
3. brush teeth twice a day
4. not make Mom angry
5. go running once a week
6. share toys with Johnny

1. I ______________________________.
2. ______________________________
3. ______________________________
4. ______________________________
5. ______________________________
6. ______________________________

G. What are your New Year's resolutions? List three of them in the future tense.

1. ______________________________
2. ______________________________
3. ______________________________

ISBN: 978-1-897164-32-7

12

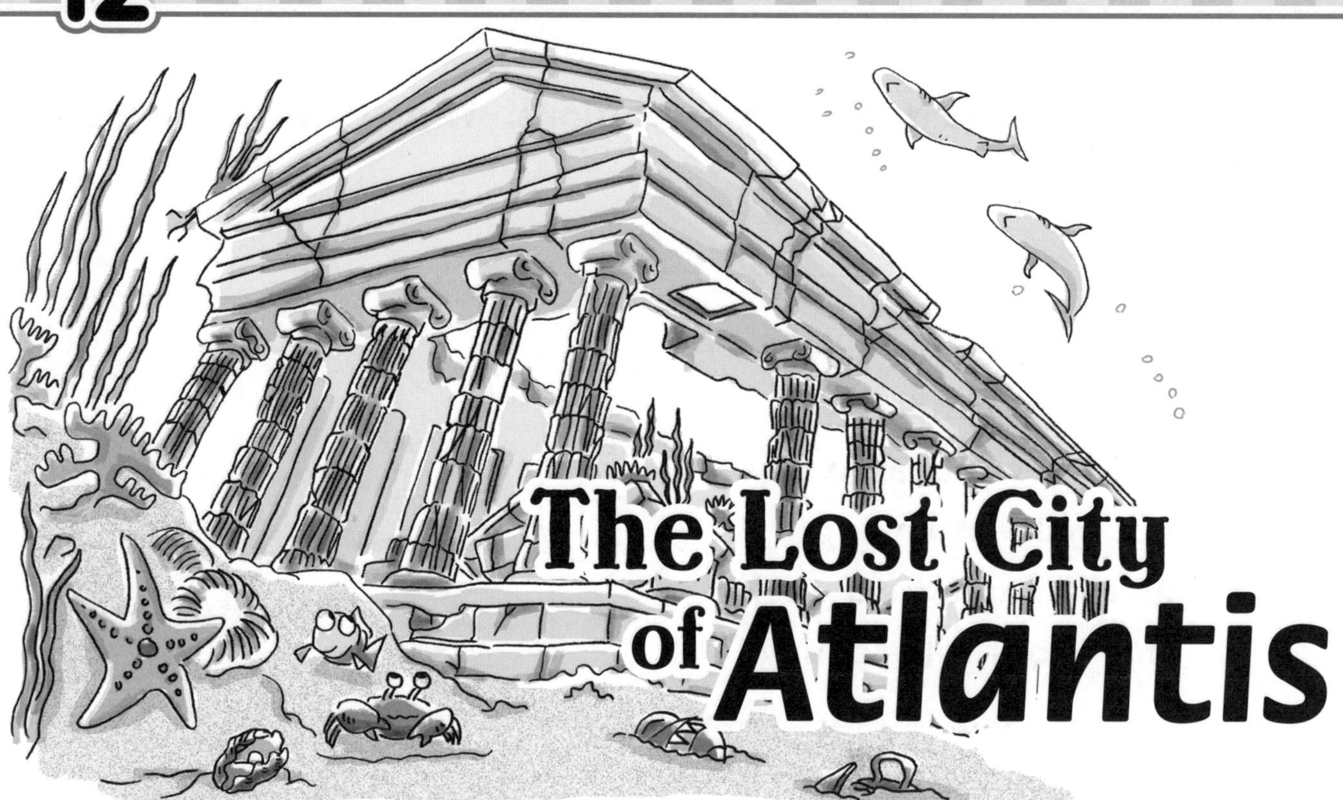

The Lost City of Atlantis

People have been writing about the "lost city" of Atlantis for centuries. Some say it was an ancient civilization that disappeared into the sea. Others say it was a place where real-life "merpeople" lived, and perhaps still do ("mer" is the French word for "ocean"). Do you think Atlantis is a real place? Do you think it still exists on the ocean floor somewhere?

Many people now believe that there is a place on Earth that can be traced back to the famous legend of Atlantis. It is a small Greek island called Santorini in the Mediterranean Sea.

Santorini is an island of stunning beauty. It has lowlands and lovely beaches at one end, but it rises up to enormous steep cliffs at the other end. When you stand on the cliffs and look out, you can see another, much smaller island.

Geologists (people who study the Earth) say this island's unusual shape is because of a volcano. Centuries ago, the island had a huge volcano on it. When it exploded around 3500 years ago, it blew the island apart.

Archaeologists have found evidence of an ancient town on Santorini. If you go there, you can see for yourself; there are walls and steps of buildings. Pot shards and cooking utensils and pieces of furniture have also been found.

Is this evidence of Atlantis or simply evidence that people lived on that lovely island centuries ago?

ISBN: 978-1-897164-32-7

A. Read the clues. Complete the crossword puzzle with words from the passage.

Across

A. story handed down from the past

B. impressive

C. periods of 100 years

Down

1. proof

2. broken pieces of pottery, glass, etc.

3. implements or containers for everyday use at home

B. Answer these questions.

1. What is so special about the landscape of Santorini?

____

____

2. Why do some people believe that Santorini was Atlantis?

____

____

ISBN: 978-1-897164-32-7

Sentences (1)

A **sentence** gives a complete thought about someone or something.

A **telling sentence** makes a statement. It ends with a period.

Example: Santorini is a small island in Greece.

An **asking sentence** asks a question. It ends with a question mark.

Example: Have you been to Greece?

C. Write "T" for telling sentences, "A" for asking sentences, and "I" for incomplete sentences.

1. Do you know where Santorini is? ______
2. Santorini, a beautiful island. ______
3. Atlantis may never have existed. ______
4. Are you interested in archaeology? ______
5. Shall we go to the library? ______
6. Just a legend. ______
7. The landscape on the island is unique. ______

D. Put the correct punctuation marks at the end of the sentences.

Have you been to the new Greek restaurant ◯ My parents took me there for dinner last night ◯ It was the first time I had tried Greek food ◯ Do you know what "Horta" is ◯ It is boiled greens ◯ It tastes good with lemon, vinegar, and oil ◯ Would you like to try it ◯

ISBN: 978-1-897164-32-7

E. Change the telling sentences to asking sentences and asking sentences to telling sentences.

1. There is a volcano on the island.

   ____

2. The volcano did not explode in the last decade.

   ____

3. People can find evidence of explosion.

   ____

4. Will Donald go to the beach this weekend?

   ____

5. Can we go boating on the lake?

   ____

   ____

F. Write two telling sentences and two asking sentences about the lost city of Atlantis.

Telling Sentences

1. ______________________________
2. ______________________________

Asking Sentences

3. ______________________________
4. ______________________________

ISBN: 978-1-897164-32-7

The Snake Dens of Narcisse

The little town of Narcisse, Manitoba is known to herpetologists all over the world. Herpetologists are people who study snakes and other reptiles. The area around Narcisse has the world's largest population of the red-sided garter snake. It is the largest community of any snakes in the world!

Around Narcisse, the ground is made with a porous rock called limestone. There are a lot of crevasses and caves underground, which make cozy dens. The garter snake spends the winter there. It is the only reptile that can survive in such a cold place, thanks to these warm winter dens. There are more than 30 snake dens in a 12-square-kilometre area around Narcisse, which is the home of well over ten thousand snakes.

Once the snow is gone, male garter snakes come out of the dens. The female snakes appear soon after, and mating season begins. It lasts for about three weeks. During this time, the snakes will form large wriggling balls together. It is an extraordinary sight to see. When mating season is over, the snakes will slither away to nearby fields and wetlands for the summer to feed.

Female garter snakes will give birth to as many as 40 offspring, but over three-quarters of them will not survive through the winter. Cold temperatures, predators, and poaching are a problem. Many snakes are also killed when they try to cross the highway. Snake tunnels have been built under the roads to help protect the snakes of Narcisse.

ISBN: 978-1-897164-32-7

A. Give one-word answers to the questions.

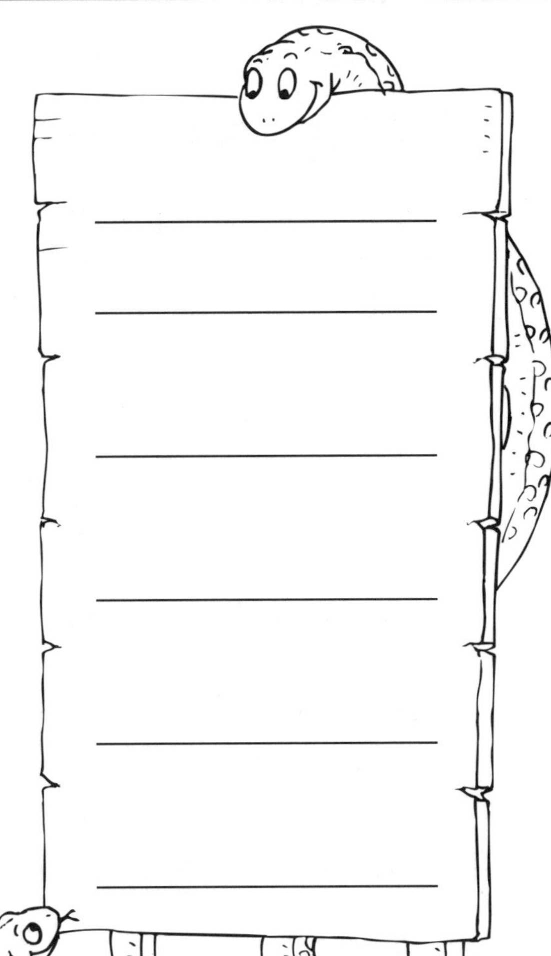

1. Where do snakes live? ____________
2. In which province is Narcisse? ____________
3. What is the ground of Narcisse made with? ____________
4. What has been built to help protect the snakes in Narcisse? ____________
5. What do we call the people who study snakes and other reptiles? ____________
6. How many weeks does the mating season of garter snakes last? ____________

B. Write an effect for each of the following causes.

1. Narcisse has the world's largest population of the red-sided garter snake.

   ____

2. The crevasses and caves in the limestone make cozy dens.

   ____

3. There are poachers for the garter snakes.

   ____

ISBN: 978-1-897164-32-7

Sentences (2)

An **imperative sentence** makes a request or gives an order. It ends with a period. The subject "you" is left out.

Example: Listen to me.

An **exclamatory sentence** expresses a strong feeling, such as surprise, happiness, or anger. It ends with an exclamation mark.

Example: That snake is real!

C. Write "I" for imperative sentences and "E" for exclamatory sentences.

1. What a big wriggling ball the snakes have formed!
2. Wow, there are so many snakes in the cage!
3. Take a picture of the snake.
4. Stay away from the bush.
5. Read the tag and write down the name of the snake specimen.
6. The snake is really long!
7. Do not stand beyond the railing.
8. I've never seen a snake with such a big head in my life!
9. Tell me the time, please.

ISBN: 978-1-897164-32-7

D. Change the following questions to imperative sentences.

1. Could you show me your ticket?

 ____

2. Will you take off the jacket?

 ____

3. Can you stop running?

 ____

4. Would you wait for me at the exit?

 ____

E. Look at the picture. Write three exclamatory sentences to show your feelings if you were one of the children.

1. ______________________________
2. ______________________________
3. ______________________________

ISBN: 978-1-897164-32-7

Ogopogo

Canada's Lake Monster

You have probably heard of Nessie, the shy monster that lives in Loch Ness, Scotland. But did you know Canada has its own "Loch Ness Monster"? It is called Ogopogo, and it lives in long, deep Lake Okanagan in British Columbia.

The Salish Native people in British Columbia have known about this lake monster for more than 100 years, long before the Loch Ness Monster became known to the world. These First Nations people called it N'ha-a-itk. Every time they needed to go onto the lake, they would look carefully for the monster before setting out. Sometimes they would throw food into the lake, so the monster would like them and leave them alone.

In 1942, the monster became known as Ogopogo. These days, we think Ogopogo is more of a friendly lake creature than a scary monster. Just like Nessie, the Loch Ness Monster, Ogopogo is believed to have a snake-like body, with several humps, a green outer skin, and a large, goat- or horse-like head. Its body is about half a metre in diameter and five or six metres long. Some people who claimed they saw it said it looked like a log! Some scientists think Ogopogo could be a kind of ancient water serpent or a primitive whale.

What do you think? Is Ogopogo a friendly creature – or just a funny story?

ISBN: 978-1-897164-32-7

A. Match the related words.

1.	green	•	• Ogopogo
2.	horse-like	•	• body
3.	snake-like	•	• head
4.	Nessie	•	• Lake Okanagan
5.	N'ha-a-itk	•	• skin
6.	British Columbia	•	• Loch Ness Monster

B. Write "T" for the true sentences and "F" for the false ones.

1. Canada has a lake called Lock Ness. ______
2. The name "Ogopogo" was adopted in 1942. ______
3. The First Nations people called the lake monster Ogopogo. ______
4. People would throw food into the lake to attract the lake monster. ______
5. Nessie and Ogopogo are believed to be the same kind of creature. ______
6. Ogopogo has several humps on its body. ______
7. Its body is about five or six metres in diameter. ______
8. Some scientists believe that Ogopogo could be a kind of primitive whale. ______

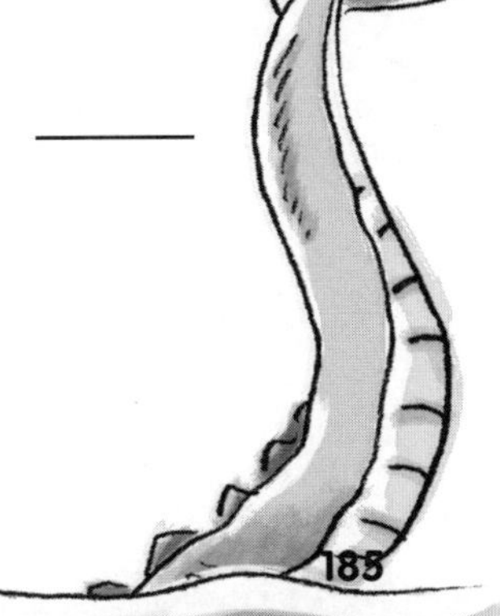

ISBN: 978-1-897164-32-7

Simple and Compound Sentences

A **simple sentence** is made up of one subject and one predicate. It gives a complete thought about someone or something.

Example: Uncle Greg has a cottage near the lake.

A **compound sentence** is made up of two or more independent clauses joined by a conjunction. An independent clause can be a sentence by itself.

Example: We visit him every summer and he takes us to a boat ride.

C. Colour "S" for simple sentences and "C" for compound sentences.

1. They want to go to Lake Okanagan and they'll stay in the lakeside town for a few days. S / C

2. Loch Ness is known for its monster Nessie and Lake Okanagan is famous for its Ogopogo. S / C

3. The head of Ogopogo is like a horse but its body is like a snake. S / C

4. The lake is 169 kilometres long and up to 300 metres deep. S / C

5. Do you think it is a friendly creature or is it just a myth? S / C

6. Ogopopo could be a kind of primitive whale. S / C

7. The monster looks weird but cute. S / C

ISBN: 978-1-897164-32-7

D. Add subjects or predicates to make simple sentences.

1. The lake monster ______________________________.
2. Lake Huron ______________________________.
3. My sister and I ______________________________.
4. ______________ go boating on the lake.
5. ______________ took a picture of the statue.
6. ______________ is just a myth.

E. Complete the sentences with the related clauses to make compound sentences.

- we will watch it tonight
- Mom wants to go shopping
- his sister chose to be Snow White
- we call it Ogopogo

1. The First Nations people call the lake monster N'ha-a-itk but ______________________________.
2. Benjamin picked a costume of the lake monster and ______________________________.
3. Dad wants to go fishing this Saturday but ______________________________.
4. Uncle Henry gave us a DVD yesterday and ______________________________.

ISBN: 978-1-897164-32-7

Review 1

A. Rewrite the sentences by replacing the underlined words with proper nouns.

1. <u>This city</u> is the capital of Ontario.

   ____

2. School starts in <u>the ninth month of the year</u>.

   ____

3. This is the picture of <u>the first prime minister of Canada</u>.

   ____

4. The club has a meeting every <u>second day of the week</u>.

   ____

   ____

B. Use the correct form of the adjectives to complete the sentences.

lovely	small	touching
few	cold	expensive

1. It is ______________ in winter than in fall.
2. Betsy has ______________ stamps than Kingsley.
3. Which lake is the ______________ of the Great Lakes?
4. This storybook is ______________ than that one.
5. The ______________ picture here is drawn by my sister.
6. That was the ______________ scene in the movie.

ISBN: 978-1-897164-32-7

C. **Find and circle 12 verbs in the word search. Then write them in the correct boxes.**

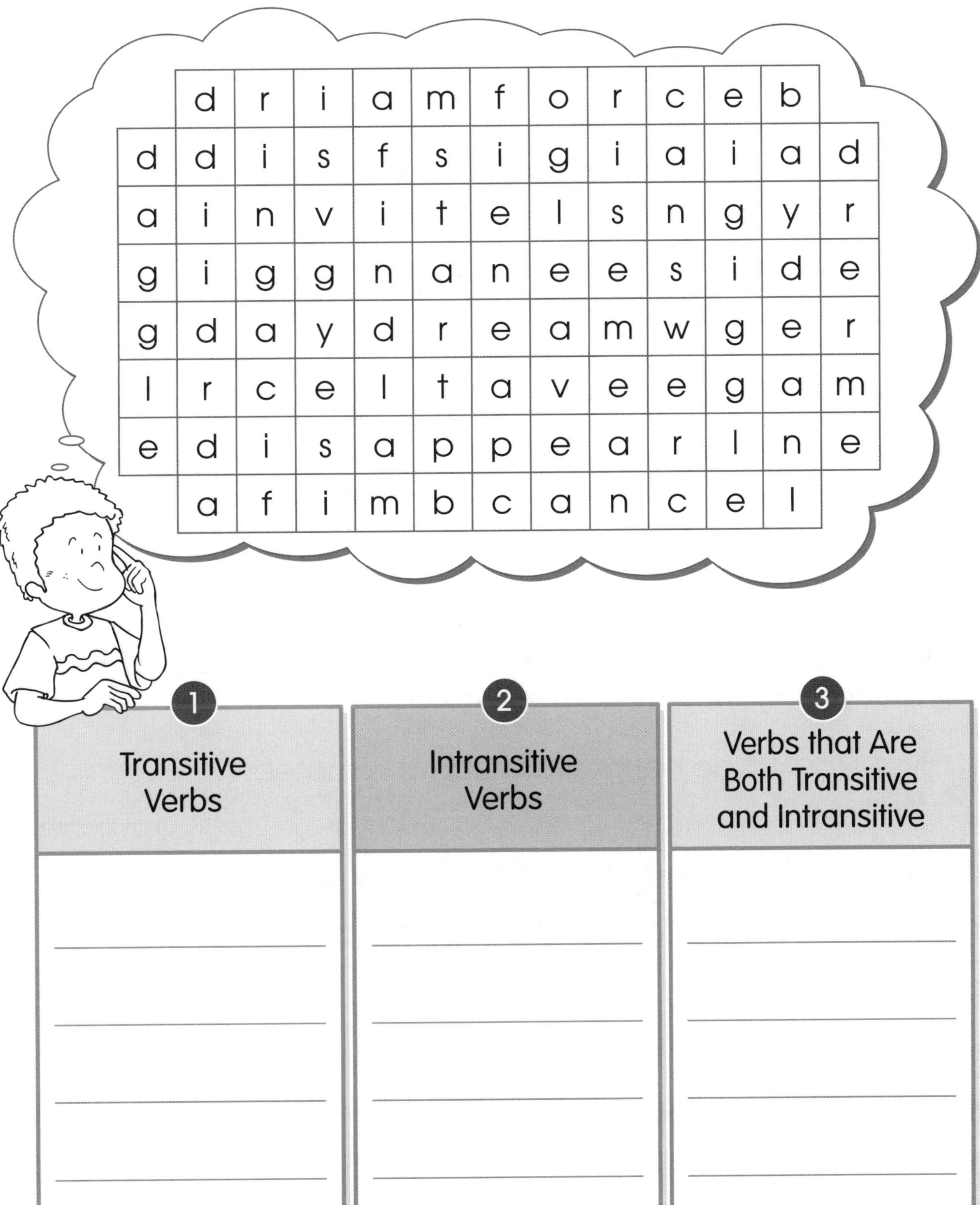

ISBN: 978-1-897164-32-7

D. Put a vertical line between the subject and the predicate in each sentence. Then circle the object of the verb if there is any.

1. The little girl opened the door to let her dog in.
2. Aunt May and Uncle Tom bought a big birthday cake for me.
3. My sister and I have borrowed some books from the library.

4. Dad took a big, colourful lollipop out from the bag.
5. All members will gather at the school entrance at eight.
6. The children tossed the empty cans into the bin.

E. Check if the underlined words agree with the subjects. Correct the wrong ones and write them on the lines.

1. Mrs. Hopkins do not hesitate about volunteering to help. ____________
2. The water in the glasses are not very clear. ____________
3. Ray and Donald are rehearsing the play. ____________
4. No one want to do badly on the test. ____________
5. The Cudneys is having a vacation in Cuba. ____________
6. He don't have any tokens left. ____________
7. Is your brother joining us too? ____________
8. We often strolls in the park after dinner. ____________

ISBN: 978-1-897164-32-7

F. Replace the underlined words with pronouns or possessive adjectives.

1. My friends and I are going to Wonderland this Sunday.

   ____

2. That bag over there is Jane's.

   ____

3. Mrs. Gifford gave some stickers to her students.

   ____

4. Could you pass Jeremy's picture to me?

   ____

G. Fill in the blanks with the correct prepositions.

Maggie is taking part 1. ________ a running race tomorrow. It will start 2. ________ nine o'clock 3. ________ the morning. Maggie is very anxious 4. ________ the race. She wants to make sure she has her T-shirt, shorts, socks, and running shoes ready tonight. But she can only find one shoe. She looks everywhere 5. ________ the other one but it is nowhere to be found. Mom says she can borrow the shoes 6. ________ her sister, but Maggie insists 7. ________ finding hers. Finally Dad finds it half buried 8. ________ the soil 9. ________ their backyard. It must have been hidden there by their naughty dog, Super.

ISBN: 978-1-897164-32-7

H. Fill in the blanks with the correct form of the verbs.

Last Wednesday, Miss Weller (tell) 1.____________ me to bring something interesting to class for show-and-tell tomorrow.

I (have) 2.____________ a shell that I (like) 3.____________ very much. I (find) 4.____________ it on a beach when my family (go) 5.____________ on a vacation in Thailand last summer. It (be) 6.____________ as big as a mug and (have) 7.____________ a bright orange colour. There (be) 8.____________ many pointed spikes around it. I (learn) 9.____________ from Mom that this (be) 10.____________ a very rare shell. I (want) 11.____________ to show it to my classmates but (be) 12.____________ afraid that I might break it. Then I (come) 13.____________ up with an idea. I (ask) 14.____________ my dad to take a picture of the shell with our digital camera. Then we (print) 15.____________ out the picture. It (be) 16.____________ like real.

Tomorrow I (show) 17.____________ the picture of my precious shell to my classmates. I (be) 18.____________ sure they (like) 19.____________ it as much as I (do) 20.____________ .

ISBN: 978-1-897164-32-7

I. Write "S" for the simple sentences and "C" for the compound sentences.

1. All grade one and grade two students can join the day camp. ____
2. Kylie prepared the materials and Rhonda made the model. ____
3. I can give you some guidelines but you have to finish the writing yourself. ____
4. Keep pressing the button or the music will stop. ____
5. Babies eat nothing but milk. ____

J. Put the words in order to form sentences.

1. **Telling Sentence**

   at morning school the eight in starts

   ____

2. **Asking Sentence**

   you call she last did give nIght a

   ____

3. **Imperative Sentence**

   play on don't road the ever

   ____

4. **Exclamatory Sentence**

   a surprise everyone great what for

   ____

ISBN: 978-1-897164-32-7

Cheese Rolling

Great Britain's Extreme Sport

You have probably heard of tomato throwing and the polar bear swim. But have you ever heard of the sport of cheese rolling?

Cheese rolling is an event that takes place every spring at Cooper's Hill, Gloucestershire (a county in England, west of London). People say that cheese rolling is one of Great Britain's oldest customs. Some say the custom started even before the Romans lived in that country 2000 years ago. Most say cheese rolling has been going on for at least a couple of centuries as a celebration of the onset of summer.

Each year, thousands of spectators come to Cooper's Hill to watch people chase a seven-pound round of Double Gloucester Cheese down the hillside. There are separate races for men and women, and now uphill races for boys and girls too. The winners get to keep the rounds of cheese they have tried so hard to catch. However, no one ever catches the cheese because it hurtles down the slope at nearly 110 kilometres per hour!

It is all quite funny to imagine people chasing a little wheel of cheese as it rolls down a hill, but perhaps it is not so funny to see it because Cooper's Hill is very steep. Every year, several of the cheese-chasers tumble down the hill. Often, people suffer broken bones. But this has not stopped the event from taking place.

Chasing cheese. Would you do it?

ISBN: 978-1-897164-32-7

A. Complete the crossword puzzle with words from the passage that are synonyms of the clue words.

Across

A. onlookers

Down

1. beginning
2. maybe
3. dashes
4. fall
5. traditions

B. Answer these questions.

1. Describe how the event goes.

2. What are the prizes for the winners?

3. Do you think the event should stop? Explain.

ISBN: 978-1-897164-32-7

Capitalization

We use **capital letters** for:

- the first word in a sentence.
- proper nouns.
- titles.
- days, months, holidays, and events.
- races, nationalities, religions, and languages.

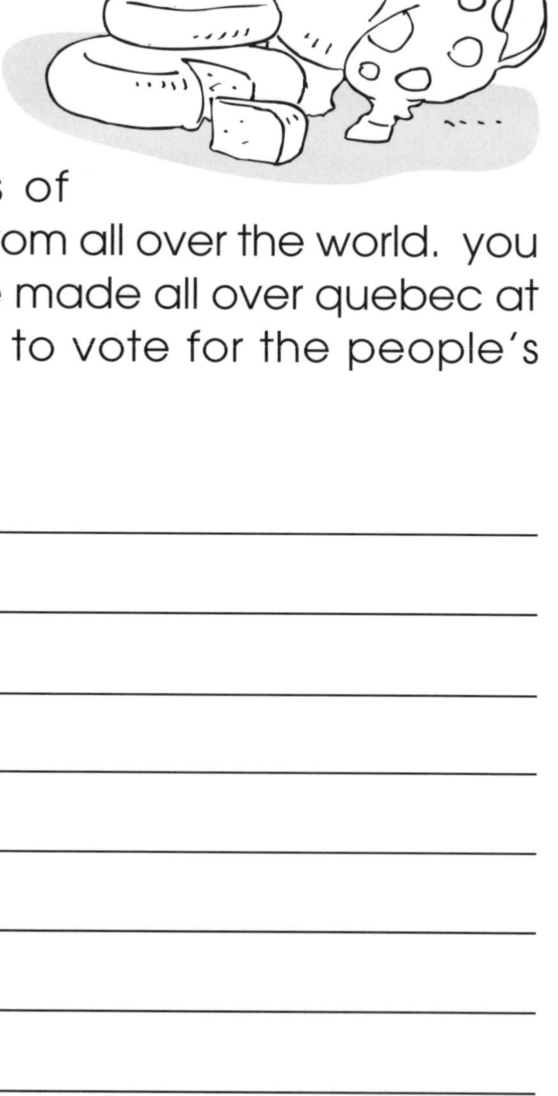

C. Rewrite the following paragraph by using capitalization correctly.

this year, the warwick cheese festival will take place from friday, june 16 to sunday, june 18. this annual event is the biggest cheese festival in north america, attracting tens of thousands of canadians and visitors from all over the world. you can sample over 100 kinds of cheese made all over quebec at the festival. attendees are invited to vote for the people's choice prize of the year.

ISBN: 978-1-897164-32-7

Commas

We use the **comma** to:

- separate words or phrases in a series.
- separate adjectives before a noun.
- set off transitional words.
- set off a direct quotation.
- set off words in apposition.

Examples: Mr. Merlot, the committee chairman, said to the members, "We should find a new, safer location for next year's event." However, Mr. Anderson, Mr. Powers, and Mrs. Streep disagreed.

D. Add commas where needed in the following sentences.

1. Vincent shouted "I shall return next year."
2. Bridget Carlson last year's winner presented the prize to Jason.
3. The participants have to chase a big heavy round of cheese down the hillside.
4. The slope the stones and the speed have caused some cases of injuries.
5. Mr. Douglas their team leader explained to them why they had lost.
6. Unfortunately the contest was put off because of the nasty weather.

ISBN: 978-1-897164-32-7

Meteorites and Craters

Meteors are large rocks that speed through space and fly into the Earth's atmosphere with a streak of bright light. Usually they break into pieces before they hit the Earth. If they land, we call them meteorites. If the meteorite is big, it will cause a lot of damage to our Earth. Some people believe that dinosaurs died out because a large meteorite hit the Earth millions of years ago.

When a meteorite hits the Earth, it forms a crater. Barringer Meteor Crater is in the United States, near the town of Winslow, Arizona. It is the best example of a crater that is easy to see. It is about 1200 metres in diameter and 170 metres deep. Scientists say this crater was made about 50 000 years ago, and was created by an iron meteorite that was only 30 m in diameter. That is a pretty small piece to make such a large crater!

We know of at least 120 craters around the world. Some are very old, and can only be seen when viewed from space. There is a crater in the Gulf of Mexico. It is 180 kilometres wide. Some scientists think this was the place where the meteorite which killed the dinosaurs landed.

Some people think that Hudson Bay is actually a crater. This would make it the largest crater on Earth by far. Do you believe it?

ISBN: 978-1-897164-32-7

A. Write "F" for facts and "O" for opinions.

1. Dinosaurs died out because a large meteorite hit the Earth millions of years ago.

2. Meteors break into pieces before they land on the Earth.

3. Barringer Meteor Crater was formed about 50 000 years ago.

4. Barringer Meteor Crater is about 1200 m in diameter.

5. The iron meteorite that created the Barringer Meteor Crater was small.

6. There are at least 120 craters that we know of in the world.

7. Some craters can only be seen when viewed from space.

B. Find words from the passage for the meanings below.

1. loss of value and usefulness ______________
2. long, thin line ______________
3. the longest line across a circle ______________
4. come against something with force ______________
5. reached the ground ______________

ISBN: 978-1-897164-32-7

Quotation Marks

Quotation marks are used in pairs. They can be used to:

- contain the exact words of a speaker or from a book.
  Example: "Freeze!" the FBI agent said.
- indicate the titles of songs, books, movies, newspapers, etc.
  Example: Do you watch the latest series of "The X Files"?

C. Add quotation marks where needed in the following sentences.

1. My dad is a great fan of Star Wars.
2. Dragon Rider is a must-read for you.
3. Wendy asked, Do dinosaurs have feathers?
4. Issac has read Harry Potter and the Goblet of Fire three times already.
5. The magician said, Count one to ten with me and then you will see.
6. All your performances were exceptionally good, the judge commented.
7. He added, Everyone deserves a big round of applause here.
8. They sang Dancing Queen in the singing contest.

ISBN: 978-1-897164-32-7

Apostrophes

We use the **apostrophe** to:

- show possession.
  Example: Mike's brother has to wait for us there.
- form contractions.
  Example: He isn't tall enough to get on the ride.

D. Check whether the underlined words are possessives (P) or contractions (C).

1. "The Invaders" <u>isn't</u> an easy game to play.
2. <u>I'll</u> beat you in the next game.
3. We will meet at <u>Joe's</u> place tomorrow.
4. The <u>teacher's</u> explanation was very clear.
5. <u>Dad's</u> telescope is very powerful.
6. They <u>didn't</u> understand how that crater was formed.

P	C

E. Add apostrophes where needed in the following sentences.

1. Candys uncle is a professor at the University of Toronto.
2. The children dont want to stop the game.
3. Theyre going to be late.
4. Mr. Greens farm is near Hudson Bay.
5. Bryans dog doesnt like this model dinosaur.

ISBN: 978-1-897164-32-7

The Highest Tides on Earth

The sizes of ocean tides are different around the world. A typical tidal range is one or two metres. The Bay of Fundy, between New Brunswick and Nova Scotia, has one of the most extreme tidal ranges. The Minas Basin at the eastern end of the Bay of Fundy has the highest tides in the world. There, the tidal range is between 12 and 16 metres!

The main reason for the immense tides in the Bay of Fundy has to do with the shape of the Bay of Fundy-Gulf of Maine coastline and the continental shelf, which is a shelf of land that juts out into the Atlantic Ocean, making the sea floor shallower.

People from all over the world come to the town of Wolfville, Nova Scotia, to see the tide for themselves. At low tide, the tiny harbour of Wolfville is empty. The mud flats of the sea bottom extend for several kilometres. In summer months, migrating shorebirds feast on the worms and crustaceans exposed at low tide.

When the tide is rushing in, tidal bores often form in the St. Croix, Meander, and Salmon Rivers, which empty into Minas Basin. Then people can watch the awesome sight of a wave of water travelling in the opposite direction of these rivers' current. Soon enough, however, the action starts moving in the opposite direction. High tide has arrived once again and the water will soon start moving out once more – in its never-ending and always fascinating cycle.

ISBN: 978-1-897164-32-7

A. Fill in the blanks with words from the passage.

1. Usually, a tidal ____________ is one or two metres.
2. The Bay of Fundy has ____________ tides.
3. The enormous tides of the Bay of Fundy are caused by the shape of the bay's ____________ and the continental ____________ .
4. At low tide, the mud flats of the sea bottom ____________ for several kilometres.
5. In summer, worms and crustaceans are ____________ at low tide.
6. The tide rushes in and out in an endless ____________ .

B. Write the main idea of each paragraph.

Paragraph One ____

____

Paragraph Two ____

____

Paragraph Three ____

____

Paragraph Four ____

____

ISBN: 978-1-897164-32-7

Connecting Words

We use **connecting words** to join ideas together. Some connecting words are used to add, contrast, show sequence, and conclude ideas.

Example: At low tides, the water will move out <u>and</u> some crustaceans will be exposed on the sand.

C. Circle the correct connecting words in the following sentences.

1. If / Since you want to see the highest tides of the world for yourself, you can go to Wolfville in Nova Scotia.

2. Nova Scotia may be a bit far to you and / but it is worth it.

3. Uncle Ray took some pictures of the tides. However / Also , he drew a few sketches of the scene.

4. Although / Because I did not see the tides for myself, I could imagine how massive they must have been.

5. Amy and I have not seen Uncle Ray when / since he left for Calgary in January.

6. He said that he would come back for Christmas and / or we could meet him in Calgary this summer.

ISBN: 978-1-897164-32-7

D. Use these connecting words to join the related sentences below.

and but after because if

- I did not expect they would reach that high
- he will record the tidal bores
- it is a long ride to get there
- the waves subsided
- Dad takes us

1. I was shocked by the heights of the tides ____________________

    ____.

2. The water became very calm ____________________

    ____.

3. The tides are beautiful ____________________

    ____.

4. I would love to go there again ____________________

    ____.

5. I will ask Dad to take a video camera with him ____________________

    ____.

ISBN: 978-1-897164-32-7

18

The Longest Train Ride

Did you know you can travel all the way from London, England to China by train? It is one of the longest regularly scheduled train rides in the world! This train journey passes through many cities, including Paris in France, Berlin in Germany, Warsaw in Poland, Moscow in Russia, Ulaan-Baatar in Mongolia, and Beijing in China.

In the past, people taking this journey had to take a hovercraft from Dover, England to the coast of France, and then get back on a train. But now, the train goes through the Channel Tunnel, connecting England with France.

The longest run of this journey without changing trains is the Trans-Siberian Railway. This railway network actually has four routes connecting Moscow with the Russian Far East, Mongolia, China, and beyond.

The Trans-Siberian route runs from Moscow to the Russian Far East at Vladivostok. It is 9288 kilometres long and crosses eight time zones.

The Trans-Manchurian route coincides with the Trans-Siberian up to Tarskaya, about 1000 km east of Lake Baikal. At Tarskaya, the route goes southeast to Beijing.

The Trans-Mongolian route coincides with the Trans-Siberian up to Ulan Ude on Lake Baikal's eastern shore. Then it heads south to Ulaan-Baatar, and then Beijing.

In 1991, a fourth route, the Baikal Amur Mainline was completed. This line branches off from Tayshet to Khabarovsk, in Russia's Pacific Northeast.

ISBN: 978-1-897164-32-7

A. Match the cities with their countries.

1.	London	Germany
2.	Berlin	Poland
3.	Moscow	England
4.	Beijing	Mongolia
5.	Warsaw	Russia
6.	Paris	France
7.	Ulaan-Baatar	China

B. Answer these questions.

1. What is so special about the Trans-Siberian Railway?

____

____

2. What allows people to travel from England to France by train?

____

____

3. From where do these routes branch off?

a. Trans-Manchurian ______________

b. Trans-Mongolian ______________

c. Baikal Amur Mainline ______________

ISBN: 978-1-897164-32-7

Abbreviations

An **abbreviation** is the shortened form of a word or words.

Example: December → Dec.

C. Underline the abbreviations in the following sentences.

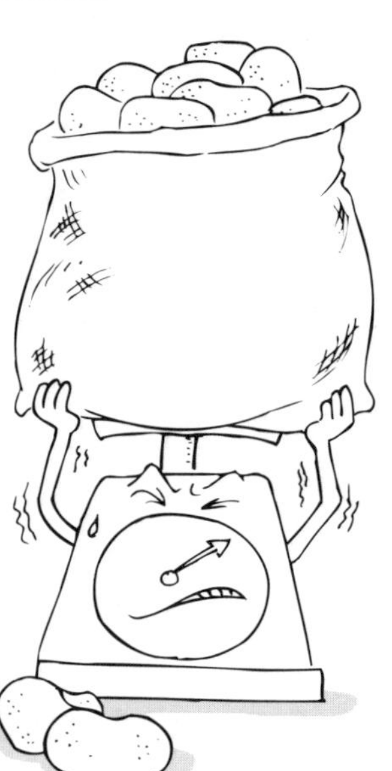

1. A bag of potatoes weighs more than 4 kg.
2. Mrs. Sorenson goes to work by train.
3. The community centre is on Sunshine Rd.
4. P. 3 of the handouts went missing.
5. We cannot go to P.E.I. by train.
6. Uncle Larry has worked for Jubilee Co. for six years.
7. The Street Festival starts from Friday, Jul. 10.
8. Lt. Paddington gave each officer a map.

D. Write the abbreviations for the words and the standard forms for the abbreviations.

1. Mountain ________ 2. compact disc ________
3. Building ________ 4. centimetre ________
5. U.S. ________________ 6. Jr. ________________
7. Tue. ________________ 8. Ltd. ________________

ISBN: 978-1-897164-32-7

Contractions

A **contraction** is a single word that is formed by combining and shortening two words. An apostrophe is used to replace letters.

Example: He has lost his day pass for the train.
He's lost his day pass for the train.

E. Form contractions from the following pairs of words.

1. there is ____________
2. do not ____________
3. should not ____________
4. they will ____________
5. we are ____________
6. you have ____________
7. did not ____________
8. I am ____________
9. will not ____________
10. that is ____________

F. Fill in the blanks with some of the contractions you formed in (E).

1. __________ going to the train station. Do you want a ride?
2. __________ ridiculous. How could he have done that?
3. Can you see that? __________ something behind the black curtain.
4. You __________ miss Lily. She is the tallest girl on the team.
5. __________ listen to him. He is a liar.
6. Polly was sick. She __________ go to the show.

ISBN: 978-1-897164-32-7

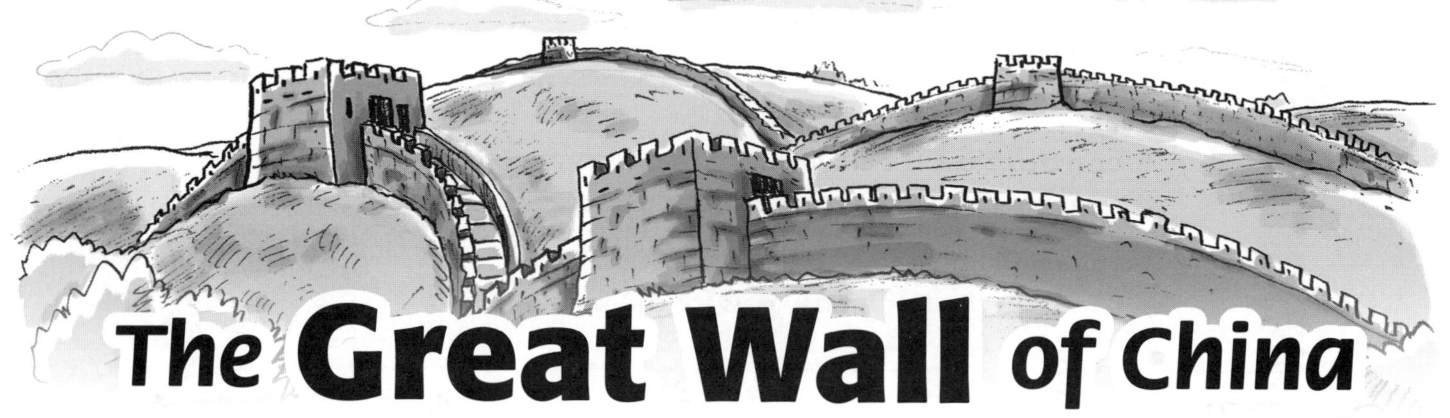

The Great Wall of China

The Great Wall of China was first built over 2200 years ago by the Emperor of the Qin (Ch'in) Dynasty. This warrior created his empire by defeating and uniting seven warring states. Then he connected four old fortification walls that had been built 500 years earlier to defend against the invading tribes.

Over the years, the Great Wall of China was built, rebuilt, and added to. The wall we see today is actually farther south than the first Great Wall. It was made with masonry, hard-packed earth, granite, bricks, and rocks. All the construction was done by hand! The walls vary in thickness, from about 4.5 to 9 metres.

A major rebuild took place from the end of the 14th century until the beginning of the 17th century, during the Ming Dynasty. The wall was expanded to 6400 kilometres. Watchtowers and cannons were built onto it.

The Great Wall of China is the biggest feat of engineering and construction ever undertaken. It stretches from Shanhai Pass on the Bohai Sea in the northeast part of China to the southeastern portion of Xinjiang province, in the far west. Today it is a major tourist attraction. It is not only proof of our construction capabilities, but also a reminder of a history of warring and separation.

ISBN: 978-1-897164-32-7

A. Choose the correct answers. Circle the letters.

1. The Great Wall of China was built by a Chinese ___ .

   A. dynasty B. emperor C. tribe

2. The Great Wall was built to ___ against the enemy.

   A. defend B. invade C. unite

3. The present wall is farther ___ than the first Great Wall.

   A. north B. east C. south

4. ___ were added onto the walls during the Ming Dynasty.

   A. Paintings

   B. Windows and doors

   C. Watchtowers and cannons

5. Which of these were not used to build the walls?

   A. masonry and granite

   B. bricks and rocks

   C. steel and wood

B. "It is not only proof of our construction capabilities, but also a reminder of a history of warring and separation." What does it mean? Explain in your own words.

ISBN: 978-1-897164-32-7

Prefixes

A **prefix** is a group of letters placed at the beginning of a base word to change its meaning.

Example: The prefix "un" of "unstable" changes the base word "stable" to its opposite.

C. In each group of words, circle the one that contains a prefix. Then write the prefix on the line.

1. invade include insignificant ________
2. defend defrost deduct ________
3. unwise unite undertaken ________
4. pressure prepaid precise ________
5. disappear disaster discipline ________

D. Use each prefix you have identified in (C) to form a new word. Use the new word to write a sentence of your own.

1. ________ ______________________________
2. ________ ______________________________
3. ________ ______________________________
4. ________ ______________________________
5. ________ ______________________________

ISBN: 978-1-897164-32-7

Suffixes

A **suffix** is a group of letters placed at the end of a base word to change its meaning.

Example: The suffix "er" of "reminder" changes the verb "remind" to a noun.

E. Complete the crossword puzzle with the base words of the clue words.

Across

A. provincial
B. construction
C. thickness
D. attractive

Down

1. noticeable
2. uniting
3. historical
4. earlier

F. Add a suffix to each of the following words to form a new word. Use the new word to write a sentence of your own.

big connect expand actual

1. ____________ ____
2. ____________ ____
3. ____________ ____
4. ____________ ____

ISBN: 978-1-897164-32-7

Tulipomania

Have you ever heard of tulipomania? It means that people went crazy for tulips, all at the same time. This is not a joke. It really happened.

About 400 years ago, tulips were becoming the most popular flower in Holland (a part of what is now called the Netherlands). Rich people spent a lot of money building lavish gardens. It seemed that the more tulips they put in their gardens, the richer they felt. This made the price of tulip bulbs go higher and higher. If the price of a tulip bulb cost 50 florins (Dutch money) on Monday, it might cost 100 florins by Wednesday.

People started to think they could make a lot of money selling tulips. Now both rich and poor people wanted tulips. If people did not have money, they traded their jewellery, their land, and their animals to buy tulip bulbs.

In late 1636, tulipomania reached its climax. One single tulip could be sold for 6000 florins, two horses, and a coach. At that time, 6000 florins would buy 50 tonnes of butter!

Soon after, tulip traders found that people were no longer willing to pay such high prices for tulips. The bubble burst. Tulips became almost worthless. People who had paid a lot of money for their tulips lost everything.

It seems hard to believe that people would spend so much money for a flower. Tulipomania was a baffling event, but it is something we can learn from.

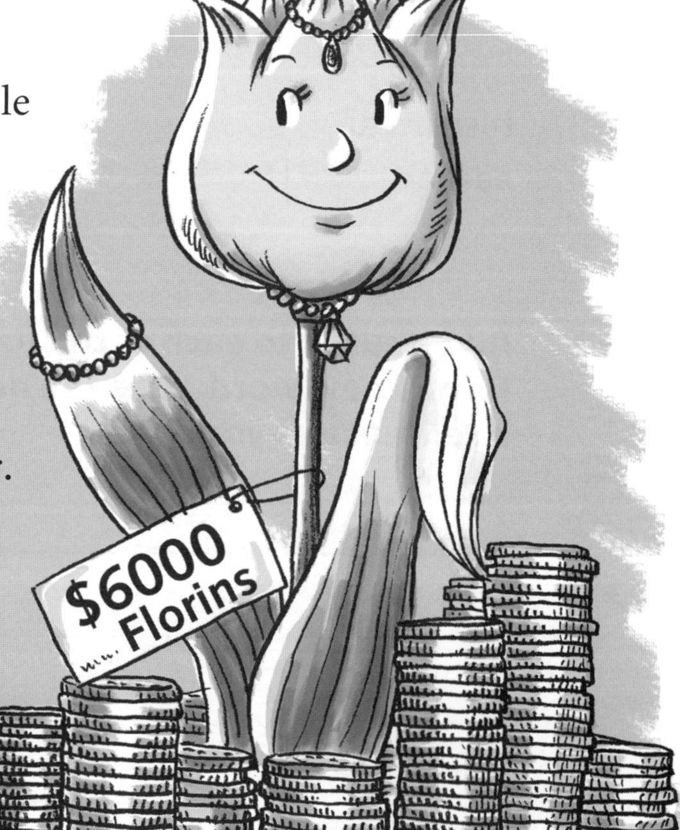

ISBN: 978-1-897164-32-7

A. Check the true sentences.

1. Tulipomania is only a story. ______
2. Holland is a part of the Netherlands. ______
3. All people in Holland spent a lot of money building lavish gardens. ______
4. They were once willing to pay any price for tulips. ______
5. People even traded their animals for tulip bulbs. ______
6. Tulipomania was most serious in 1936. ______
7. Florin is a kind of tulip. ______
8. A single tulip once cost more than a horse. ______

B. Quote a sentence from the passage to support each of the following sentences.

1. A tulip once cost a fortune.

____

2. The price of tulips went up quickly.

____

____

3. People would pay any price for tulips.

____

____

ISBN: 978-1-897164-32-7

Compound Words

A **compound word** is formed when two words are put together to form a new word of a different meaning.

Example: flower + pot → flowerpot

C. Underline the compound words in the paragraph. Then circle them in the word search below.

This morning we got up early because we had to meet Grandma and Grandpa at the airport. They went to the Netherlands to celebrate Grandma's 50th birthday. I saw Grandma coming out from the gate before anybody else. I was attracted by her big tulip hairpin. Grandpa said they had been upgraded to business class because the economy class had been overbooked. How lucky they were!

G	r	h	u	p	g	r	a	d	e	d	G	a
r	h	a	i	r	p	i	n	h	d	p	r	i
a	b	i	r	h	d	a	y	a	G	r	a	r
n	i	r	o	a	b	o	b	i	r	a	n	p
d	r	o	v	e	r	b	o	o	k	e	d	o
e	t	t	G	r	a	n	d	m	a	d	p	r
b	i	r	t	h	d	a	y	a	n	y	a	t

ISBN: 978-1-897164-32-7

D. Unscramble the letters to form compound words.

1. price + [ ] (essl) ____________
2. grass + [ ] (popher) ____________
3. thunder + [ ] (morst) ____________
4. [ ] (rafe) + well ____________
5. [ ] (rowth) + while ____________
6. [ ] (sharm) + mallows ____________
7. [ ] (letab) + cloth ____________

E. Fill in the blanks with the compound words you formed in (D).

1. We threw Tim a ____________ party yesterday.
2. We bought some ____________ for dessert.
3. Mom laid the new floral-patterned ____________ on the table.
4. Can you see the ____________ on that tulip?
5. Wendy was late because of the ____________ .
6. She said that it was ____________ coming all the way from downtown.
7. To me, our friendship is ____________ .

ISBN: 978-1-897164-32-7

The Amazing Story of a Japanese Soldier

Hiroo Onoda was a Second Lieutenant in the Japanese army. During World War II, he was sent to fight in Lubang, the Philippines. When Japan lost the war and surrendered, soldiers from the United States took custody of the Japanese soldiers in the Philippines. Onoda and several of his comrades did not want to surrender. They ran into the jungle.

Over time, his comrades died and Onoda was alone. People who saw him told him that the war was over, but he did not believe them. He was sure they were just trying to trick him. In 1960, Onoda was declared legally dead in Japan. Later, a Japanese student, Norio Suzuki, found him. He went back to Japan with photos of himself and Onoda to prove that this old soldier was still alive.

The Japanese government found Onoda's commanding officer, Major Taniguchi and asked him to go to the Philippines and convince Onoda to come out. Taniguchi went to Lubang and told Onoda that Japan had lost the war. Finally, Lieutenant Onoda came out of the jungle and surrendered. He handed over his sword and his rifle, which was still in good condition. Onoda was given permission to return to Japan. He had lived in the jungle for 29 years!

Later, Onoda decided to move to Brazil and became a cattle rancher there. He wrote a book about his life called *No Surrender: My Thirty-Year War*. In 1996, Onoda returned to Lubang Island and donated over ten thousand dollars to the local school there.

ISBN: 978-1-897164-32-7

A. Write numbers to put the events in order.

_____ Onoda was declared legally dead in Japan.

_____ Onoda was sent to Lubang.

_____ A Japanese student found Onoda.

_____ Onoda surrendered and returned to Japan.

_____ Japan lost the war and Onoda ran into the jungle.

_____ Major Taniguchi went to Lubang to convince Onoda.

_____ Onoda wrote *No Surrender: My Thirty-Year War.*

B. Read the clues. Complete the crossword puzzle with words from the passage.

Across

A. imprisonment while awaiting trial

B. allowing somebody to do something

C. companions involved in the same activity

Down

1. stop resisting an enemy
2. a kind of gun
3. persuade

ISBN: 978-1-897164-32-7

Synonyms and Antonyms

A **synonym** is a word that is similar in meaning to another word.

Example: rush – dash

An **antonym** is a word that is opposite in meaning to another word.

Example: win – lose

C. State whether each pair of words are synonyms or antonyms.

1. alive dead ________________
2. leave return ________________
3. fault mistake ________________
4. goal objective ________________
5. stress pressure ________________

D. Fill in the blanks with the correct synonyms of the words in parentheses.

criticized **respected** **task** **pail**

1. The soldier poured some water into the (bucket) ________________ .
2. His first (duty) ________________ was to wash the uniforms of his superiors.
3. He was (blamed) ________________ for being too slow.
4. He (admired) ________________ his major for his leadership.

ISBN: 978-1-897164-32-7

E. In each sentence, underline the antonym of the word in parentheses.

1. All of his comrades survived the war. (none)
2. The soldiers failed to return to their barracks. (managed)
3. Their barracks were destroyed by bombs in just one night. (protected)
4. Ivan was forbidden to join the march in the ceremony. (allowed)
5. The soldiers are well-trained to stay calm in ambush. (frantic)
6. The refugees received food and drugs from developed countries. (donated)

F. Complete the story with synonyms or antonyms of the words in parentheses.

popular big started over meaningful

Dad has a (small) 1.____________ collection of toy soldiers. He (began) 2.____________ collecting these figurines since he was in grade six. Lido soldiers were the most (common) 3.____________ figures in his childhood. He has collected (under) 4.____________ 100 toy soldiers. Each of them is (meaningless) 5.____________ to him.

ISBN: 978-1-897164-32-7

Ellen MacArthur

The Fastest Solo Sailor in the World

On February 7, 2005, Ellen MacArthur, a 28-year-old British woman, sailed around the world. Actually, sailing around the world is no longer an extraordinary feat. People have been doing it in sailboats and cruise ships for <u>ages</u>. But Ellen did it in the fastest time so far – 71 days, 14 hours, 18 minutes and 33 seconds – and she did it all by herself!

But this was not Ellen's first experience as a record-breaker. In the 2001 Vendée Globe <u>race</u>, she sailed around the world solo in 94 days. At that moment, she became the fastest woman and youngest person to sail solo around the world.

During this trip, she videotaped her experiences. She suffered from loneliness much of the time. If there was a problem, she had to <u>fix</u> it herself. For example, during a storm, Ellen was injured by a flying object inside her small cabin. She had to stitch up the cut herself. She was cook, sailor, doctor, repairman, mechanic – and her only companion.

When asked about her achievement, Ellen said it was not an easy thing to do. But the support of the public around the world was what kept her going to reach her goal. She thanked her team on land that made it possible. And she said that there are other records, such as the transatlantic <u>record</u>, that she would like to break. We know she will give it her best <u>shot</u>.

ISBN: 978-1-897164-32-7

A. Check the meanings of the underlined words as they are used in the passage.

1. **ages**
   - A a very long time
   - B lengths of time that a person has lived

2. **race**
   - A a subdivision of mankind sharing physical characteristics
   - B contest

3. **shot**
   - A try
   - B act of shooting a gun

4. **record**
   - A videotape
   - B best performance ever reached

5. **fix**
   - A repair
   - B fasten something firmly to something

B. Write the main idea of each paragraph.

Paragraph One: ______________________

____

Paragraph Two: ______________________

____

Paragraph Three: ______________________

____

Paragraph Four: ______________________

____

ISBN: 978-1-897164-32-7

Homophones

A **homophone** is a word that sounds the same as another word, but has a different meaning and spelling.

Example: sail – sale

C. Circle the homophones of these words in the word search.

ours
crews
feet
teem
maid
brake
sew
daze

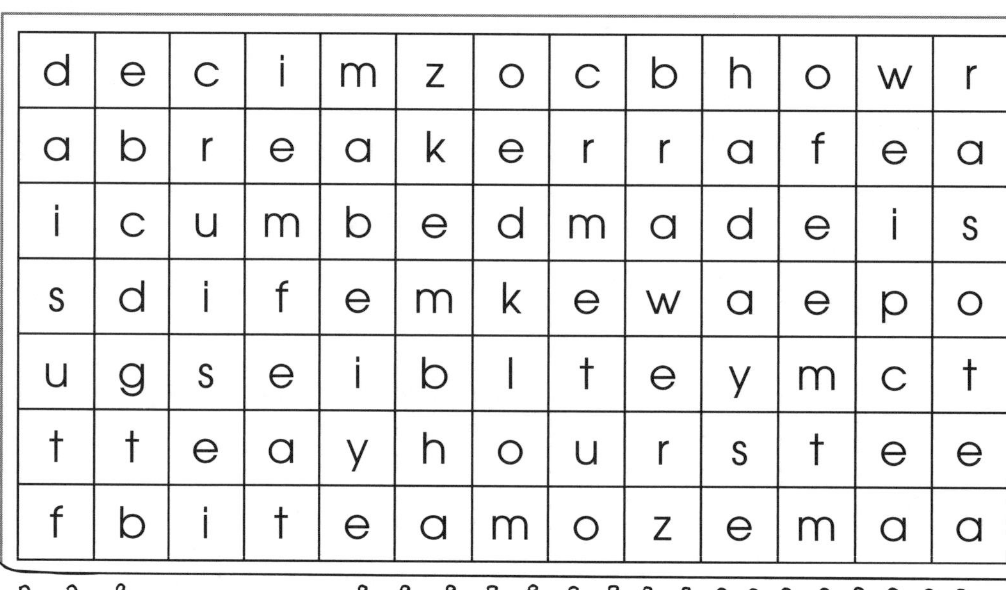

d	e	c	i	m	z	o	c	b	h	o	w	r
a	b	r	e	a	k	e	r	r	a	f	e	a
i	c	u	m	b	e	d	m	a	d	e	i	s
s	d	i	f	e	m	k	e	w	a	e	p	o
u	g	s	e	i	b	l	t	e	y	m	c	t
t	t	e	a	y	h	o	u	r	s	t	e	e
f	b	i	t	e	a	m	o	z	e	m	a	a

D. Fill in the blanks with homophones of these words.

peak **blew** **role** **sealing** **knight**

1. Peter can touch the ______________ of the cabin.
2. We want to ______________ at Uncle John's note.
3. Kylie likes the ______________ of the sea water.
4. Uncle John thinks that it is tranquil to sail at ______________ .
5. Kylie helped him ______________ up the sail on the mast.

ISBN: 978-1-897164-32-7

Frequently Confused Words

We may be confused by words that have similar spellings or sound alike. To ensure that we use the proper word, we can look up the dictionary to clarify the meaning.

Examples: His boat is bigger <u>than</u> ours.
We should check the weather first. <u>Then</u> we will decide if we go sailing tomorrow.

E. Circle the correct words for the following sentences.

1. Its / It's such a good day to go sailing.
2. We should waste / waist no time and set sail to the island.
3. Feel free to seek advise / advice from your leaders.
4. A team of boats with colourful sails sailing off the coast is an awesome site / sight .
5. It seems that the rope is a bit loose / lose .
6. He wants to take a beginner's coarse / course before we go sailing again.
7. Everyone except / accept Daniel enjoyed the sailing trip.
8. Whose / Who's cap is this?
9. Maybe / May be we should take it to the "Lost and found".

ISBN: 978-1-897164-32-7

A Mystery

On November 7, 1872, the Mary Celeste left New York to sail to Italy. Captain Briggs, his wife and daughter, and seven crew members were on board. But something terrible happened. The captain of another ship found the Mary Celeste floating in the middle of the Atlantic Ocean on December 4, 1872. There were no people on the wooden sailing ship and they were never found.

What happened? Why did the crew and passengers leave the ship? There were no obvious reasons. The Mary Celeste was undamaged. Everything was neat and tidy, with no sign of fighting. There was plenty of food and drinking water and no sign of fire or smoke damage. But Captain Briggs, his family, and the crew abandoned the Mary Celeste very quickly. We can tell because there was half-eaten food on the table. The crew also left all their clothing behind. Even their boots were beside their beds.

How and when did the people leave? Although some people claim that the lifeboat was still on the ship, others say it was missing. The captain's journal was still on the ship and the last entry was made on November 24. So, we can only guess that they left sometime between then and December 4.

An investigator, Mr. Flood, went to the ship several times to search for the answers to all the questions. But he could not find anything. No one else has solved the mystery either.

What do you think happened to those people on the ship?

ISBN: 978-1-897164-32-7

A. Match the words with their meanings. Write the letters.

1. crew ____
2. obvious ____
3. abandoned ____
4. entry ____
5. investigator ____

A item written

B clear; easily seen

C person who looks into something

D all people working on a ship

E deserted

B. Answer these questions.

1. How many people had gone missing when the Mary Celeste was found?

   ____

2. How do you know the people left the ship very quickly?

   a. ______________________________

   b. ______________________________

   c. ______________________________

3. What happened on these days?

   a. Nov. 7, 1872:

   ____

   b. Nov. 24, 1872:

   ____

   c. Dec. 4, 1872:

   ____

   ____

ISBN: 978-1-897164-32-7

Journals

A **journal** is a daily written record of things happened and experiences.

C. Imagine you are Captain Briggs. Write a journal for November 24, 1872.

You can write about an event that might lead to the abandoning of the ship later on.

November 24, 1872

ISBN: 978-1-897164-32-7

Forming Questions

We can begin a question with a question word like "What", "When", "Where", "Who", "Whom", "Whose", "Why", or "How".

Example: Where was the ship found?

D. Complete the questions with question words.

1. ____________ did the crew and passengers leave the ship?
2. ____________ can we see the northern lights?
3. ____________ are those things in the corner?
4. ____________ can solve the problem?
5. ____________ does this machine work?
6. ____________ did you call just then?
7. ____________ can't you join us?
8. ____________ journal is this?

E. You have a chance to ask Mr. Flood, the investigator, five questions about the mysterious case of the Mary Celeste. What will you ask him? Use the question words you have learned.

1. ______________________________
2. ______________________________
3. ______________________________
4. ______________________________
5. ______________________________

ISBN: 978-1-897164-32-7

Inukshuk

Have you ever seen an inukshuk? If you have seen the flag of Nunavut, you have seen one. The word "inukshuk" means "likeness of a person" in Inuktitut, the language of the Inuit people.

An inukshuk is a stone figure made by balancing rocks on top of each other. Inuksuit (the plural form of inukshuk) are an important part of Inuit culture and are created for various reasons. Depending on how the rocks are placed, an inukshuk may be built to warn others of nearby dangers, mark a place of respect, such as a gravesite, or show directions for later travellers to follow.

Building an inukshuk is an important part of hunting for the Inuit people. An inukshuk may be built to give other hunters information about the location of caribou herds or spook the caribou during the hunt, causing the animals to run to an area where other hunters lie in wait.

An inukshuk may be large or small, and the rocks used will be of any size and shape. An inukshuk may consist of only one stone too, although most are made of several rocks. It is forbidden to destroy or remove an inukshuk.

There are important things to consider when building an inukshuk. The rocks must fit together in harmony, and balance each other. Those making the inukshuk must work together. In Canada's Arctic territories, one can still see these amazing structures. Some are centuries old, still standing as a symbol of harmony and cooperation.

ISBN: 978-1-897164-32-7

A. Fill in the blanks with words from the passage.

1. An inukshuk is the symbol on the flag of ______________ .
2. An inukshuk can show travellers ______________ .
3. Inuksuit are important to lives of Inuit people, especially ______________ .
4. People build inuksuit with rocks of any ______________ and ______________ .
5. The rocks must ______________ each other when building an inukshuk.
6. Removing or destroying an inukshuk is ______________ .
7. An inukshuk stands as a symbol of ______________ and ______________ .
8. Some inuksuit found in Canada's Arctic territories are ______________ old.

B. List five uses of an inukshuk.

1. ______________________________
2. ______________________________
3. ______________________________
4. ______________________________
5. ______________________________

ISBN: 978-1-897164-32-7

Tricky Usage

Some words often cause confusion. Be sure to check the correct usage of these words in the dictionary to avoid mistakes.

Example: They are already for the competition. (✗)
They are all ready for the competition. (✓)

C. Read the explanations and complete the sentences with the correct choices. You may change the form where necessary.

1. **among and between**

"Among" refers to more than two people or things while "between" refers to two people or things.

a. ___________ the six stones, the bottom one is the biggest.

b. You need to put one flat stone ___________ the two round ones.

2. **lay and lie**

"Lay" is a transitive verb meaning "to place something down". "Lie" is an intransitive verb meaning "to rest in a certain position".

a. The doctor asked me to ___________ down on the bed.

b. Please ___________ the picnic blanket on the grass.

ISBN: 978-1-897164-32-7

3. **raise and rise**

"Raise" means "to make higher". You have to do something to something else. "Rise" means "to get up".

a. They all __________ when there is a score.

b. They are __________ the flags of the teams they support.

4. **bring and take**

"Bring" means "to carry from a more distant place to a nearer one". "Take" means the opposite.

a. Please __________ the drinks over here.

b. I helped Dad __________ the garbage out today.

5. **good and well**

"Good" is an adjective and it describes nouns. "Well" is an adverb and it describes verbs.

a. The necklace is __________ on you.

b. He dances __________ .

6. **amount and number**

"Amount" is used with uncountable nouns whereas "number" is used with countable nouns.

a. A large __________ of beads were used to make this belt.

b. There is only a small __________ of alcohol in the dessert.

ISBN: 978-1-897164-32-7

25

Our Wonderful Rainforests

Rainforests are called "the lungs of the world" because we breathe oxygen with our lungs, and the dense growth of trees there make the much-needed oxygen.

Rainforests can be divided into four layers. The forest floor is the ground level. It is very dark down there because very little sunlight gets past all the leaves in the trees above. When dead leaves and animals are on the ground, they are broken down into organic matter by the heat and the many small insects.

The understorey starts from the ground to about 20 metres. It is made up of the trunks of taller trees, plants, and smaller trees. It is still quite dark at this level, so the trees grow slowly. Some of these trees grow tall and pointed at the top to reach the sunlight. Other plants, like vines, cling onto the trees and get a free ride towards the sunlight.

The canopy layer is made up of the limbs and leaves of trees. This is a very thick layer: 20 to 50 m off the ground. Insects, birds, reptiles, and monkeys live in this layer. This layer of leaves and branches catch the sunlight and also most of the rain.

The top layer is called the emergent layer. The top of the tallest trees can stretch more than 50 m high. These trees are old and big but there are not too many of them. These trees have huge leafy heads that stretch wide because they have more room to grow.

ISBN: 978-1-897164-32-7

A. Name the layers of the rainforest, from the bottom (1) to the top (4). Then match the activities with the layers by writing the letters in the boxes.

1. ______________________ ☐
2. ______________________ ☐
3. ______________________ ☐
4. ______________________ ☐

(A) Vines cling onto trees to reach the sunlight.

(B) Huge leafy heads of trees stretch wide.

(C) Dead leaves are broken down into organic matter.

(D) Insects, birds, reptiles, and monkeys live here.

B. Answer these questions.

1. Why are rainforests called "the lungs of the world"?

____

____

2. What breaks down the dead leaves and animals on the ground of the rainforest?

____

____

3. Why are some trees in the understorey pointed at the top?

____

ISBN: 978-1-897164-32-7

Writing Paragraphs

A **paragraph** is a group of sentences that expresses a common idea. It is made up of a topic sentence and body sentences.

A **topic sentence** introduces the main idea. Usually, it is the first sentence in a paragraph. It tells us what to expect in the rest of the paragraph.

C. For each paragraph, check the appropriate topic sentence.

1. Rainforests clean and recycle water. The rainforest plants remove carbon dioxide from the atmosphere and give out much of the Earth's oxygen. Rainforests affect the greenhouse effect, which traps heat inside the atmosphere.

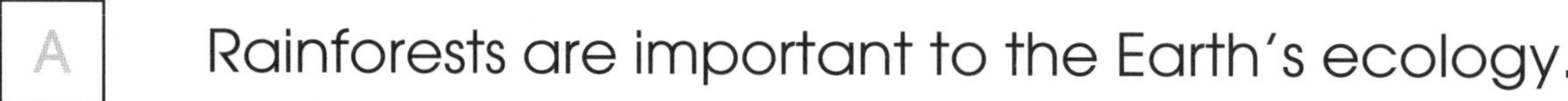

A Rainforests are important to the Earth's ecology.

B Rainforest plants generate much of our oxygen.

2. The whole restaurant was decorated like a real rainforest. There were monkeys swinging in the trees. A crocodile kept opening and closing its mouth and an elephant kept curling up its trunk. There was a big aquarium filled with colourful fish. We could also hear the sounds of different animals, such as birds, gorillas, and elephants.

A I felt as if I were in a rainforest.

B Dad took us to a special restaurant for lunch.

ISBN: 978-1-897164-32-7

D. Write a topic sentence for each of the following paragraphs.

1. Topic sentence: ____________________

____

You can find wax figures of famous people in the museum – Elvis Presley, John Lennon, John F. Kennedy, and Pierre Elliot Trudeau, to name a few. These figures were carved in detail. You may find your favourite movie stars standing beside you. So, be prepared.

2. Topic sentence: ____________________

____

I woke up early and put on my "out in the sun" T-shirt. Mom had already finished packing our food and drinks. Dad loaded everything into the trunk and off we went. It took us almost an hour to get to the beach.

3. Topic sentence: ____________________

____

He went into the forest alone after his wife passed away. His children had tried to convince him to come home time and again but he refused to leave. Mr. Sanderson has not had his hair cut since he left home 20 years ago. He finally came out on their 30th wedding anniversary.

26

Our Window Box Herb Garden

My family live in a small apartment. We do not have a backyard, but we love plants. One day, Mom and I decided to make a window box herb garden.

First, we went to the library to read about how to grow herbs in window boxes. Then we went to the gardening store and bought a long window box with a long "dish" that fits under it, some soil, and packets of seeds. Then we went for a "coffee talk" at a doughnut shop and talked about what delicious meals we would make with our herbs.

At home, we put some small stones into the bottom of the box. The stones allow extra water to drain out of the soil and into the dish under it. If there is no drainage, the soil gets soggy and the herbs do not grow well.

Mom and I both love pizza, so we made sure to plant a lot of basil. I love the smell of fresh basil! We also planted rosemary, which tastes good with roast lamb. That smells wonderful too. We planted mint because Mom wanted to try making fresh mint tea. We planted dill too because it goes so well in potato salad.

We placed the window box on top of the fridge and waited for the seeds to sprout. Then we put the box on the shelf outside the kitchen window to get the sunlight. My mom and I love to smell our fresh herbs. We couldn't wait to see them grow and prosper!

ISBN: 978-1-897164-32-7

A. Colour the herbs that the writer planted. Then write the herbs for the dishes.

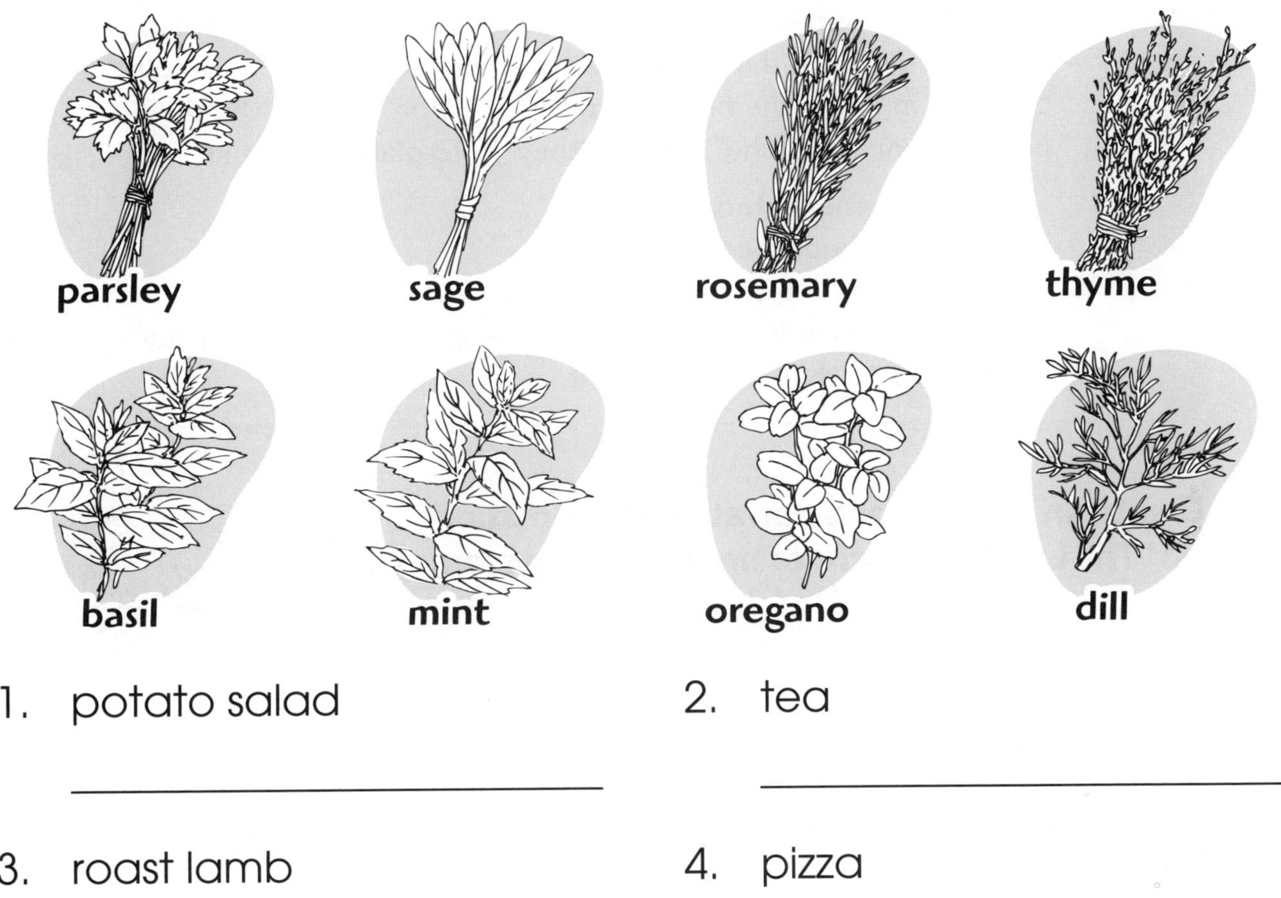

1. potato salad ________________

2. tea ________________

3. roast lamb ________________

4. pizza ________________

B. Put what the writer and her mom did in order. Write the letters on the lines.

A. They put the box on the shelf outside the kitchen window.

B. They placed some stones in the box and planted the herbs.

C. They read about how to grow herbs in window boxes.

D. They put the box on top of the fridge and let the seeds sprout.

E. They bought a window box, some soil, and packets of seeds.

______ , ______ , ______ , ______ , ______

ISBN: 978-1-897164-32-7

Narrative Writing

In **narrative writing**, we tell a story, true or imagined. We usually write the events in the order in which they happen. We may tell the story in either the first person (using "I" or "we") or the third person (using "he", "she", "it", or "they"). To plan, we should:

- think of a general storyline.
- set the time and place for the story.
- list the events in the story in the order in which they happen.
- include a concluding paragraph that wraps up the story or leads the reader to think more about it.

C. Create an outline for a narrative composition on "The Last Day at school" in the third person.

Topic: ______________________

General storyline: ______________________

____

____

Time and place: ______________________________

____

Events: ______________________________________

____

____

____

____

Conclusion: __________________________________

____

ISBN: 978-1-897164-32-7

Paragraphs in a Narrative Composition

Introductory paragraph: This sets up the story. It tells where and when the story takes place, who is involved, and what the story is about.

Body paragraphs: They contain details of the events.

Concluding paragraph: This ends the story.

D. Based on your outline in (C), write a finished copy of your story.

Title: ____________________

Introduction: ____________________

____

____

____

Body paragraphs: ____________________

____

____

____

____

____

____

Conclusion: ____________________

____

____

____

____

Summer Holiday

ISBN: 978-1-897164-32-7

27

Our Summer at the Farm

Last summer, my parents took my little sister and me to my grandpa's old farmhouse. Grandpa was born in the house. He says that when he was a boy, there were many farmers living in the area around the old farmhouse. There are not so many now.

Mom wanted to plant a vegetable garden, so Grandpa tilled the soil before we arrived. In late May, we planted onions, potatoes, peas, beans, carrots, leeks, corn, and Chinese cabbages. By the end of June, there were a lot of weeds in our garden, so we had a lot of hoeing to do.

The onions came up first. By the middle of July, we had so many onions! We ate them in salads and egg sandwiches, and gave a lot away. But where were our carrots, leeks, and Chinese cabbages? Grandpa said the grasshoppers had eaten the tops off them! But at least they did not get the peas and beans.

By the middle of August, the grasshoppers were starting to eat the leaves off all the potato plants, so we picked the potatoes quickly, and they were small. We ate a lot of potato salad. Small potatoes are yummy! The corn did not get very big, either. There were just too many weeds. But we still had fun eating our own delicious potatoes, onions, peas, and beans.

By the end of August, our garden was empty. But the memories of our special summer on the farm will be with us forever!

ISBN: 978-1-897164-32-7

A. Write "T" for the true sentences and "F" for the false ones.

1. The writer went to his grandpa's farmhouse with his parents and brother. ____
2. There are not many people living around their farmhouse now. ____
3. The writer's grandpa tilled the soil before they arrived. ____
4. Carrots were the first to come up. ____
5. Some of their vegetables were eaten off by grasshoppers. ____
6. The carrots, leeks, and Chinese cabbages were untouched by the grasshoppers. ____
7. They gave many vegetables away. ____

B. Write one thing that the writer and his family did in each period of time.

1. Late May

____

2. Late June

____

3. Mid-July

____

4. Mid-August

____

ISBN: 978-1-897164-32-7

Descriptive Writing

Descriptive writing describes a person, a thing, or an event in great detail to create a picture in the reader's mind. We can make our writing more interesting by using vivid adjectives and adverbs.

C. Write two adjectives to describe each of the following nouns.

1. farmhouse ____________, ____________
2. garden ____________, ____________
3. grandpa ____________, ____________
4. day ____________, ____________

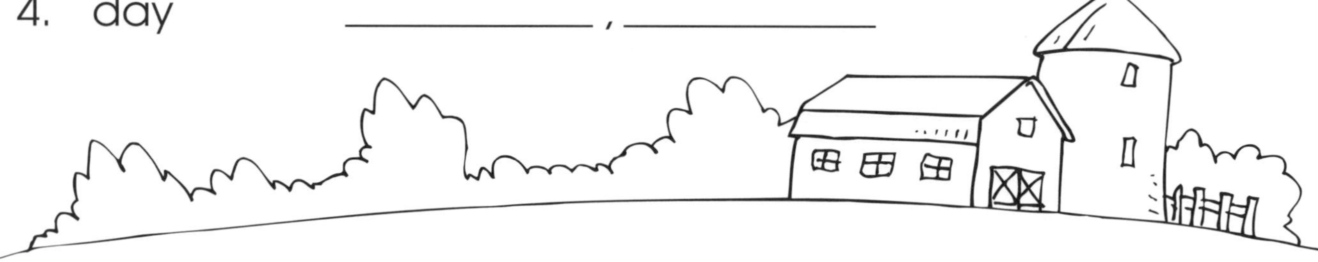

D. Underline the adverb in each of the following sentences. Then circle its synonym.

1. The field needs tilling and watering badly.

   desperately / well

2. The weeds are almost as tall as my sister.

   mostly / nearly

3. The birds are chirping cheerily in the trees.

   happily / loudly

4. They really enjoyed the rural experience on the farm.

   truly / actually

ISBN: 978-1-897164-32-7

Using Senses in Descriptive Writing

We may develop our **descriptive writing** according to our senses – sight, hearing, touch, and sometimes smell and taste too.

E. Complete the table by listing and describing what you sensed in your last outing, e.g. a day at a farm, the zoo, or the beach.

	What you sensed	Description (in detail)
Sight		
Hearing		
Smell		

F. Based on the table in (E), write a short paragraph about the outing. Be as descriptive as you can.

ISBN: 978-1-897164-32-7

28

The World Is Ours

Venezuela! France! Sudan!
China and Afghanistan!
I'll go here, then I'll go there.
I want to learn about everywhere!

I want to ask, "How are you feeling?"
In Ushuaia and Darjeeling.
I'll play soccer with kids like me
From the Amazon River to the Caspian Sea.

Come with me!
The world is ours!
We'll learn – we've got secret powers.

In Vietnam, we'll plant some rice.
Then fly to Tibet, and touch the skies.
We'll make our way to Timbuktu –
Tuktoyaktuk and Kalamazoo!

Iceland! Spain! Cambodia!
Ethiopia! Bolivia!
Indonesia! Mexico!
So many places we will go.

We'll have fun, but we'll take a stand
When our friends need help in far-off lands.
It's up to me. It's up to you.
Together we will make it true.

The world is mine.
The world is yours.

The world is ours.

ISBN: 978-1-897164-32-7

A. Complete the crossword puzzle with words from the passage that rhyme with the clue words.

Across

A. Afghanistan
B. go
C. there
D. me

Down

1. Cambodia
2. you
3. eyes
4. ours

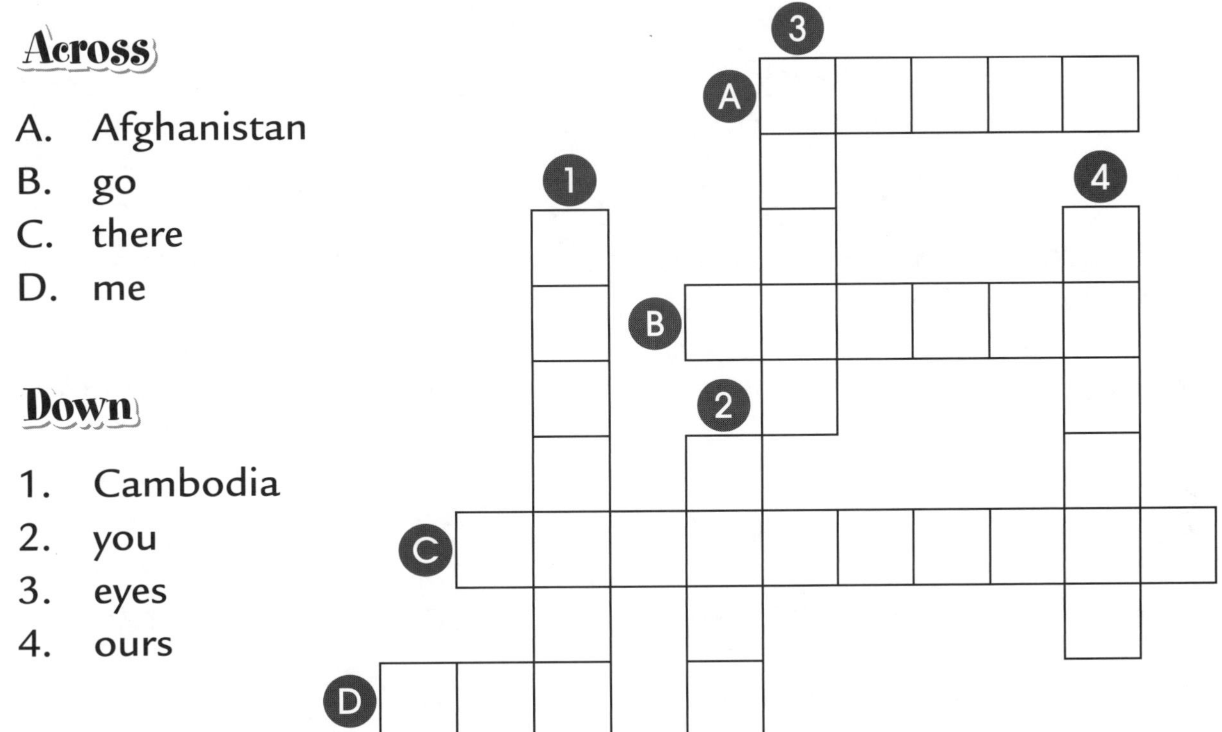

B. Complete the verse that can be added after the fourth one "In Vietnam...Kalamazoo!"

A verse is a group of lines forming a unit in a poem.

In England, we'll have fish and chips.

Writing Poems

Rhyme is one of the most frequently used tools in **poems**.

Example: Sunshine, blue sky, lullaby,
It is time to say goodbye.

C. In each group of words, cross out the one that does not rhyme with the word on the left.

1. **Canada**	Lydia	conquer	Australia
2. **there**	fair	chair	dead
3. **plane**	plan	drain	rain
4. **soccer**	locker	sober	sorry
5. **popcorn**	warn	poppy	horn
6. **dream**	dim	supreme	scream

D. Add a line that rhymes with each of the given ones.

1. Roll, roll, roll the snow.

   ____

2. In goes my favourite lemonade.

   ____

3. Look at this and look at that.

   ____

4. From the Rocky Mountains to the St. Lawrence River.

   ____

ISBN: 978-1-897164-32-7

Acrostic Poems

An **acrostic poem** is a poem in which the first letters of the lines form a word or words. The word or words formed is usually the theme of the poem.

Example: Eric is an active boy.
Riding his bike with buddy Roy.
Into the woods and around the park.
Can't stop until it's dark.

E. Write an acrostic poem with your first name. Make the lines rhyme where possible.

F. Write another acrostic poem, this time with your favourite season.

ISBN: 978-1-897164-32-7

Review 2

A. Rewrite the sentences using the correct capitalization and adding commas, apostrophes, and quotation marks.

1. theyll invite dr. hogan to the special event held next sunday.

2. have you seen the musical beauty and the beast before?

3. edwin our team leader reminded us Dont forget to take a compass a map and enough water with you.

4. lesters sister speaks english french spanish and japanese.

5. the banner with the big bright words Come and Join Us! has been put up since june.

ISBN: 978-1-897164-32-7

B. Circle the correct connecting words to complete the sentences.

1. Janice locked the door before / after she left.
2. The trip will be cancelled if / because it rains tomorrow.
3. He has had great improvement until / since he started the training.
4. You'll be able to get there on time because / however it's not far away from here.
5. Catherine lost the game but / although she was not discouraged.

C. Underline the wrong word in each of the following sentences. Write the correct word on the line.

1. I like to lay on the grass and look at the sky. ____________
2. Rise your hand before you ask a question. ____________
3. A large amount of birds live in this forest. ____________
4. The dress is too lose around the waist. ____________
5. Thank you for your advise. ____________
6. It was dark when we reached the sight. ____________

ISBN: 978-1-897164-32-7

D. Rewrite the sentences using abbreviations and contractions.

1. Mister Adams does not live on Maple Avenue.

___

2. Let us do a project on Mount Alberta.

___

3. We are going to Prince Edward Island in August.

___

4. The ribbon is 60 centimetres long.

___

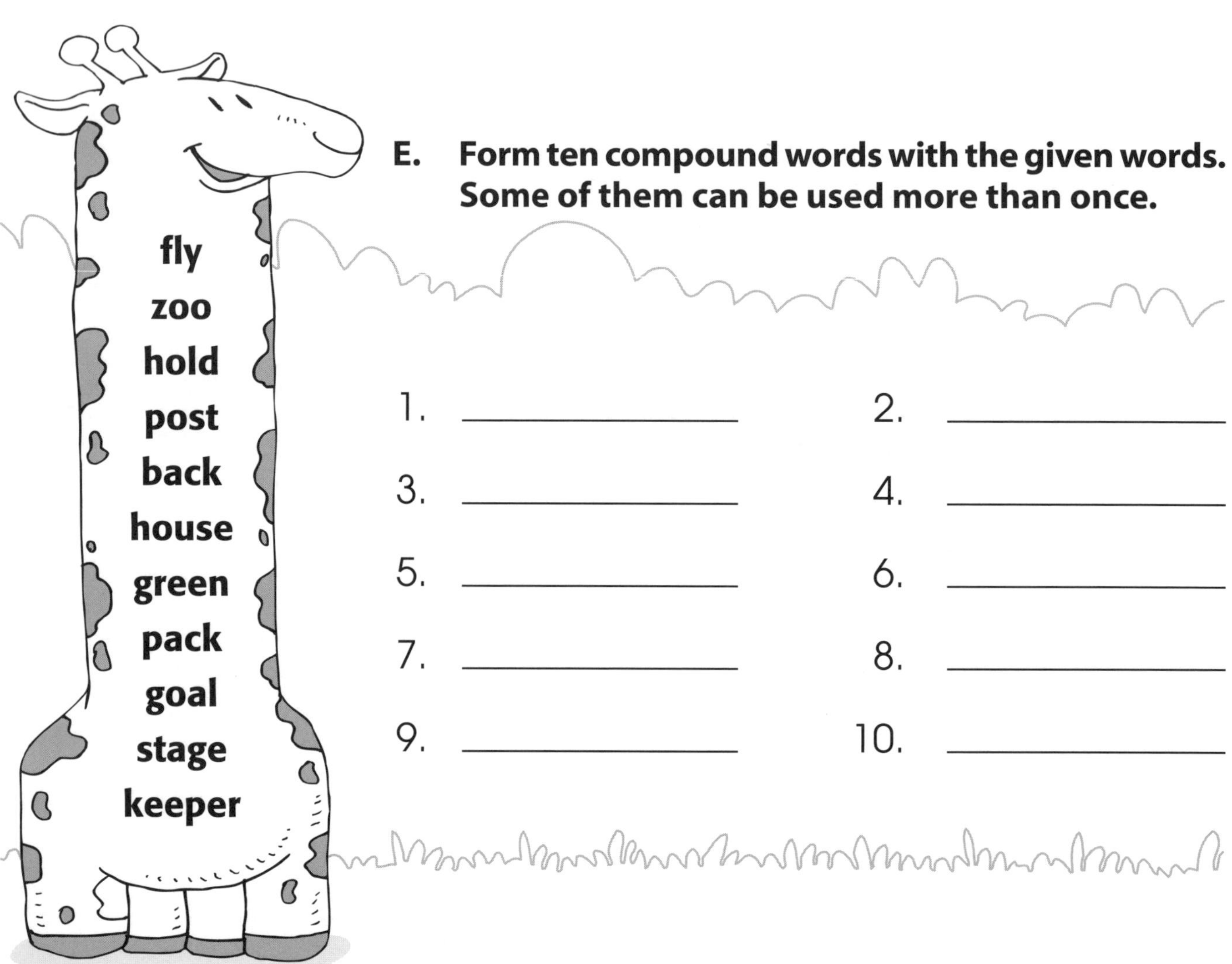

fly
zoo
hold
post
back
house
green
pack
goal
stage
keeper

E. Form ten compound words with the given words. Some of them can be used more than once.

1. ___ 2. ___

3. ___ 4. ___

5. ___ 6. ___

7. ___ 8. ___

9. ___ 10. ___

ISBN: 978-1-897164-32-7

F. Read the clues. Add prefixes and suffixes to form new words with the root word "direct".

1. opposite of "direct"

   ____

2. instructions

   ____

3. readdress

   ____

4. adverb of "direct"

   ____

5. give the wrong direction

   ____

6. person in charge of a company

   ____

G. Write questions for the answers.

1. ______________________________________

   <u>The blue whale</u> is the largest mammal on Earth.

2. ______________________________________

   Blue whales can be found <u>in all oceans around the world</u>.

3. ______________________________________

   A blue whale is <u>greyish-blue in colour</u>.

4. ______________________________________

   There are <u>no more than 2000</u> blue whales in the world.

5. ______________________________________

   The blue whale is an endangered species <u>because of pollution and illegal whaling</u>.

ISBN: 978-1-897164-32-7

H. **Complete the crossword puzzle with synonyms, antonyms, or homophones of the clues words.**

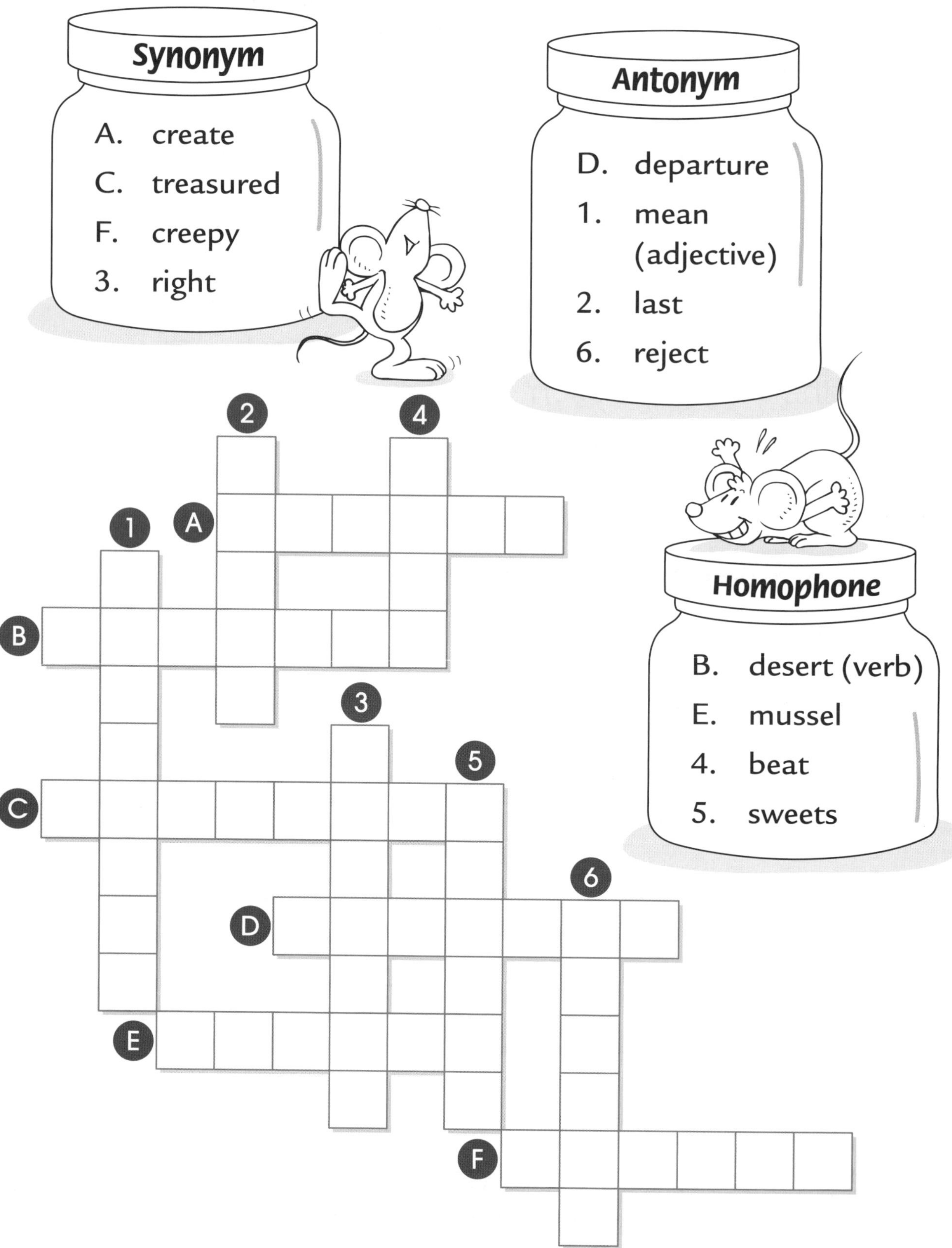

Synonym
A. create
C. treasured
F. creepy
3. right
Antonym
D. departure
1. mean (adjective)
2. last
6. reject
Homophone
B. desert (verb)
E. mussel
4. beat
5. sweets
1
2
3
4
5
6
A
B
C
D
E
F

ISBN: 978-1-897164-32-7

I. Write a descriptive paragraph on "A Summer Day". Put the topic sentence in parentheses ( ). Circle all the adjectives and underline the adverbs used.

A Summer Day

J. Write a rhyming word for each of the words below. Then write a poem with the three rhyming pairs. Give a title to your poem.

1. breezy ________
2. sing ________
3. giggle ________

ISBN: 978-1-897164-32-7

ISBN: 978-1-897164-32-7

ISBN: 978-1-897164-32-7

1

The Feudal System

In medieval times, kings, nobles, and knights had **land** and **power** over peasants and serfs. This was the feudal system.

A. Fill in the blanks with the given words.

serf manor land vassal obey
oath grow king knight

1. A fief was a land grant given to a __________ by a lord or to a noble by the __________ .

2. A __________ was a knight or noble who held land granted to him.

3. A fealty was an __________ sworn by a vassal to __________ and support the one who granted him land.

4. A __________ was an agricultural estate held by a lord.

5. I'm a __________ . I work my lord's __________ . I can also use it to __________ my own food.

ISBN: 978-1-897164-32-7

B. Show the medieval power structure. Unscramble the letters and label the pyramid.

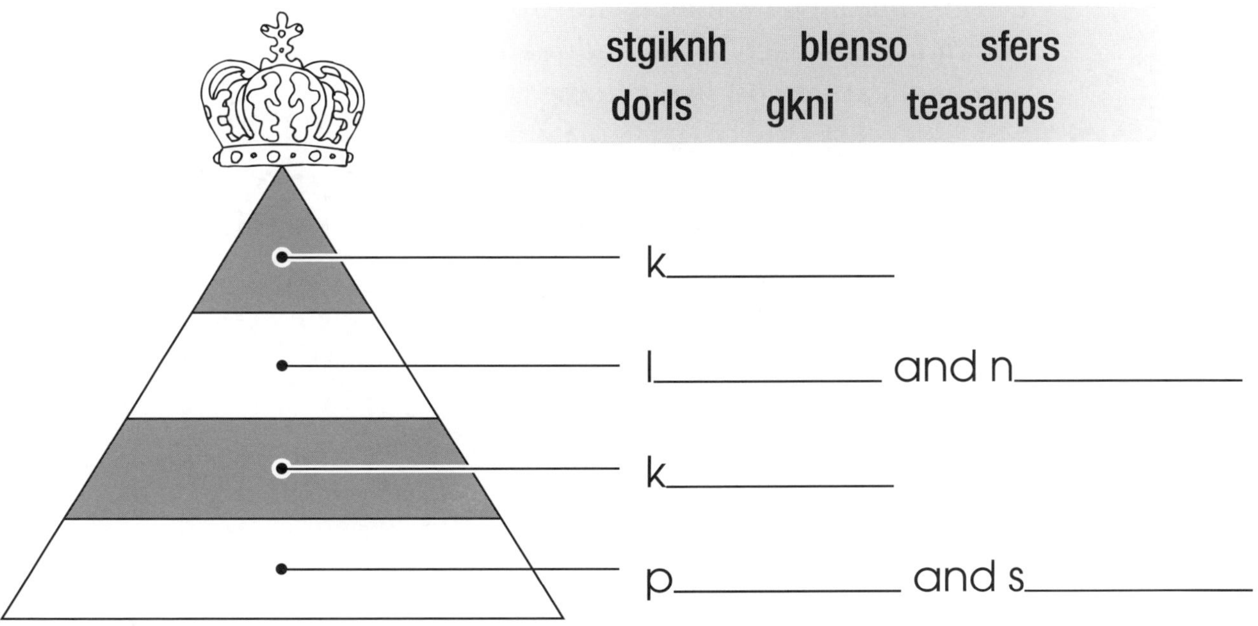

C. Read what this knight says and read his oath. Then write an oath of your own that can be used today.

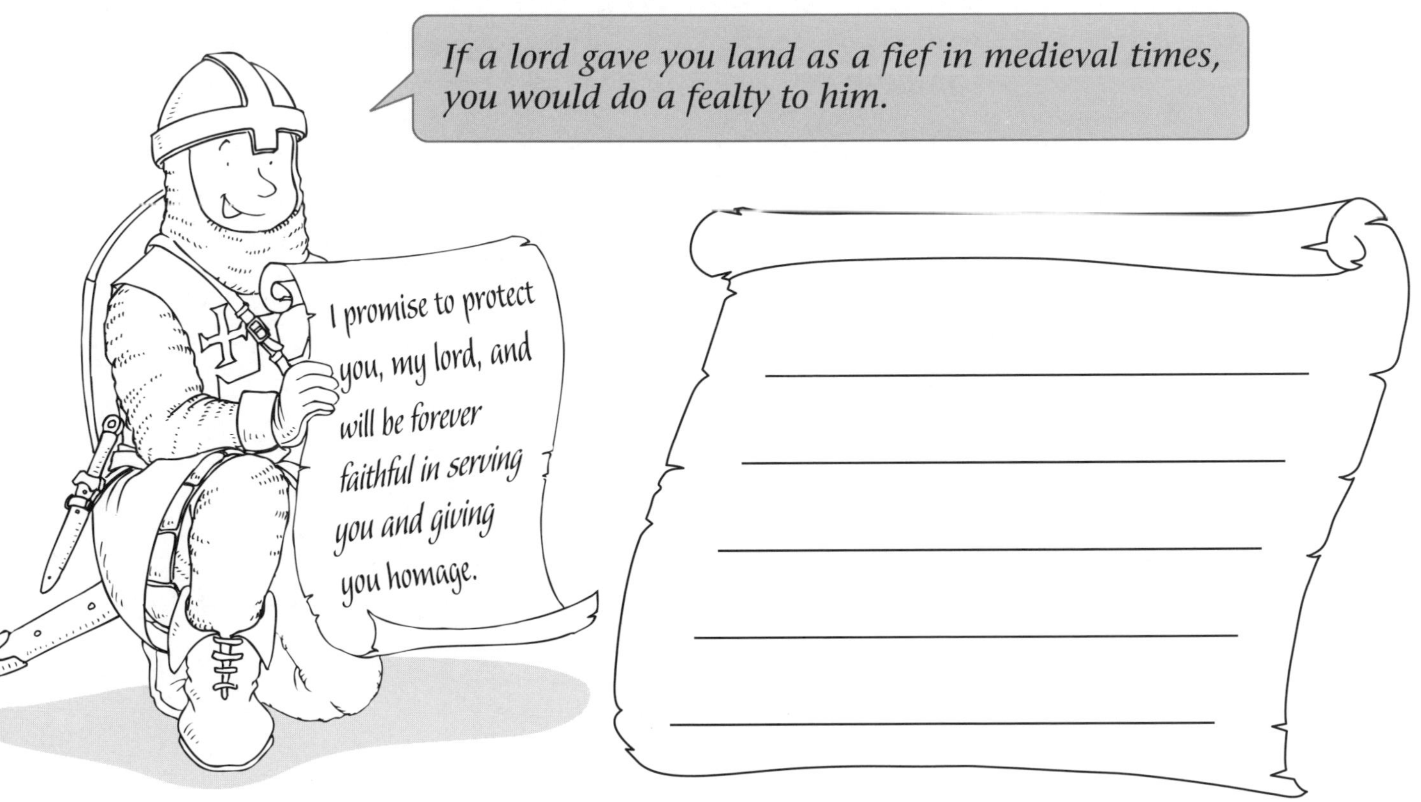

If a lord gave you land as a fief in medieval times, you would do a fealty to him.
I promise to protect you, my lord, and will be forever faithful in serving you and giving you homage.

ISBN: 978-1-897164-32-7

2

Medieval Castles

During medieval times in Europe, castles were built to protect communities. Each castle had features for **attack** and **defence**. It also had features just like a home.

A. Look at this castle. Then write the correct word for each description.

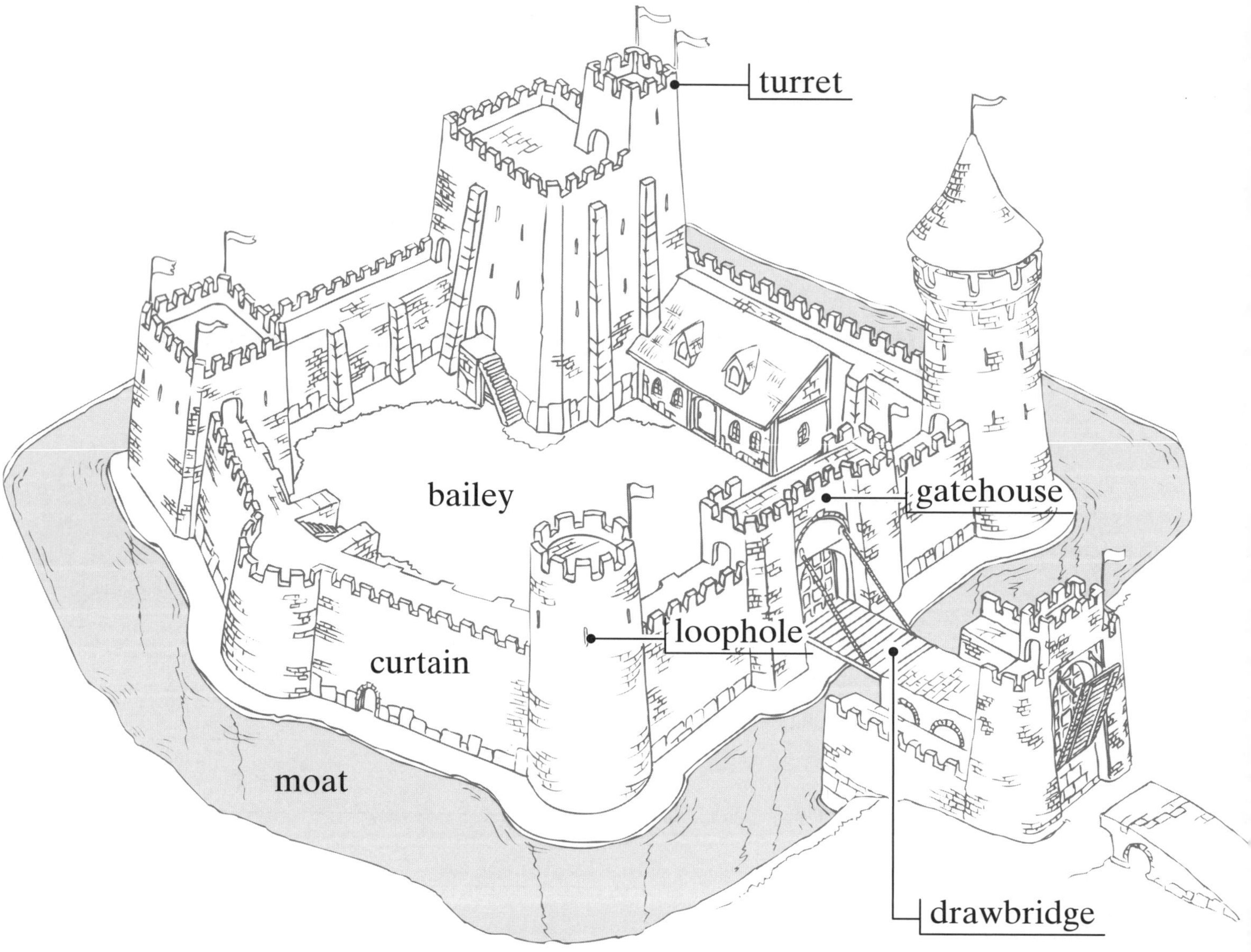

turret
gatehouse
bailey
loophole
curtain
moat
drawbridge

ISBN: 978-1-897164-32-7

1. courtyard of the castle ______________
2. encloses the entire bailey ______________
3. place for keeping watch ______________
4. water-filled ditch around the castle ______________
5. small window for shooting out arrows ______________
6. castle entrance which is often fortified with murder holes ______________
7. wooden bridge that is lowered for entry and raised for protection ______________

B. Read these descriptions and fill in the blanks with the given words.

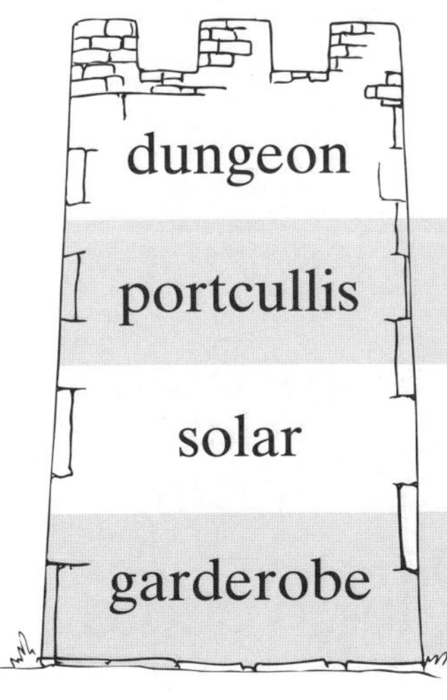

- place for keeping prisoners
- falls to shut the entrance
- place to sit and relax
- where the toilet is

1. Lock is to door as ______________ is to castle entrance.
2. Bathroom is to house as ______________ is to castle.
3. Jail is to town as ______________ is to castle.
4. Living room is to house as ______________ is to castle.

ISBN: 978-1-897164-32-7

Knights (1)

The knight's **armour** changed over time in medieval times. The earlier mail armour protected against swords but not arrows like the later plate armour. A knight's life, however, remained unchanged throughout.

A. Draw lines to match these armour terms with the meanings.

1.

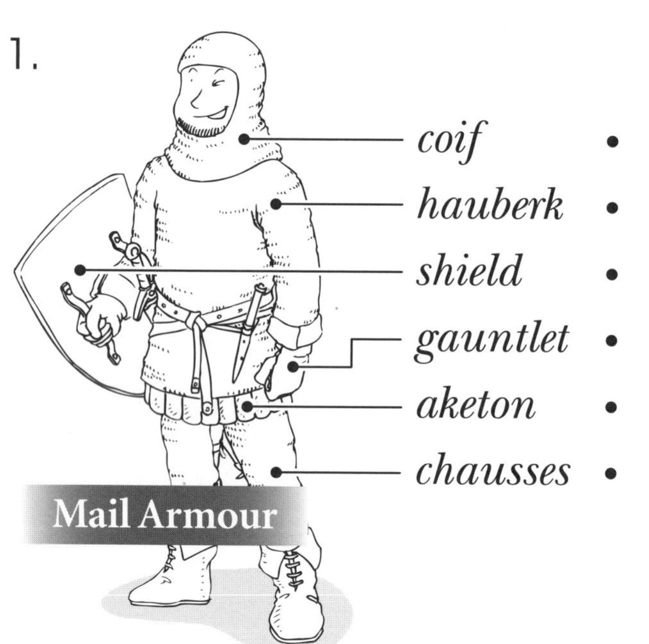

coif •	• glove
hauberk •	• leggings
shield •	• defensive device
gauntlet •	• extra protection
aketon •	• shirt
chausses •	• hood

2.

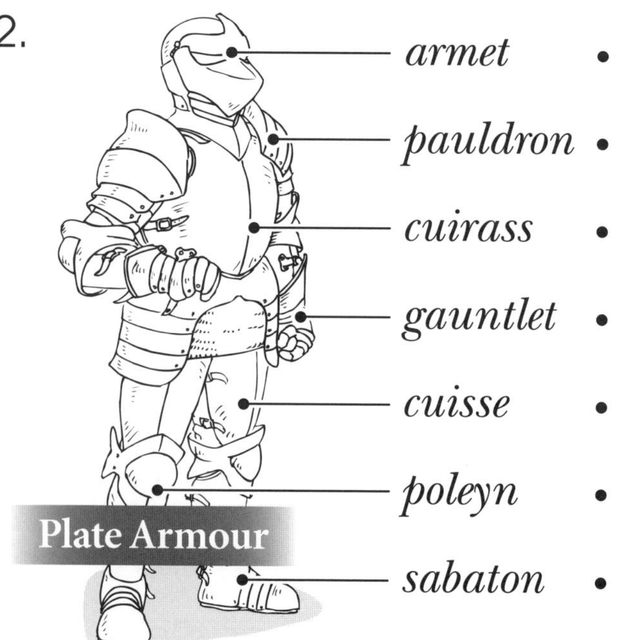

armet •	• glove
pauldron •	• body armour
cuirass •	• thigh guard
gauntlet •	• knee guard
cuisse •	• shoulder guard
poleyn •	• foot armour
sabaton •	• helmet

ISBN: 978-1-897164-32-7

B. Fill in the blanks with the given words to tell about the life of a knight.

swords	training	horse	noble	knighthood	ceremony
lord	battlefield	armour	knight	vows	clean

A boy from a 1. ______________ family is sent to a lord's house to begin his 2. ______________ as a page.

He learns how to hunt and how to ride a 3. ______________ . He also learns how to use 4. ______________ .

He becomes a squire and assists his knight on and off the 5. ______________ . He practises for his own 6. ______________ .

He helps his knight care for and 7. ______________ his 8. ______________ , and gets used to wearing his own.

When he is deemed ready, he is dubbed a knight in a special 9. ______________ .

He upholds the 10. ______________ he took on becoming a 11. ______________ , and goes to battle for his 12. ______________ when necessary.

ISBN: 978-1-897164-32-7

Knights (2)

Knights used many different **weapons**. Each knight also had a **coat of arms**, which was a symbol used to identify him.

A. Label these medieval weapons with the given words.

battle-axe lance sword crossbow bow and arrow
pollaxe spiked club mace club flail dagger

1. d________
2. s________
3. c________
4. f________
5. m________
6. l________
7. b________
8. cr________
9. s________
10. p________
11. b________ and a________

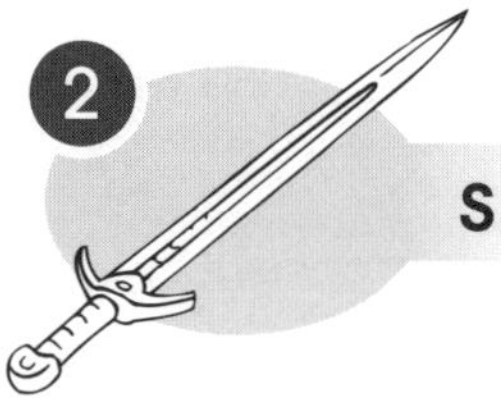

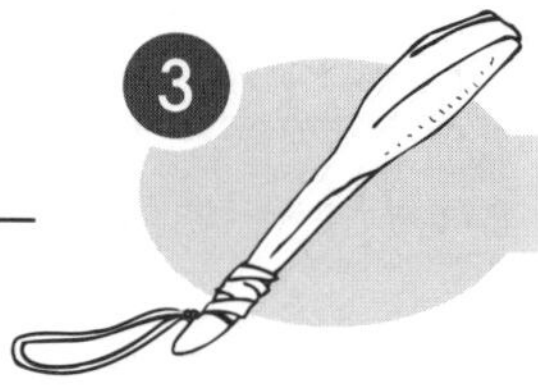

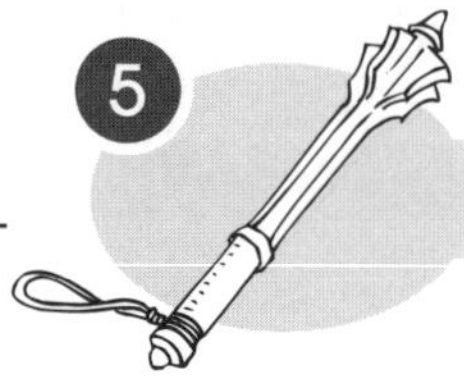

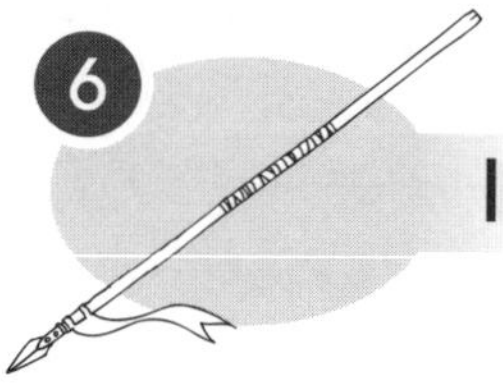

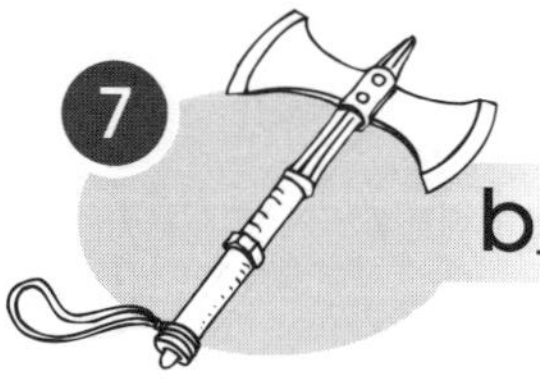

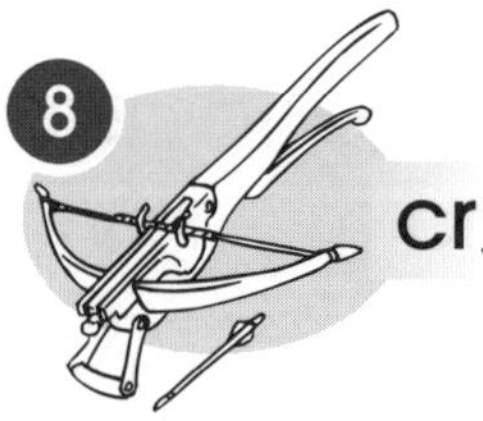

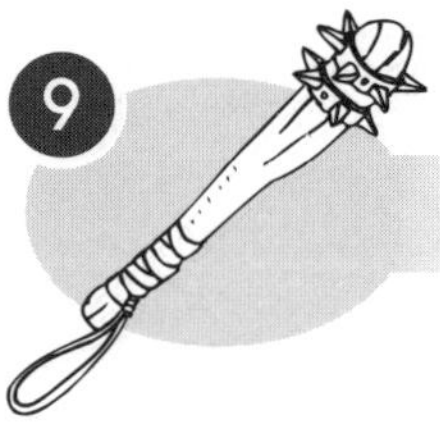

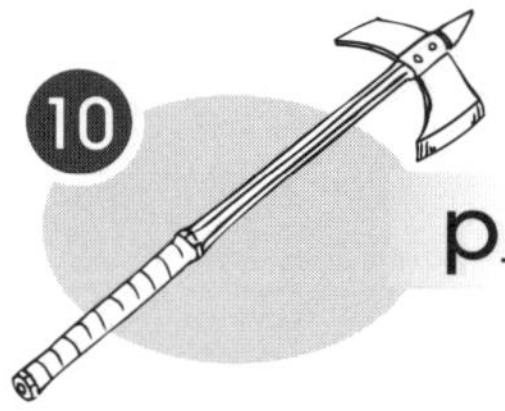

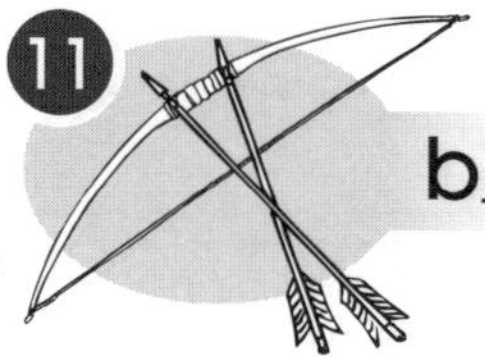

ISBN: 978-1-897164-32-7

B. Read what this noble son says about coats of arms. Colour his parents' coats of arms. Then draw and colour his own.

Coats of arms began as a way to identify knights in armour. They were important symbols to knights, and were often seen on their shields. Later, lords and ladies started to have their own coats of arms, like my parents. Because I'm their son, I have both of their coats of arms on my shield, one on each half.

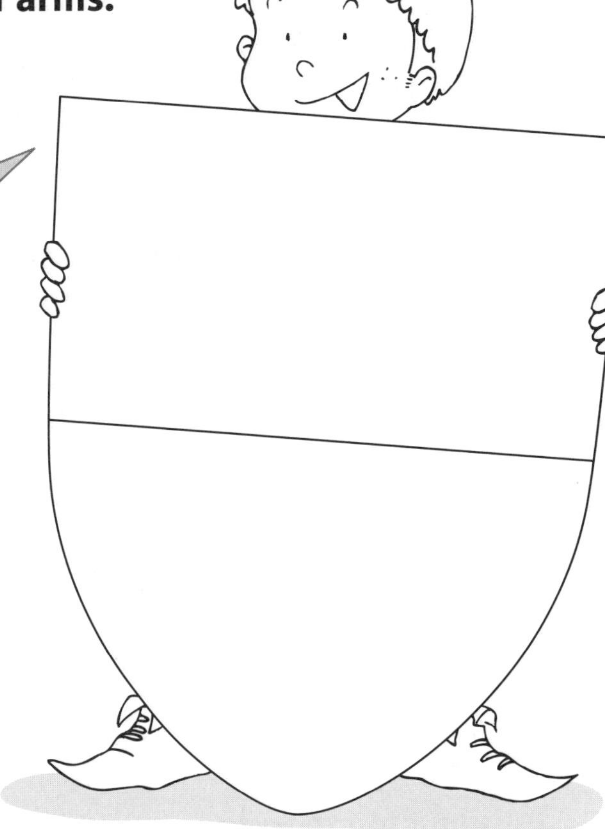

Father

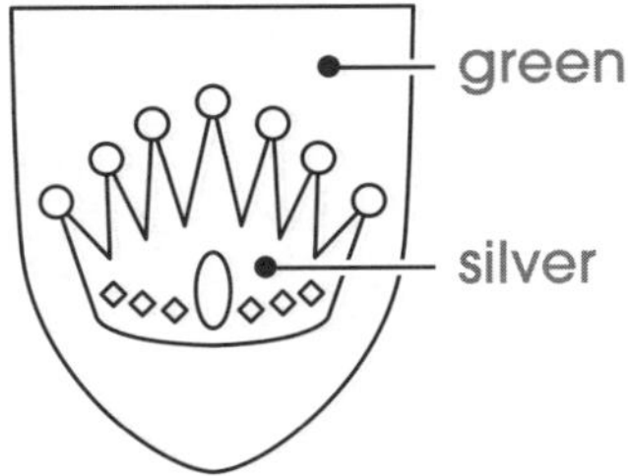

Mother

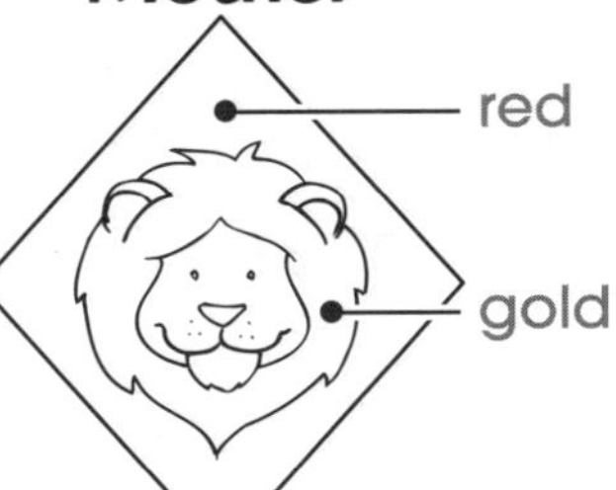

C. Draw and colour your own coat of arms using pictures of things that are important to you.

Rules:

1. Use red, blue, green, purple, or black with gold or silver.
2. Divide your coat of arms in one of these ways:

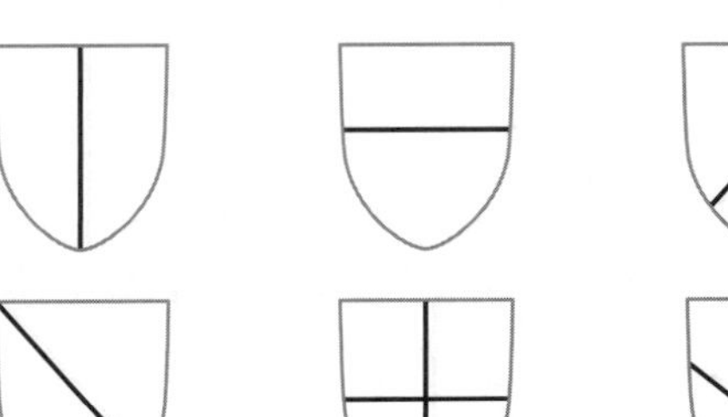

ISBN: 978-1-897164-32-7

5

Medieval Life

Peasants and serfs worked through all seasons of the year. They used a variety of tools to get their chores done.

A. Read about these chores and look at the pictures. Then write "Spring", "Summer", "Fall", or "Winter".

1. ____________

- harvest corn with jointed sticks called a **flail**
- grind corn into flour
- pick ripe grapes to make wine
- take pigs to the woods to feed on wild nuts

2. ____________

- cut tall meadow grass with a **scythe** and turn it into hay for animals' winter food
- shear sheep
- harvest wheat using a **sickle**

3. ____________

- prune trees and grape vines
- pull weeds growing among crops
- plough and cultivate fields using a **harrow**
- repair buildings and tools damaged over winter

4. ____________

- gather firewood
- slaughter pigs for winter meat
- maintain tools and equipment
- hunt

ISBN: 978-1-897164-32-7

B. Circle "T" for the true sentences and "F" for the false ones.

1. was harvested in spring. T F

2. Meadow grass was made into in fall. T F

3. and were pruned in spring. T F

4. was gathered in winter. T F

5. were ploughed in summer. T F

6. were repaired in spring. T F

C. Look at the tools in (A) and match them with these descriptions. Write the correct tool names.

1. This tool has a long handle and a long blade to cut tall grass. ____________

2. This tool with sharp spikes is dragged by an ox to break up hard soil. ____________

3. This tool has two jointed sticks and is used to separate grain from husks. ____________

4. This hand-held tool has a sharp, curved blade that cuts wheat. ____________

ISBN: 978-1-897164-32-7

Medieval Food

To keep the soil fertile, serfs and peasants practised something called **crop rotation**. They ate a lot of bread and vegetables. Although their food was different from the food of lords and nobles, everyone avoided drinking water and cow's milk.

A. Read what this tool says. Then complete the diagram and fill in the blanks.

Serfs and peasants practised crop rotation. For example, they moved peas and wheat from one field to another year after year. One of the fields would be left empty once every three years.

1.

Year	Field A	Field B	Field C
1200	peas in spring	wheat in fall	empty
1201	empty	peas in spring	
1202			

2. Peas were always planted in ________ .

3. Wheat was always planted in ________ .

4. Each crop was planted in a field once every ________ years.

ISBN: 978-1-897164-32-7

B. Read these holiday menus and write "Peasant" or "Lord".

- *Bread*
- *Pottage* – *a thin stew of bones and vegetables like peas and beans*
- *Bacon, eggs, and cheese*
- *Ale*

- *Roasts*
- *Stews*
- *Pudding* – *with honey and almonds*
- *Swan* – *served in gold leaf*
- *Spices*
- *Wine*

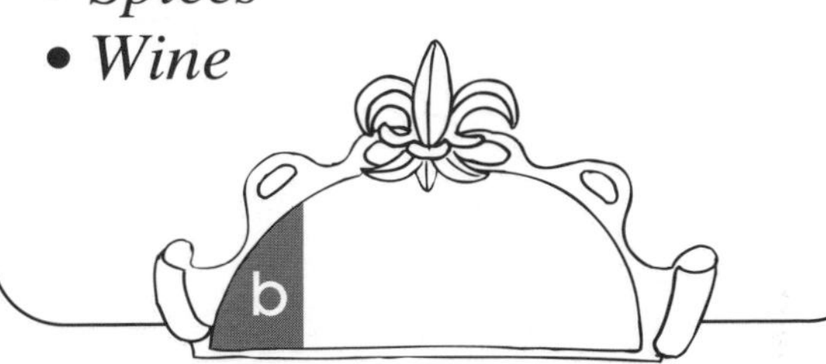

C. Read to find out what was unsafe to drink in medieval times. Help Tom circle the correct answers.

In medieval times, cow's milk was not always safe to drink. It was hard to keep fresh, and often contained dangerous germs. For recipes requiring milk, cooks made their own milk with crushed nuts and water. But because garbage and human waste littered the streets and streams, even water was sometimes unsafe to drink. It was safe to drink ale and wine.

1. Unsafe to drink:

   cow's milk / ale / wine / almond milk / water

2. Things for making milk required in certain recipes:

   crushed nuts / cow / water / ale / cheese / peas

ISBN: 978-1-897164-32-7

7

Medieval Trade Guilds

Merchants and **craftspeople** organized themselves into guilds in medieval times. Each guild had its own badge. These guilds were there to promote high standards in workmanship and set prices to give guild members a good income.

A. Sort these workers into their guilds. Write the correct names.

mason

tailor

butcher

carpenter

spinster

brewer

baker

shearman

tiler

1. Clothing Guilds

   ____

   ____

   ____

2. Builders Guilds

   ____

   ____

   ____

3. Food Guilds

   ____

   ____

   ____

ISBN: 978-1-897164-32-7

B. Label these badges with the given words.

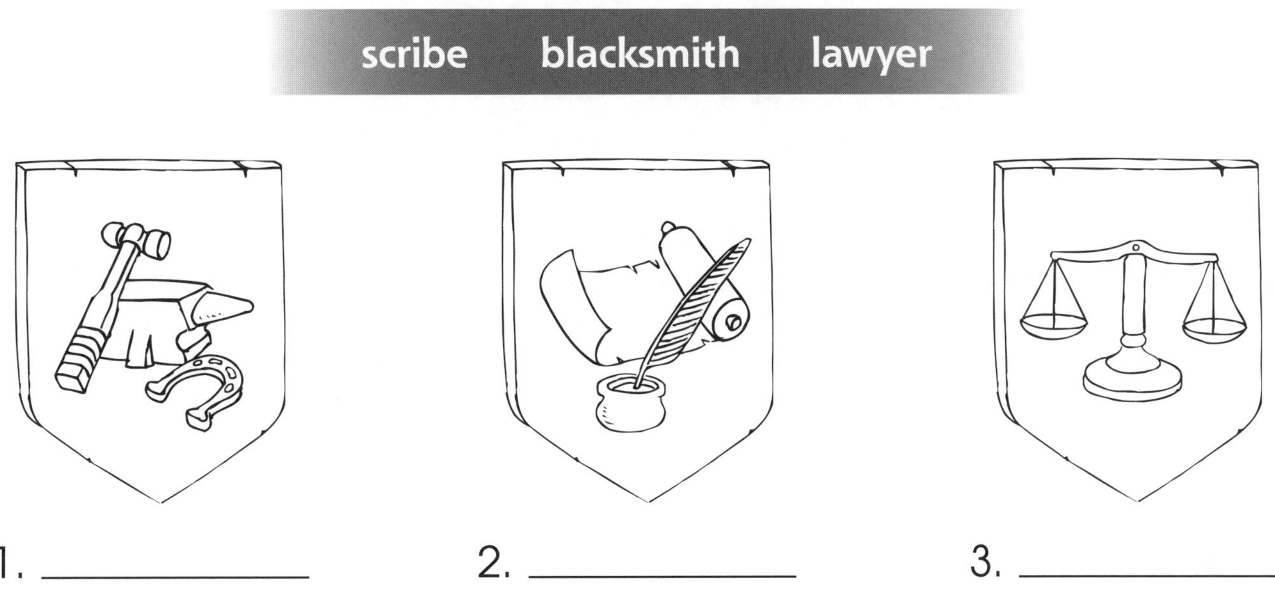

1. ______________ 2. ______________ 3. ______________

C. What did a man need to be before becoming a master of his trade? Follow the path in this medieval maze to find out.

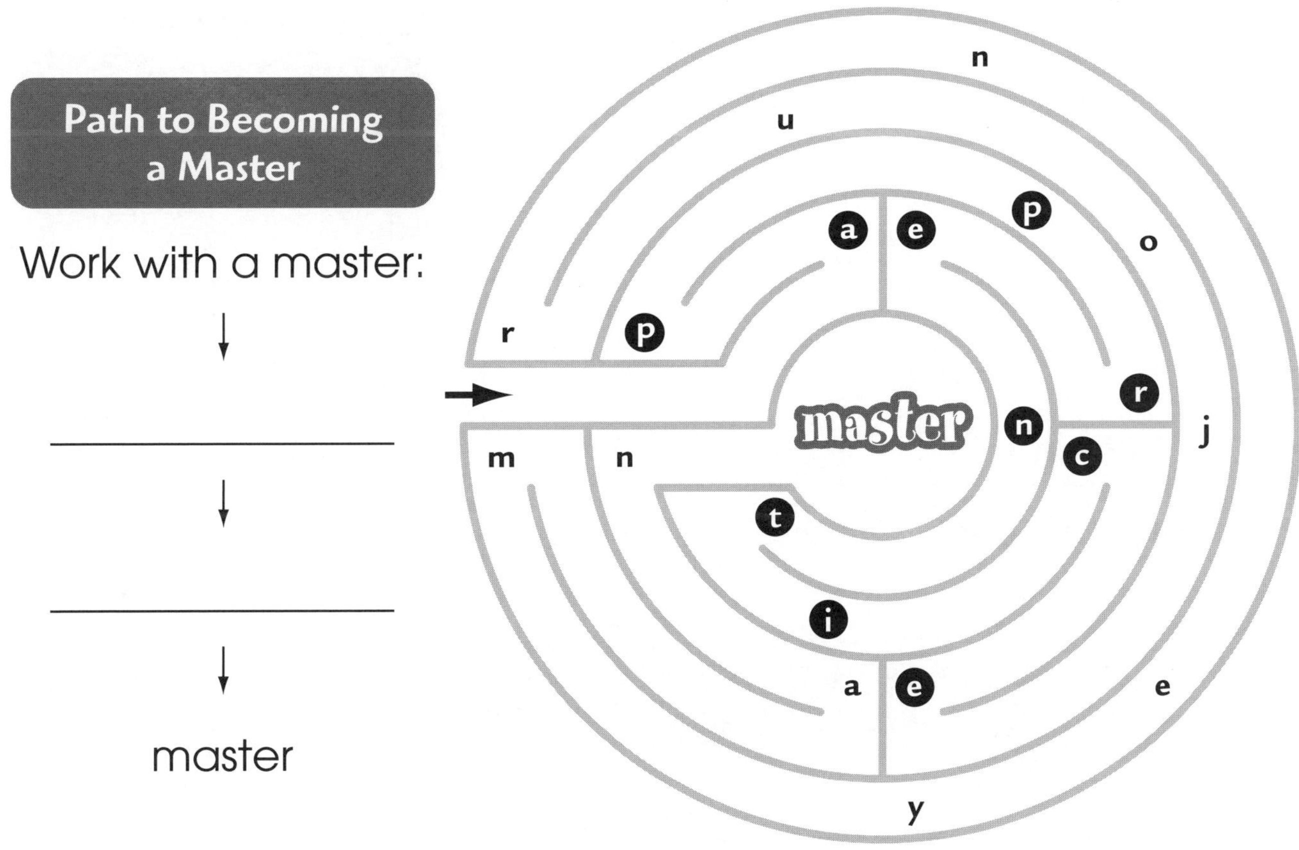

ISBN: 978-1-897164-32-7

8

Medieval Buildings

Medieval buildings were built with bricks and stones that had **masons' marks**. Each mark was like a mason's signature. Many buildings from this period still exist today and are very well-known.

A. Help the masons draw a mark on each of their bricks. Then count and make a tally and answer the question.

1. Mason John – E

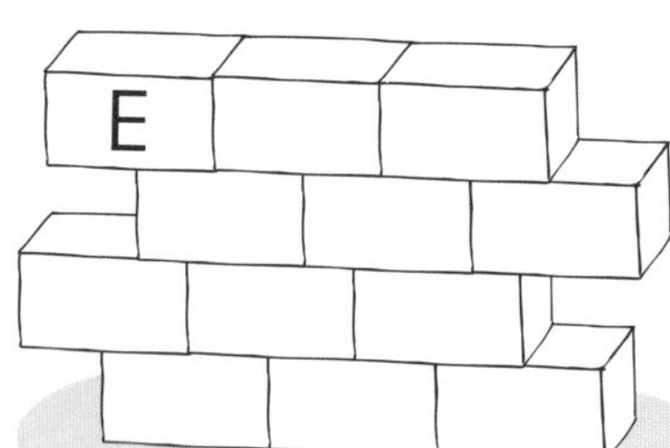

Mason Pierre – ✳

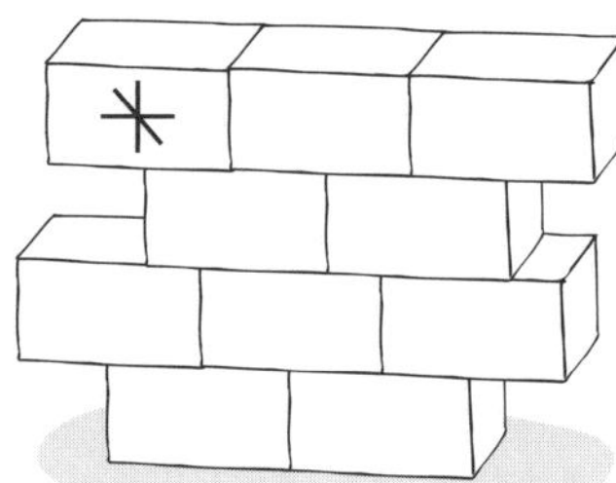

Mason David – Z

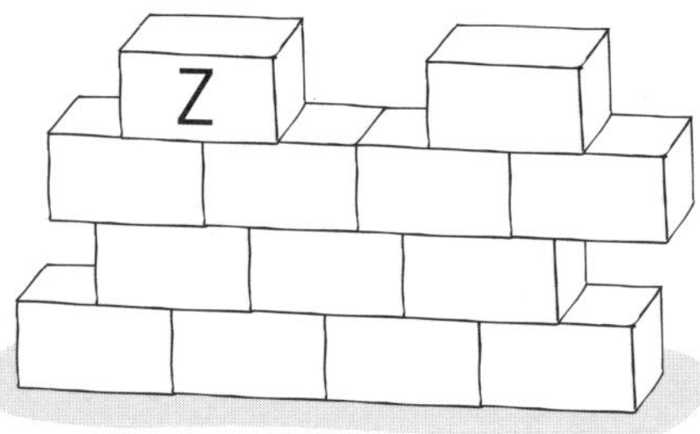

Mason Simon – ☆

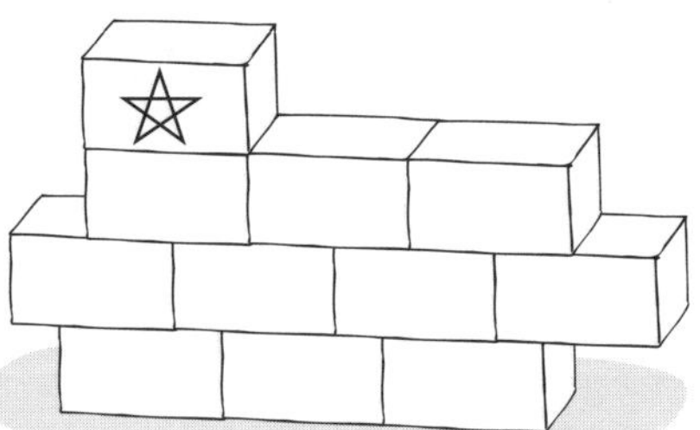

2.

Mason	John	Pierre	David	Simon
Brick Count	卌 卌 ||			

3. *We chisel a mark into each brick we make to get paid for our amount of work. So, who got the highest pay?*

____

ISBN: 978-1-897164-32-7

B. Look at these medieval buildings and read the clues. Draw lines to match them with the names.

- Dover Castle
- Leaning Tower of Pisa
- Notre Dame Cathedral
- Westminster Abbey

C. Read what this gargoyle says. Then complete the face of each gargoyle by drawing its other half.

We look hideous, but we're useful because we direct water from the walls of medieval buildings.

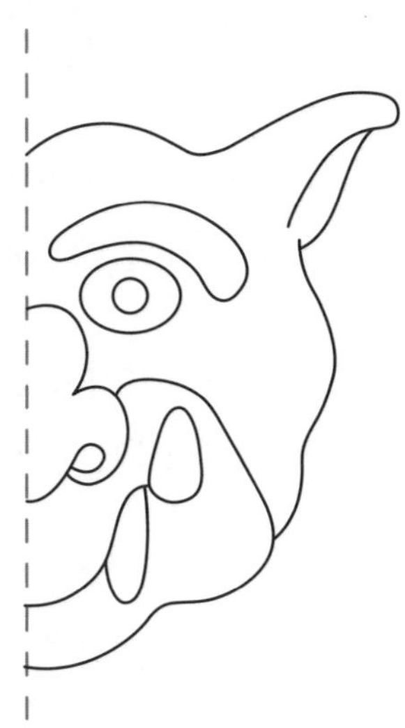

ISBN: 978-1-897164-32-7

9

Medieval Technology

Many inventions from the East made their way into Europe during the medieval times. Many of them are still in use today. Some of them have changed, but some look pretty much the same.

A. Match the descriptions with the inventions. Write the correct words.

cannon mirror windmill magnet spectacles compass paper printing press wheelbarrow

1. a thin sheet made from wood pulp ____________
2. a surface that reflects a clear image ____________
3. an instrument with a needle pointing north ____________
4. uses wind power to grind grain ____________
5. lenses that help the near-sighted and far-sighted see better ____________
6. a small cart with a wheel that carries heavy loads ____________
7. a piece of heavy artillery that shoots metal balls to attack enemies ____________
8. a machine that uses type or plates to print text and pictures ____________
9. a piece of iron that attracts other iron-containing metals ____________

ISBN: 978-1-897164-32-7

B. **Look at these things from today. Label them with the correct words from (A).**

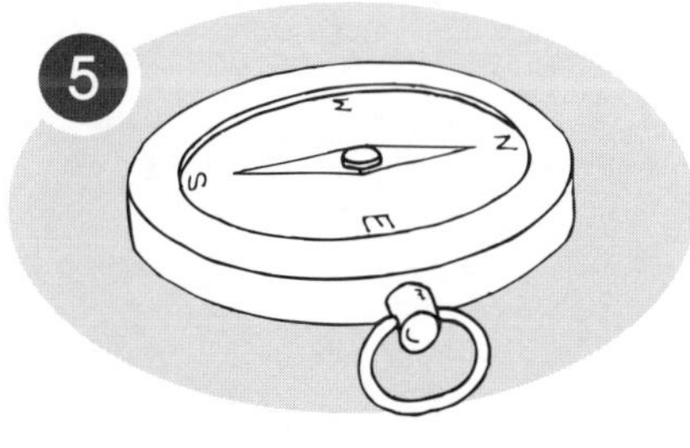

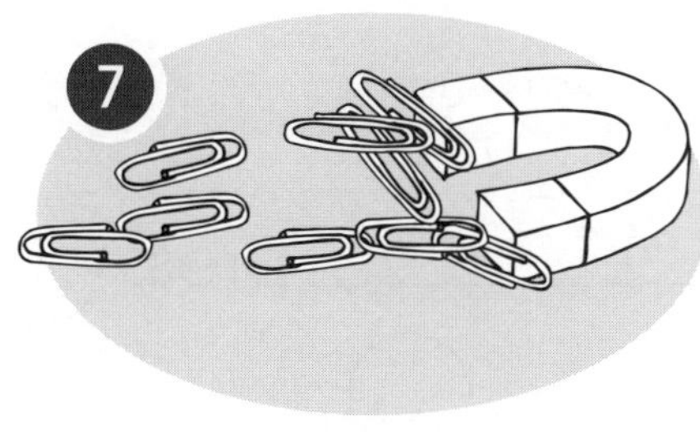

ISBN: 978-1-897164-32-7

Another Look at the Medieval Times

The medieval times lasted many years. Many important events happened throughout. This period was also full of entertainment. Some of the things from this period still exist today.

A. Fill in the blanks with the given words to complete this timeline. Then check the events that happened in the medieval times.

Black Canada Roman printing Christianity millennium China

CE	Event
0	beginning of ________ ◯
fall of Western ________ Empire ◯
500
1000	first millennium ◯
first Crusade ◯
Marco Polo's journey to ________ ◯
________ Death ◯
1500	invention of the ________ press ◯
forming of ________ ◯
2000	second ________ ◯

Medieval Times (500–1500)

ISBN: 978-1-897164-32-7

B. Look at these picture clues of medieval entertainment. Circle the entertainment words in the word search.

hurdy-gurdy juggler clown minstrel acrobat harp lute

a	n	a	c	l	u	e	t	r	l	e	m	i	n	s	t
b	h	c	l	h	e	j	u	g	g	e	l	u	t	e	a
a	a	l	o	l	j	u	g	g	l	e	r	l	t	u	c
c	r	o	w	o	c	h	a	c	r	o	b	a	t	t	r
d	p	w	n	w	n	h	a	n	w	l	c	t	e	b	o
u	h	u	r	d	y	-	g	u	r	d	y	u	l	e	a
c	u	r	w	n	a	m	i	n	s	t	r	e	l	o	t

C. Check the medieval item in each group. Then circle the medieval item that is still common today.

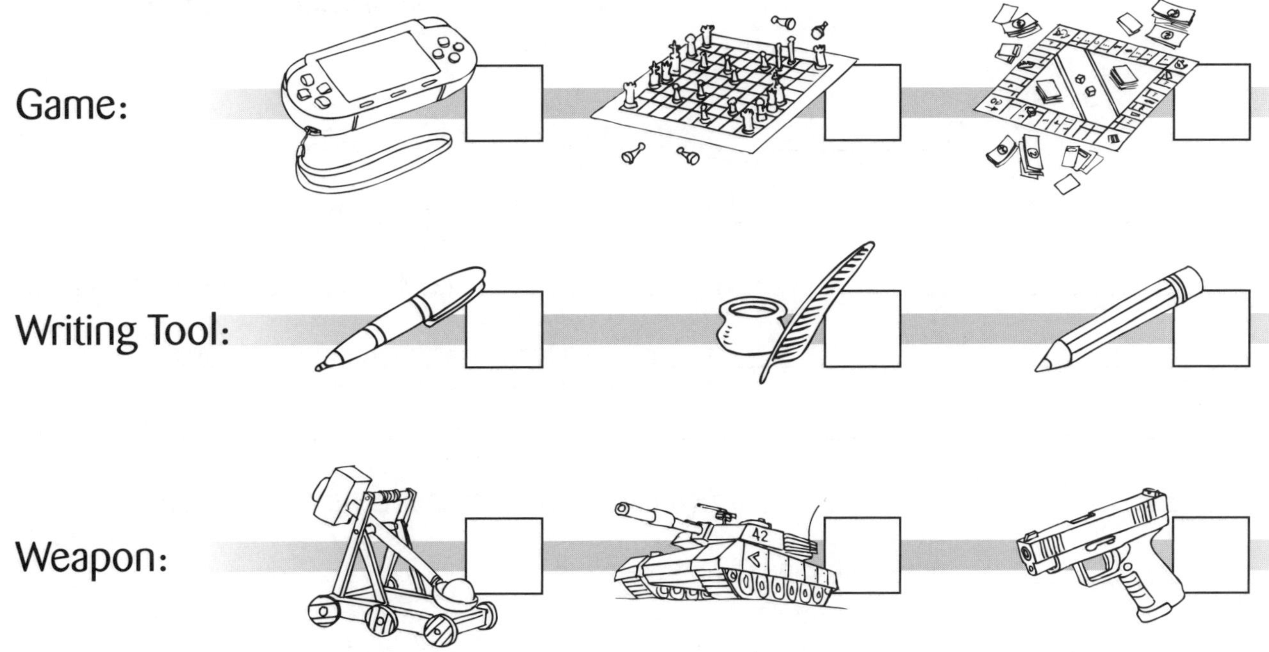

ISBN: 978-1-897164-32-7

11

Canada

Canada can be divided into areas of land that share physical characteristics. These are Canada's **physical regions**.

A. Look at this map of Canada's physical regions. Write the region names beside the meanings. Then answer the questions.

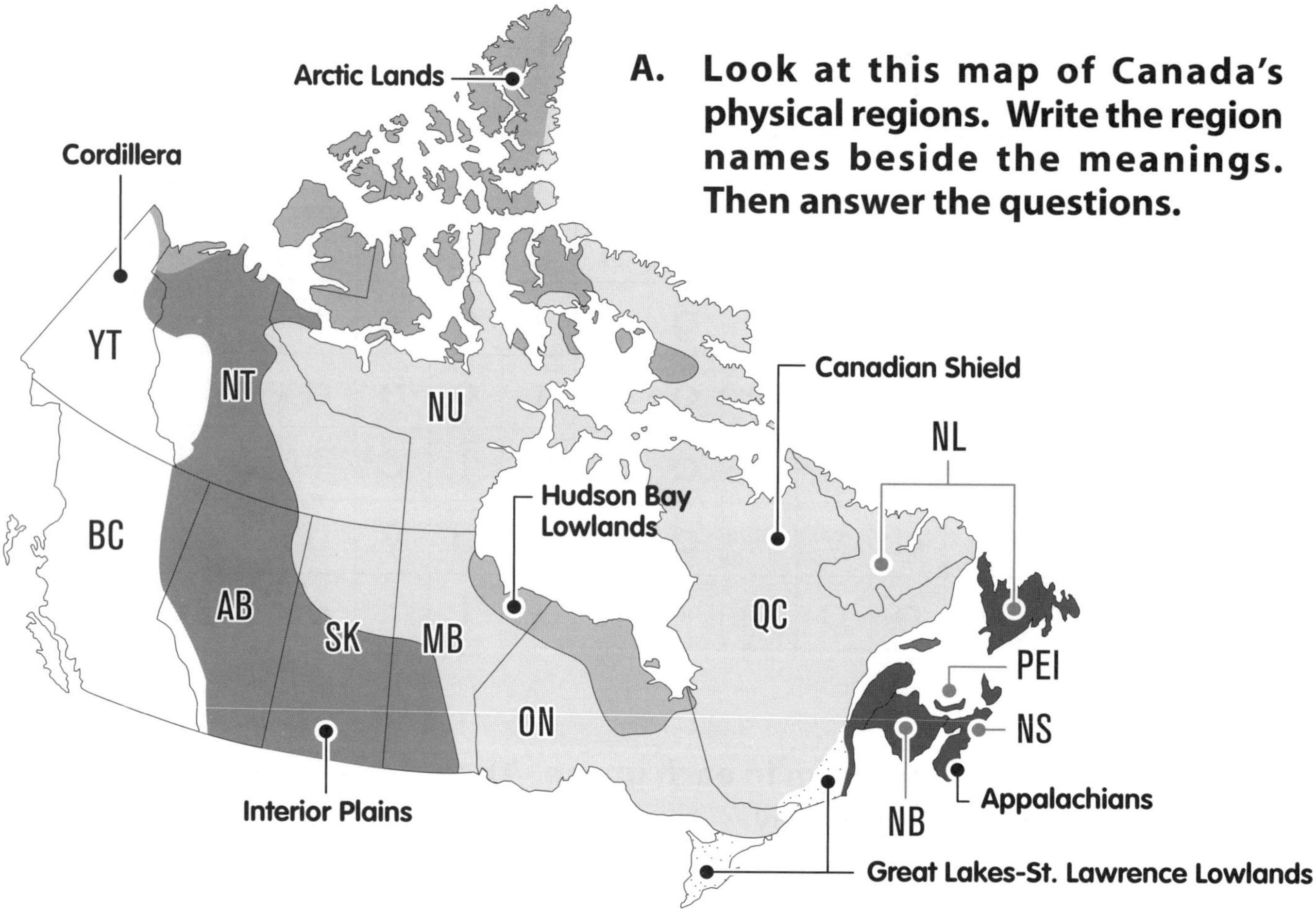

Arctic Lands
Cordillera
YT
NT
NU
BC
AB
SK
MB
ON
QC
NL
PEI
NS
NB
Canadian Shield
Hudson Bay Lowlands
Interior Plains
Appalachians
Great Lakes-St. Lawrence Lowlands

1. C__________ S__________ : ancient rock and thick forests

   A______________ : weathered mountains and large coastal bays

   H__________ B__________ L__________ : level coast land with lots of swamps

   A__________ L__________ : continuously frozen ground and ice caps

   G__________ L____________________ L__________ : lush farmland

   I__________ P__________ : rich deposits of dinosaur bones, oil, and gas

   C__________ : mountain ranges and plateaus

ISBN: 978-1-897164-32-7

2. Which provinces and territories are within the Canadian Shield?

____

3. Which region surrounds the banks of lakes and a river?

____

4. Which region is BC in? _______________

5. What is the northernmost region? _______________

6. What is the easternmost region? _______________

7. Which region is shared by MB, SK, and AB? _______________

B. Where do these places belong? Write the names of the physical regions.

a _______________

b _______________

c _______________

d _______________

ISBN: 978-1-897164-32-7

Yukon

Yukon is one of Canada's three territories. It is home to **gold mines** and the highest mountain of the country: Mount Logan.

A. Colour the coat of arms of Yukon. Then fill in the blanks with the given words.

Yukon River fur trade husky
explorers gold mountains mineral

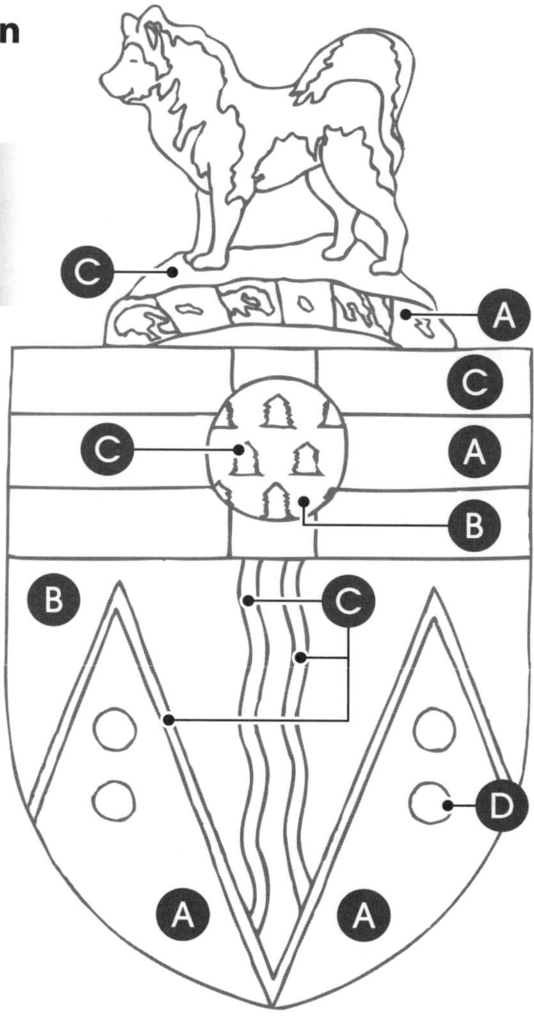

1. The coat of arms of Yukon is a shield that is red, blue, white, and ____________ , with a ____________ on top.

2. The wavy white and blue stripes represent the ____________ .

3. The red, triangle-like shapes represent the ____________ of the territory and the gold circles represent the territory's famous ____________ .

4. The cross at the top of the shield represents the early English ____________ , who played an important role in the ____________ .

ISBN: 978-1-897164-32-7

B. Look at this map of Yukon. Write the names of Yukon's neighbours in the four directions.

N: ______________________

S: ______________________

E: ______________________

W: ______________________

C. Read the clues and complete this crossword puzzle about Yukon.

Across

A. frozen ground that never thaws

B. Yukon's physical region

Down

1. Yukon's flower symbol
2. type of reindeer
3. Canada's highest mountain

					1							
					F		2			3		
							C			M		
		A	P		R	M		F				T
							R					
					W							
							B					
					D		U			L		
B	C			D		L						
										N		

The Northwest Territories

The Northwest Territories is made up of many physical regions. The land here means different things to different people, depending on what they use it for.

A. Label the physical regions of the Northwest Territories.

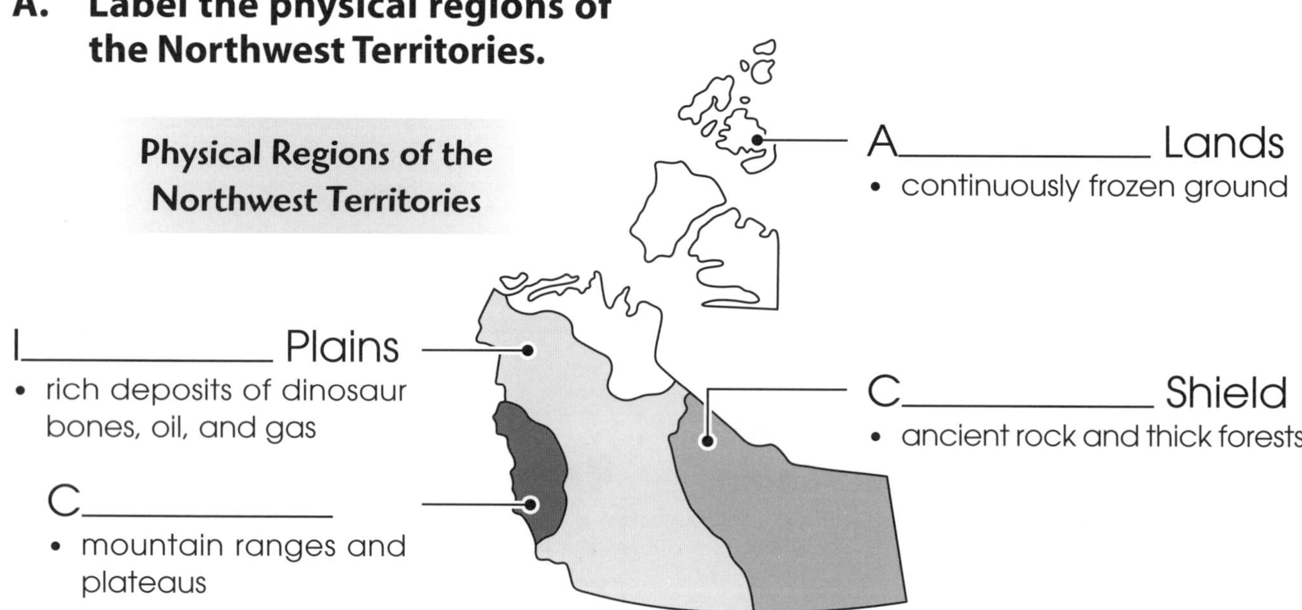

B. Colour the coat of arms of the Northwest Territories. Then fill in the blanks with the correct physical region names from (A).

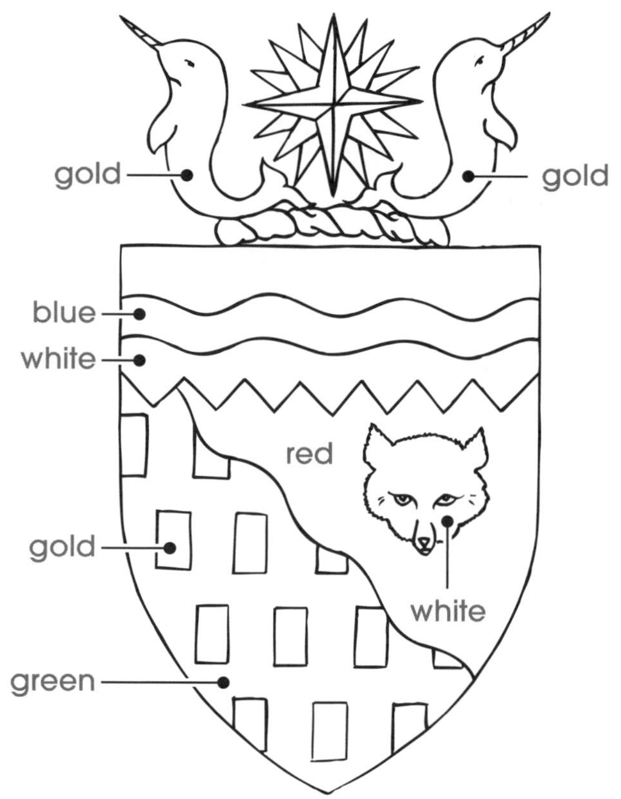

The red part of the coat of arms represents frozen ground, which is the ____________________ .

The green part represents the southern forests, which are part of the ____________________ .

ISBN: 978-1-897164-32-7

C. **Read what Sam says. Then find out what the Northwest Territories means to each person and write the correct word in bold.**

To the Aboriginal people who live there, the Northwest Territories is their ***homeland****. To others, it is a* ***frontier****, waiting to be conquered and used, with its many raw materials like natural gas, oil, diamonds, and gold.*

We need only two things to survive on this wonderful land: seal and caribou.

1. ________________

There is money to be made from the gold in this land, symbolized by those gold bars on the coat of arms!

2. ________________

My company supplies the world with the raw materials that this open land has to offer.

3. ________________

My people have lived here for many generations. No one has the right to take it away from us.

4. ________________

ISBN: 978-1-897164-32-7

Nunavut

Nunavut is Canada's youngest and largest territory. Its population is mostly **Inuit**.

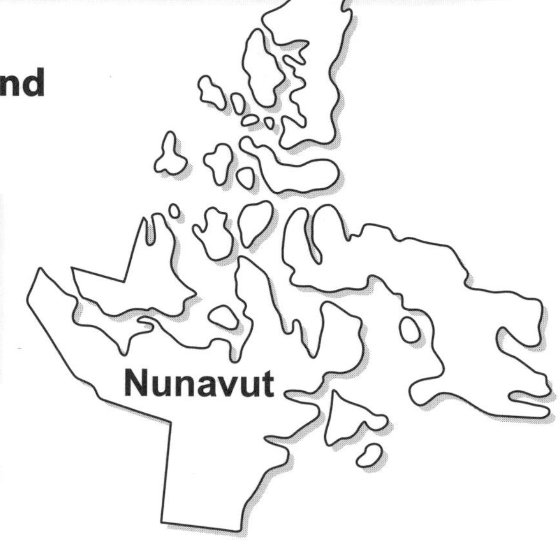

A. Fill in the blanks with the given facts and figures of Nunavut.

Mt. Barbeau purple saxifrage
communities Inuit
20% 1999 30 000 24

1. Nunavut became a territory on April 1, ________________ .
2. There are about ________________ people living in the territory.
3. The ________________ make up 85% of the population.
4. The land area of Nunavut makes up about ________________ of all the land in Canada.
5. Nunavut has 26 ________________ ranging from very small to fairly large.
6. The territory's official flower is the ________________ , chosen on May 1, 2000.
7. Nunavut is home to the highest mountain in eastern North America, called ________________ .
8. Iqaluit, the capital city, receives ________________ hours of sunlight every day in June.

ISBN: 978-1-897164-32-7

B. Match the symbols on Nunavut's coat of arms with the meanings. Write the correct letters.

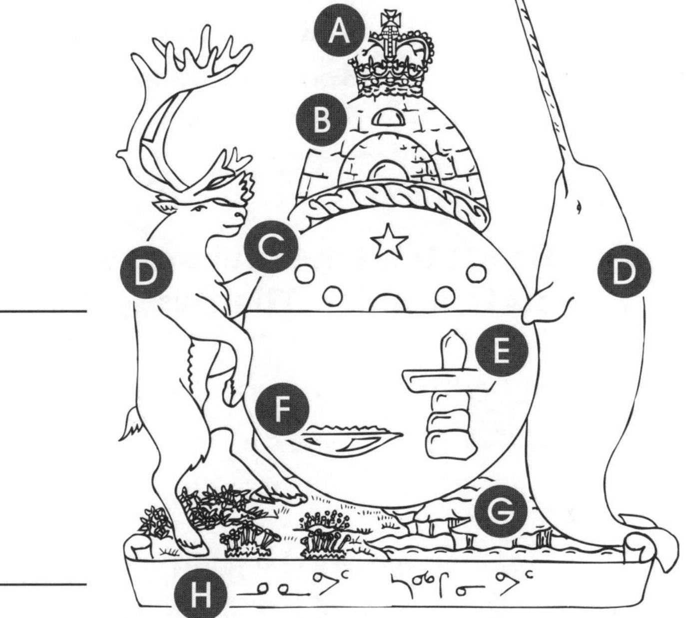

1. The Inukshuk symbolizes the stone monuments that guide the people of the land. It is also used to mark sacred places. ____

2. The caribou and the narwhal are the land and sea animals that are part of Nunavut's heritage. ____

3. The crown symbolizes the government of Nunavut and shows that it is part of Canada. ____

4. The igloo symbolizes survival and Nunavut's traditional way of life. ____

5. The arc of the five golden circles stands for the life-giving qualities of the sun. ____

6. The quiliq, which is an Inuit stone lamp, symbolizes the warmth of family and community. ____

7. The motto is in Inuktitut, one of the native languages in Nunavut. It reads, "Nunavut Sanginivut", meaning "Nunavut, our strength". ____

8. The base of the coat of arms portrays both land and sea, showing three types of arctic plants. ____

ISBN: 978-1-897164-32-7

Newfoundland and Labrador

Newfoundland and Labrador was once home to the now extinct **Beothuk** people. The province is home to many **natural features**, like mountains, rivers, and islands.

A. Read about the coat of arms of Newfoundland and Labrador. Then write the correct answers.

Coat of Arms of Newfoundland and Labrador

• created in 1637

This elk represents the caribou herds of the province.

These two people are the Beothuk, the Aboriginal people of the province.

This motto is in Latin, meaning "Seek ye first the kingdom of God".

1. The name of the extinct Aboriginal people of Newfoundland and Labrador: ____________
2. The animal that represents the caribou herds of the province: ____________
3. The language of the motto at the bottom of the coat of arms: ____________
4. "Seek ye first the ________ of God": ____________
5. The year that this coat of arms was created: ____________

ISBN: 978-1-897164-32-7

B. Find the natural features on the map of Newfoundland and Labrador. Write their names on the chart.

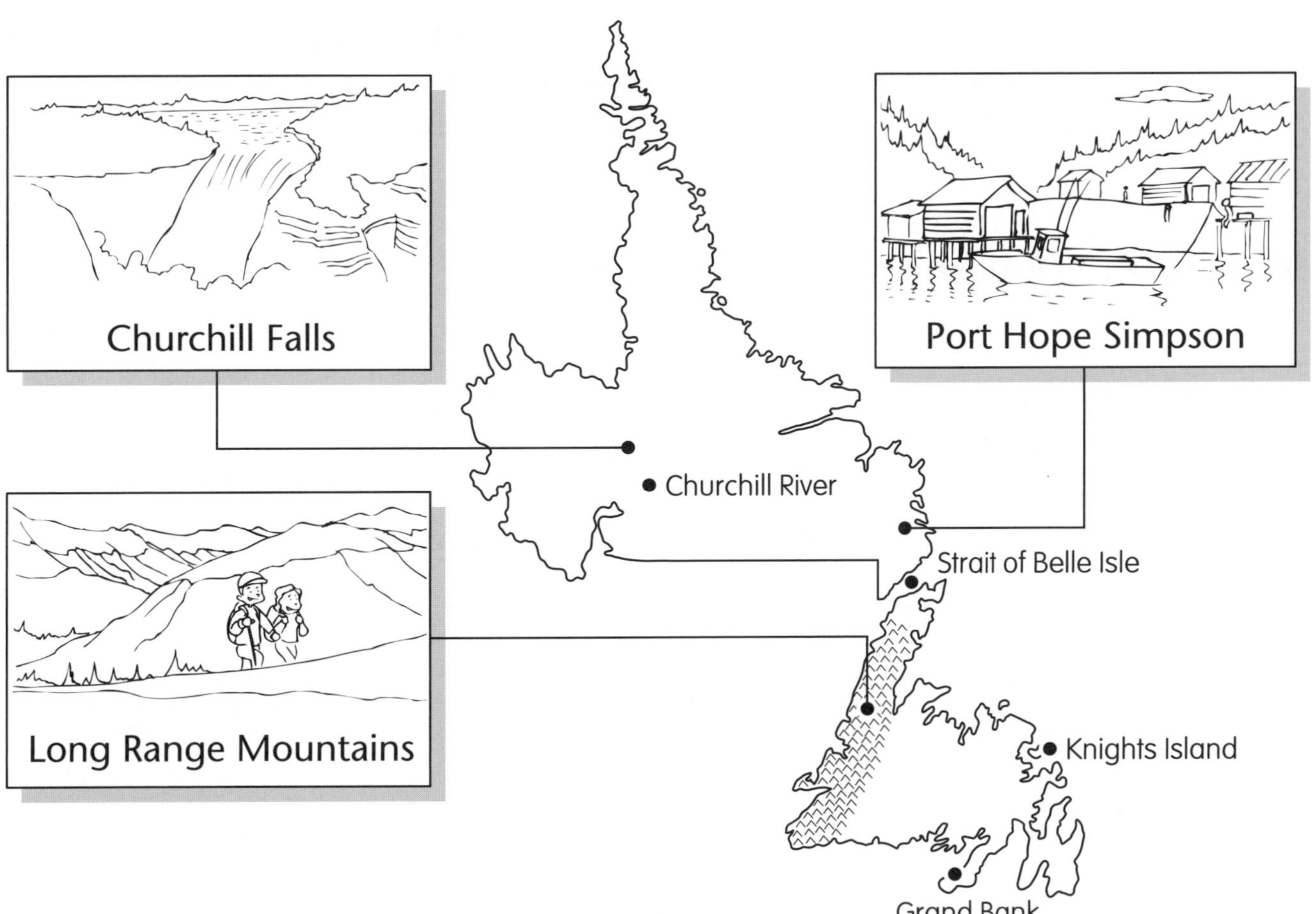

Natural Feature	Name of Natural Feature on the Map
Falls	
River	
Bank	
Strait	
Port	
Island	
Mountains	

ISBN: 978-1-897164-32-7

16

Prince Edward Island

The rich soil and surrounding area of Prince Edward Island are ideal for **agricultural activity** and **seafood harvesting**. The beautiful setting of the island also attracts many tourists every year.

A. Write the industry name for each picture.

Agriculture

Fishing

Manufacturing

Tourism

1. ____________________

2. ____________________

3. ____________________

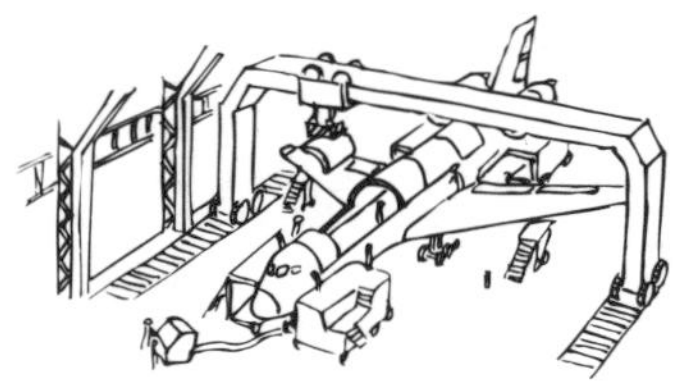
4. ____________________

5. ____________________

6. ____________________

7. ____________________

8. ____________________

9. ____________________

ISBN: 978-1-897164-32-7

B. Unscramble the letters to complete each sentence about PEI.

1. PEI is in the Gulf of St. ____________ (arewLnec).
2. PEI is the smallest ____________ (rvoicpen) in Canada.
3. The soil in PEI is ____________ (der) because of its unique iron-oxide content.
4. The capital of PEI is ____________ (halorCtteownt).
5. PEI is the setting of Lucy Maud Montgomery's novel, *Anne of Green* ____________ (*aGelbs*).

C. Read about the coat of arms of PEI and find the items in bold. Write the correct letters.

A. *a **rose** for PEI's English background*

B. *the **blossom** of a potato plant*

C. *a **lily** for the country France*

D. *a necklace **net** to fish the sea*

E. *a **leaf** from PEI's official oak tree*

F. *a prickly **thistle** to represent Scotland*

G. *an Irish **shamrock***

H. *a **Royal Crown***

I. *an **eight-pointed star**, the Mi'kmaq's sun-symbol*

ISBN: 978-1-897164-32-7

17

Nova Scotia

Nova Scotia is one of the provinces where the **Mi'kmaq** people live. Its coat of arms is the most detailed of all the provinces and territories. It is also where **Bluenose**, the schooner on the Canadian dime, was built.

A. Write "NOVA SCOTIA" in the boxes to complete the Mi'kmaq words. Then draw lines to match the meanings with the pictures.

☐ **ajiwsget**
go fishing

☐ **onegun**
portage (with moccasins)

☐ The Mi'kmaq language has no words beginning with "v".

☐ **kum**
snowshoe

☐ **eboo**
river

☐ **hegaoo**
bass fish

☐ **otool**
my canoe

☐ **ia'muei**
moose meat

☐ **nuipi**
native paddle

☐ **be**
bow

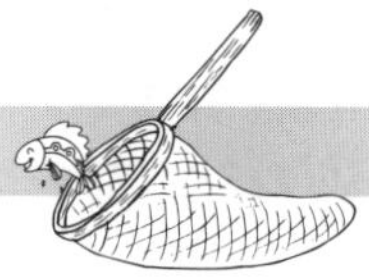

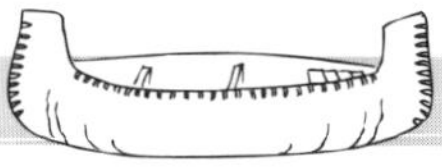

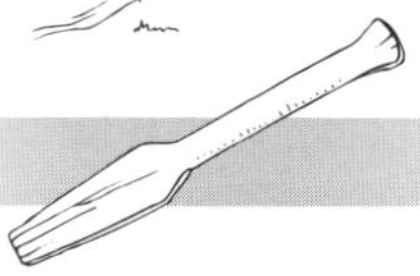

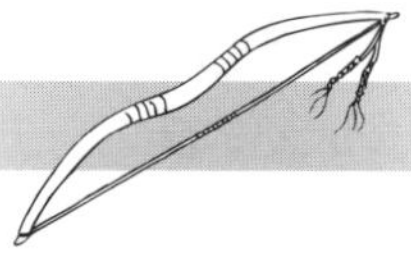

ISBN: 978-1-897164-32-7

B. Look at the coat of arms of Nova Scotia and fill in the blanks with the given words.

Scottish　　New Scotland　　above　　below

The coat of arms of every province and territory has its motto ______________ the shield, but the one for Nova Scotia has its motto ______________ the shield. This is a ______________ tradition. In fact, Nova Scotia is Latin for ______________ .

C. Look at the picture clues on this timeline and put the sentences about Bluenose in order. Write 1 to 5.

☐ Bluenose was built by hand in Nova Scotia and launched on March 21, 1921 as both a fishing schooner and a racing boat. It was crowned "the fastest in the world".

☐ The memory of Bluenose is kept alive as her image is displayed on the Canadian dime.

☐ Bluenose sank during a storm in the Caribbean Sea in 1942.

☐ Bluenose II was built by hand again in Nova Scotia in 1963, and currently sails the coasts of Canada and the United States, a proud symbol of Nova Scotia.

☐ Bluenose was sold to work in the West Indies because schooners lost their importance after World War II.

ISBN: 978-1-897164-32-7

New Brunswick

New Brunswick is a province in eastern Canada, close to Newfoundland, Nova Scotia, and PEI. It has many **natural resources**, and is one of the provinces with lots of rain.

A. Find and circle the things in bold on New Brunswick's coat of arms. Then fill in the blanks to tell what these symbols represent.

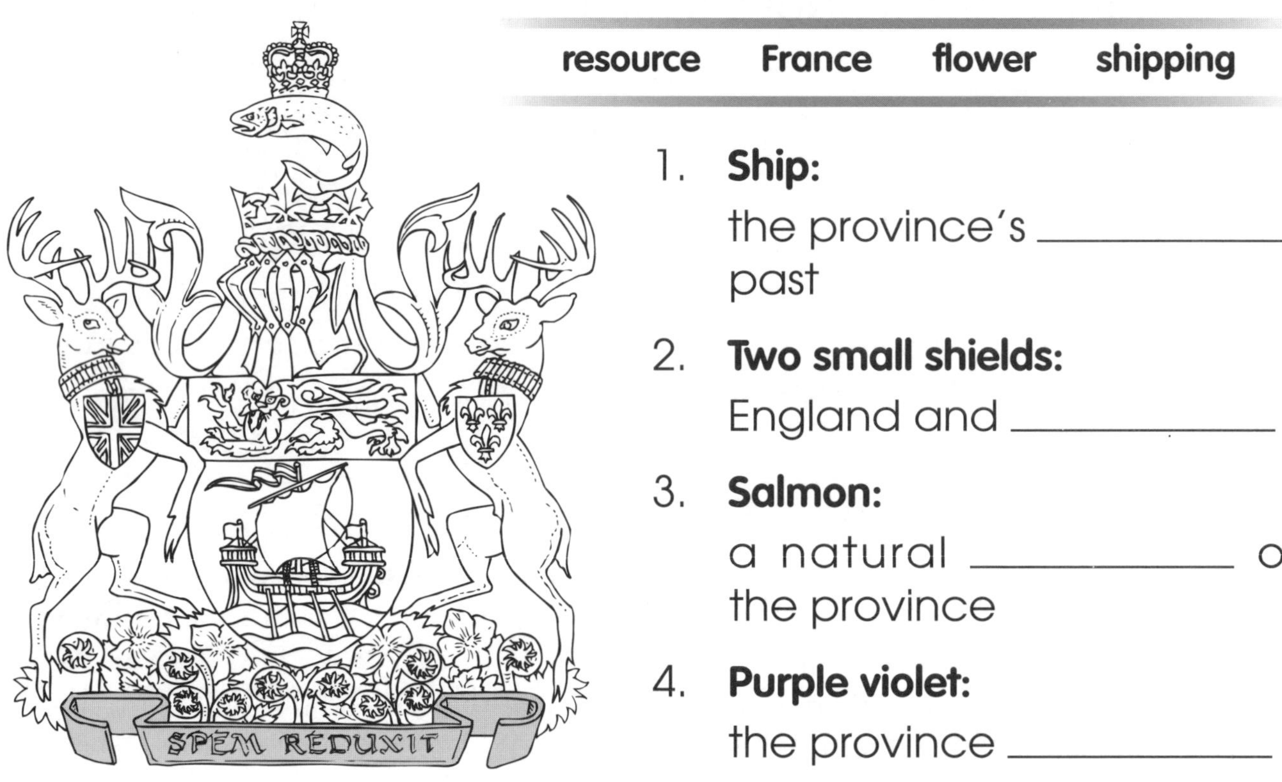

resource **France** **flower** **shipping**

1. **Ship:** the province's ____________ past
2. **Two small shields:** England and ____________
3. **Salmon:** a natural ____________ of the province
4. **Purple violet:** the province ____________

B. Look at these natural resources of New Brunswick. Unscramble the letters.

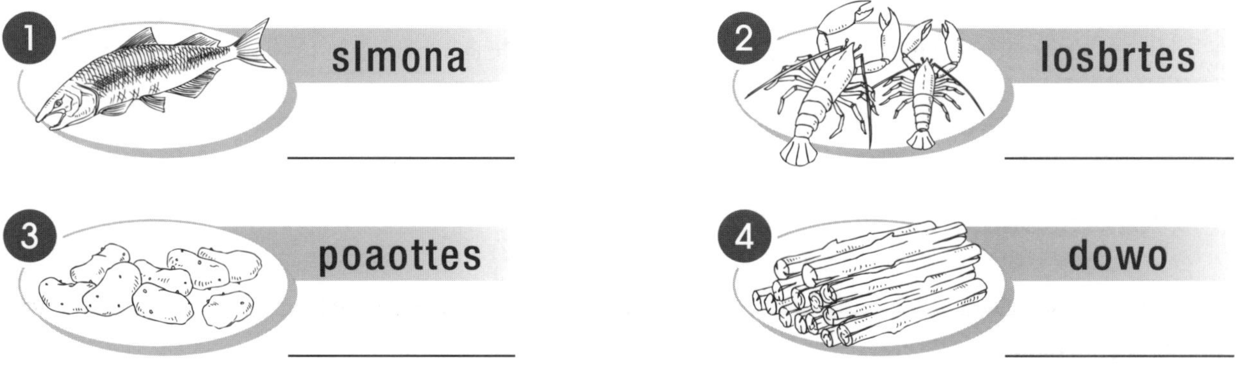

1. slmona ____________
2. losbrtes ____________
3. poaottes ____________
4. dowo ____________

ISBN: 978-1-897164-32-7

C. Look at this bar graph showing the rainfall of some Canadian cities. Answer the questions and circle the correct answer.

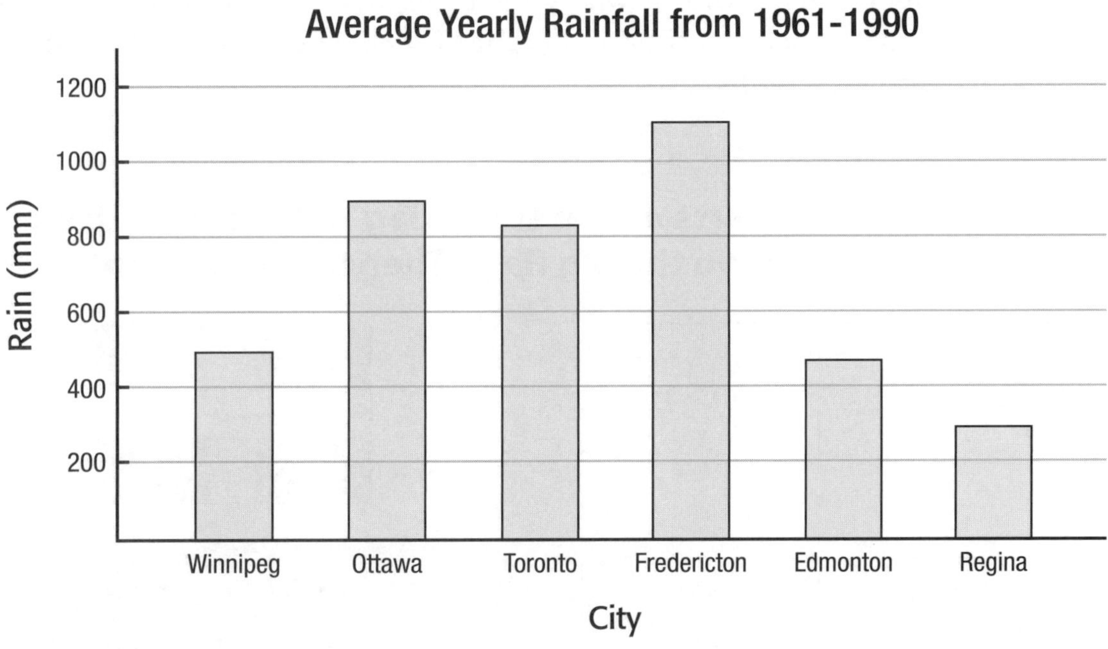

1. The city with the most rain on the graph: ____________

2. The city with the least rain on the graph: ____________

3. Cities in the Interior Plains get very little rain. Which cities do you think are in this region?

   ____

4. New Brunswick is a province with lots of rain. Which city do you think is in this province?

   ____

5. New Brunswick gets lots of rain because it is a province

   in the Canadian Shield / close to the sea .

Graph adapted from Statistics Canada <http://www.statcan.ca/english/kits/cyb1999/environment/art1.htm>, July, 2006

ISBN: 978-1-897164-32-7

Quebec

Quebec is a province with very strong French roots, where most people speak French. Its capital, Québec City, is the only North American city with **city walls**.

A. Look at the shaded parts of the small flag of Quebec. Use blue to colour the same parts on the big flag. Then fill in the blanks.

purity white
blue France

Like the ancient royal flags of ____________, the flag of Quebec has a ____________ cross. The white flowers on ____________ fields are symbols of ____________ .

B. Fill in the blanks with the given words to tell about Quebec's coat of arms.

England Canada
I remember France

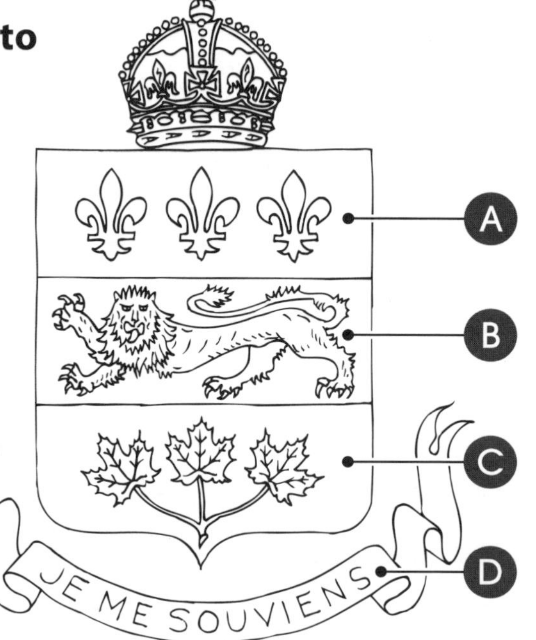

1. Ⓐ represents ________________ .
2. Ⓑ represents ________________ .
3. Ⓒ represents ________________ .
4. Ⓓ means ________________ .

ISBN: 978-1-897164-32-7

C. Look at the picture clues and circle the correct words.

1. Québec City is the capital / province of Quebec. It is the only city in North America with shields / city walls , built by French people long ago to protect the city. "I remember", Quebec's motto, means to remember the history of the province.

2. Most of Quebec is in the Appalachians / Canadian Shield . Some of it is in the fertile / frozen Great Lakes-St. Lawrence region, where agriculture / tourism plays a big part in Quebec's economy.

D. Look at this circle graph of the languages spoken in Quebec. Fill in the blanks.

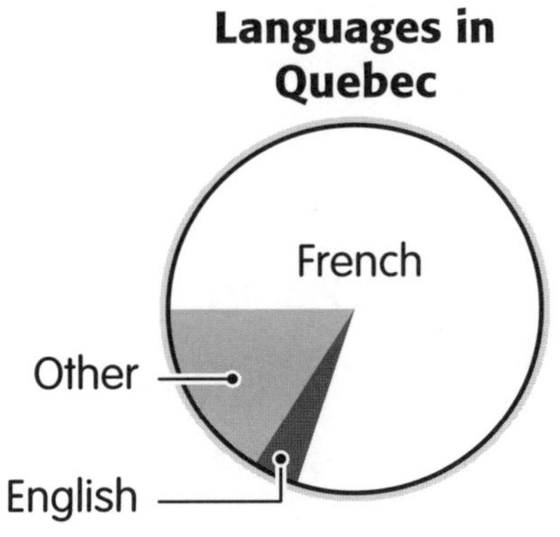

1. Most of the people living in Quebec speak __________ .

2. There are more people in Quebec who speak __________ languages than people who speak __________ .

ISBN: 978-1-897164-32-7

Ontario

Ontario is close to the **St. Lawrence River** and the five **Great Lakes**, which were very important to the early settlers of Canada. Today, the province is full of both urban and rural activities.

A. Read the clues and check the coat of arms of Ontario. Then answer the questions.

Clues
- a black bear at the top
- a motto at the bottom
- the Cross of St. George
- maple leaves on the shield
- a moose and a deer supporting the shield

1.

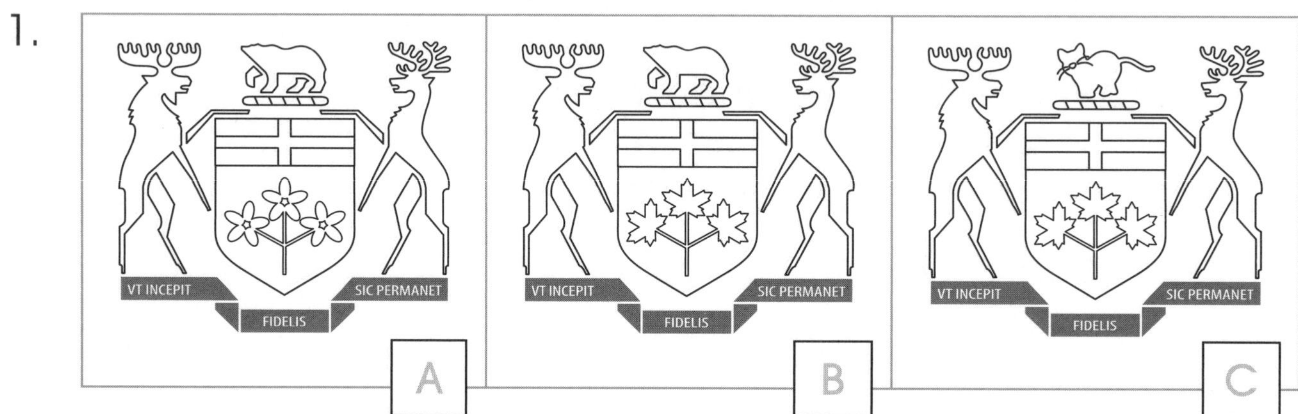

2. How many maple leaves are there on the shield?

____

3. What is the symbol of England on the shield?

____

4. What is "Loyal she began, loyal she remains"?

____

ISBN: 978-1-897164-32-7

B. Trace the outline of Ontario. Then use the map and the compass rose to write the correct answers.

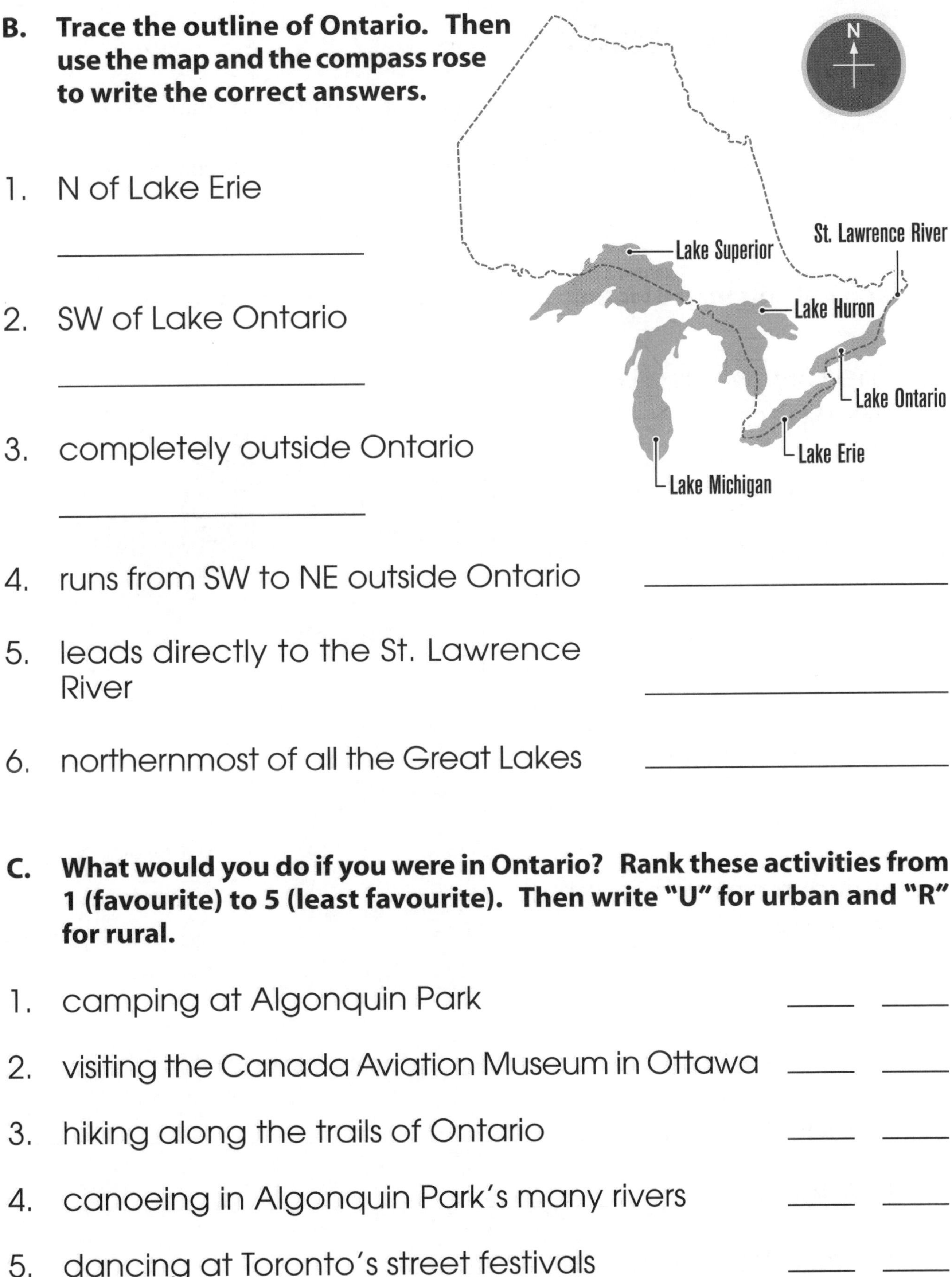

1. N of Lake Erie ____________________

2. SW of Lake Ontario ____________________

3. completely outside Ontario ____________________

4. runs from SW to NE outside Ontario ____________________

5. leads directly to the St. Lawrence River ____________________

6. northernmost of all the Great Lakes ____________________

C. What would you do if you were in Ontario? Rank these activities from 1 (favourite) to 5 (least favourite). Then write "U" for urban and "R" for rural.

1. camping at Algonquin Park ____ ____
2. visiting the Canada Aviation Museum in Ottawa ____ ____
3. hiking along the trails of Ontario ____ ____
4. canoeing in Algonquin Park's many rivers ____ ____
5. dancing at Toronto's street festivals ____ ____

ISBN: 978-1-897164-32-7

Manitoba

There are three physical regions in Manitoba: Hudson Bay Lowlands, Canadian Shield, and Interior Plains. Most of the province is **rural**, symbolized by the **wheat**, trees, and water on its coat of arms.

A. Look at this map of Manitoba and write the correct answers.

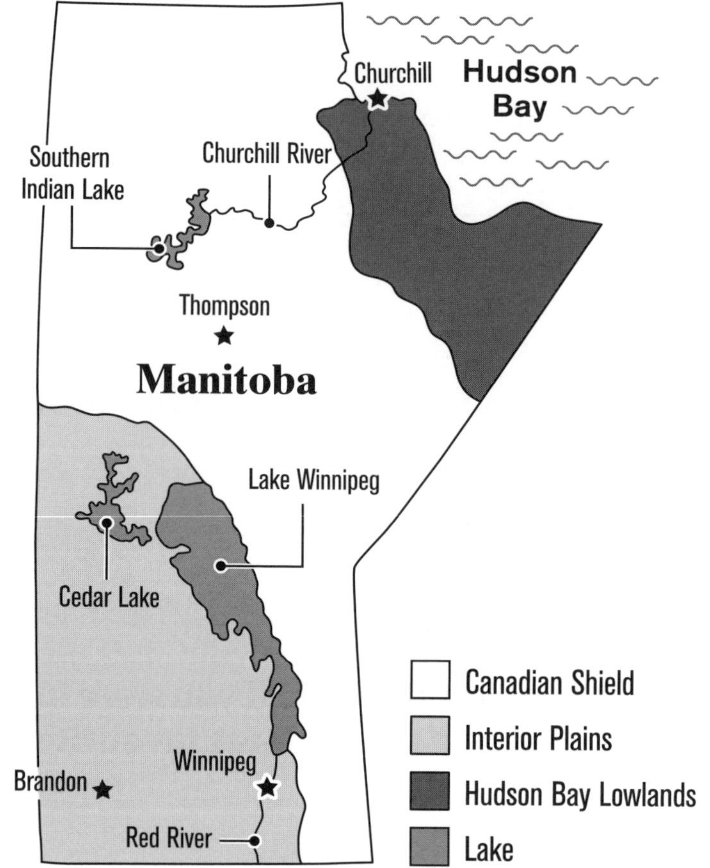

1. The city that is west of Winnipeg:

   ____

2. The biggest lake on the map:

   ____

3. The city that is closest to Hudson Bay:

   ____

4. A river running through Winnipeg:

   ____

5. Write the place names found in these physical regions:

   Canadian Shield: ______________________________

   Interior Plains: ______________________________

   Hudson Bay Lowlands: ______________________________

ISBN: 978-1-897164-32-7

B. Look at the map in (A) again and complete the names of these Manitoba cities. Then use the picture clues to write "urban" or "rural" under the names.

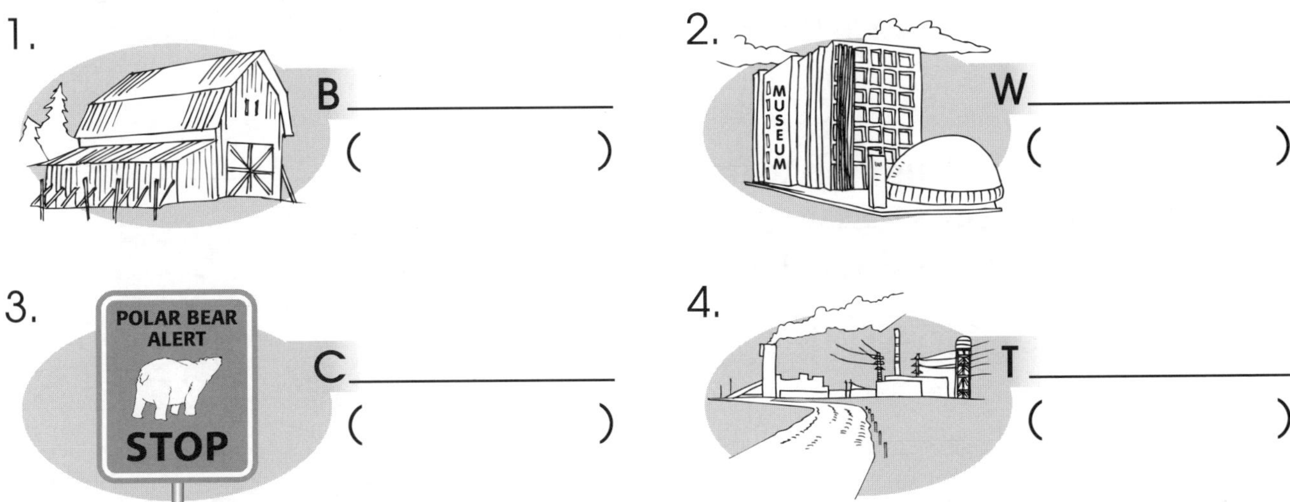

1. B_____________ ( )
2. W_____________ ( )
3. C_____________ ( )
4. T_____________ ( )

C. Tell what these things represent on Manitoba's coat of arms. Write the correct given words.

Manitoba's flower   Canada   Manitoba's water
Manitoba's agriculture   England   Manitoba's forests

GLORIOSUS · ET · LIBER

ISBN: 978-1-897164-32-7

22

Saskatchewan

Saskatchewan is a province that is shaped almost like a rectangle. A big part of it is in the Interior Plains, so it produces many **crops**.

A. Use the grid on this map to find the locations of these Saskatchewan cities and answer the question.

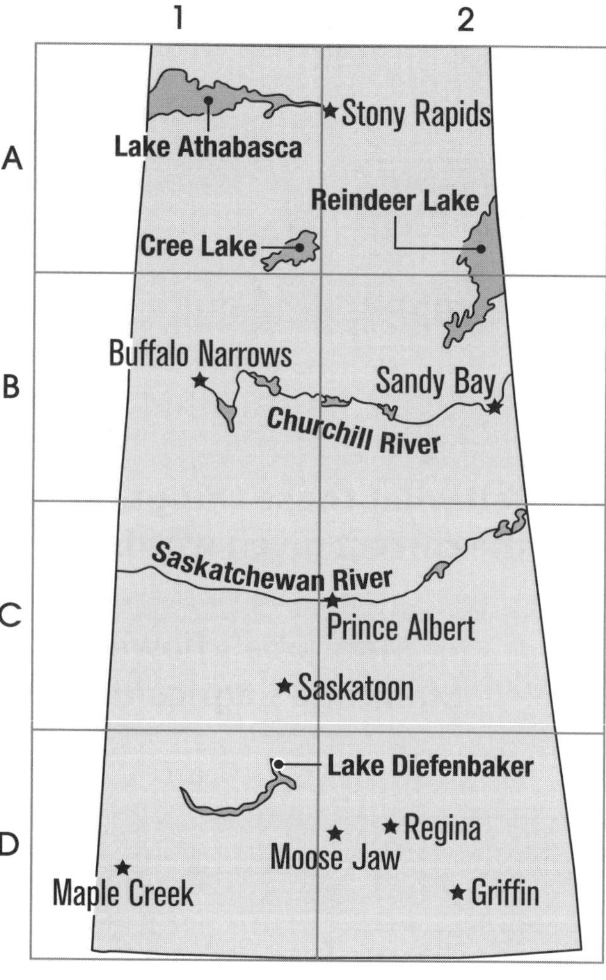

1. Locations of the Cities

Prince Albert C2

Saskatoon ______

Moose Jaw ______

Maple Creek ______

Regina ______

Griffin ______

Stony Rapids ______

Sandy Bay ______

Buffalo Narrows ______

2. *Which river or lake is in each of these locations?*

A1: ______________________

C1: ______________ D1: ______________

A2: ______________ C2: ______________

ISBN: 978-1-897164-32-7

B. Look at these Saskatchewan crops. Unscramble the letters.

1. theaw ____________

2. 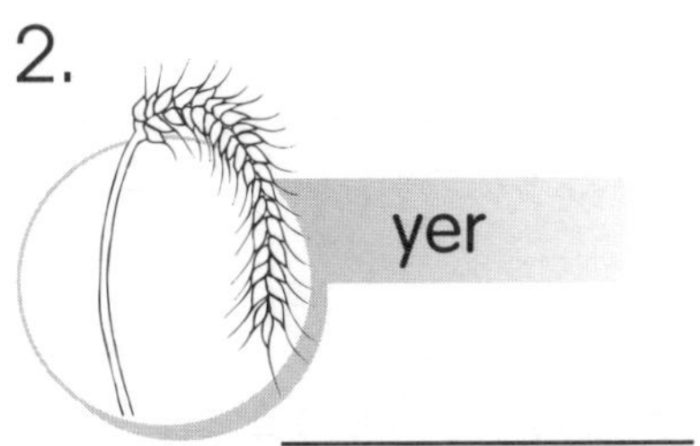

____

3. 

____

4. 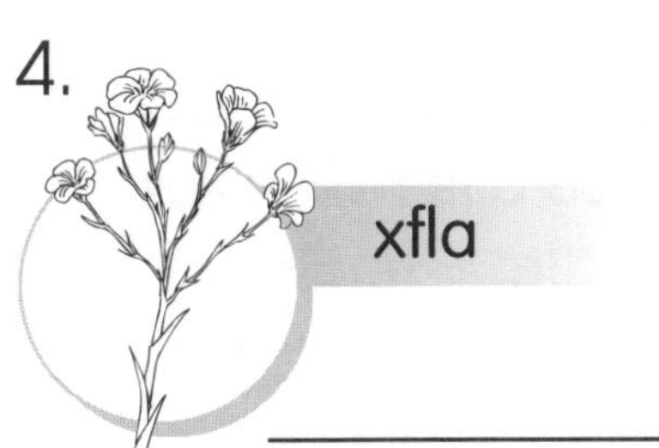

____

5. 

____

6. 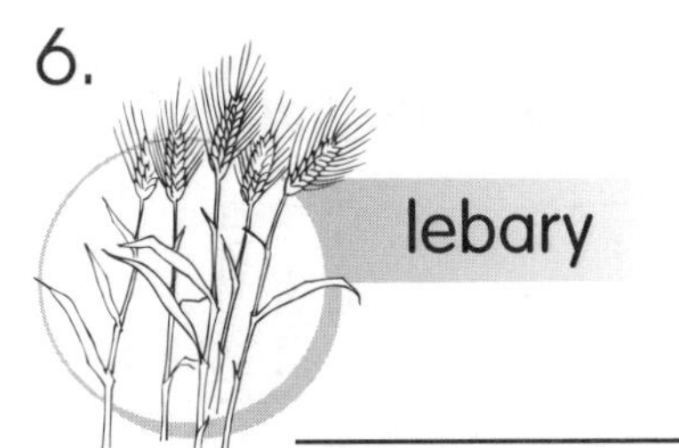

____

C. Tell what the symbols on Saskatchewan's coat of arms represent. Write the correct given words.

Saskatchewan's agriculture Saskatchewan's flower
Canada England

ISBN: 978-1-897164-32-7

23 Alberta

There are three physical regions in Alberta: Interior Plains, Cordillera, and Canadian Shield. The province produces both crops and **oil**.

A. Label the physical regions of Alberta and describe them with the given words.

Physical Regions of Alberta

Canadian Shield	ancient rock	
Interior Plains	Cordillera	lakes
mountains	flat	fertile

C________ S________

- forests, ________ , ________

I________ P________

- ________ and ________ land

C________________

- ________________

B. Match the symbols on Alberta's coat of arms with the descriptions. Write the correct letters.

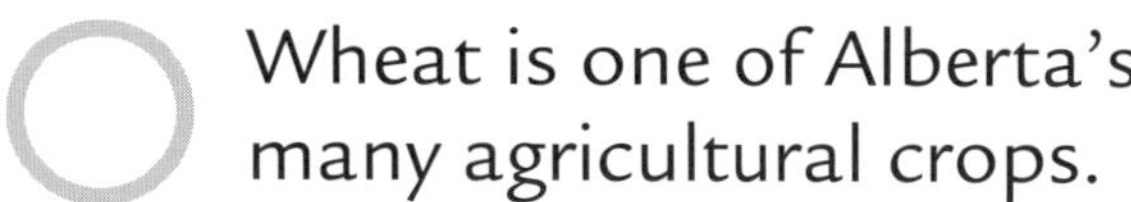 Wheat is one of Alberta's many agricultural crops.

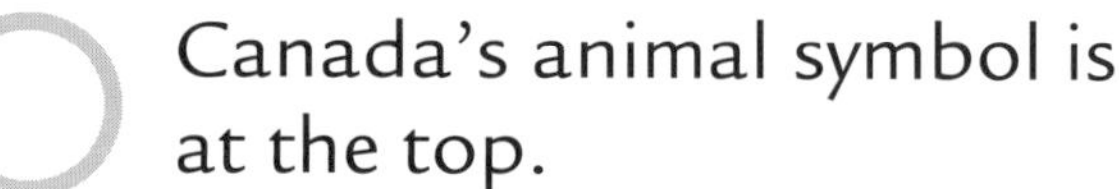 Canada's animal symbol is at the top.

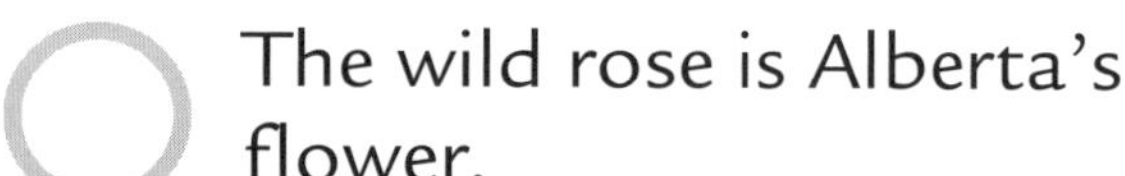 The wild rose is Alberta's flower.

 The Cordillera is represented on the shield.

ISBN: 978-1-897164-32-7

C. **Fill in the blanks with the given words to tell about Alberta's oil industry. Then circle the oil words in the word search.**

ground fuel plant plastics

Animal and __________ fossils are the source of Alberta's thriving oil industry. The oil is pumped out of the __________ and refined to make products like __________ and motor __________ .

petroleum gasoline refinery pollutants pipeline drilling energy oil sands well fossil fuel

p	e	t	r	d	r	i	l	l	i	n	g	i	s	a	g
p	e	p	o	l	l	u	t	a	n	t	s	z	r	p	a
e	n		p	o	l	l	u	t	e	f	u	e	e	i	
t	o	i	l		s	a	n	d	s	p	e	r	f	p	
r	e		f	i	u	l	f	u	e	i	y	e	i	e	
o	r	w	a	e	n	e	r	g	y	p	r	t	n	u	
l	o	e	s	l	g	g	a	s	f	e	o	n	e	a	
e	i	l	s	i	n	i	p	e	r	l	r	e	r		
u	s	l	i	g	p	o	w	e	l	i	g	g	y		
m	l	r	l	g	a	s	o	l	i	n	e	e			
d	f	o	s	s	i	l		f	u	e	l	s			

ISBN: 978-1-897164-32-7

24

British Columbia

Many place names in British Columbia have an interesting history. Because this province has **mountains** but is next to the **ocean**, it has regions with very different climates and vegetations.

A. Match these name histories with the place names on this BC map. Write the correct place names.

1. This northern city was named after a famous explorer.

   ____

2. This city was named after the Queen of England at the time.

   ____

3. This is the largest city of the province, named after a Pacific north coast explorer.

   ____

4. This city is northwest of Vancouver, and its name is a shortened version of "komuckway", an Aboriginal word meaning "plenty".

   ____

5. There used to be lots of salmon here.

   ____

6. This old mining town is near the centre of the province and was named after a businessman who first struck it rich here.

   ____

ISBN: 978-1-897164-32-7

B. Match these pictures with the descriptions of two BC regions. Write the correct letters.

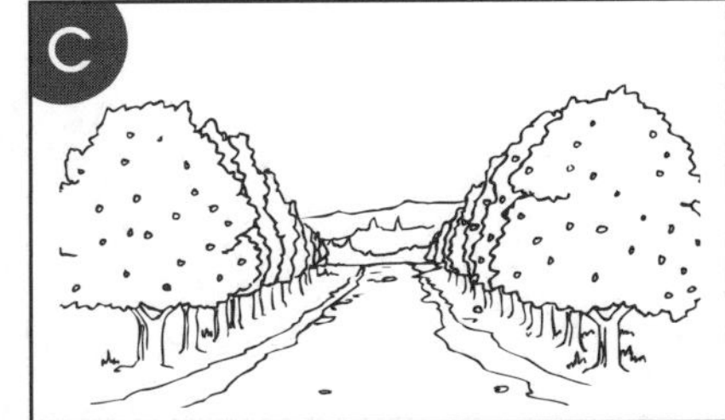

Northwest Coast

- *whales*
- *inlets*
- *rainforest*
- *mountains*

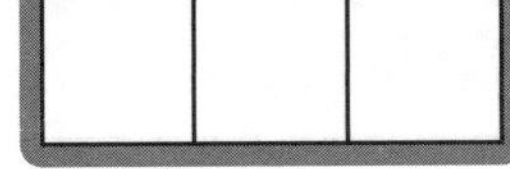

Okanagan Valley

- *desert climate*
- *irrigation for growing fruit*

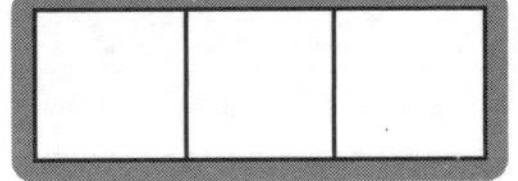

C. Look at the coat of arms of BC and circle the correct answers.

1. There is a Canadian / British flag.
2. There is a setting sun / moon .
3. There are three crowns / dogwood flowers .
4. There are seven crowns / dogwood flowers near the motto.

ISBN: 978-1-897164-32-7

Review

A. Jason is showing Linda the medieval power structure. Help him write the correct word and letter in each level.

lords king serfs knights

Ⓐ We obey our lord, work on his land and use it to grow food for his family and for ourselves.

Ⓑ We wear an armour and know how to ride a horse. We go to battle for our lords whenever needed.

Ⓒ We dine on delicious meals of roasts, stews, and pudding. We love wine, and especially enjoy eating swan.

Ⓓ I live in a huge castle guarded by knights. I am above everyone in the entire kingdom.

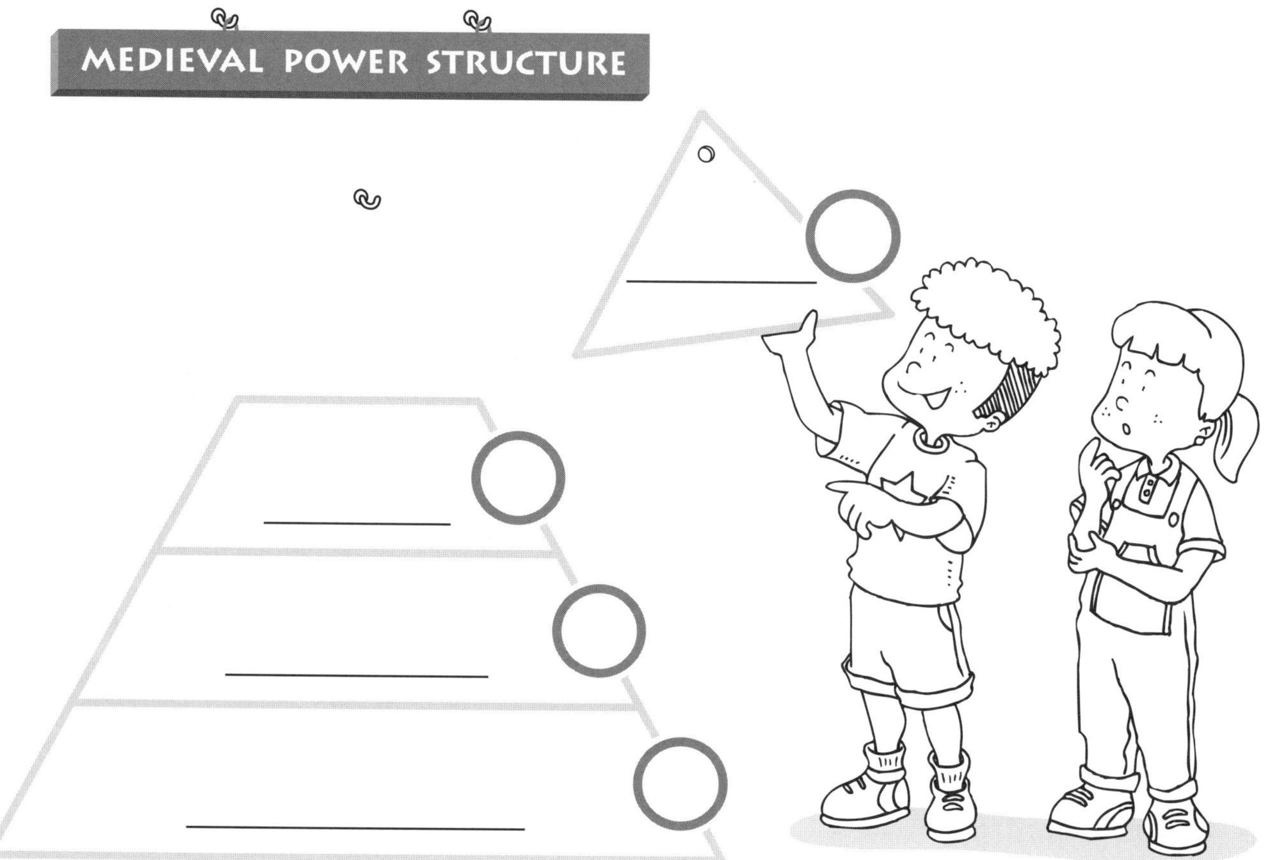

ISBN: 978-1-897164-32-7

B. Jason shows Linda his model castle. Help him label the pictures and draw lines to match them with the correct descriptions.

gatehouse moat loopholes turret drawbridge

- encloses the courtyard
- entrance to the castle
- place for keeping watch
- small windows for shooting out arrows
- can be lowered for entry and raised for protection
- water-filled ditch around the castle
- courtyard of the castle

ISBN: 978-1-897164-32-7

Review

C. Jason is pretending to be a medieval mason. Help him circle or write the correct answers.

1. A medieval mason belonged to a ________ .
   - A. food guild
   - B. builders guild
   - C. clothing guild

2. A builders guild included ________ .
   - A. carpenters, masons, and tilers
   - B. carpenters, masons, and spinsters
   - C. tailors, bakers, and brewers

3. A clothing guild included ________ .
   - A. tailors, spinsters, and brewers
   - B. spinsters, shearmen, and tailors
   - C. shearmen, butchers, and carpenters

4. Masons chiselled a mark on each of their bricks to ________ .
   - A. show their chiselling skill
   - B. get praised for their work
   - C. get paid for their work

5. Write "mason", "baker", or "tailor" for these badges:

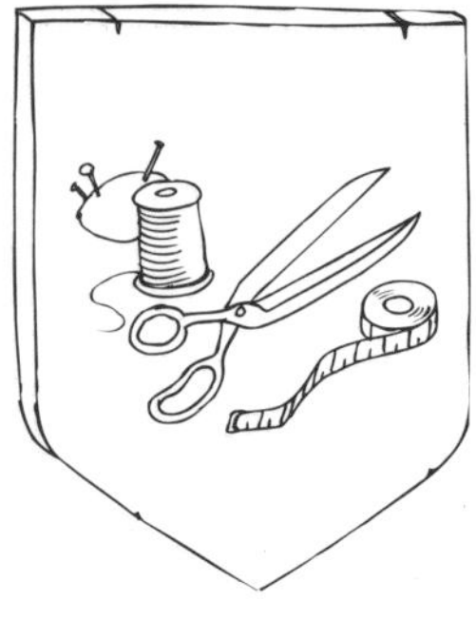 ____________________

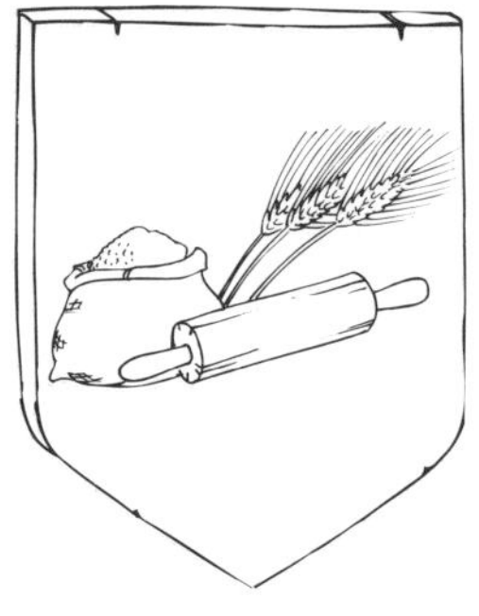 ____________________

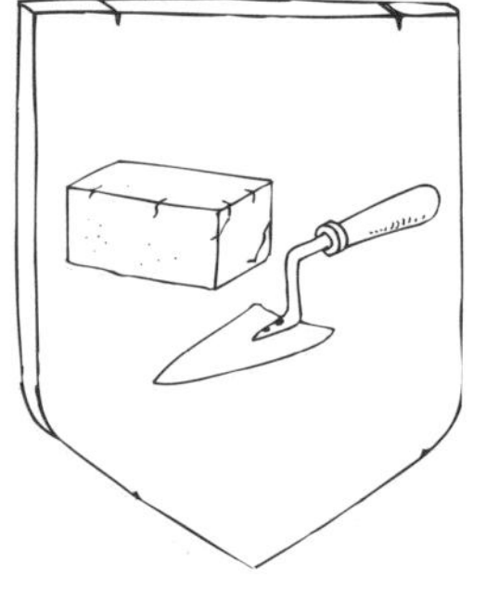 ____________________

ISBN: 978-1-897164-32-7

D. Jason tells Sam about medieval farmers' chores. Help him circle the correct answers.

Medieval farmers used flails / scythes to harvest corn, which was made into wine / flour . During the spring / fall season, they picked ripe grapes / oranges to make wine. In order to have enough meat, they needed to fatten up the cows / pigs by taking them to the woods so that they could feed on wild nuts / animals .

E. Sam shows Jason the coats of arms of two Canadian territories. Label them and tell what mineral is symbolized on both.

Territories: Yukon Nunavut Northwest Territories
Minerals: gold silver diamond

1

Territory: ______________

Mineral: ______________

2

Territory: ______________

Mineral: ______________

ISBN: 978-1-897164-32-7

F. Use the clues on these coats of arms and your knowledge of Canada's provinces to fill in the blanks.

1. Cordillera (Canadian Rockies):

   ____

2. Interior Plains (flat and fertile land):

   ____

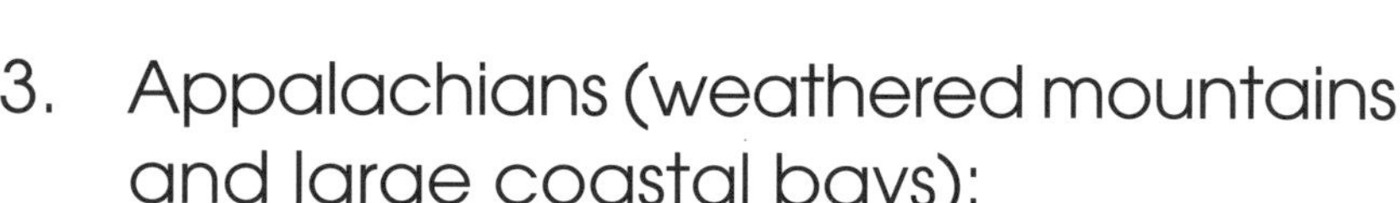

3. Appalachians (weathered mountains and large coastal bays):

   ____

4. Seafood can be found in:

   ____

5. Wheat can be harvested in:

   ____

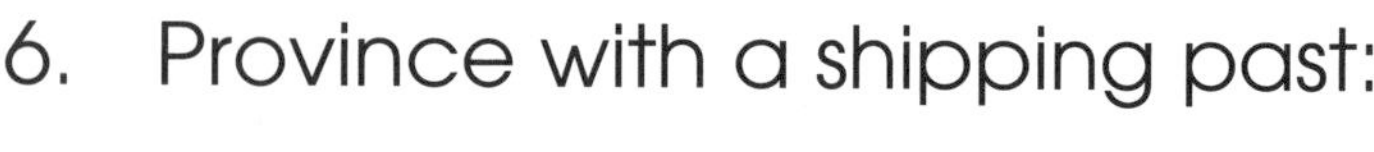

6. Province with a shipping past:

   ____

ISBN: 978-1-897164-32-7

G. Sam and Jason are looking at a map of Canada. Help them match the physical regions with the descriptions. Then circle the correct answers.

Hudson Bay Lowlands Great Lakes-St. Lawrence Lowlands
Cordillera Arctic Lands Canadian Shield

1. ____________________ : *ancient rock and thick forests*
2. ____________________ : *continuously frozen ground and ice caps*
3. ____________________ : *mountain ranges and plateaus*
4. ____________________ : *lots of swamps*
5. ____________________ : *lush farmland*

6. Mountains / Forests make up much of Ontario, which is in the Cordillera / Canadian Shield .

7. The Great Lakes-St. Lawrence Lowlands is a fertile / dry region. It plays an important role in the economy of Manitoba / Quebec .

8. The Cordillera covers Yukon, the Northwest Territories, British Columbia, and Saskatchewan / Alberta . The region is in Eastern / Western Canada.

ISBN: 978-1-897164-32-7

ISBN: 978-1-897164-32-7

ISBN: 978-1-897164-32-7

1

Habitats

- *A habitat is a place where plants and animals live and grow.*
- *Plants and animals must have everything they need for health in their habitats.*

A. Look at the favourite food and things of the animals. Write the animals' habitats on the lines.

wetlands cave carpet desert savanna underground

Trumpeter Swan

Food:
aquatic plants, snails

Things:
grassy areas, water

Habitat:

1. ____________

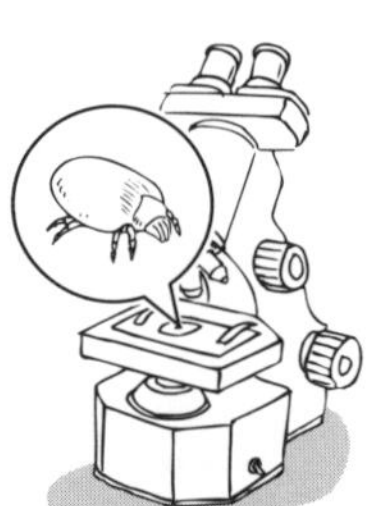

Dust Mite

Food:
human skin flakes

Things:
warmth, humidity

Habitat:

2. ____________

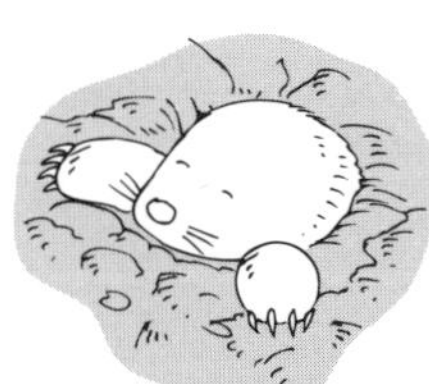

Mole

Food:
worms

Things:
dark, damp places

Habitat:

3. ____________

Roadrunner

Food:
lizards, insects

Things:
space to run

Habitat:

4. ____________

Giraffe

Food:
tree leaves, grass

Things:
dry, open space, tall trees

Habitat:

5. ____________

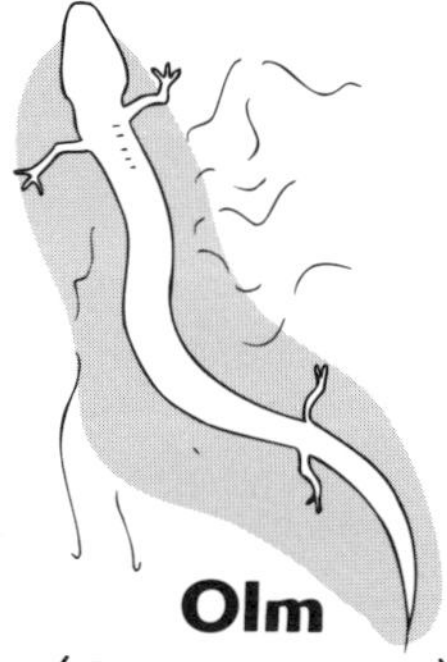

Olm
(Cave Salamander)

Food:
worms, can go years without food

Things:
dark, wet places

Habitat:

6. ____________

ISBN: 978-1-897164-32-7

B. Help the zookeeper prepare the correct habitat for each animal. Put a check mark in the correct boxes.

	Polar Bear	Black Bear
Ice floes		
Chilly water		
Forest		
Shrubs and berries		
Fresh fish and seal meat		
Fish streams		
Large space to roam		

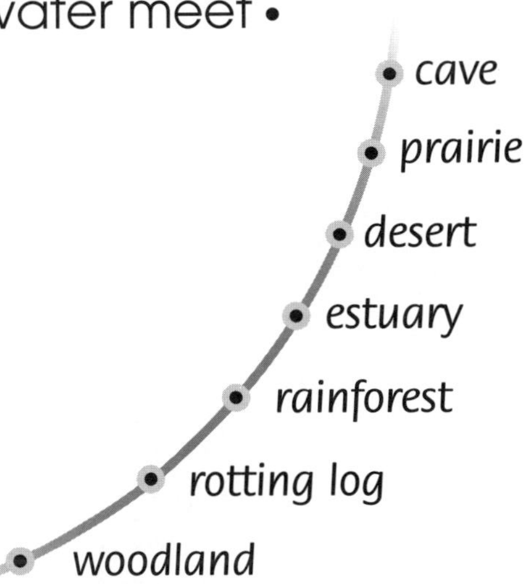

C. Draw lines to match the descriptions with the habitats.

1. a place where salt water and fresh water meet •
2. dry and hot, with little plant life •
3. dark, rocky, and often wet •
4. a decomposing structure •
5. very wet and forested •
6. flat, grassy land •
7. forest of trees •

• cave
• prairie
• desert
• estuary
• rainforest
• rotting log
• woodland

Science Fact

The habitat of an insect can be as small as a space in your backyard, while the habitat of a whale can be as large as all the world's oceans.

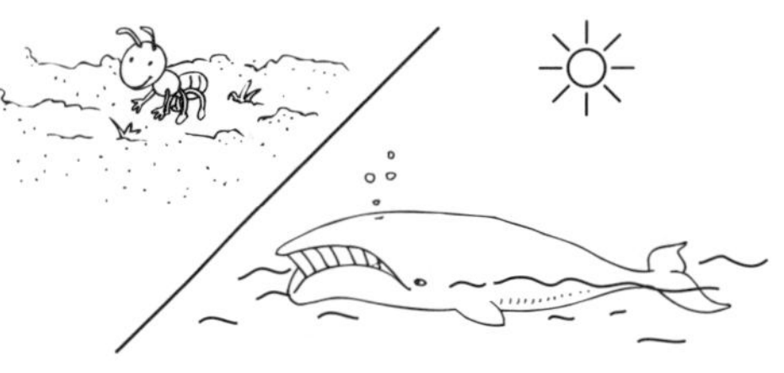

ISBN: 978-1-897164-32-7

2

Producers and Consumers

- Living things are either producers or consumers.
- Animals can be grouped by the type of food they eat.

A. Read what they say. Help them fill in the blanks with the words in bold. Then sort the things by writing the letters in the circles and draw one more item for each group.

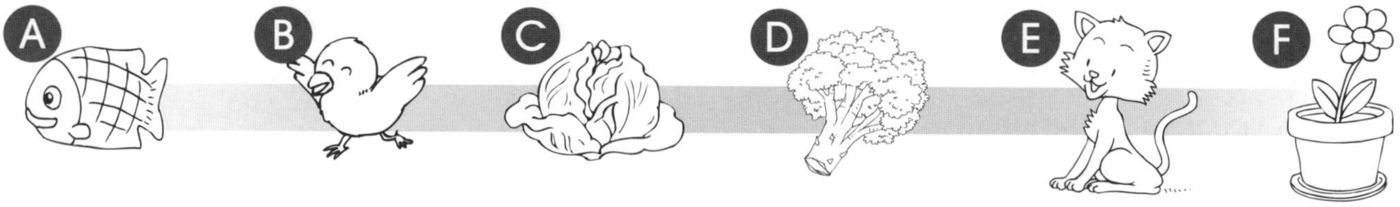

A B C D E F

Plants are **producers** because they make their own food with energy from the sun.

____

Animals are **consumers** because they get their energy by eating plants or other animals.

____

ISBN: 978-1-897164-32-7

B. Fill in the missing letters to complete the words. Then help the animals find their favourite food. Circle the answers.

Types of Animals

H__ __b__ __o__e
(eat plants only)

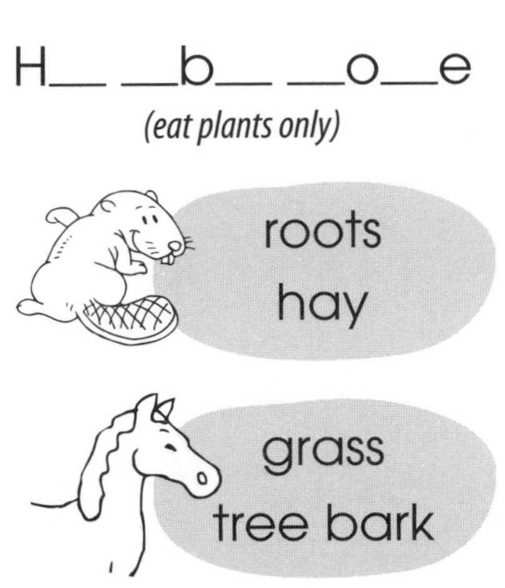

__ar__ __ __or__
(eat animals only)

__m__ __v__r__
(eat both plants and animals)

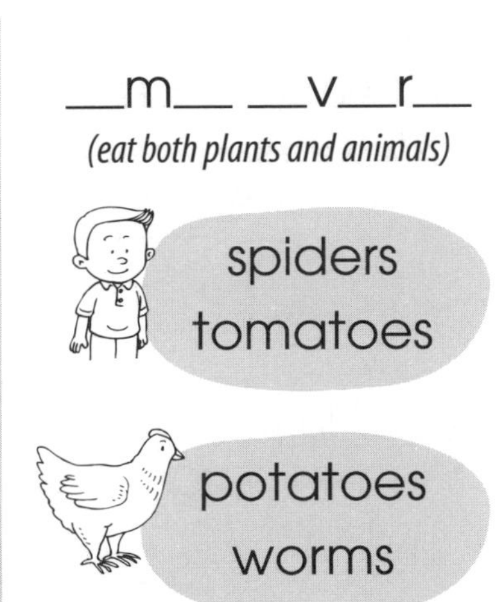

C. Colour the dinosaurs that were probably carnivores.

Most carnivorous dinosaurs had strong, sharp teeth for tearing flesh. They could run quickly to catch their prey and grasp them with strong claws.

Science Fact

A panda bear is physically a carnivore, though it behaves like a herbivore by eating only plant material.

ISBN: 978-1-897164-32-7

3

Food Chains

- *A food chain shows the order that animals eat plants and other animals.*

A. Draw the missing link in each food chain with the help of the given pictures.

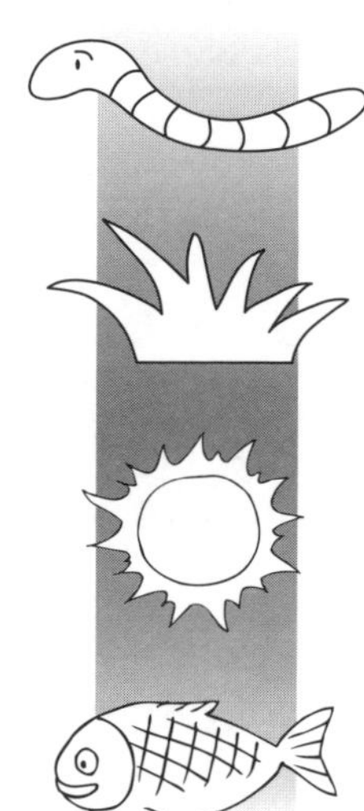

1. sun ➔ ☐ ➔ cow
2. sun ➔ algae ➔ ☐
3. sun ➔ leaf ➔ ☐ ➔ small bird
4. ☐ ➔ grain ➔ hen ➔ human

B. Circle the correct words to complete the sentences.

1. Every food chain starts with the plant / sun .

2. The link following the sun in any food chain is the producer / consumer .
3. The arrow (➔) in a food chain means "provides food for" / "eats" .
4. In any food chain, the animals are always producers / consumers .

ISBN: 978-1-897164-32-7

C. Find the animals that eat the salmon at its different life stages. Write the letters.

As salmon go through their life cycle, their habitat changes. As their habitat changes, they become a part of different food chains.

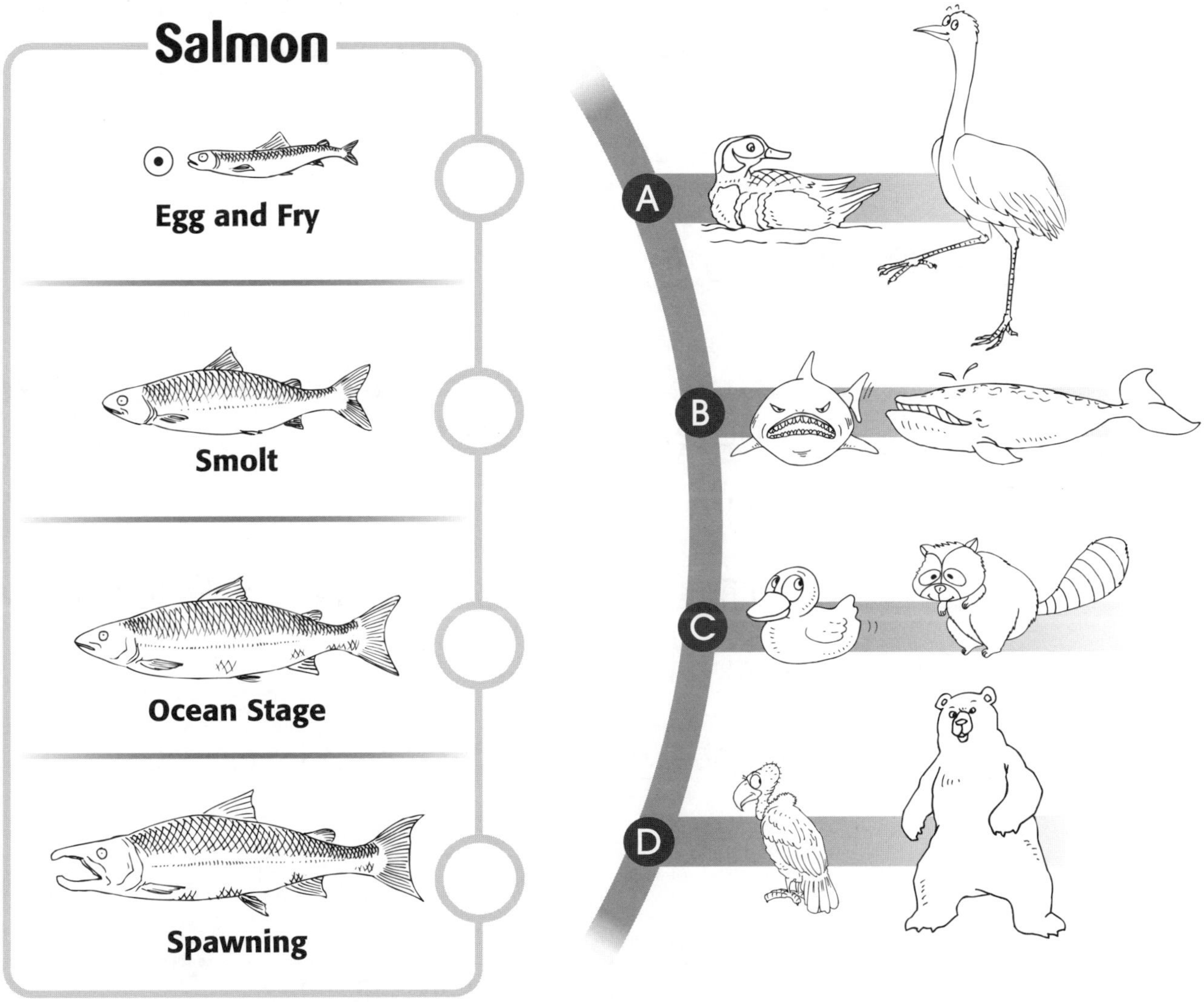

Salmon

Egg and Fry	
Smolt	
Ocean Stage	
Spawning	

A
B
C
D

Science Fact

A food chain can be thought of as a cycle. As the consumers die and provide food for decomposers like fungi, they in turn provide food for new plants.

ISBN: 978-1-897164-32-7

Adaptations

I can change colours to adapt to different environments.

- *Adaptations are traits animals or plants develop to survive in a habitat.*
- *An adaptation can be physical or something about the way an animal or a plant behaves.*

A. Fill in the blanks with the given words to tell the reasons for adaptations. Then find the animals that show these kinds of adaptations.

defence movement feeding

Reasons for Adaptations

- ______________ – to protect themselves against predators and extreme weather

  e.g. __________

- ______________ – to find and reach the available food easily

  e.g. __________

- ______________ – to get where they need to go easily

  e.g. __________

Ⓐ  fur changes to colour of snow in winter

Ⓑ  long beak can reach nectar

Ⓒ  long toes help move on mud

Ⓓ 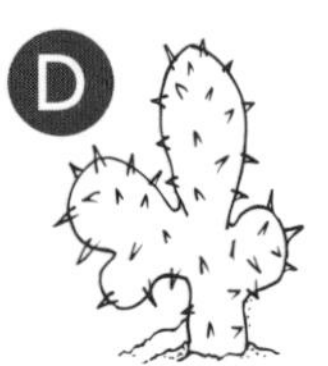 store water for drier times

Ⓔ  small horns on head protect when fighting

ISBN: 978-1-897164-32-7

B. Read the poem. Tell what each line describes. Fill in the blank with "behavioural" or "physical".

Why do geese travel in groups?
Why do bees fly loop-the-loop?
Why do a sea lion's nostrils close?
Why do some birds have only three toes?

- 1st line: the ________________ adaptation of geese
- 2nd line: the ________________ adaptation of bees
- 3rd line: the ________________ adaptation of the sea lion
- 4th line: the ________________ adaptation of some birds

C. Draw lines to match the sentences with the correct feet.

1. An eagle can grasp and carry a fish from water to nest with its feet.
2. A duck moves well in water.
3. A finch can rest on the thinnest tree branch.
4. A chicken is unable to fly or swim, but it scratches for food on the ground.

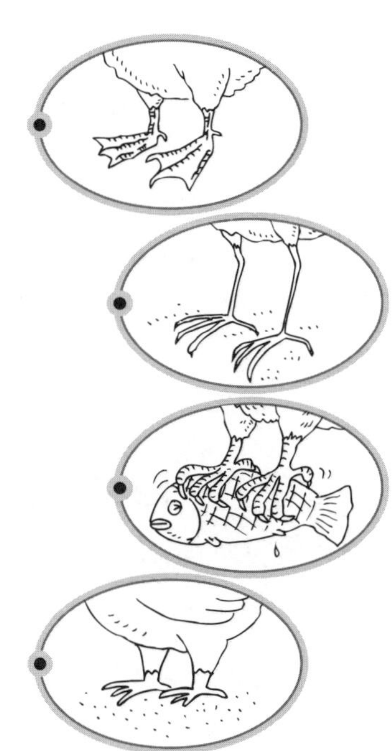

Science Fact

The web-footed gecko's webbed feet are adapted not for swimming, but for staying atop a sandy desert.

ISBN: 978-1-897164-32-7

5

Habitat Destruction

- *Humans depend on plants and animals and their habitats.*
- *When we take things from nature, habitats can be harmed or destroyed.*
- *We recognize and categorize the plants and animals at risk of disappearing.*

A. See how we use animals, plants, and their habitats in our lives. Fill in the blanks with the correct words. Then cross out the one that does not belong in each group.

Building Material Clothing Energy
Food Medicine Recreation

1. ______________

cotton fur
leather plastic

2. ______________

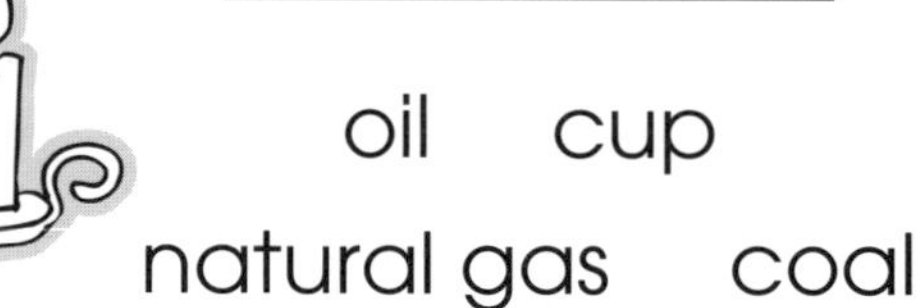

oil cup
natural gas coal

3. ______________

jello ginseng
aspirin aloe gel

4. ______________

rock quarry hay
lumber wheat

5. ______________

skiing boating
hiking cleaning

6. ______________

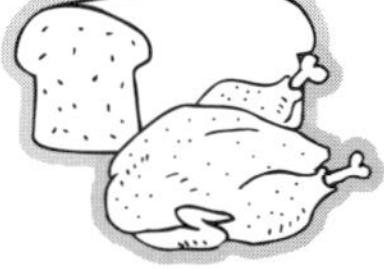

wheat meat
pencil corn

ISBN: 978-1-897164-32-7

B. Find the different ways human activities can harm or destroy different habitats. Match the pictures with the descriptions. Write the letters.

Loss of habitat due to human activity:

- ( ) Oil extraction
- ( ) Oil spill
- ( ) Hydroelectric dam
- ( ) Air pollution
- ( ) Development
- ( ) Logging

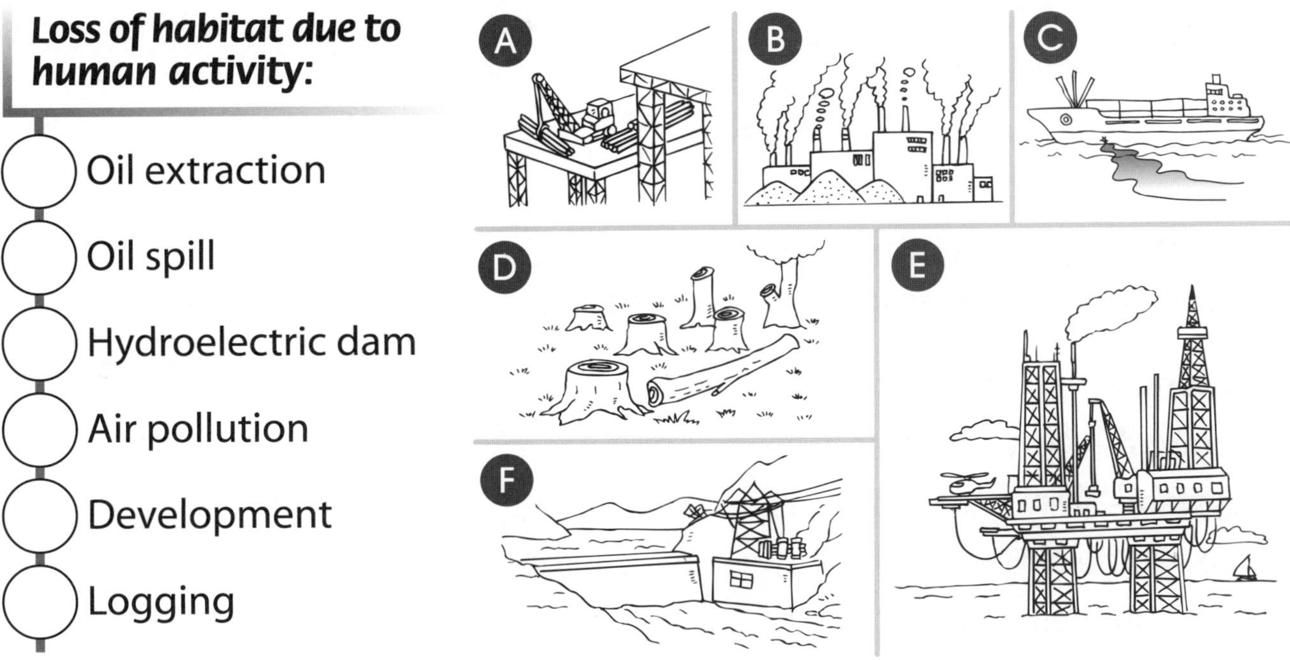

C. See how we define the different levels of danger for species at risk. Write the words in bold on the lines to complete the chart.

Endangered species:
This species is facing future extinction or extirpation.

Species of special concern:
Something has happened to put the species at risk.

Extirpated species:
This species no longer exists in Canada.

Threatened species:
Something must be done to prevent this species from becoming endangered.

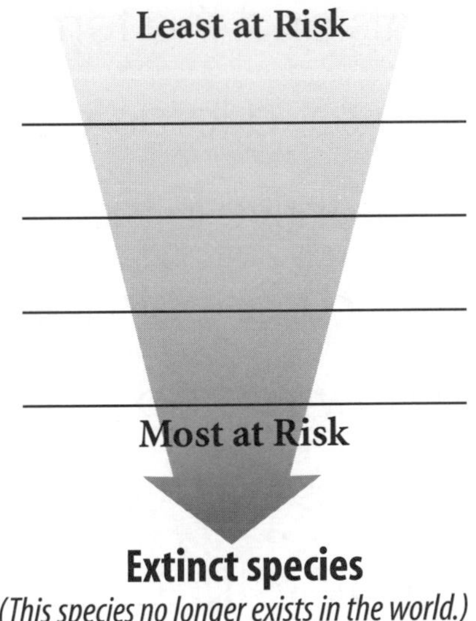

Extinct species
(This species no longer exists in the world.)

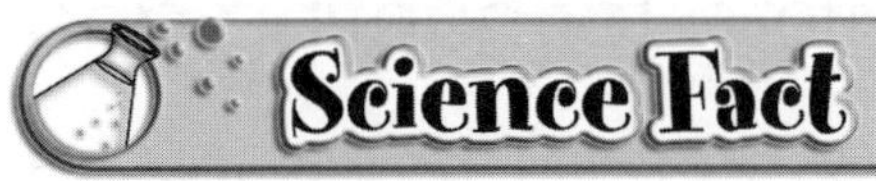

Landfills take up space and habitats. Reduce your garbage to help save the homes of some plants and animals.

ISBN: 978-1-897164-32-7

6

The Arctic

- *The Arctic is habitat for animals and plants adapted to cold weather.*
- *A food web can show the relationships among Arctic animals.*

A. Fill in the blanks with the given words to complete the passage about the Arctic.

community – group of living things
permafrost – frozen earth that never thaws
ecosystem – living things and their environment
biome – large environment with the same characteristics
tundra – northern land in climates too cold for most plants
ecological niche – the role a living thing has in support of its ecosystem

Much of the Arctic is treeless 1.____________ . There is little soil for plants and the temperature is extremely cold in the dark winter. Even so, a large community of perfectly adapted animals and plants thrive in the Arctic 2.____________ . The permanently frozen ground beneath the shallow soil excludes deep-rooted plants, but shallow-rooted plants grow happily above the 3.____________ . Birds, insects, and many marine and land animals are also part of the Arctic 4.____________ . Food is abundant in the summer, and the long daylight hours give plenty of time for hunting and growing. All living things in the Arctic have a role to play: an 5.____________ that drives the Arctic 6.____________ .

ISBN: 978-1-897164-32-7

B. **Read the clues. Complete the Arctic food web and answer the questions.**

Polar Bears

Killer Whales

Ringed Seals

Squid

Arctic Cod

Plankton

Arctic Food Web

- Squid eat **krill.**
- **Caribou** are eaten by polar bears.
- **Bowhead whales** eat plankton.

1. Killer whales and ringed seals both eat: ____________________
2. Plankton is eaten by: ______________________________

C. **Match the descriptions with the things that humans wear in similar weather.**

1. Caribou have wider hooves than their southern relatives, better for walking on snow.
2. Polar bears have an extra eyelid to help prevent snow blindness.
3. The Arctic fox is a short-eared fox. A body part that sticks out is one that loses heat fast.
4. The long, thick coat of a musk-ox will get it through the worst winter storm.

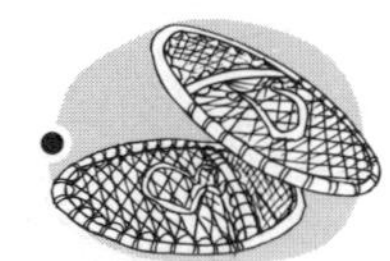

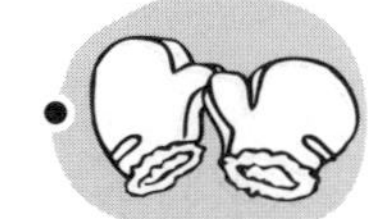

Science Fact

The reindeer of northern Europe is the same species as the caribou of northern Canada.

ISBN: 978-1-897164-32-7

7

Light

I'm brighter.

OFF

- *Light is a form of energy that is found naturally or artificially in the universe.*
- *Light travels in straight lines, reflecting off some objects, and bending as it passes from one medium to another.*

A. Look at the "light" in each picture. Classify it with the given words.

natural / artificial **light producer / light reflector**

1.

Moon:

______________ ; ______________

Cat:

______________ ; ______________

Flashlight:

______________ ; ______________

Lightning:

______________ ; ______________

2.

Sun:

______________ ; ______________

Water:

______________ ; ______________

Candle:

______________ ; ______________

Sunglasses:

______________ ; ______________

ISBN: 978-1-897164-32-7

B. Read the properties of light. Then draw lines to match them with the movie posters that illustrate the properties.

Properties* of Light

* Properties are the special things or powers that an object has.

Light travels in straight lines. •

Light can pass through some things but not others. •

Light can be reflected by shiny objects. •

Light bends as it passes from one medium to another. •

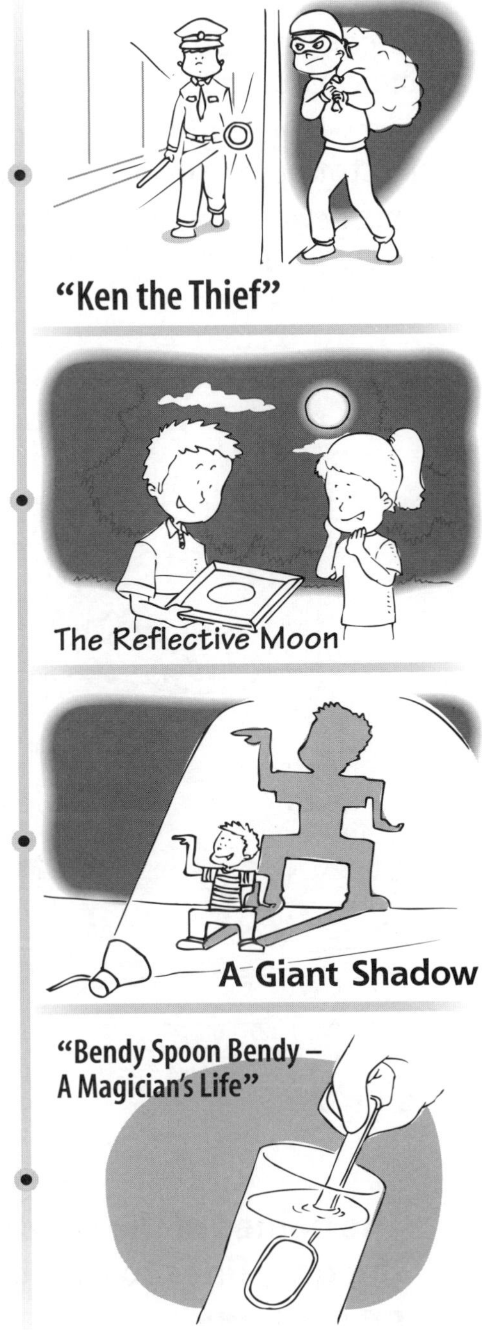

Science Fact

Light travels at more than one billion kilometres in an hour.

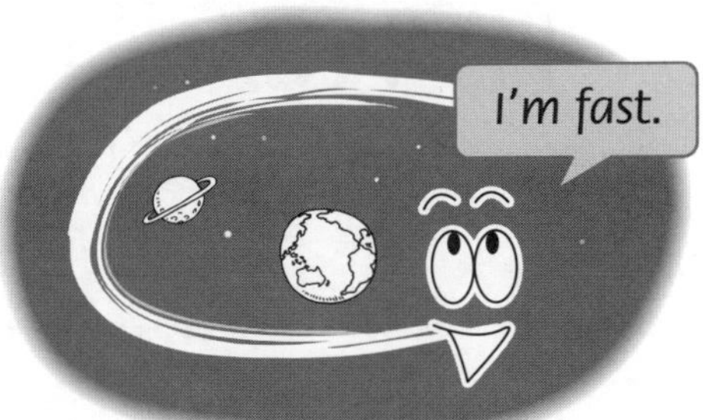

ISBN: 978-1-897164-32-7

8

Light – Reflection and Refraction

- We can see something because light is bouncing or reflecting off that thing.
- Lenses bend light, or refract it, making objects appear smaller or larger.
- Some devices use reflection and refraction to help us see things better.

A. Colour the objects that reflect green and the objects that refract red.

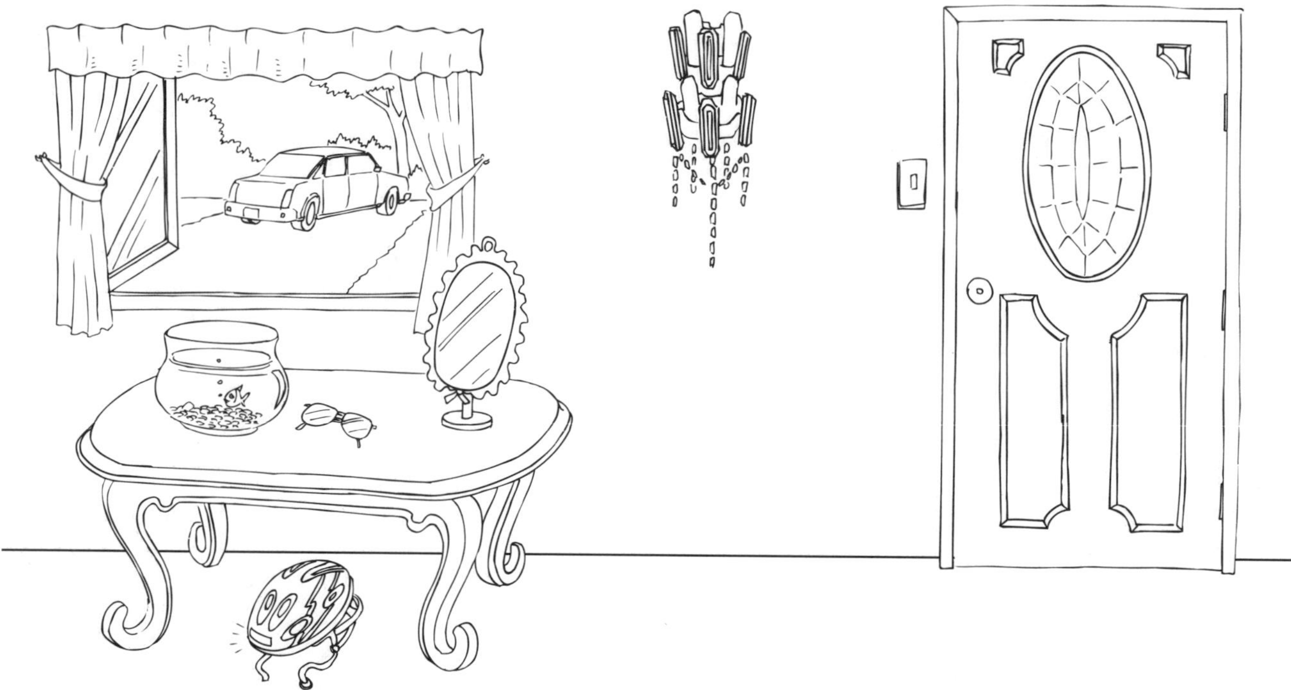

B. The names of the children are reflected in a mirror. Put a mirror along the grey lines to find out their names in normal form and write them on the lines.

NANCY

BRIAN

My name is ________________ .

My name is ________________ .

ISBN: 978-1-897164-32-7

C. **Read the clues and fill in the missing letters to complete the names of the devices. Then draw lines to match the devices with their images.**

kaleidoscope microscope telescope

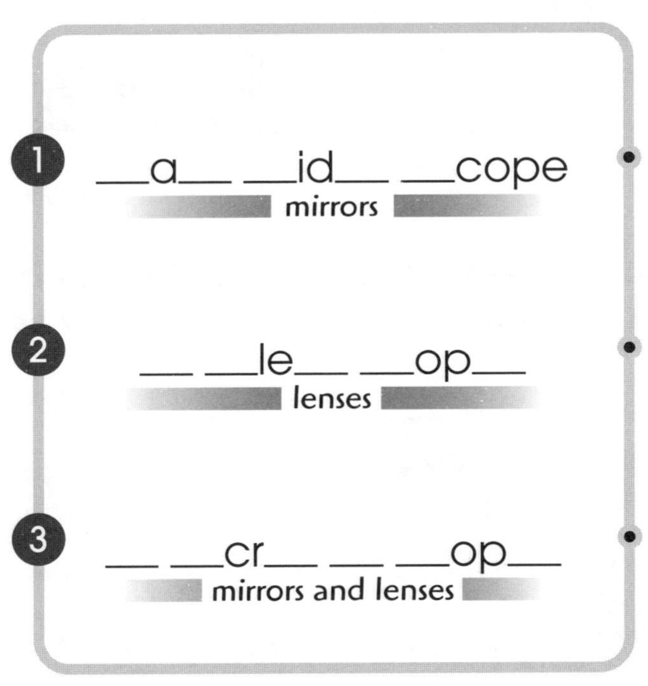

1
__a__ __id__ __cope
mirrors
2
__ __le__ __op__
lenses
3
__ __cr__ __ __op__
mirrors and lenses

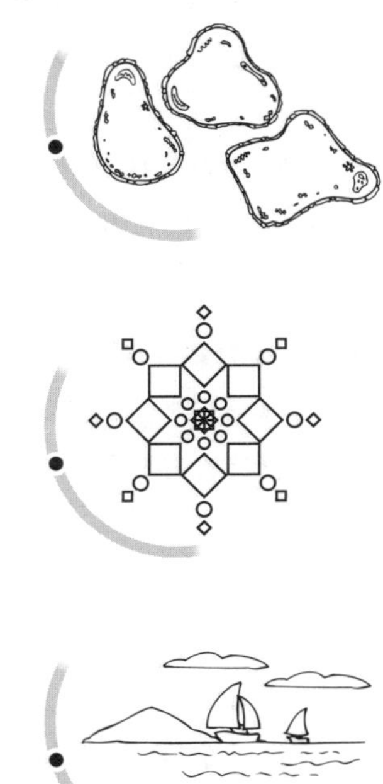

Experiment – Fun with Refraction

Put a penny into a soup bowl on a table. With the bowl in front of you, sit down and slouch in your chair so that when you look at the bowl, the penny is just barely out of sight. Then, without changing your position or moving your head, pour water into the bowl. What do you see?

____

____

Science Fact

A periscope makes it possible to see things from a hidden position. It is widely used on submarines.

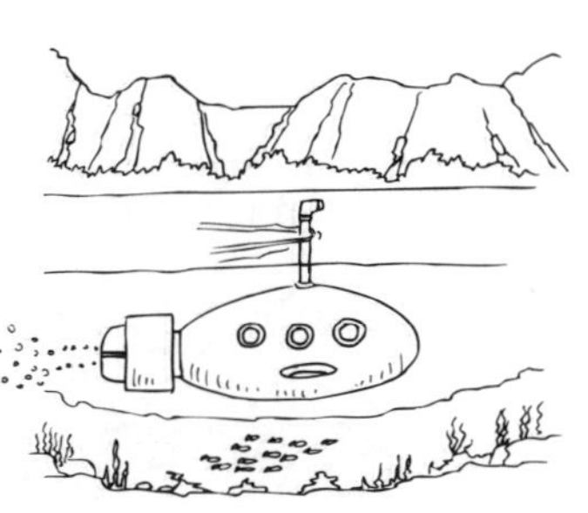

ISBN: 978-1-897164-32-7

9

Light – Transparency

- *Materials that easily allow light to pass through are said to be transparent. A translucent material allows some light to pass through, while an opaque material doesn't allow light to pass through it at all.*
- *Shadows are a result of light not being able to pass through objects.*

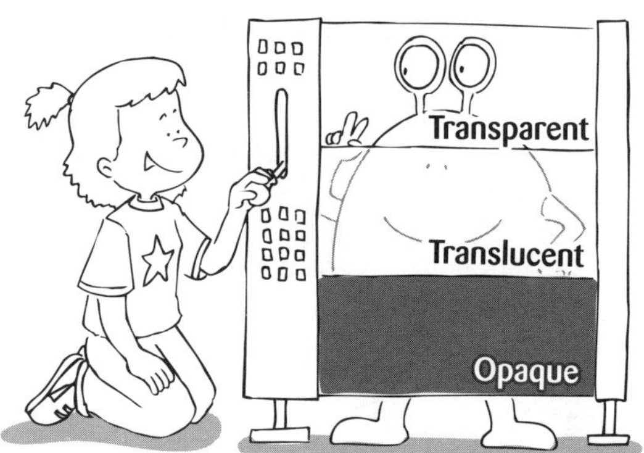
Transparent
Translucent
Opaque

A. Choose the best word to describe the material being talked about in each picture. Then give an example that has the same property as the one mentioned.

transparent translucent opaque

1.

This unit provides the total darkness that these plants need, at least for the time being.

____

Example:

____

2.

I can see the clothes clearly through this clean and nice window.

____

Example:

____

3.

This weave will allow just the perfect amount of late afternoon light to enter your lovely living room.

____

Example:

____

ISBN: 978-1-897164-32-7

B. Read what Judy says. Look at the location of the shadow in each picture. Put a check mark in the circle if it is correct; otherwise, put a cross and draw the correct one in the picture.

Light travels in a straight line and opaque objects absorb light. Therefore, the length of the shadow of an opaque object depends on where the light is coming from in relation to the object.

Experiment – Shadow Puppets

Take a flashlight with you into a dark room. You should stand about 1 m away from a clear wall and make different puppets with your hands in front of the flashlight. Look at the shadows cast on the wall.

Science Fact

The sundial was an ancient timepiece that used the shadow cast by the sun to tell time. As the sun travelled across the sky, the shadow would move and mark the time of day on the dial.

ISBN: 978-1-897164-32-7

10

Light and Colour

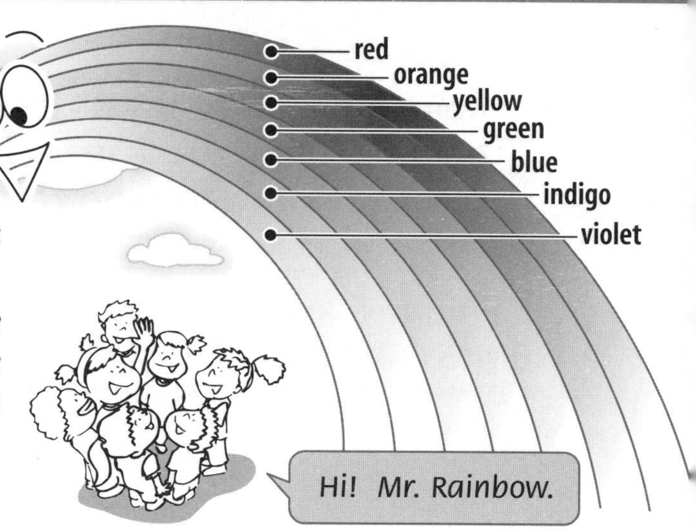

- *White light is made up of all the spectral colours of the rainbow.*
- *We can see the colour of an object because the object absorbs all the other colours of the spectrum, except the one seen. The colours seen is the colour reflected.*
- *Colours can be mixed to produce other colours.*

A. Read what Judy says. Help her colour the spectrum.

The glass prism has bent the beam of light into the spectral colours that make up white light. The order of the colours is the same as the one in the rainbow.

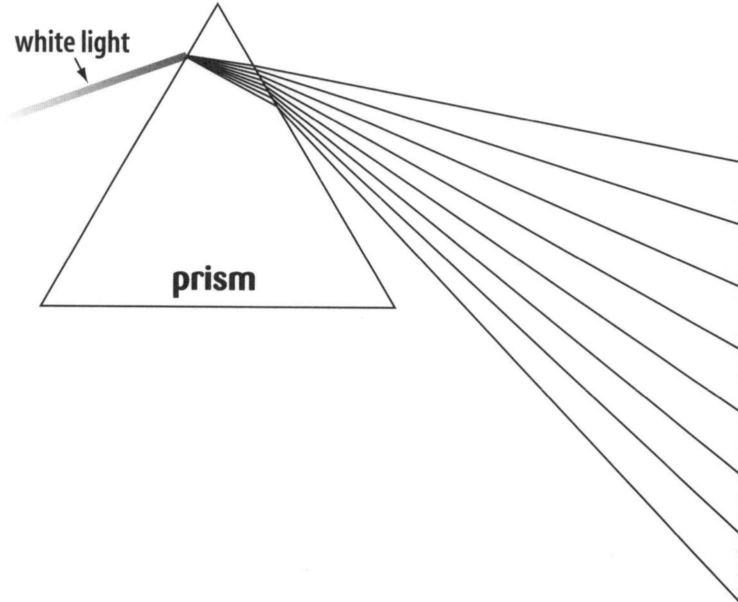

B. Fill in the blanks with "absorbs" or "reflects" to complete the sentences.

1. The grass looks green because it ____________ all colours except green.
2. A black cat is black because it ____________ all the colours that make up light.
3. A clean, white shirt appears white because it ____________ all the colours of the rainbow found in the white light that strikes it.

ISBN: 978-1-897164-32-7

C. **Colour the circles with acrylic paint. Then write what colours you can see in the overlapping area.**

- red + yellow = ____________
- red + blue = ____________
- yellow + blue = ____________

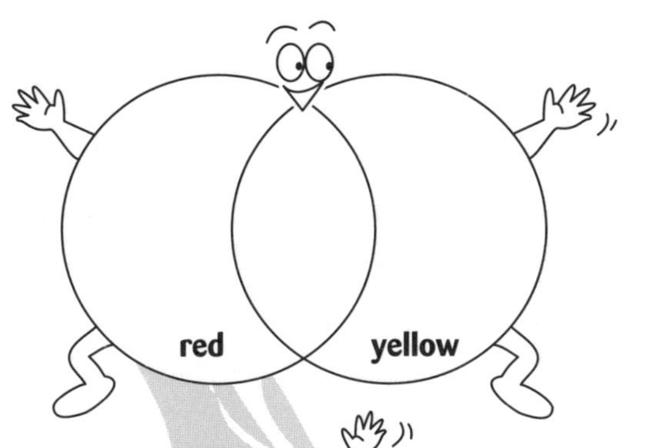

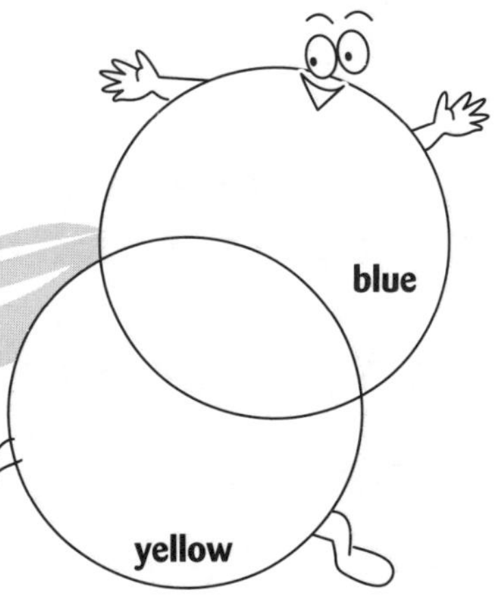

red blue

Try this

Trace the circles with tracing paper. Colour each section with a different colour in the given order. Cut out the whole thing and glue it on a cardboard. Use a sharp pencil to pierce the cardboard wheel through the centre, and place the pencil point on a table. Then spin it like a top.

Order of the colours: (from outside to inside)
red, orange, yellow, green, blue, indigo, violet

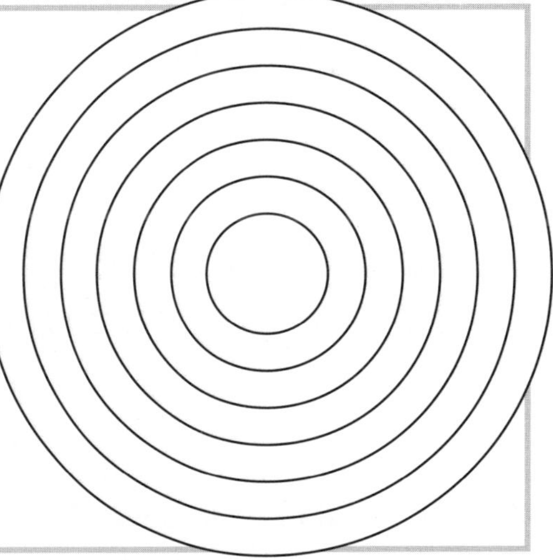

Science Fact

The light that we see is the "visible" part of something known as the electromagnetic spectrum (a bunch of types of radiation). Infrared light is often thought of as heat, and ultraviolet light is the invisible light that gives us sunburns if we stay too long in the sun.

ISBN: 978-1-897164-32-7

Sound

I like the low pitch of your drum.

- *Sounds are caused by vibrations. The faster something vibrates, the higher the pitch.*
- *The larger the vibration, the louder the sound.*
- *The human ear is a complex organ designed to detect vibrations, thus giving us information about our environment.*

A. Identify the animal that makes the sound. Tell whether the pitch is high or low.

Fruit Bat
African Elephant
Bottle-nosed Dolphin
Saint Bernard Dog
Humpback Whale

1. This very large pet does not bark very much.

   ____________________ ; __________ pitch

2. The clicking noise that this flying mammal makes allows it to "echolocate". It hunts and captures its food by using sound.

   ____________________ ; __________ pitch

3. Sounds made by this animal travels through the ground to tell family group members of its whereabouts.

   ____________________ ; __________ pitch

4. This animal uses squeals to communicate emotions as well as clicks to echolocate.

   ____________________ ; __________ pitch

5. *This water animal can make sounds, called "songs", that can be heard several hundred kilometres away.*

   ____________________ ; __________ pitch

ISBN: 978-1-897164-32-7

B. Fill in the blanks with the words given in the diagram.

Cross-Section of an Ear

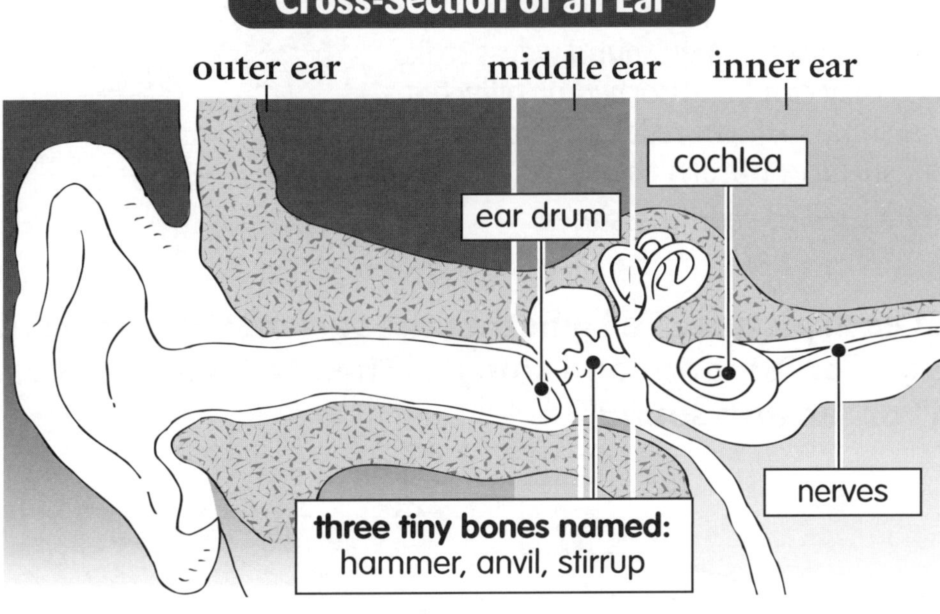

Sound is collected by the 1. ________________, which is made up of an earflap and a tunnel that leads to the 2. ________________, a thin-skinned structure. There are three tiny little bones your 3. ________________. These bones, the 4. ________________, 5. ________________, and 6. ________________ make the vibrations larger and send these vibrations to the 7. ________________. It is in this part, the 8. ________________, where the motion of the vibrations is changed into signals that are carried by 9. ________________ to your brain.

Science Fact

Vibrations cause sound, and the colliding of air molecules transmits the sound to us. There is no sound in space because there are no air molecules there.

ISBN: 978-1-897164-32-7

More about Sound

- *Sound travels in waves. When sound waves strike other things, they can be absorbed or reflected. Smooth and shiny surfaces reflect sound waves, while rough surfaces absorb them.*
- *Sound can be used to send messages.*

A. Look at each picture. Tell whether the surface the arrow is pointing at is "rough" or "smooth and shiny". Then tell whether it can "reflect sound" or "absorb sound".

1. 

_______________ ; _______________

2. 

_______________ ; _______________

3.

_______________ ; _______________

4. 

_______________ ;

____

5.

_______________ ; _______________

ISBN: 978-1-897164-32-7

B. Sound can be used to convey messages. Match the sounds with the correct messages.

1. "Wake up!" ◯
2. "Someone's stealing." ◯
3. "Get out of the house!" ◯
4. "Someone wants to talk to you." ◯

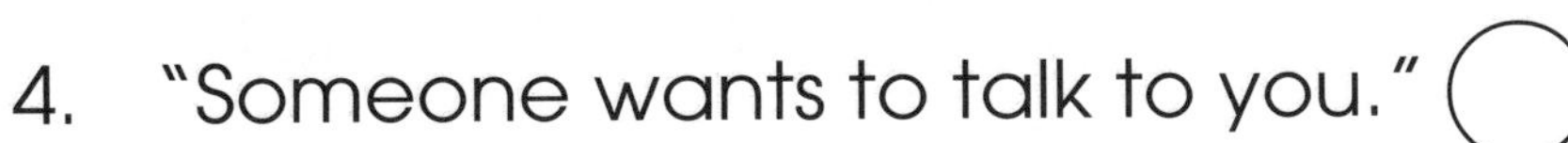

5. "Move your car to the right and stop!" ◯
6. "Someone outside wants your attention." ◯

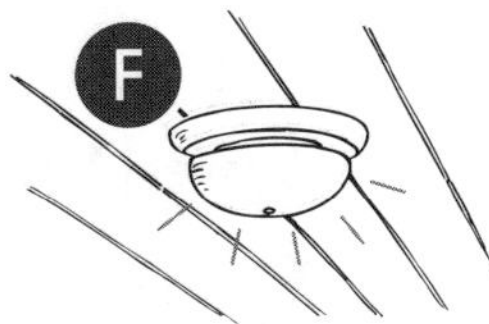

Experiment

You can do this experiment to see how well different materials absorb sound.

***Things needed*:**

- *1 shoe box with lid*
- *a tick-tock clock*
- *paper strips, dish towels, wood chips, etc. to use as insulators*

1. Put the shoe box on the table with the clock inside it and close the lid.
2. Open the box and fill it with a quantity of the first packing material you choose. Close the lid.
3. Stand back 1 metre and take note of how the loudness of the ticking of the clock has changed. Test with the other materials.

Science Fact

Sound travels at about 340 m/s. In 1947, Air Force pilot Chuck Yeager broke the sound barrier using a rocket-powered Bell X-1. This flight marked the first time a plane moved faster than the speed of sound. This speed resulted in a crashing sonic boom.

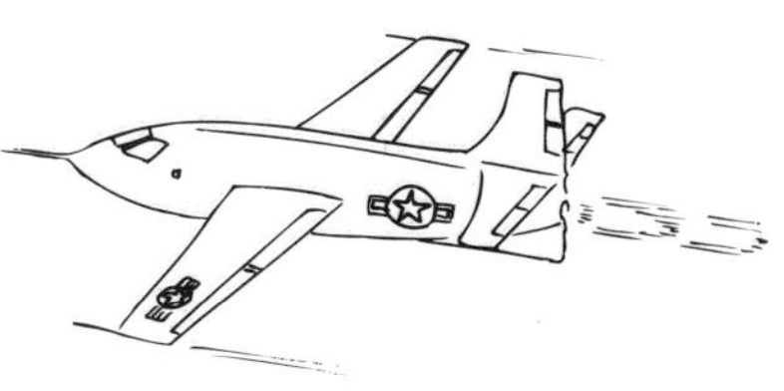

ISBN: 978-1-897164-32-7

Special Wheels – Gears and Pulleys

- Gears and pulleys are wheel-like simple machines that make our work easier. Gears have teeth and a pulley has a groove.
- When gears are linked together, they can change the speed and direction of movement.
- Sometimes we make our work easier by changing the direction of movement with the help of pulleys.

We make the work a lot easier.

A. Tell whether each object contains gears or pulleys in its mechanism. Write "gears" or "pulleys" on the line. Leave it blank if the mechanism contains neither.

1\.

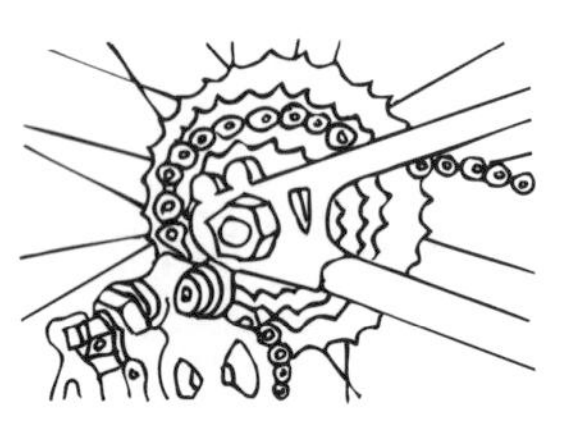

____

2\.

____

3\.

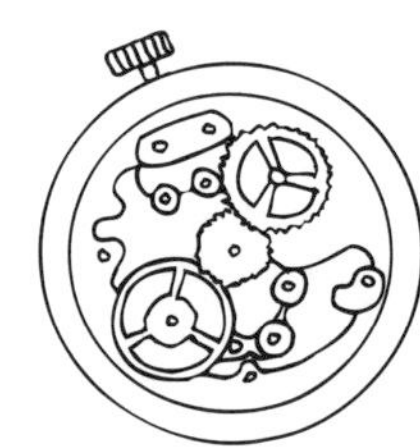

____

4\.

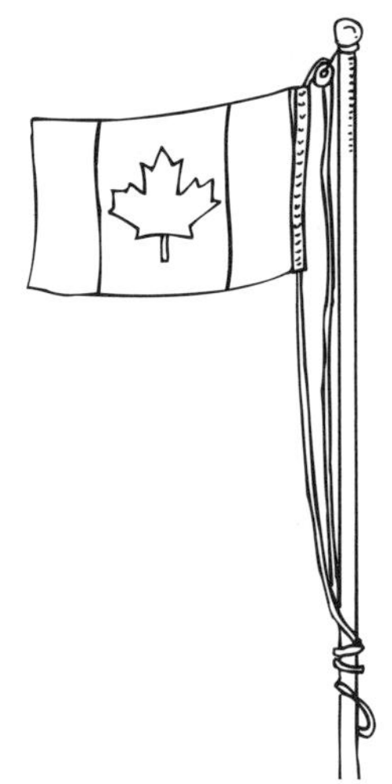

____

5\.

____

6\.

____

7\.

____

ISBN: 978-1-897164-32-7

B. Look at the gears. Draw arrows to show the directions that the shaded gears will turn. Then use the given words to describe how fast they turn.

as fast as faster than slower than

1. It turns ________________ the one on the left.

2. 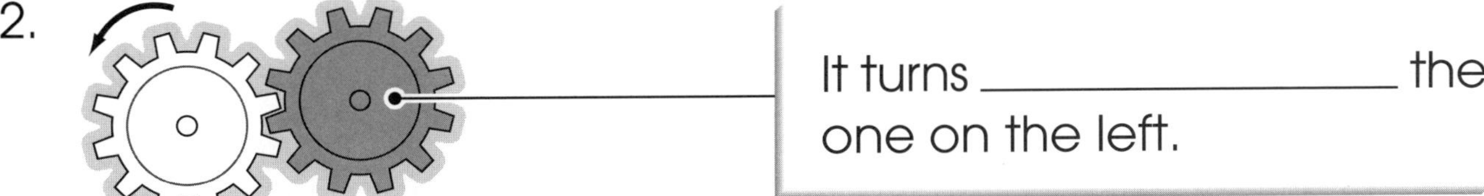

It turns ________________ the one on the left.

3. 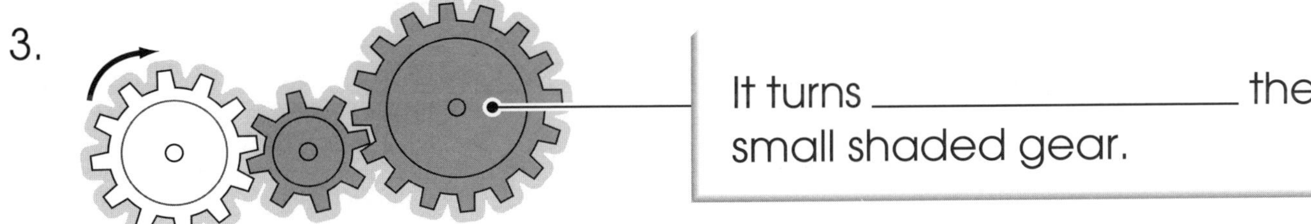

It turns ________________ the small shaded gear.

C. Look at the picture. Answer the question.

You can consider my weight.

How are the pulleys helping the mouse?

____

____

____

Science Fact

The world's highest flagpole is in North Korea. It is 157.5 m tall, and the flag at the top of it weighs 270 kg.

ISBN: 978-1-897164-32-7

14

Minerals

- *Minerals are non-living, solid substances that occur naturally.*
- *Minerals are what rocks are made of.*

A. Fill in the blanks with the given words.

non-living	**inorganic**	**lead**
tools	**shapes**	**mineralogists**
colours	**minerals**	**heaviness**
hardness	**diamond**	**food**

Salt, gold, 1. ______________, and 2. ______________ are all examples of minerals. They are different from plants and animals because they are 3. ______________. Because they have never been alive, we call them 4. ______________. Minerals come in different 5. ______________, 6. ______________, 7. ______________, and 8. ______________. These are just some of the ways that 9. ______________ use to compare and identify minerals. 10. ______________ are commoner in our lives than we may think. They are the ingredients of rocks, which can be made up of one or many minerals. From rocks, we mine minerals and use them for 11. ______________, jewellery, 12. ______________, and many more.

ISBN: 978-1-897164-32-7

B. Fill in the missing letters to complete the names of the minerals. Then colour the precious minerals the colour they are most often prized for.

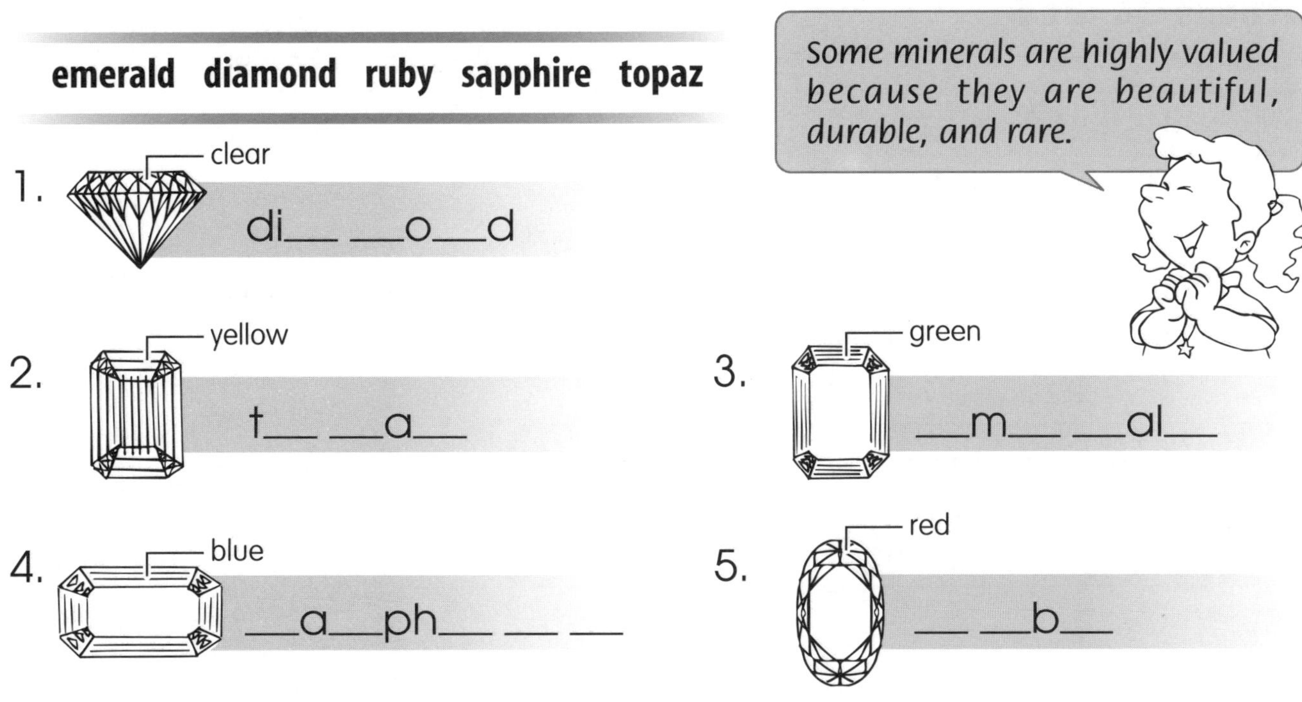

emerald diamond ruby sapphire topaz
Some minerals are highly valued because they are beautiful, durable, and rare.

C. Complete the crossword puzzle with the given rocks.

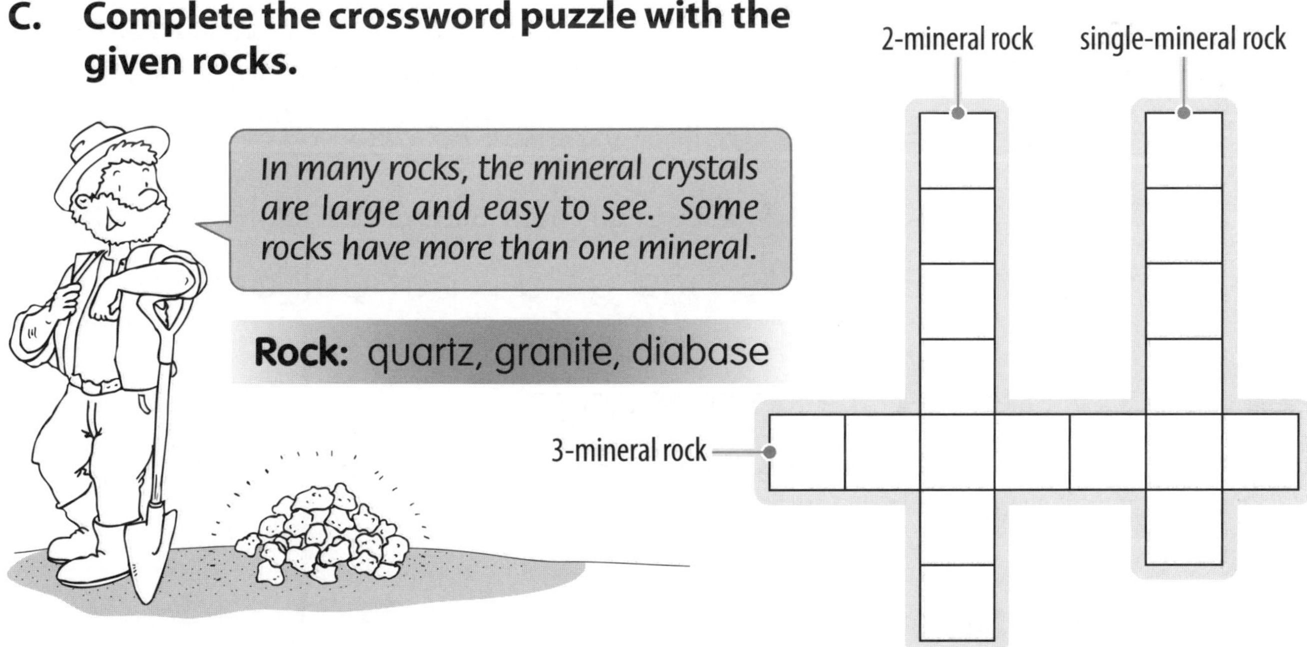

In many rocks, the mineral crystals are large and easy to see. Some rocks have more than one mineral.
Rock: quartz, granite, diabase
2-mineral rock
single-mineral rock
3-mineral rock

Science Fact

Rubies and sapphires are different coloured specimens of the same mineral: corundum.

ISBN: 978-1-897164-32-7

15

More about Minerals

It's hard. I think it's quartz.

- *Minerals are identified by their physical properties.*
- *The Mohs Scale of Hardness is a tool used to measure one property of minerals: its hardness.*

A. Read what the mineralogist says. Match the comparison with the property being compared. Write the letter.

Pyrite looks and feels so much like real gold that it is nicknamed "fool's gold". A mineralogist can tell the difference by looking at special properties.

Gold and Pyrite

- **A** Pyrite leaves a black streak of powder when rubbed on a piece of unglazed porcelain. Real gold leaves a yellow streak.
- **B** Gold and pyrite have similar shades of yellow.
- **C** Gold is much heavier than a similar sized sample of pyrite.
- **D** The look of both pyrite and gold is not dull or waxy, but metallic.
- **E** Gold and pyrite are both opaque.
- **F** It takes a harder mineral to scratch pyrite than it does to scratch gold.

Properties of Minerals

◯ colour	◯ hardness	◯ specific gravity
◯ lustre	◯ streak	◯ transparency

ISBN: 978-1-897164-32-7

B. Use arrows to place the minerals in the "Mohs Scale of Hardness" chart. Then answer the questions.

1.

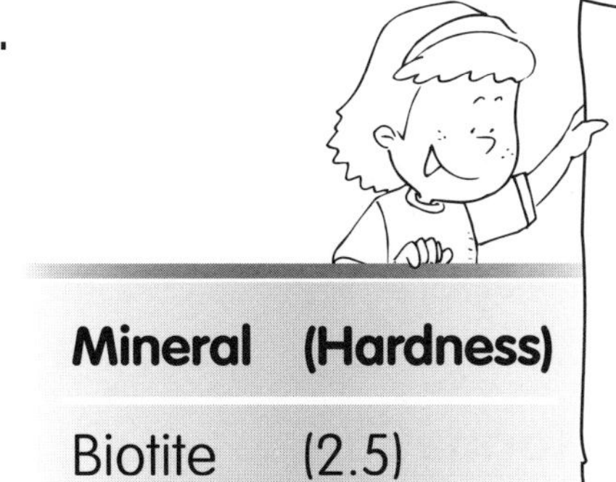

Mineral	(Hardness)
Biotite	(2.5)
Obsidian	(5 – 5.5)
Bakerite	(4.5)
Melanite	(6.5)
Nealite	(4)
Copper	(2.5 – 3)

Mohs Scale of Hardness

1. Talc
2. Gypsum
3. Calcite
4. Fluorite
5. Apatite
6. Orthoclase
7. Quartz
8. Topaz
9. Corundum
10. Diamond

2. Name two minerals that

a. can cut copper. ________________

b. can be scratched by a diamond. ________________

c. are softer than apatite. ________________

d. are harder than calcite but softer than quartz. ________________

Science Fact

Mercury does not have a hardness rating. Because of its unusual characteristic of being liquid at room temperature, mercury cannot scratch or be scratched.

ISBN: 978-1-897164-32-7

Rocks

- *Rocks are all around us.*
- *Almost all rocks are solid and made from non-living substances on Earth.*
- *Many people study rocks and things to do with rocks.*

A. Look at each picture. Name the natural rock formation.

bedrock mountain boulder clay sand pebbles silt rock

1. 

   ____

2. 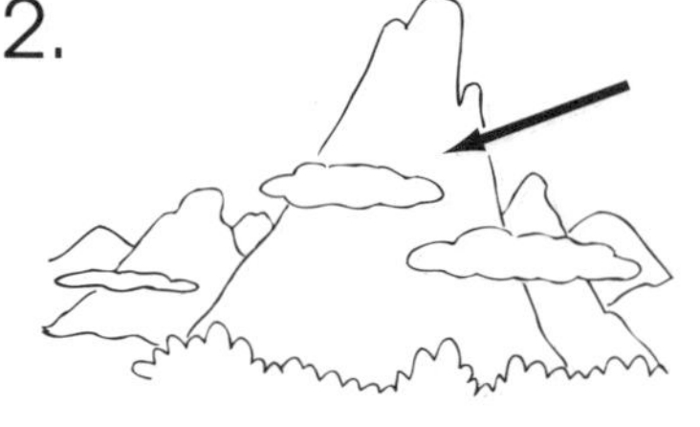

   ____

3. 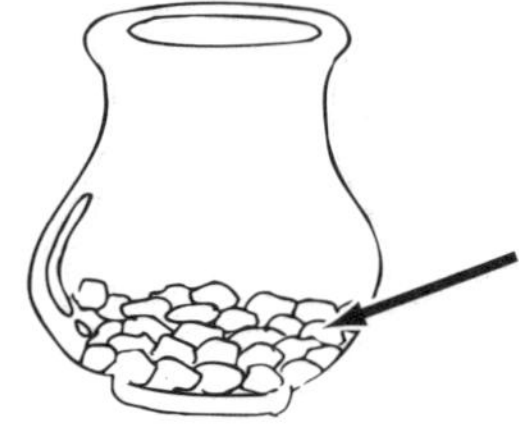

   ____

4. 

   ____

5. 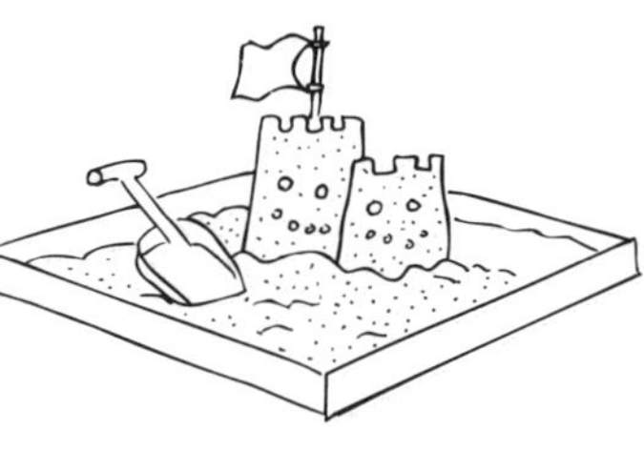

   ____

6. 

   ____

7. 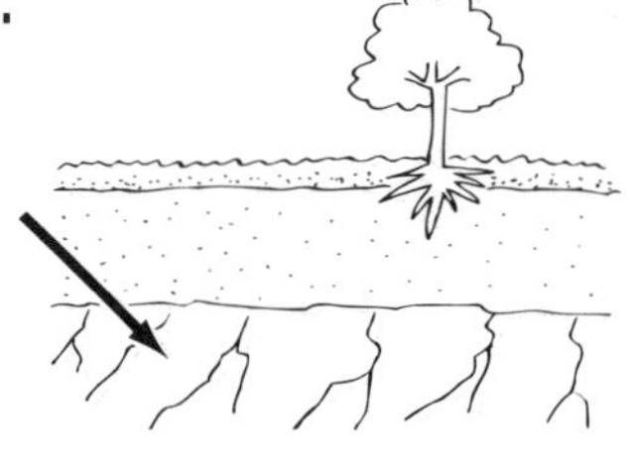

   ____

8. 

   ____

ISBN: 978-1-897164-32-7

B. Draw a line to match the unusual rock with the definition.

1. meteorite •
2. lava •
3. coal •

• Unlike most other rocks, this is made from plant matter.

• This rock is from outer space.

• When it first flows above ground, this is liquid rock.

C. How do we name the people who work closely on minerals? Write the letters.

- (A) gemologist
- (B) geologist
- (C) mineralogist
- (D) paleontologist
- (E) petrologist
- (F) prospector
- (G) rock hound
- (H) volcanologist

One who...

1. studies fossils ◯
2. studies rocks ◯
3. studies minerals ◯
4. studies volcanoes ◯
5. searches for minerals ◯
6. studies precious stones ◯
7. collects rocks or minerals ◯
8. studies features of the Earth and its history ◯

Science Fact

Liquid rock is called magma when it is below the Earth's surface. Above the surface it is called lava, even after it hardens.

ISBN: 978-1-897164-32-7

Igneous Rocks

- *Igneous rocks form when hot molten lava cools.*
- *Intrusive igneous rocks form beneath the Earth's surface. They are exposed by erosion.*
- *Extrusive igneous rocks form from volcanic eruptions.*

A. Fill in the blanks with the given words.

in above extrusive intrusive

- ____________ igneous rock – forms ____________ the ground

  Hot molten magma below the Earth's surface gets trapped in an underground pocket. It is slow to cool, but when it finally hardens, it is igneous rock.

- ____________ igneous rock – forms ____________ the ground

  Hot molten magma is forced from the inside of the Earth through a volcano or opening in the crust to the Earth's surface. When it is above ground, it is lava. Hot molten lava cools quickly, and another kind of igneous rock is formed.

B. Complete the chart with the names in bold to tell whether each formation of igneous rock is intrusive or extrusive.

1. The stripe of **diabase** in this rock is called a dike. It seeped into a crack in the rock, hardened, and after millions of years of erosion, it is exposed.
2. **Obsidian** is a rock that is smooth as glass. It cools quickly, so no crystals have a chance to form in the rock.
3. This **basalt** formed when magma seeped through an opening in the ocean floor.
4. This **granite** cliff is easy to see now, but it was once underground! After this earth was forced upward to make a mountain, soft rock around it eroded, exposing the granite.

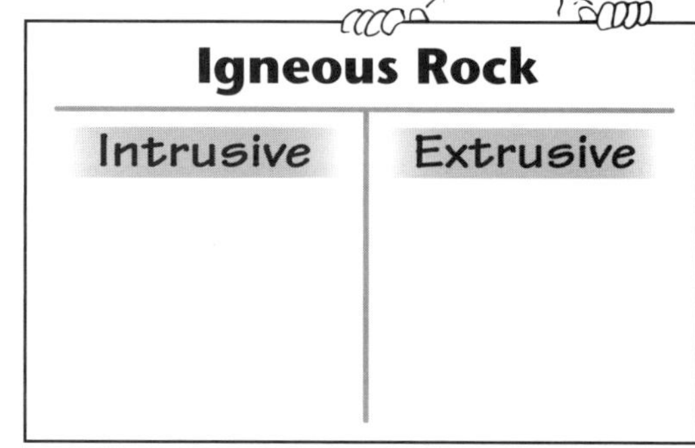

Igneous Rock

Intrusive	Extrusive

ISBN: 978-1-897164-32-7

C. **Colour the igneous rock words to find the path leading to ground surface.**

	diabase		
	molten		
fossil	crystals	plant	soil
glass	volcano	extrusive	animal
clay	silt	intrusive	grass
mud	boulder	lava	
obsidian	magma	granite	
basalt	sand	wood	

Experiment *What makes hot molten magma rise?*

Things needed:

- *a large, clear jar*
- *a small jar*
- *a long string*
- *food colouring*
- *hot and cold water*

Steps:

1. Tie a long string to the top of a small jar and fill the jar with hot water.
2. Add a few drops of red food colouring to the small jar.
3. Slowly immerse the small jar into the large jar filled with cold water.

What happens to the coloured hot water?

____

____

Science Fact

Can rock look like long thin strands of hair? An igneous rock called Pele's hair looks just like that. It forms when lava flies through the air under the right conditions.

ISBN: 978-1-897164-32-7

18

Sedimentary Rocks

- *Small pieces of rock break off from bigger rocks and are carried through water as sediment.*
- *In time, with chemicals from water, they become sedimentary rocks.*

Hi! Mr. Sedimentary.

A. Match the sentences with the correct pictures to show how sedimentary rocks are formed.

Formation of Sedimentary Rocks

1. Rivers tumble sand into the sea.
2. Sand builds up over thousands of years.
3. Chemicals in seawater cement grains together.
4. Sandstone layers are revealed as sea recedes.

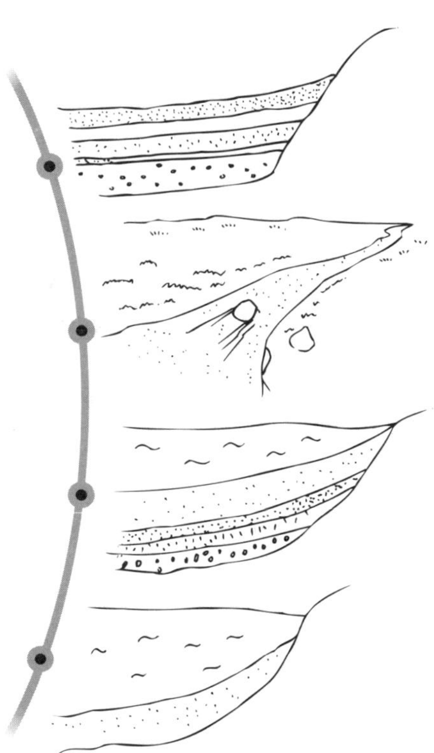

B. Fill in the blanks to find the origins of the sedimentary rocks.

Origin	Sedimentary Rock
1. s__ __ __	sandstone
2. m__ __	shale
3. s__ __ __ __ __	limestone
4. river p__ __ __ __ __ __	conglomerate

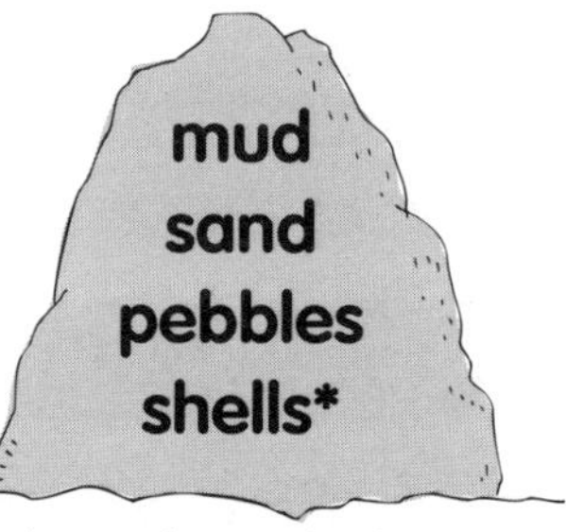

* rich in a chemical substance called calcium carbonate

ISBN: 978-1-897164-32-7

C. **Where do sedimentary rocks form? What kinds of sedimentary rocks are there? Write the names of the rocks and draw the correct pictures.**

Place				Sedimentary Rock
shells	muddy water	flowing river	dry seabed	rock salt conglomerate limestone shale

1. Minerals in water provide the cement for this rock.

   ____

2. For this rock to form, slow moving or still water is needed.

   ____

3. This rock forms when seabeds dry up.

   ____

4. This rock began with secretions from different sea animals.

   ____

Science Fact

Limestone is an exception to the rule that rocks are made from inorganic (non-living) substances. It is formed from the crushed shells of living animals.

ISBN: 978-1-897164-32-7

Metamorphic Rocks

- *Metamorphic rocks are made from extreme heat or pressure in the Earth.*
- *The rock cycle shows the relationship among the different rock types.*

A. Read what Susan says. Draw an arrow in each circle to show the direction of pressure.

The right amount of heat and pressure below the Earth's surface can change a rock into another kind of rock.

Sedimentary rocks under pressure | **Metamorphic rocks formed**

1.

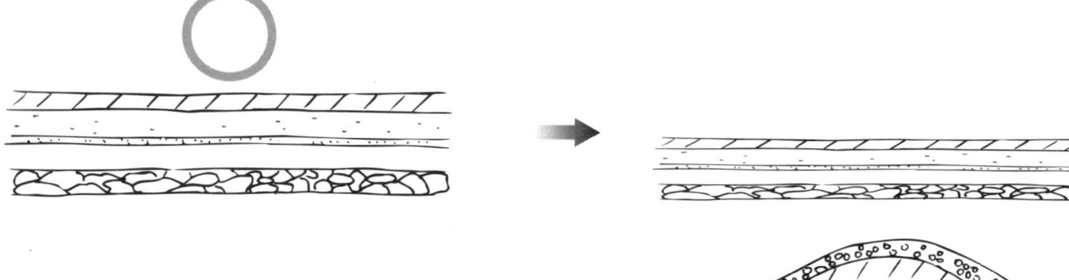

2.

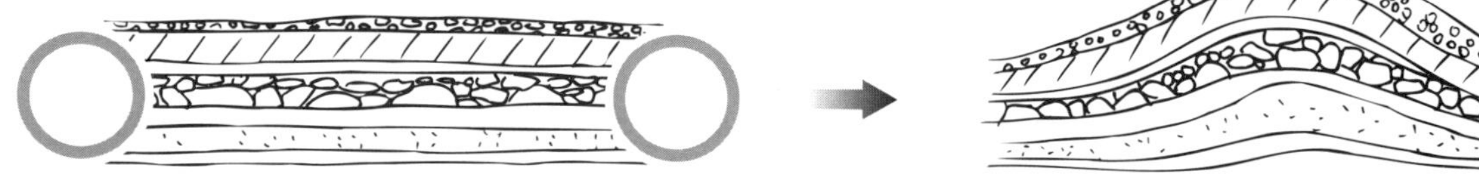

B. Read what Michael says. Complete the pattern on each rock. Then label each rock with the words in bold.

The igneous rock ***granite*** *changes to the metamorphic rock* ***gneiss*** *when it is under extreme heat or pressure.*

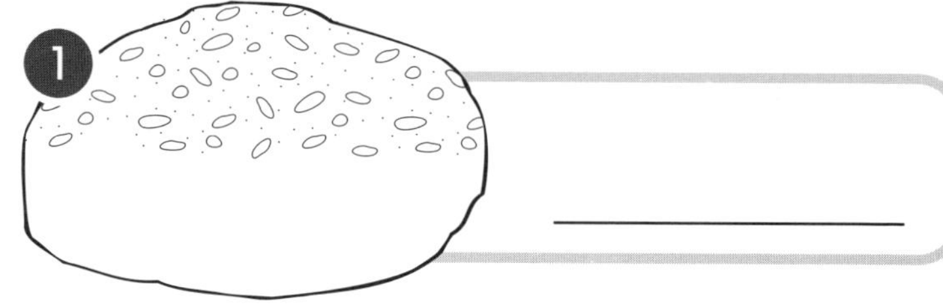

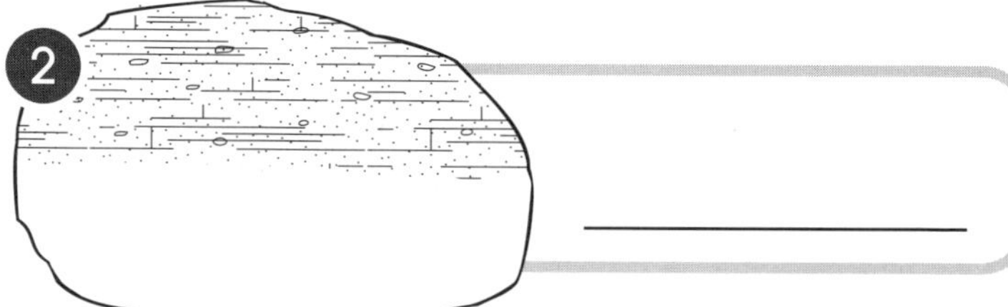

ISBN: 978-1-897164-32-7

C. Fill in the missing letters to find out what type of metamorphic rock the given rock will turn to under the right amount of heat and pressure.

Metamorphic Rock

- *slate*
- *gneiss*
- *marble*
- *quartzite*

1. sandstone → ___ ___ar___ ___i___ ___
2. shale → ___ ___at___
3. granite → ___ne___ ___s
4. limestone → ___a___b___ ___

D. Look at the rock cycle. Fill in the blanks.

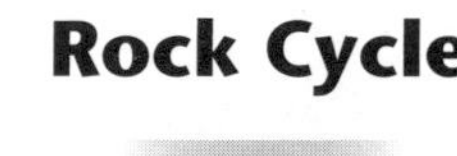

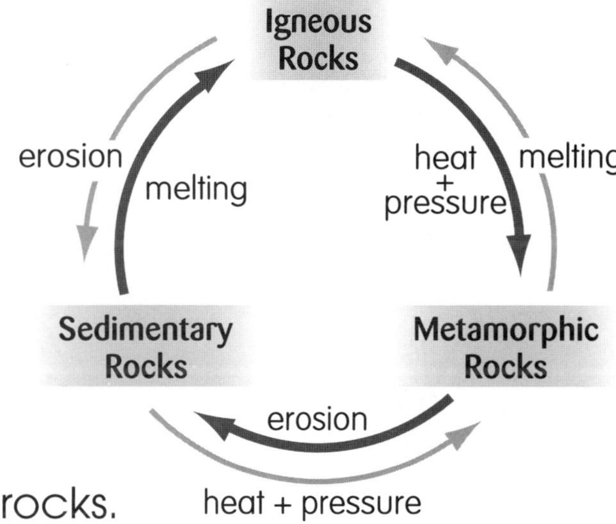

1. Metamorphic rocks can become ________________ rocks when they melt into hot molten magma.
2. When ________________ and ________________ undergo intense heat or pressure, they become metamorphic rocks.
3. Metamorphic rocks may become ________________ when they break down into small pieces and are carried off into the sea.

Science Fact

Conditions can be too extreme for metamorphic rocks to form. If temperatures are high enough, rocks will turn to hot molten magma instead.

ISBN: 978-1-897164-32-7

How We Use Rocks and Minerals

- *Rocks and minerals are used in almost every aspect of our lives.*

A. Colour the things that are made of rocks and minerals.

1.

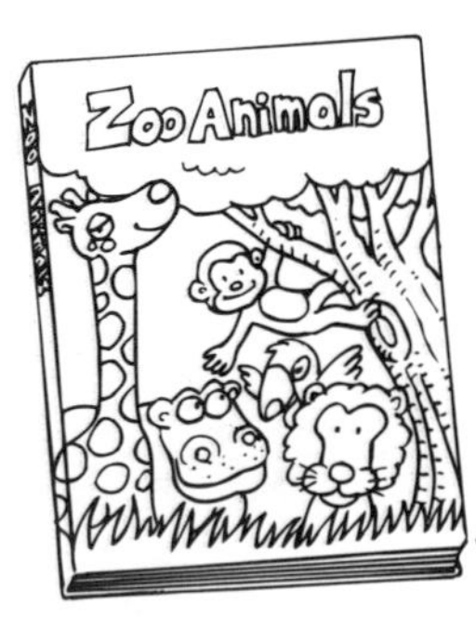

2.

3.

4.

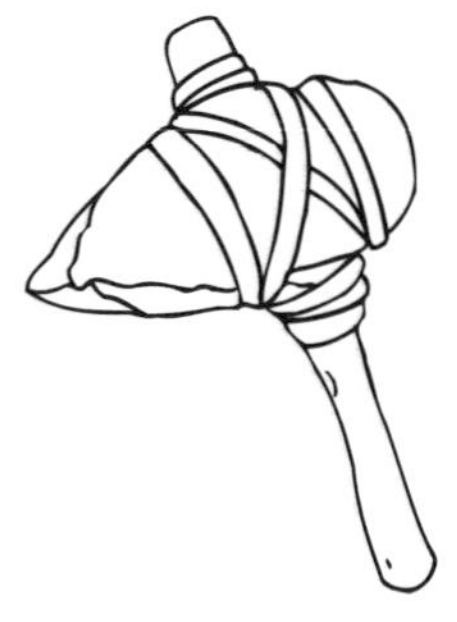

5.

8.

6.

7.

ISBN: 978-1-897164-32-7

B. Use the rock-base materials to make a house. Draw it in the box and label the materials you use.

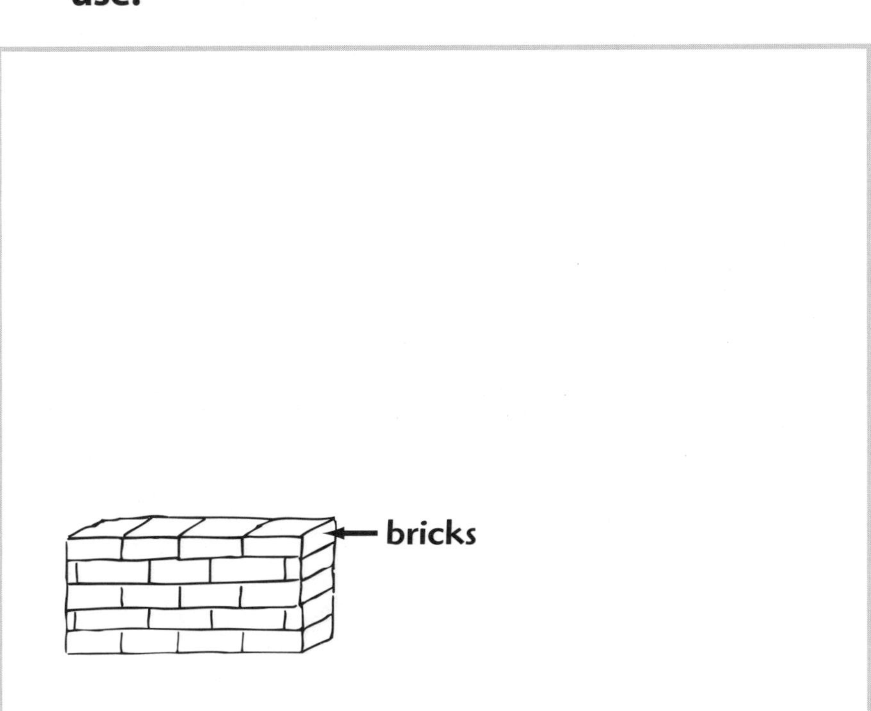

Materials:

concrete (made from crushed limestone and pebbles)

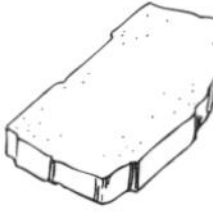

granite

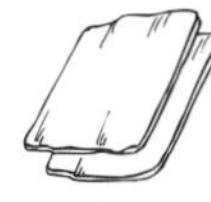

slate sheets

stones

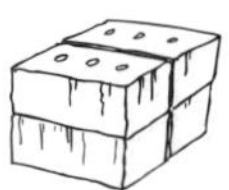

bricks (made from sand)

glass (made from sand)

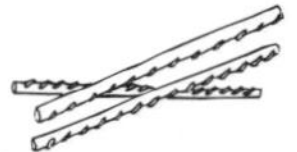

steel bars

C. Read the descriptions to find the colours of these minerals.

Minerals are often a source of colour pigments.

Minerals

- Hematite – ____________ (colour of an apple)
- Malachite – ____________ (colour of grass)
- Azurite – ____________ (colour of the sky)
- Charcoal – ____________ (colour of a shadow)

Science Fact

Sometimes minerals can be dangerous to us. Asbestos is a mineral with qualities that make it very useful. Unfortunately, it also causes serious lung disease.

ISBN: 978-1-897164-32-7

21

Erosion

- *Erosion causes rocks to break off, break down, and move to another place.*
- *Erosion has many different causes.*

A. Fill in the blanks to show the progress of erosion.

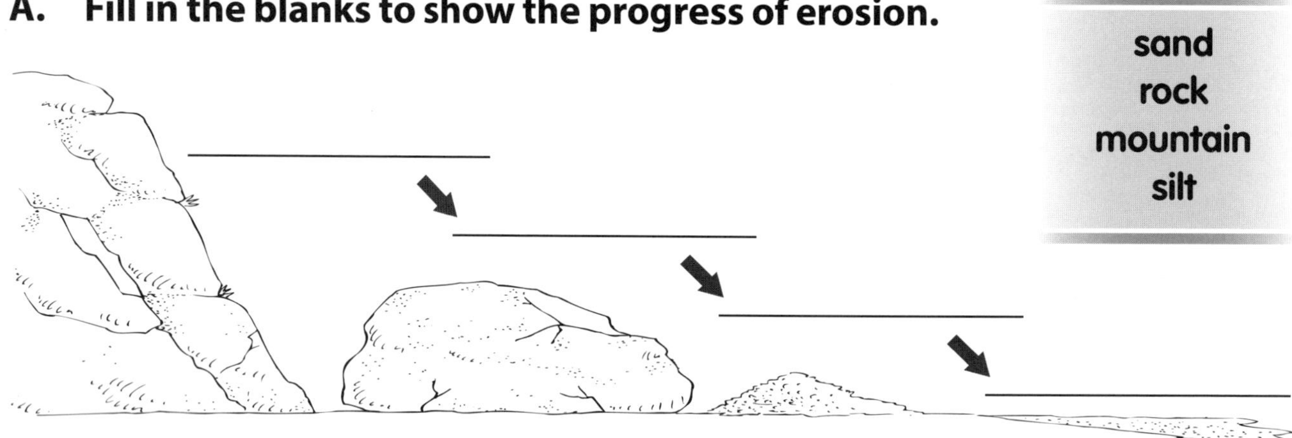

B. Tell what type of erosion occurs in each picture. Write "ice", "wind", or "moving water" on the line. Then draw a line to match each type of erosion with another example.

Types of Erosion

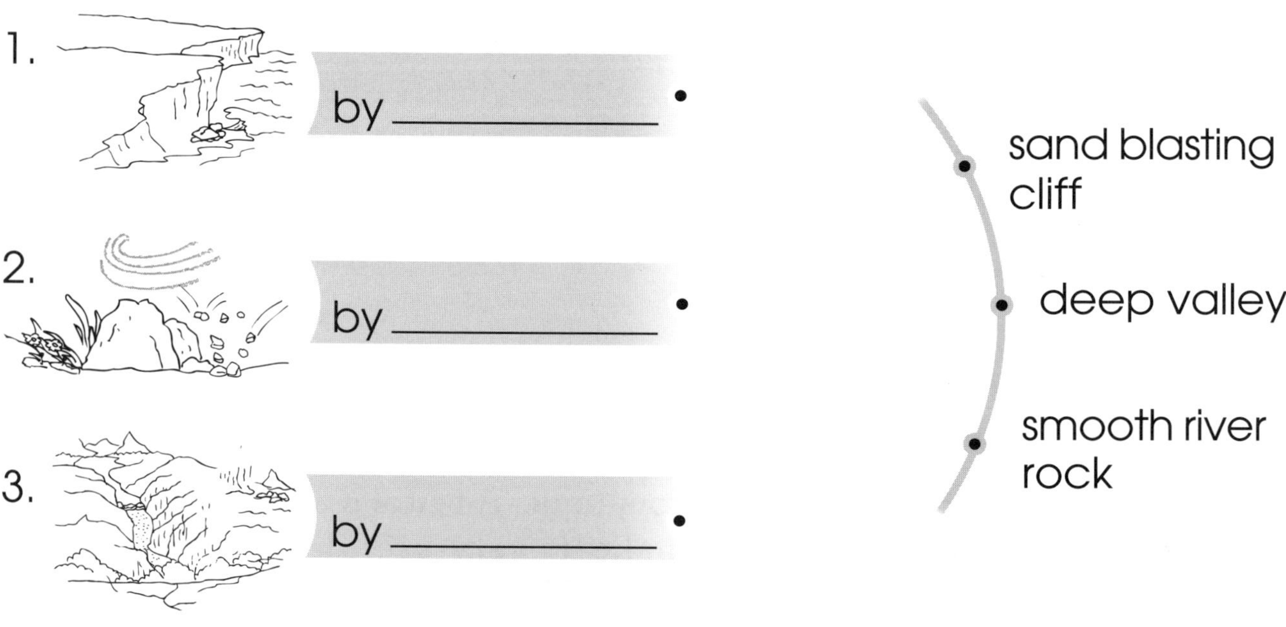

ISBN: 978-1-897164-32-7

C. **Read the descriptions. Draw lines to show the causes of erosion. Then fill in the blanks to tell what the causes are.**

glacier landslide tide plant roots

Causes of Erosion

1. Rock will not stop it from growing.

2. The twice-a-day rise and fall is powerful enough to break down rocks.

3. This will slowly carve valleys between mountains.

4. The erosion of this mountainside happened in minutes, not thousands of years.

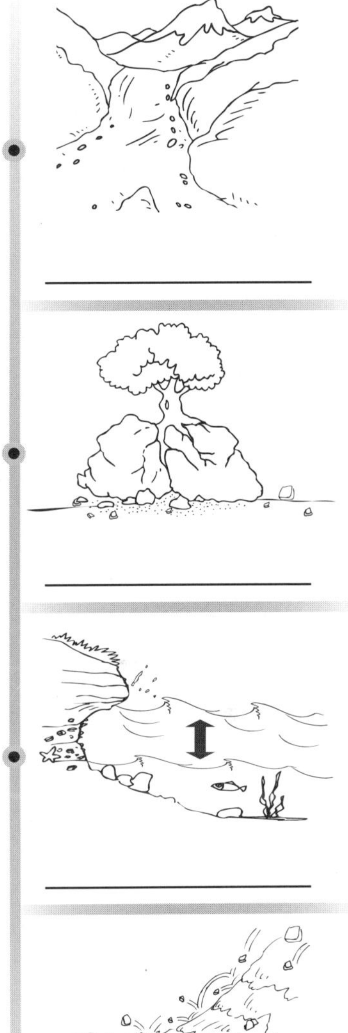

One of the most disastrous consequences of a drought is soil erosion. With no plants to keep the soil together, and lack of rain causing the soil to dry, winds easily carry good soil away.

ISBN: 978-1-897164-32-7

22

Fossils

- Fossils are traces of things that lived in prehistoric times.
- Fossils can be the preserved body of a plant or an animal, or an imprint of it.

A. Put the formation of each fossil in order. Write the letters.

Ammonite fossil formation:

____ , ____ , ____ , ____

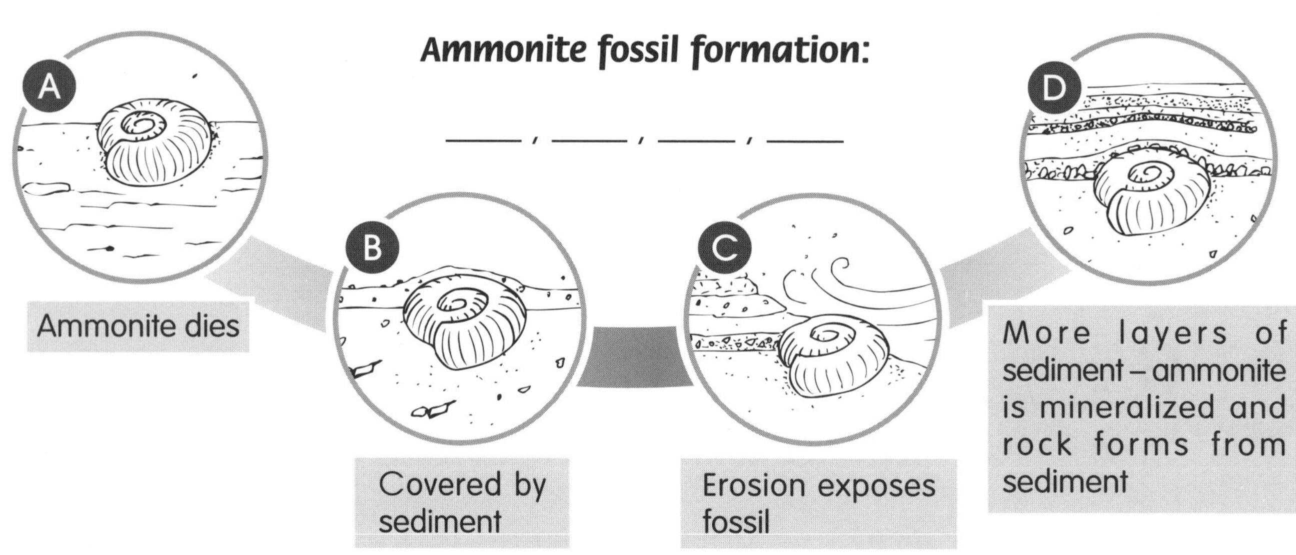
A
Ammonite dies
B
Covered by sediment
C
Erosion exposes fossil
D
More layers of sediment – ammonite is mineralized and rock forms from sediment

Leaf imprint fossil formation:

____ , ____ , ____ , ____

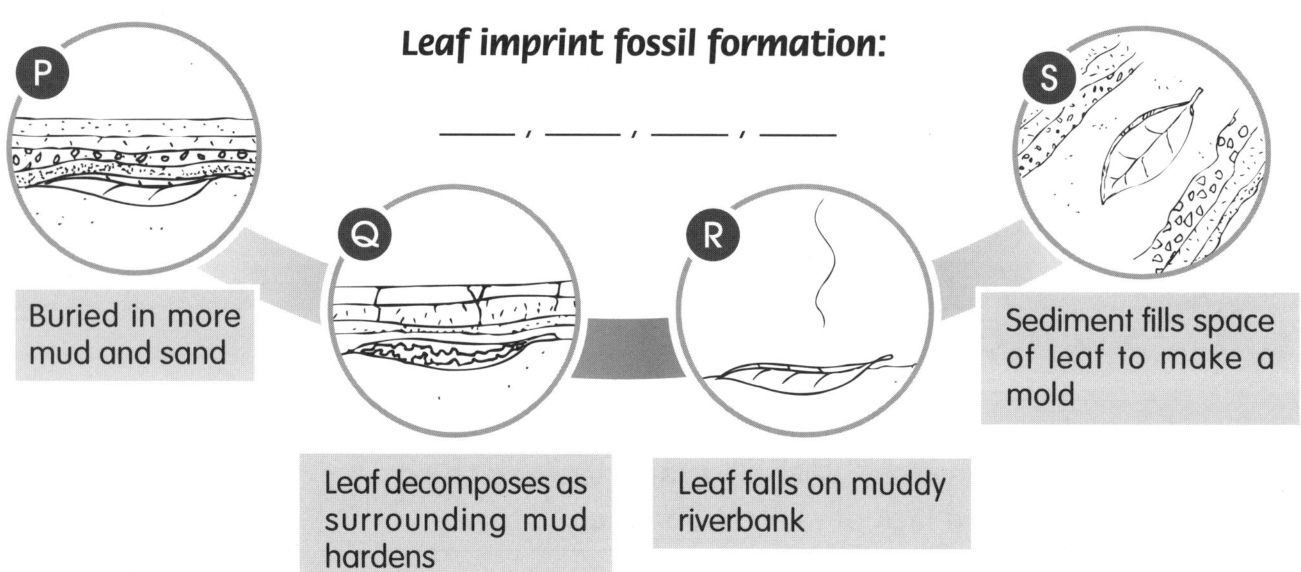
P
Buried in more mud and sand
Q
Leaf decomposes as surrounding mud hardens
R
Leaf falls on muddy riverbank
S
Sediment fills space of leaf to make a mold

ISBN: 978-1-897164-32-7

B. Label the fossils with the given words. Then tell which fossils are used to find out the following about each animal.

bones teeth tracks egg nest dung

1. **Fossil**

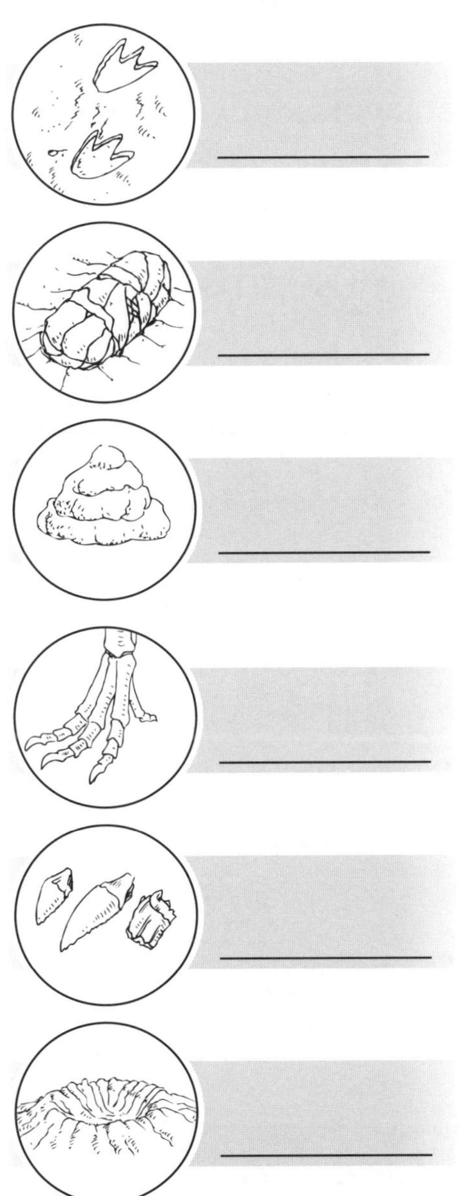

2. Which fossils tell us

a. if the animal walked on two legs?

_______ ; _______

b. how an animal defended itself?

_______ ; _______

c. what an animal ate?

_______ ; _______

d. that an animal was a carnivore?

_______ ; _______

e. how an animal moved?

_______ ; _______

f. the size of a baby animal?

_______ ; _______

Science Fact

Fossils of dinosaur droppings that are bigger than a small dog have been found. Scientists call these fossils coprolites.

ISBN: 978-1-897164-32-7

23

More about Fossils

- Fossils are only found in places where the conditions were right for making fossils.
- Most fossils are never discovered. The ones we find are exposed through erosion or quarrying.

A. Where are fossils found? Circle the correct answers.

1. Fossils are most often found in ____ .

   sedimentary rocks   magma   museums

2. Insects are sometimes found in amber, which is fossilized ____ .

   apples   seeds   tree resin

3. Some fossils are from animals that got stuck in ____ .

   a tree   tar pits   a line-up

4. The Burgess Shale is rich in fossils. Once in the tropics at sea level, it is now at the top of the ____ .

   Rocky Mountains   Swiss Alps   CN Tower

5. 

   Sometimes, fossilized animals are found in dry desert ____ .

   air   water   sand

ISBN: 978-1-897164-32-7

B. Read what the archaeologist says. Help him circle the correct tools for removing fossils from rock.

When rock erodes, fossils appear at the surface. If they are not removed, they will erode too.

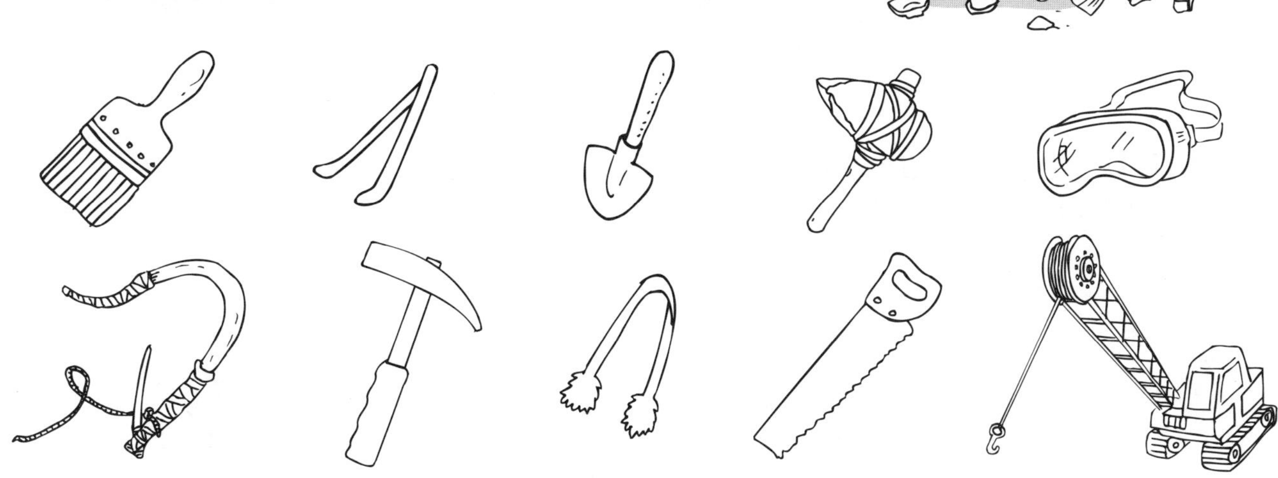

C. Label the parts of a dinosaur skeleton. Write the words on the lines.

back vertebrae skull rib tail vertebrae leg bone

1. ____________
2. ____________
3. ____________
4. ____________
5. ____________

Science Fact

Fossils are not found in igneous or metamorphic rocks because the heat that creates the rocks destroy the fossils.

sedimentary rock

fossil

ISBN: 978-1-897164-32-7

24

Caves

- *The special environment of caves allows unique structures to form over many thousands of years.*

A. Read the passage. Then write a word to match each description.

Water flowing or dripping over limestone gradually erodes the soft rock. In fact, most caves are formed exactly because of this. Limestone caves with water flowing develop speleothems, or decorations, caused by water dissolving limestone and then letting it collect when the water evaporates. With each drip from a cave's ceiling, a stalagmite grows higher. Mineral deposits also build from the dripping point, and a stalactite grows downward. If the two ever meet, they form a column of the mineral calcite.

1. What cave "decorations" are called ________________
2. A mineral that stalactites and stalagmites are made of ________________
3. A speleothem grows down from the cave ceiling ________________
4. A speleothem grows up from the cave floor ________________
5. A kind of rock that most caves are made from ________________
6. A structure that is formed when a stalagmite and a stalactite meet ________________

ISBN: 978-1-897164-32-7

B. Label the structures in the cave.

stalagmite stalactite column

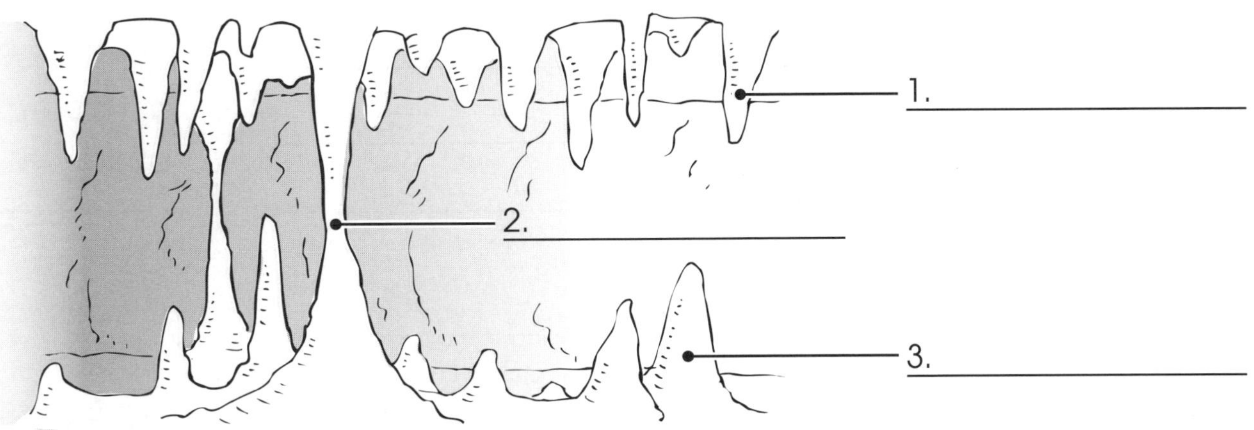

Experiment – Making Stalagmites

Things needed:

- 2 jars
- washing soda
- hot water
- a small plate
- a cotton string

Steps:

1. 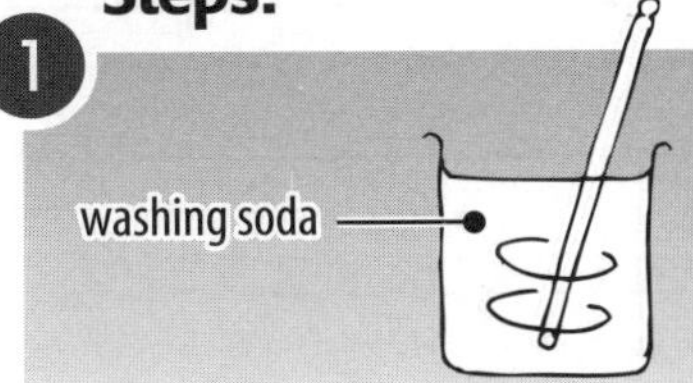

Fill the jars with hot water to about $\frac{3}{4}$ full. Stir in washing soda until it no longer dissolves.

2. 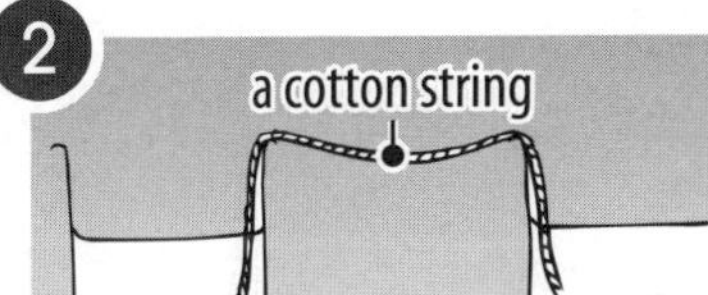

Let one end of the string hang in one jar of water, and the other end in the second jar. Allow the string to hang just above the plate.

3. 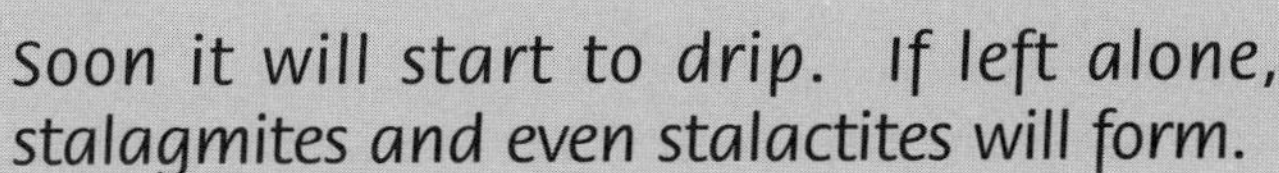

Science Fact

Other speleothems made from calcite are found in caves too! "Soda straws" and "drapes" hang from ceilings, and flowstone can take the shape of ice cream scoops.

ISBN: 978-1-897164-32-7

Review

A. Identify what types of animals they are. Then help them find their favourite food and habitats.

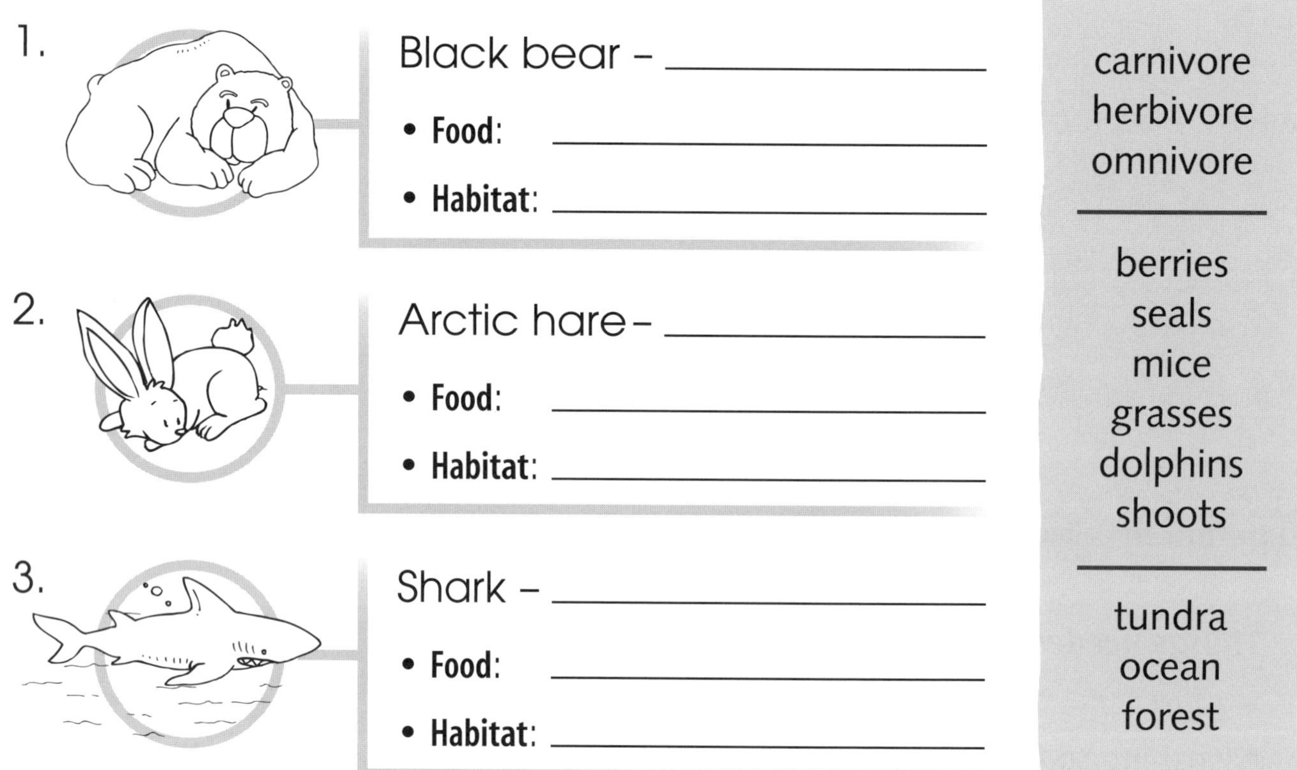

Types of Animals
1.
Black bear – ______
• Food: ______
• Habitat: ______
2.
Arctic hare – ______
• Food: ______
• Habitat: ______
3.
Shark – ______
• Food: ______
• Habitat: ______
carnivore
herbivore
omnivore
berries
seals
mice
grasses
dolphins
shoots
tundra
ocean
forest

B. Read the sentences. Complete the Arctic Food Web with the words in bold.

- **Plankton** is eaten by **Arctic cod**, krill, and **bowhead whales**.
- Arctic cod are eaten by **ringed seals** and **polar bears**.
- **Caribou** are eaten by polar bears.

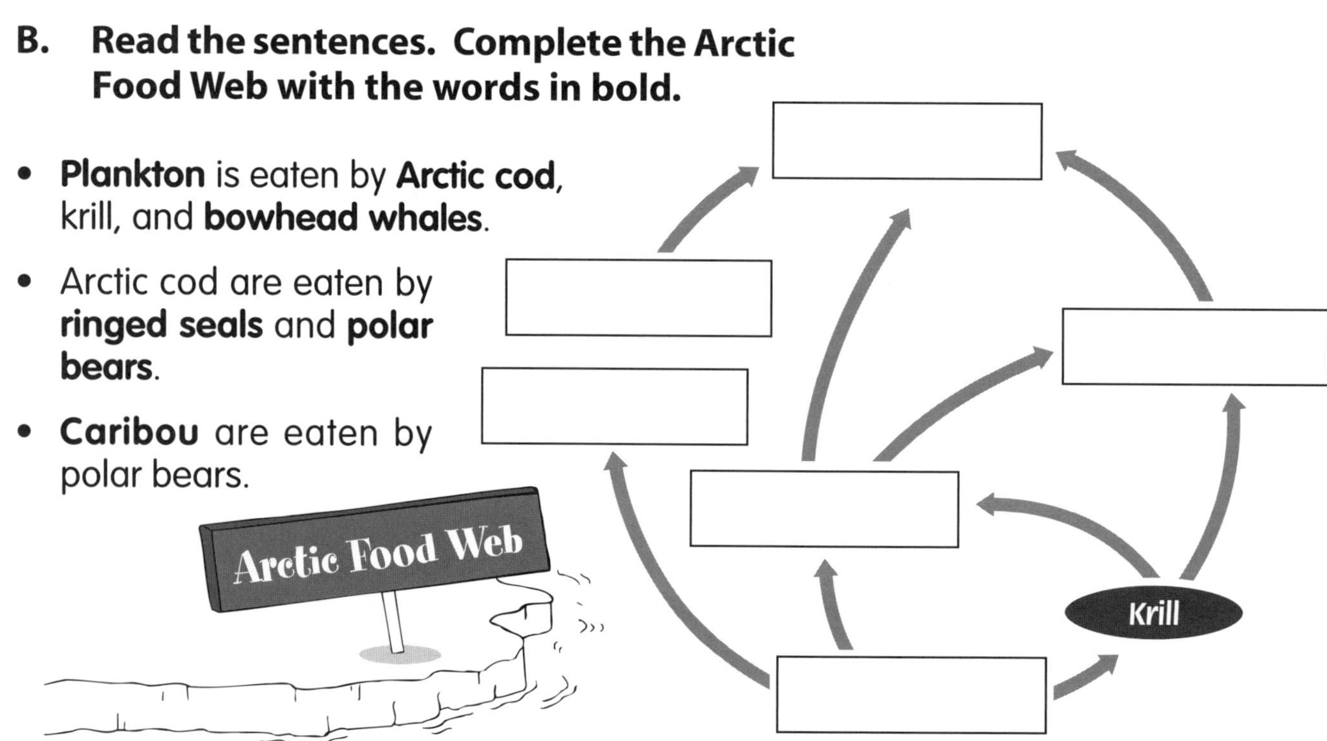

ISBN: 978-1-897164-32-7

C. Circle the correct words to complete the sentences.

Properties of Light

1. Light travels in straight / curved lines.
2. Light can pass through some / all the things.
3. Light can be reflected by rough / shiny objects.
4. Light runs / bends as it passes from one medium to another.

D. Cross out the thing that does not belong in each group. Then draw lines to match the groups with the correct materials.

1. •
2. •
3. •

Materials

- transparent
- translucent
- opaque

ISBN: 978-1-897164-32-7

E. Label the diagram with the words in bold and identify the parts of an ear.

When a sound is made outside the outer ear, our **earflap** in the **outer ear** will collect the sound waves and the sound waves travel along the canal and strike the **eardrum**. The eardrum vibrates and sends the vibrations to the **middle ear** which contains the three tiny bones – the **hammer**, **anvil**, and **stirrup**. These three bones make the vibrations larger and pass them to the **cochlea** in the **inner ear**. Then the motion of the vibrations is changed into signals that are carried by **nerves** to the brain.

Cross-Section of an Ear

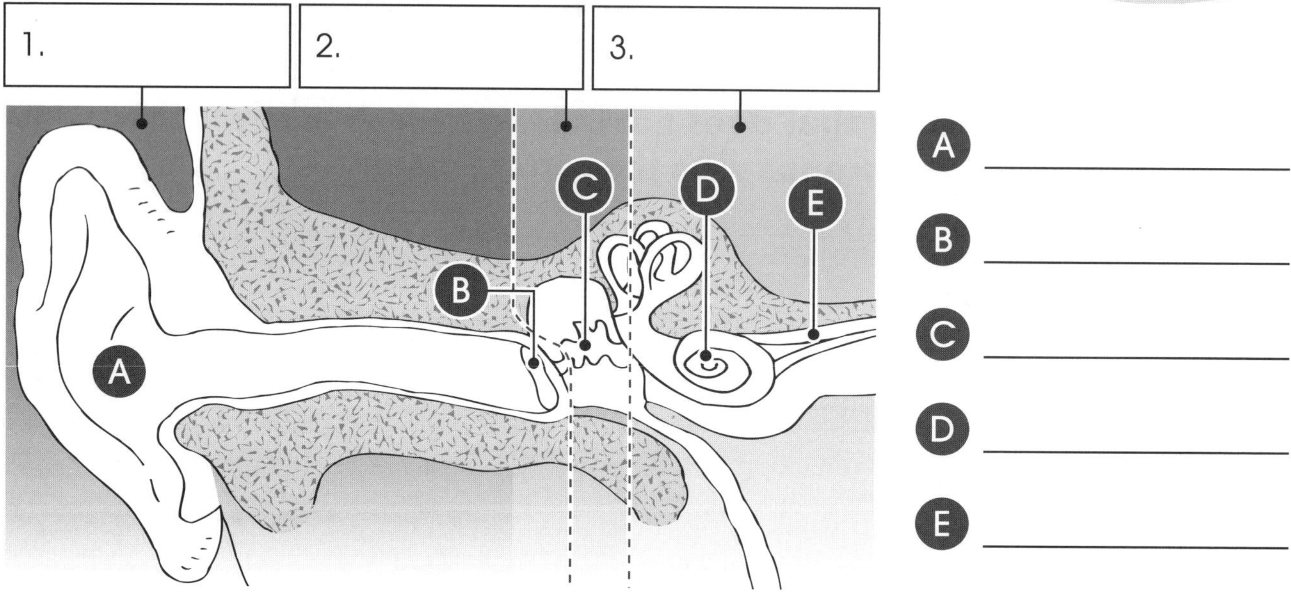

A ______

B ______

C ______

D ______

E ______

F. Tell whether each surface "reflects sound" or "absorbs sound".

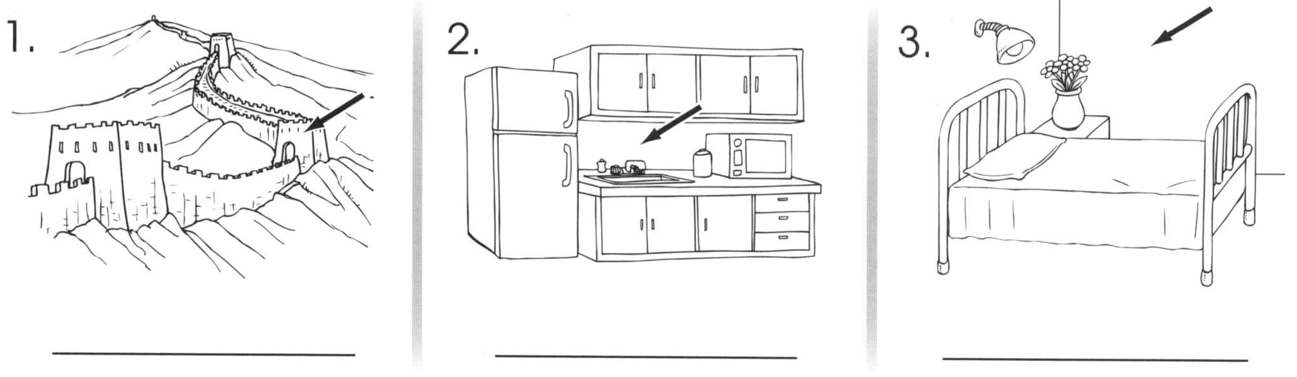

1. ______ 2. ______ 3. ______

ISBN: 978-1-897164-32-7

G. **Look at the gears. Draw arrows to show the directions that the shaded gears will turn. Then describe how fast they turn compared to the one on the left.**

faster equally fast slower

1\.

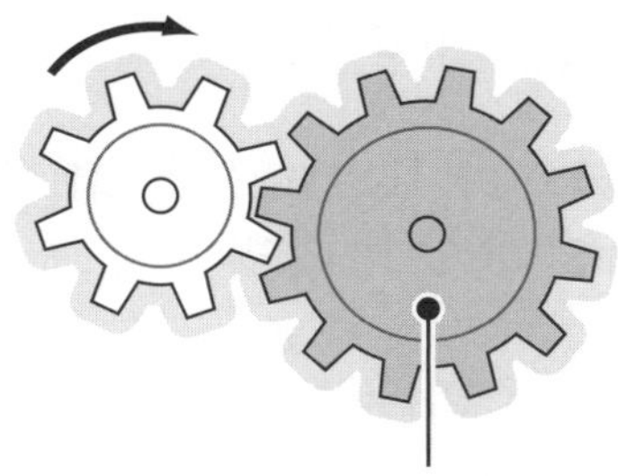

____

2\.

____

H. **Fill in the blanks to complete what the mineralogist says. Then help him complete the "Mohs Scale of Hardness" chart.**

heaviness colours salt diamond hardness inorganic shapes

Minerals are ____________ substances. They come in different ____________, ____________, ____________, and ____________. Gold, ____________, and ____________ are all examples of minerals.

- **Diamond** can scratch all minerals.
- **Topaz** is harder than **quartz**, but softer than corundum.
- **Gypsum** can cut talc, but not calcite.

Mohs Scale of Hardness

1. Talc
2. ____________
3. Calcite
4. Fluorite
5. Apatite
6. Orthoclase
7. ____________
8. ____________
9. Corundum
10. ____________

ISBN: 978-1-897164-32-7

Review

I. Draw lines to match the words with the correct descriptions.

1. limestone
2. sedimentary rock
3. fossils
4. igneous rock
5. stalagmite
6. stalactite
7. metamorphic rock
8. lava
9. meteorite
10. coal

- a rock formed by compressed sediment deposited in layers
- a kind of rock that most caves are made from
- traces of things that lived in prehistoric times
- a speleothem that grows up from the cave floor
- This kind of rock is formed when hot molten lava cools.
- a speleothem that grows down from the cave ceiling
- When it first flows above ground, this is a liquid rock.
- a rock made from extreme heat or pressure in the Earth
- Unlike most other rocks, this is made from plant matter.
- This rock is from outer space.

ISBN: 978-1-897164-32-7

J. Check the correct answers.

1. The process of erosion

   (A) mountain → sand → rock → silt

   (B) silt → sand → rock → mountain

   (C) mountain → rock → sand → silt

2. What type of erosion occurs in the picture?

   (A) by moving water

   (B) by ice

   (C) by wind

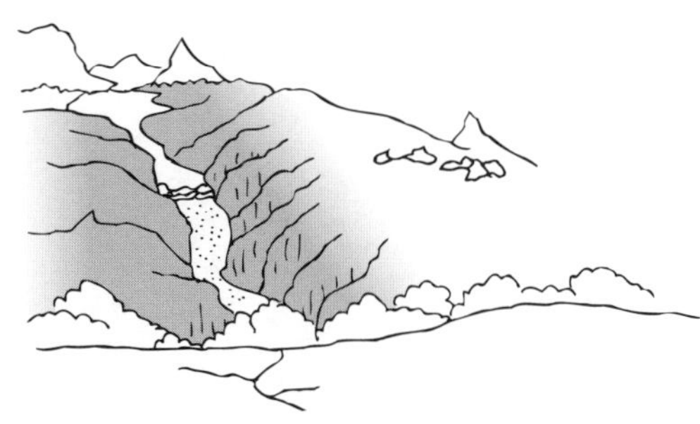

3. Which fossil tells us how an animal moved?

   (A) 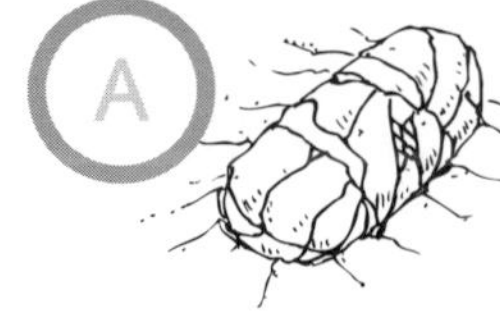

   (B) 

   (C) 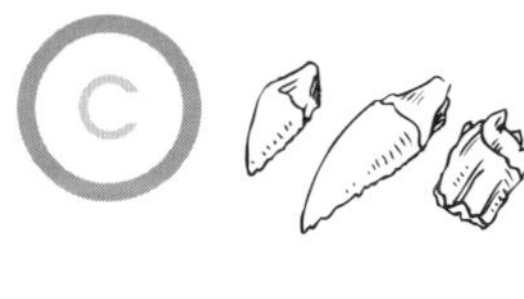

4. Which tool is for removing fossils from rock?

   (A) 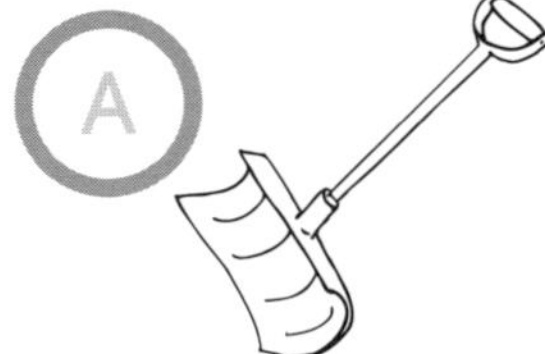

   (B) 

   (C) 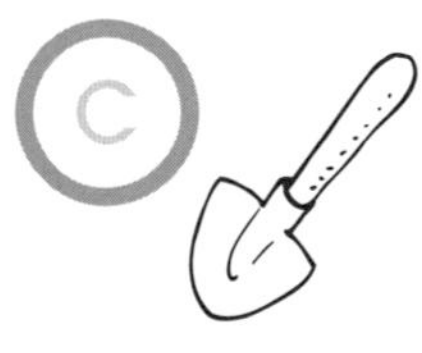

5. Which structure is stalactite?

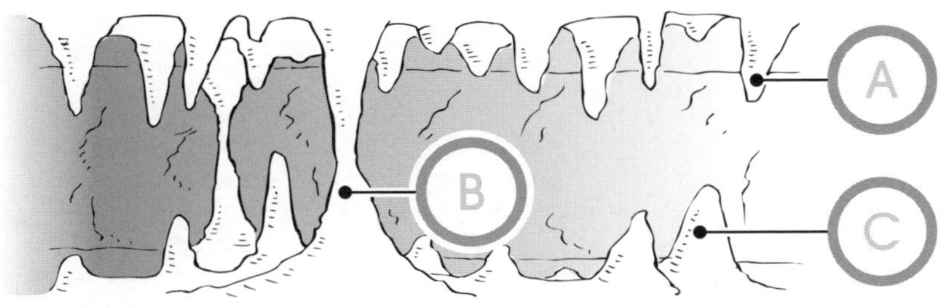

ISBN: 978-1-897164-32-7

ISBN: 978-1-897164-32-7

ANSWERS

ISBN: 978-1-897164-32-7

1 Numbers to 10 000

1. 3 ; 5 ; 4 ; 2 ; 3542
2. 2 ; 8 ; 2 ; 3 ; 2823
3. 2 ; 5 ; 7
4. 9 ; 6 ; 4
5. 7260
6. 6084
7. 800 ; 6
8. 3000 ; 40

9-12. (Suggested answer for the number in between)

9. 9621 ; 1269 ; 1296
10. 8543 ; 3458 ; 3485
11. 5442 ; 2445 ; 2454
12. 9730 ; 3079 ; 3097
13. 3825 4276 3766 4063 ;
    3000 4000 5000
    4276, 4063, 3825, 3766
14. 5161 5116 5611 6151 6511 ;
    5000 5200 5400 5600 5800 6000 6200 6400 6600
    5116, 5161, 5611, 6151, 6511
15. 7000 ; 500 ; 60 ; 3
16. 6000 ; 900 ; 10 ; 4
17. 2000 ; 400 ; 80 ; 5
18. 3000 ; 800 ; 70 ; 9
19. 6530 ; 6500 ; 7000
20. 3870 ; 3900 ; 4000
21. 4130 ; 4100 ; 4000
22. 9480 ; 9500 ; 9000
23. 5030 ; 5000 ; 5000
24. 7750 ; 7800 ; 8000
25. 465
26. 790
27. 650
28. 5267

2 Addition and Subtraction of 3-Digit Numbers

1. 549
2. 341
3. 405
4. 505
5. 680
6. 333
7. 634
8. 431
9. 601
10. 591 ; $\begin{array}{r} 300 \\ +\ 300 \\ \hline 600 \end{array}$
11. 587 ; $\begin{array}{r} 400 \\ +\ 200 \\ \hline 600 \end{array}$
12. 391 ; 200 + 200 = 400
13. 693 ; 600 + 100 = 700
14. Tim: 164 ; Elaine: 129 ; Adam: 133 ; Tiffany: 229 ; Gary: 270 ; David: 466 ; Louis: 181 ; Nancy: 207 ; Gloria: 255 ; Sam: 433
15. David
16. Elaine
17. Tiffany
18. Adam
19. 196
20. 231 ; $\begin{array}{r} 370 \\ -\ 130 \\ \hline 240 \end{array}$
21. 183 ; $\begin{array}{r} 440 \\ -\ 250 \\ \hline 190 \end{array}$
22. 509 ; $\begin{array}{r} 150 \\ +\ 360 \\ \hline 510 \end{array}$
23. 603 ; $\begin{array}{r} 310 \\ +\ 290 \\ \hline 600 \end{array}$
24. A: ✔ ; 452
    B: ✘ ; 246 ; $\begin{array}{r} 256 \\ +\ 467 \\ \hline 723 \end{array}$
    C: ✘ ; 425 ; $\begin{array}{r} 525 \\ +\ 379 \\ \hline 904 \end{array}$
    D: ✘ ; 389 ; $\begin{array}{r} 289 \\ +\ 296 \\ \hline 585 \end{array}$
    E: ✘ ; 134 ; $\begin{array}{r} 143 \\ +\ 166 \\ \hline 309 \end{array}$
    F: ✔ ; $\begin{array}{r} 208 \\ +\ 376 \\ \hline 584 \end{array}$
25.

Month	January	February	March
No. of Men	389	225	218
No. of Women	463	448	486
Total	852	673	704

26. 389 + 225 + 218 ; 832 ; 832
27. 463 + 448 ; 911 ; 911
28. 463 – 448 ; 15 ; 15
29. 389 – 225 ; 164 ; 164
30. 204 – 29 ; 175 ; 175

3 Addition of 4-Digit Numbers

1. 6669
2. 3997
3. 7486
4. $\begin{array}{r} {}^{1} \\ 1859 \\ +\ 2016 \\ \hline 3875 \end{array}$
5. $\begin{array}{r} {}^{1} \\ 475 \\ +\ 3141 \\ \hline 3616 \end{array}$
6. $\begin{array}{r} {}^{1} \\ 3881 \\ +\ 4914 \\ \hline 8795 \end{array}$
7. 4609
8. 6648
9. 2069
10. 3999
11. $\begin{array}{r} 1053 \\ +\ 1215 \\ \hline 2268 \end{array}$
12. $\begin{array}{r} 3164 \\ +\ 2032 \\ \hline 5196 \end{array}$
13. $\begin{array}{r} 876 \\ +\ 1014 \\ \hline 1890 \end{array}$
14. $\begin{array}{r} 1351 \\ +\ 948 \\ \hline 2299 \end{array}$
15. A: 1793 B: 1163
    C: 3204 D: 1079
    E: 3326 F: 1639
    G: 3506 H: 4749
    I: 3259
16. 2956 ; $\begin{array}{r} 1793 \\ +\ 1163 \\ \hline 2956 \end{array}$
17. 1481 ; $\begin{array}{r} 1079 \\ +\ 402 \\ \hline 1481 \end{array}$

ISBN: 978-1-897164-32-7

18. 6530 ; $\begin{array}{r} 3204 \\ +\ 3326 \\ \hline 6530 \end{array}$

19. 4875 ;
800 + 60 + 15 ;
4000 + 800 + 70 + 5
$\begin{array}{r} 3529 \\ +\ 1346 \\ \hline 4875 \end{array}$

20. 6351 ;
5000 + 1300 + 40 + 11 ;
6000 + 300 + 50 + 1
$\begin{array}{r} 4714 \\ +\ 1637 \\ \hline 6351 \end{array}$

21. 7679 ;
7000 + 500 + 170 + 9 ;
7000 + 600 + 70 + 9
$\begin{array}{r} 3588 \\ +\ 4091 \\ \hline 7679 \end{array}$

22. $\begin{array}{r} 3\ 4\ 6\ 5 \\ +\ 2\ 5\ 8\ 2 \\ \hline 6\ 0\ 4\ 7 \end{array}$

23. $\begin{array}{r} 2\ 3\ 3\ 6 \\ +\ 1\ 7\ 1\ 4 \\ \hline 4\ 0\ 5\ 0 \end{array}$

24. $\begin{array}{r} 1\ 6\ 7\ 3 \\ +\ 2\ 5\ 1\ 9 \\ \hline 4\ 1\ 9\ 2 \end{array}$

25. 3623 ; 5

26. 8772 ; 3774 = 2 + 3772
27. 6573 ; 2577 = 4 + 2573
28. 3419 ; 1425 = 1419 + 6
29. 7831 ; 4836 = 4831 + 5
30. 8051 ; 7058 = 7051 + 7

31. 3172 ; $\begin{array}{r} 1586 \\ +\ 1586 \\ \hline 3172 \end{array}$

32. 2124 ; $\begin{array}{r} 1008 \\ +\ 1116 \\ \hline 2124 \end{array}$

4 Subtraction of 4-Digit Numbers

1. 2141 2. 4142 3. 2107
4. 2792 5. 1116 6. 7418
7. 3322 8. 4036 9. 5209
10. 1019 11. 621 12. 1344
13. A: 1526 B: 704 C: 1043
D: 930 E: 1163 F: 2259
14. 1526 – 704 ; 822 ; \$822
15. 1043 – 930 ; 113 ; \$113
16. 1163 – 322 ; 841 ; \$841
17. 2259 – 425 ; 1834 ; \$1834
18. 1289 19. 1596 20. 2136
21. 237 22. 1367 23. 2899

24. A: 1963 ; $\begin{array}{r} 4651 \\ -\ 2688 \\ \hline 1963 \end{array}$

B: 5888 ; $\begin{array}{r} 9682 \\ -\ 3794 \\ \hline 5888 \end{array}$

C: 1799 ; $\begin{array}{r} 2586 \\ -\ 787 \\ \hline 1799 \end{array}$

D: 1509 ; $\begin{array}{r} 6103 \\ -\ 4594 \\ \hline 1509 \end{array}$

E: 751 ; $\begin{array}{r} 7337 \\ -\ 6586 \\ \hline 751 \end{array}$

F: 5479 ; $\begin{array}{r} 8064 \\ -\ 2585 \\ \hline 5479 \end{array}$

25. 1766 ;
3 ; 3000 ; 3000 ; 1763 ;
1763 ; 3 ; 1766 ;
$\begin{array}{r} 4763 \\ -\ 2997 \\ \hline 1766 \end{array}$

26. 1291 ;
Add 4 to 4996, it is 5000. ;
6287 – 5000 = 1287 ;
1287 + 4 = 1291
$\begin{array}{r} 6287 \\ -\ 4996 \\ \hline 1291 \end{array}$

27. 1682 – 372 ; 1310 ; 1310 biscuits
28. 2885 – 394 ; 2491 ; 2491 m

5 Addition and Subtraction of 4-Digit Numbers

1. 3941 2. 2151 3. 2468
4. 869 5. 8234 6. 5259
7. 358 8. 8912 9. 1861
10. 4303 11. 1503 12. 1805
13. 5395 14. + 15. –
16. + 17. + 18. +

19. $\begin{array}{r} 2083 \\ +\ 1689 \\ \hline 3772 \end{array}$; $\begin{array}{r} 2083 \\ -\ 1689 \\ \hline 394 \end{array}$

20. $\begin{array}{r} 5287 \\ +\ 3249 \\ \hline 8536 \end{array}$; $\begin{array}{r} 5287 \\ -\ 3249 \\ \hline 2038 \end{array}$

21. A: 1400 ; 2900 ; 4300
B: 4100 ; 1800 ; 5900
C: 2400 ; 2000 ; 4400
22. 1500 23. 100
24. A: ✔ ; 3657

B: ✘ ; 1518 ; $\begin{array}{r} 1418 \\ +\ 2583 \\ \hline 4001 \end{array}$

C: ✘ ; 3207 ; $\begin{array}{r} 3217 \\ +\ 3849 \\ \hline 7066 \end{array}$

D: ✔ ; $\begin{array}{r} 6102 \\ -\ 858 \\ \hline 5244 \end{array}$

E: ✔ ; $\begin{array}{r} 1388 \\ +\ 4795 \\ \hline 6183 \end{array}$

ISBN: 978-1-897164-32-7

25. A: ✔; 1467
+ 2783
4250

B: ✘ ; 5782 ; 5882
− 3918
1964

C: ✘ ; 278 ; 268
+ 5996
6264

D: ✔; 5100
− 1899
3201

E: ✘ ; 1395 ; 1295
+ 2888
4183

26. a. 2885 – 1692 ; 1193 ; 1193 stickers
b. 2885 + 480 ; 3365 ; 3365 stickers
27. a. 4765 + 3688 ; 8453 ; 8453 hamburgers
b. 4765 – 3688 ; 1077 ; 1077 fewer
28. 1000 – 145 ; 855 ; 855 candies

6 Multiplication (1)

1. 27
2. 36
3. 20
4. 18
5. 56
6. 15
7. 36
8. 42
9. 9
10. 30
11. 32
12. 49
13. 54
14. 63
15. 16
16. 0
17. 21
18. 48
19. 9
20. 5
21. 3
22. 9

23. 7 ; 28
x 4
28

24. 3 ; $24
x 8
24

25. 4 ; 24 balls
x 6
24

26. 3 ; 27 boxes
x 9
27

27. 8 ; $40
x 5
40

28. 2 ; 18 kg
x 9
18

29. 3 ; 15 cm
x 5
15

30. 5 ; 40¢
x 8
40

31. 36
32. 48
33. 217
34. 128
35. 306
36. 246
37. 540
38. 148
39. 205
40. 189
41. 186 ; 248
42. 126 ; 189
43. 160 ; 280
44. 106 ; 159
45. a. 4 x 21 ; 84 ; 84 hats
b. 20 x 5 ; 100 ; $100
46. a. 11 x 9 ; 99 ; $99
b. 3 x 12 ; 36 ; 36 roses
47. a. 2 x 34 ; 68 ; 68 cows
b. 3 x 23 ; 69 ; 69 chickens
48. 4 x 32 ; 128 ; 128 chocolates

7 Multiplication (2)

1. ⑤
37
x 8
296

2. ①
52
x 7
364

3. ④
45
x 9
405

4. ①
73
x 4
292

5. ②
64
x 5
320

6. ④
28
x 6
168

7. 343
8. 504
9. 165
10. 76
11. 102
12. 396
13. 360
14. 312
15. 108
16. 112 ; 140 ; 196
17. $57 ; $133 ; $152
18. $162 ; $324 ; $432
19. $70 ; $175 ; $315
20. 80 ; 560
21. 90 ; 540
22. 20 ; 180
23. 4 ; 4
24. 8 ; 8
25. 5 ; 5
26. 7 ; 7
27. 5 ; 5
28. 3 ; 3
29. 252
30. 96
31. 120
32. 528
33. 4 x 42 ; 168 ; 168 stickers
34. 8 x 67 ; 536 ; $536
35. 54 x 9 ; 486 ; 486 ribbons
36. 7 x 16 ; 112 ; 112 cans

8 Division (1)

1. 4
5 ⟌ 20
20

2. 8 R 2
5 ⟌ 42
40
2

3. 9 R 1
7 ⟌ 64
63
1

4. 7
5. 6R3
6. 9
7. 5R3
8. 4
9. 8R1
10. 6R1
11. 8R4
12. 7R5
13. 6R5

14. 4 R 3
9 ⟌ 39
36
3

15. 5 R 4
8 ⟌ 44
40
4

16. 7 R 3
6 ⟌ 45
42
3

ISBN: 978-1-897164-32-7

17. blue → 5 R 8 ← red
9) 5 3 ← green
4 5
yellow: 9
8 ← red

18. 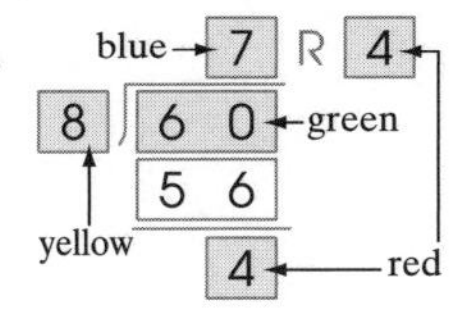

19. 16 ÷ 7 = 2 R 2
green yellow blue red

20. 43 ÷ 5 = 8 R 3
green yellow blue red

21. a. 6 ; 3 ; 39 ; 6
b. 28 ÷ 5 = 5R3 ; 3
c. 6R1 ; 43 ; 7 ; 6 ; 1
d. 50 ÷ 8 = 6R2 ; 6
e. 7R4 ; 67 ; 9 ; 7 ; 4

22. 4 R 2
8) 3 4
3 2
2

23. 9 R 1
5) 4 6
4 5
1

24. 5 R 4
7) 3 9
3 5
4

25. 6 R 3
9) 5 7
5 4
3

26. 6 R 5
6) 4 1
3 6
5

27. 8 R 2
4) 3 4
3 2
2

28. 6R2 29. 8R6 30. 9R2
31. 7R3 32. 3R1 33. 5R2
34. 9R2 ;

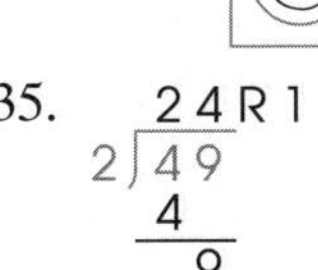

35. 2 4 R 1
2) 4 9
4
9
8
1

36. 2 1 R 2
4) 8 6
8
6
4
2

37. 3 2 R 2
3) 9 8
9
8
6
2

38. 1 1 R 1
6) 6 7
6
7
6
1

39. 1 0 R 4
5) 5 4
5
4

40. 3 2 R 1
2) 6 5
6
5
4
1

41. 11R3 42. 10R3 43. 10R2
44. 21R1 45. 11R4 46. 11R1
47. 68 ÷ 3 ; 22R2 ; 22 beads ; 2 beads left

9 Division (2)

1. 1 5 R 1
3) 4 6
3
1 6
1 5
1

2. 2 8 R 1
2) 5 7
4
1 7
1 6
1

3. 1 6 R 1
4) 6 5
4
2 5
2 4
1

4. 1 7 R 1
5) 8 6
5
3 6
3 5
1

5. 2 4 R 2
3) 7 4
6
1 4
1 2
2

6. 1 5
6) 9 0
6
3 0
3 0

7. 1 1 R 4
8) 9 2
8
1 2
8
4

8. 1 8
4) 7 2
4
3 2
3 2

9. 1 4 R 1
6) 8 5
6
2 5
2 4
1

10. 16R1

11. 13 12. 11R4 13. 12R5
14. 11R4 15. 13R1

16. 12 ;
1 2
5) 6 0
5
1 0
1 0

17. 16 ; 2 ;
1 6 R 2
3) 5 0
3
2 0
1 8
2

18. 15 ; 1 ;
1 5 R 1
3) 4 6
3
1 6
1 5
1

19. 15 ; 2 ;
1 5 R 2
4) 6 2
4
2 2
2 0
2

20. 1 8 R 1
4) 7 3
4
3 3
3 2
1

21. 1 3 R 2
5) 6 7
5
1 7
1 5
2

ISBN: 978-1-897164-32-7

22. 14 R 4
6) 88
6
28
24
4

23. 80 ÷ 5 ; 16 ; 16
24. 92 ÷ 8 ; 11R4 ; 11 ; 4
25. 75 ÷ 6 ; 12R3 ; 12 ; 3
26. a. 5) 85 = 17 (5, 35, 35) ; 17 ; 4) 72 = 18 (4, 32, 32) ; 18
    b. George
27. a. 4) 68 = 17 (4, 28, 28) ; 17 ; 0 ; 6) 68 = 11 (6, 8, 6, 2) ; 11 ; 2
    b. 2 cupcakes

10 More about Multiplication and Division

1. 600	2. 7000	3. 350
4. 9000	5. 2700	6. 420
7. 81 000	8. 3200	9. 940
10. 5000	11. 1000	12. 1000
13. 10	14. 10	15. 100
16. 100	17. 10	18. 1000
19. 4	20. 80	21. 60
22. 7	23. 5	24. 18
25. 205	26. 4	27. 100
28. 10	29. 100	30. 10
31. 10	32. 1000	33. 10
34. 100	35. ÷	36. x
37. x	38. ÷	39. ÷

40. ÷
41. ✔ ; 25 ; 3 ; 75 ; 75 ; 1 ; 76
42. ✔ ; 22 x 2 = 44 ; 44 + 1 = 45
43. ✘ ; 12R5 ; 12 x 7 = 84 ; 84 + 4 = 88
44. ✔ ; 15 x 6 = 90 ; 90 + 5 = 95
45. 17R1 ; 17 x 4 = 68 ; 68 + 1 = 69
46. 12R3 ; 12 x 6 = 72 ; 72 + 3 = 75
47. 11R4 ; 11 x 7 = 77 ; 77 + 4 = 81
48. 15 R 2 ; 15 x 3 = 45 ; 45 + 2 = 47
3) 47
3
17
15
2

49. 12 R 3 ; 12 x 7 = 84 ; 84 + 3 = 87
7) 87
7
17
14
3

50. $50
51. 460 hockey cards
52. 16 000 cm
53. 130 jellybeans

11 Length and Distance

1. km	2. cm
3. m	4. mm
5. a. cm	b. mm
6. a. km	b. cm
c. m	d. m
7. 600	8. 8000
9. 50	10. 70
11. 80	12. 6
13. 3	14. 9
15. 4	16. 10
17. 40 ; 4 cm	18. 800 ; 8 m
19. 900 ; 11 dm	20. 3000 ; 3 km

21. A: 92 B: 116 C: 110
Draw a string 110 mm long.
22. 11
23. 18
24. 55
25. (Individual estimates)

Height
CN Tower: 550 m
Rogers Centre: 100 m
Building A: 300 m

Distance between CN Tower and the bird: 250 m
Building A: 450 m

ISBN: 978-1-897164-32-7

26.

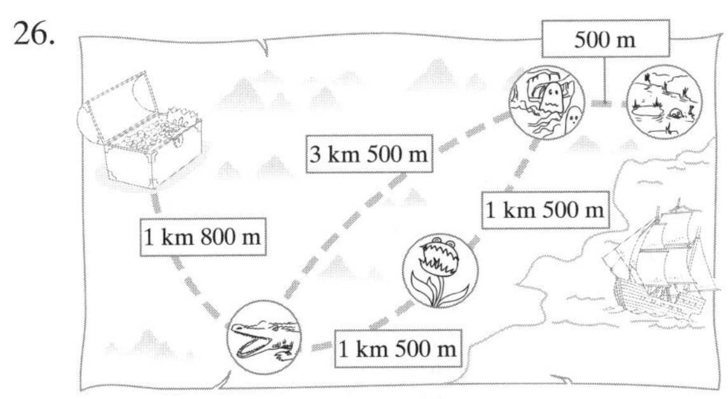

27. 1 km 500 m 28. 5 km 300 m

12 Perimeter and Area

1. square: 47 mm ; 188 mm
   rectangle: 73 mm ; 42 mm ; 230 mm
   pentagon: 32 mm ; 160 mm
   octagon: 22 mm ; 176 mm
   hexagon: 24 mm ; 144 mm
   triangle: 48 mm ; 144 mm
2. A: 28 m B: 29 km
   C: 172 mm D: 26 km
3. km 4. dm 5. m
6. mm 7. cm 8. cm
9. Area 10. Perimeter
11. Area 12. Perimeter
13. (Suggested answers)

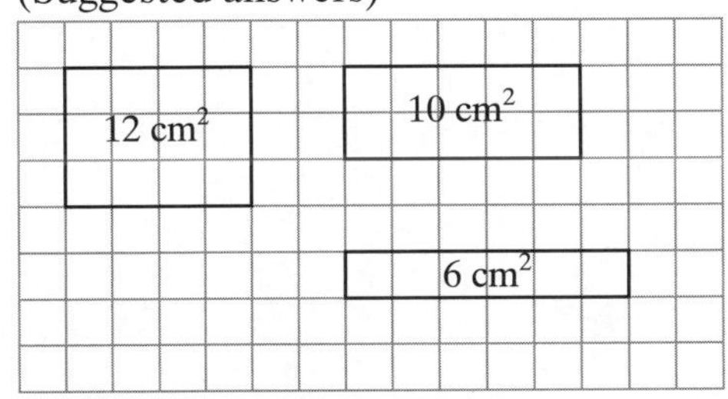

14. A: 10 cm ; 6 cm²
    B: 4 cm ; 3 cm ; 14 cm ; 12 cm²
    C: 5 cm ; 4 cm ; 18 cm ; 20 cm²
    D: 2 cm ; 5 cm ; 14 cm ; 10 cm²
    E: 3 cm ; 4 cm ; 14 cm ; 12 cm²
    F: 5 cm ; 3 cm ; 16 cm ; 15 cm²
15. Yes 16. Yes

13 Time

1. A: 17 ; 5 B: 9 ; 10
   C: 7:43 ; 17 min to 8 D: 1:24 ; 24 min past 1
   E: 4:53 ; 7 min to 5 F: 2:50 ; 10 min to 3
2. 3. 4.
5. a. 45 min b. Yes
   c. 7:25
6. a. 70 min or 1 h 10 min
   b. No c. 2:40
7. 8 85 ;
   9 : 25
   − 5 : 48
   3 : 37
   3 h 37 min
8. 3 93 ;
   4 : 33
   − 1 : 52
   2 : 41
   2 h 41 min
9. 11 73 ;
   12 : 13
   − 10 : 35
   1 : 38
   1 h 38 min
10. 5 78 ;
    6 : 18
    − 3 : 42
    2 : 36
    2 h 36 min
11. 2 h 35 min 12. 5:43 13. 3
14. 40 15. 6 16. 50
17. 8 18. 300 19. 90
20. 6 21. 1812 22. 30 years old
23. 6 ; 60

14 Mass, Capacity, and Volume

1. g 2. kg 3. g
4. 2000 5. 3 6. 5000
7. 9 8. 1200 9. 1060
10. 5004 11. 4800 12. B ; A ; C
13. C ; B ; A 14. mL 15. L
16. mL 17. L
18. A: 1040 mL B: 8500 mL
    C: 3060 mL D: 3600 mL
    B, D, C, A
19. P: 1200 mL Q: 500 mL
    R: 1050 mL S: 9500 mL
    S, P, R, Q
20. A ; F ; B ; E ; D ; C
21. 10 22. 6 23. 14
24. 10 25. 11
26. A: 14 ; 4 ; 18 B: 10 ; 8 ; 18
    C: 18 ; 9 ; 27
27. C 28. Q

Review 1

1. 4 ; 5 ; 6 ; 3 2. 7 ; 9 ; 5
3. 6000 ; 8 4. 9167

ISBN: 978-1-897164-32-7

5. a. 5000 ; 600 ; 20 ; 9
   b. 5600
6. a. 3000 ; 700 ; 50 ; 1
   b. 4000
7. ✘ ; 186 ; $196 + 209 = 405$
8. ✘ ; 444 ; $443 + 287 = 730$
9. ✔ ; $69 + 879 = 948$
10. ✔ ; $338 + 165 = 503$
11. SUM: 1253 + 8444 = 9697
    DIFF.: 8444 – 1253 = 7191
12. SUM: 2176 + 1439 = 3615
    DIFF.: 2176 – 1439 = 737
13. SUM: 5006 + 3814 = 8820
    DIFF.: 5006 – 3814 = 1192
14. SUM: 8010 + 753 = 8763
    DIFF.: 8010 – 753 = 7257
15.

No. of Visitors	1st Half of the Year	2nd Half of the Year	Whole Year
Men	4653	3750	8403
Women	3815	4502	8317

16. 4653 + 3815 ; 8468 ; 8468 visitors
17. 3750 + 4502 ; 8252 ; 8252 visitors
18. 8403 – 8317 ; 86 ; 86 more
19. 63
20. 234
21. 360
22. $65 \div 7 = 9R2$ (7 into 65; 63; remainder 2)
23. $92 \div 6 = 15R2$ (6 into 92; 6; 32; 30; remainder 2)
24. $85 \div 5 = 17$ (5 into 85; 5; 35; 35)
25. 296
26. 258
27. 23
28. 11R2
29. 306
30. 243
31. 10R3
32. 22R2
33. 8 x 34 ; 272 ; 272 cookies
34. 58 ÷ 2 ; 29 ; 29 packs
35. 54 ÷ 8 ; 6R6 ; 7 packs
36. ✔ ; 17 x 4 = 68 ; 68 + 1 = 69
37. ✘ ; 11R5 ; 12 x 7 = 84 ; 84 + 2 = 86
38. ✘ ; 15R4 ; 16 x 6 = 96 ; 96 + 2 = 98
39. ✔ ; 10 x 5 = 50 ; 50 + 3 = 53
40. 92 mm ; 114 mm ; 106 mm
41. a. 18 mm b. 23 mm
42. km
43. cm
44. dm
45. m
46. mm
47. cm
48. A: 14 cm ; 8 cm^2 B: 14 cm ; 9 cm^2
    C: 16 cm ; 16 cm^2 D: 10 cm ; 6 cm^2
49. 
    7 ; 14
50. 
    22 min to 10
51. 
    7 min to 3
52. a. 60 min or 1 h b. Yes
    c. 4:35
53. A: 9 ; 900 B: 11 cm^3 ; 1100 g
    C: 9 cm^3 ; 900 g D: 8 cm^3 ; 800 g
    E: 9 cm^3 ; 900 g

15 Fractions

1. 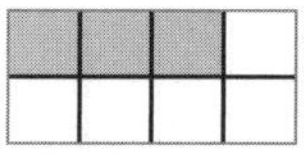 ; $\frac{3}{8}$
2. 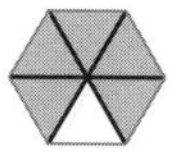 ; $\frac{5}{6}$
3. 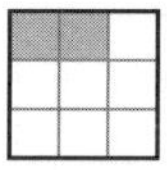 ; $\frac{2}{9}$
4. 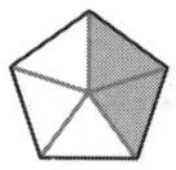 ; $\frac{2}{5}$
5. 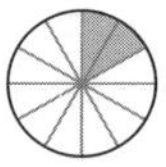 ; $\frac{2}{12}$
6. 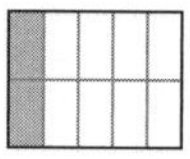 ; $\frac{2}{10}$
7. 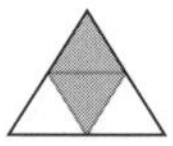 ; $\frac{2}{4}$
8. 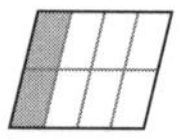 ; $\frac{2}{8}$
9. $\frac{5}{6}$, $\frac{7}{10}$, $\frac{9}{10}$, $\frac{7}{12}$
10. $\frac{3}{5}$, $\frac{2}{3}$, $\frac{1}{4}$
11. 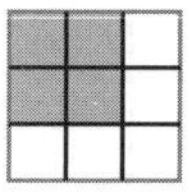
12. 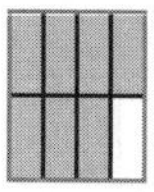
13. 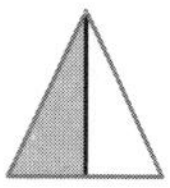
14. 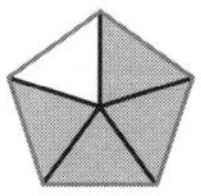
15. 
16. 
17. A: $\frac{2}{6}$ B: $\frac{1}{3}$ C: $\frac{3}{5}$
    $\frac{2}{6}$; $\frac{1}{3}$
18. A: $\frac{6}{9}$ B: $\frac{5}{10}$ C: $\frac{1}{2}$
    $\frac{5}{10}$; $\frac{1}{2}$

19-21. (Suggested drawings)
19. 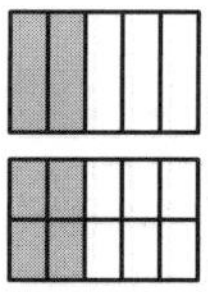
20. 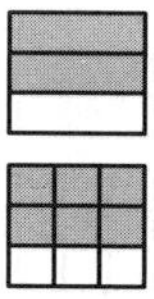
21.

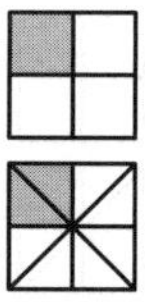

ISBN: 978-1-897164-32-7

22. $\frac{3}{6} < \frac{4}{6}$ 23. $\frac{8}{12} > \frac{3}{6}$ 24. $\frac{3}{10} < \frac{3}{5}$

25. $\frac{3}{4} > \frac{2}{4}$ 26. $\frac{7}{8}$ 27. $\frac{9}{10}$

28. $\frac{1}{3}$ 29. $\frac{4}{5}$ 30. $\frac{6}{7}$

31. $\frac{8}{9}$ 32. $\frac{1}{3}$; $\frac{3}{5}$; $\frac{9}{10}$

33. $\frac{1}{5}$; $\frac{3}{8}$; $\frac{3}{4}$ 34. $\frac{1}{4}$; $\frac{3}{10}$; $\frac{5}{9}$

35. Joe

16 Decimals

1. 0.9 ; 9 2. 1.4 ; 1 ; 4
3. 2.3 ; 2 and 3 tenths
4. 4.8 ; 4 and 8 tenths
5.   ; 2 and 7 tenths
6. 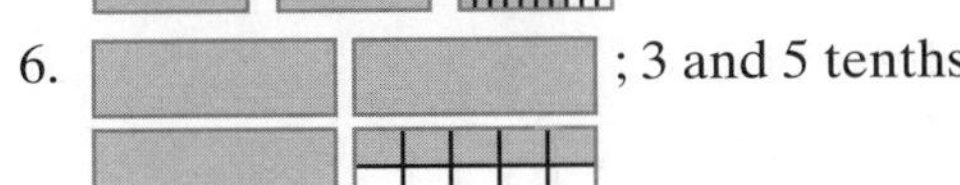 ; 3 and 5 tenths
7. 0.6 8. 7 9. 30
10. 0.8 11. 0.2 12. 90
13. 5 14. 0.4 15. 4
16. 6.2 ; 5.9 17.  11.6 ; 20.1

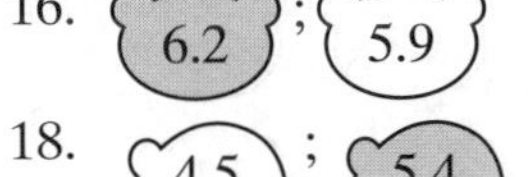

18. 4.5 ; 5.4 19.  13.1 ; 1.3

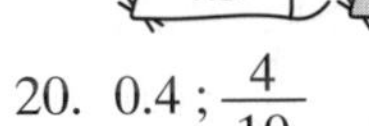

20. 0.4 ; $\frac{4}{10}$ 21. 0.7 ; $\frac{7}{10}$ 22. 0.3 ; $\frac{3}{10}$
23. 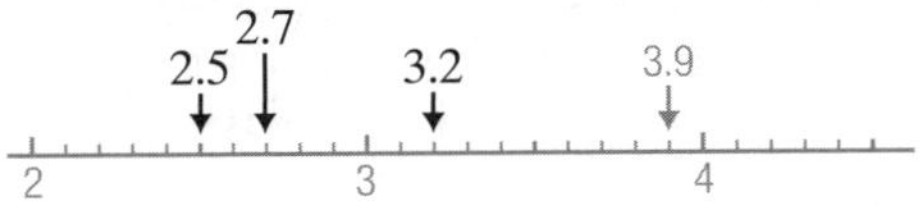 2.5, 2.7, 3.2, 3.9 (number line 2 – 4) ;

2.5, 2.7, 3.2, 3.9
24. 5.9, 6.5, 6.8, 7.4 (number line 5 – 7) ;

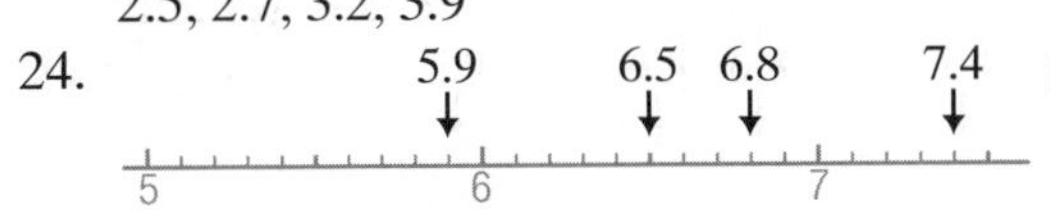

7.4, 6.8, 6.5, 5.9
25. 4.0, 4.8, 5.1 (number line 3 – 6)
26. 8.4, 9.5, 9.8, 10.3 (number line 8 – 11)

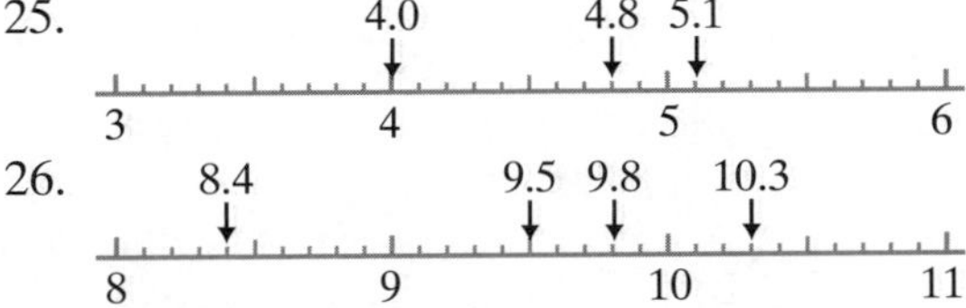

27. 0.3 28. 0.5 29. 9.7
30. 8.1 31. 8.1 32. 4.9
33. 6.8 ; 7.0 ; 7.6 34. 9.1 ; 8.9 ; 8.8
35. 6.0 ; 6.5 ; 7.5 36. 10.9 ; 11.9 ; 12.9
37. A: 0.6 B: 1.2
C: 1.9 D: 2.7

38. D 39. 0.3 m
40. 0.6 m 41. 0.8 m

17 Addition and Subtraction of Decimals

1. 8.1 2. 11.8 3. 14.0
4. 13.4 5. 16.7 6. 9.2
7. 22.1 8. 23.2 9. 24.1
10. 23 ; $16.8 + 6.2 = 23.0$ 11. 41 ; $19.5 + 21.5 = 41.0$
12. 16.6 13. 17.2
14. 11.4 15. 27
16. Tim: $9.6 + 5.8 = 15.4$ Ray: $8.1 + 11.9 = 20.0$ Mark: $12.5 + 6.3 = 18.8$

Lucy: $7.6 + 6.6 = 14.2$ Sue: $10.7 + 3.3 = 14.0$ Lily: $8.2 + 4.4 = 12.6$

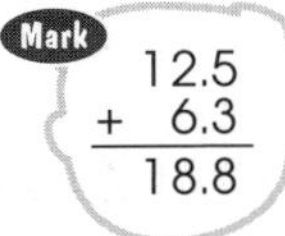
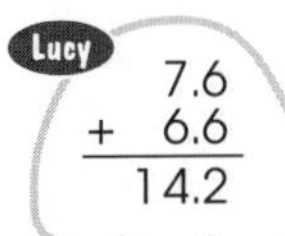

17. Ray 18. Lily
19. 15.4 + 20 + 18.8 ; 54.2 ; 54.2
20. 14.2 + 14 + 12.6 ; 40.8 ; 40.8
21. the boys' team
22. 8.9 ; $14.7 - 5.8 = 8.9$ 23. 5.6 ; $10.2 - 4.6 = 5.6$
24. 5.8 ; $8.5 - 2.7 = 5.8$ 25. 4.6 ; $8.0 - 3.4 = 4.6$
26. 7.1 ; $14.0 - 6.9 = 7.1$ 27. 6.8 ; $20.0 - 13.2 = 6.8$
28. 1.8 29. 3.7
30. 6.9 31. 5.2
32. 1 [5] . [9] − 6 . 8 = 9 . 1 33. 2 [0] . 3 − 8 . [7] = 1 1 . 6
34. [3] 5 . [4] − 1 [1] . 6 = 2 3 . 8
35. 12.2 36. 11.8 37. 4.5
38. 1.6 39. 16.2 40. 22.3
41. 1.3 – 0.8 ; 0.5 ; 0.5 L
42. 0.8 + 0.8 ; 1.6 ; 1.6 kg
43. 1.3 + 0.4 ; 1.7 ; 1.7 m
44. 38.2 – 16.4 ; 21.8 ; 21.8 m
45. 1.4 + 1.4 + 1.4 + 1.4 ; 5.6 ; 5.6 L

ISBN: 978-1-897164-32-7

18 Money

1. (Individual estimates)
   A: 70 ; 85 ; 70.85
   B: 77 dollars 10 cents or $77.10
   C: 61 dollars 28 cents or $61.28
   D: 50 dollars 65 cents or $50.65
2. A: $20 $20 $5 25¢ 25¢ 10¢ 1¢ 1¢ 1¢
   B: $50 $2 $1 10¢ 5¢ 1¢ 1¢
   C: $50 $20 $20 $5 $2 25¢ 25¢ 5¢
   D: $20 $10 $2 25¢ 25¢ 25¢ 5¢ 1¢ 1¢
3. $45.63 + $32.82 = $78.45 ; $53.17 + $32.82 = $85.99
4. $97.55 − $53.17 = $44.38 ; $97.55 − $45.63 = $51.92
5. Uncle Ben's Toyland

Item	Cost
Mr. Frog	$ 2.59
Mr. Frog	$ 2.59
Robot	$28.75
Total	$33.93
Cash	$50.00
Change	$16.07

6. Uncle Ben's Toyland

Item	Cost
Tricycle	$39.24
Doll	$20.88
Puzzle	$ 8.69
Total	$68.81
Cash	$70.01
Change	$ 1.20

7. Uncle Ben's Toyland

Item	Cost
Doll	$20.88
Puzzle	$ 8.69
Mr. Frog	$ 2.59
Total	$ 32.16
Cash	$ 40.00
Change	$ 7.84

8. Uncle Ben's Toyland

Item	Cost
Mr. Frog	$ 2.59
Tricycle	$39.24
Puzzle	$ 8.69
Total	$50.52
Cash	$ 51.00
Change	$ 0.48

9. $45.64 – $28.75 ; $16.89 ; $16.89
10. $39.24 – $28.66 ; $10.58 ; $10.58
11. a. $32.65 ; $65.30
    $32.65 + $32.65 = $65.30
    b. $40.00 ; $7.35
    $40.00 − $32.65 = $ 7.35
12. a. $40.89 ; $12.89
    $40.89 − $28.00 = $12.89
    b. $40.89 ; $48.54
    $40.89 + $ 7.65 = $48.54
13. a. $59.77 ; $16.79
    $59.77 − $42.98 = $16.79
    b. $42.98 ; $85.96
    $42.98 + $42.98 = $85.96

19 2-D Shapes (1)

1. 2 ; 5 ; 4 ; 6 ; 2 ; 3 ; 2 ; 5 ; 1

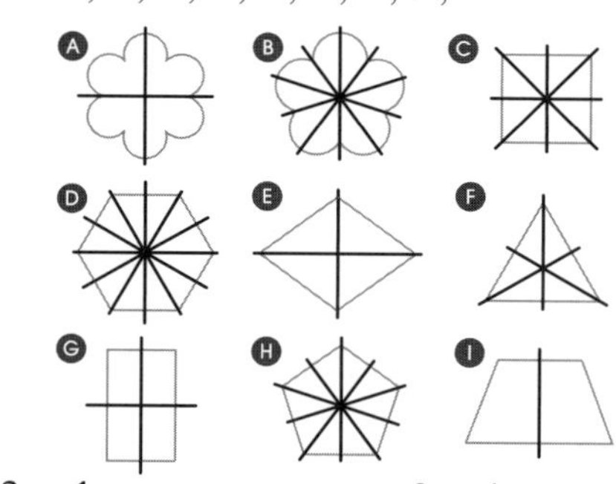

2. ✔
3. ✔
4. ✘
5. ✘
6. 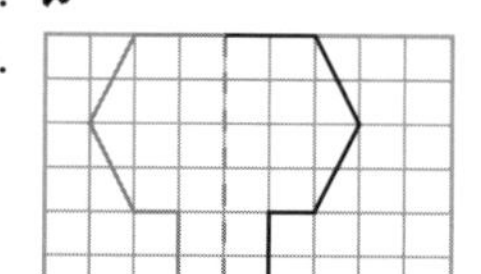
   hexagon, square
7. rectangle, pentagon
8. 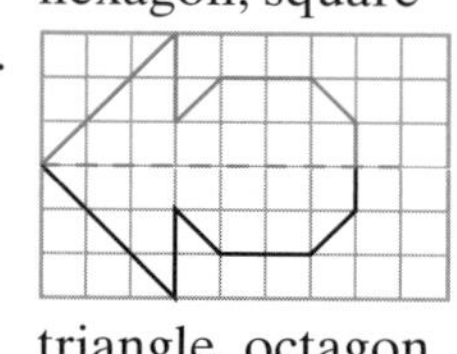
   triangle, octagon
9. 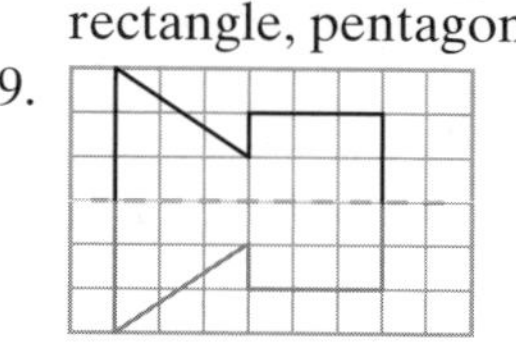
   trapezoid, rectangle
10. A: square
    B: trapezoid
    C: parallelogram
    D: rectangle
    E: rhombus
11. 2.2 ; 2.2 ; 3 cm ; 3 cm ; 2.1 cm ; 2.1 cm ; 2.1 cm ; 2.1 cm ; 3 cm ; 3 cm ; 4 cm ; 4 cm

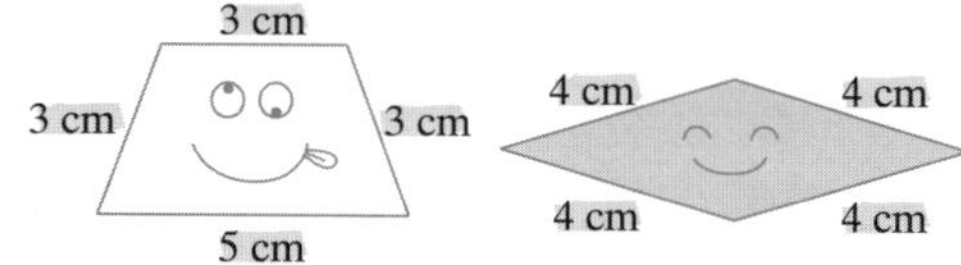

12. 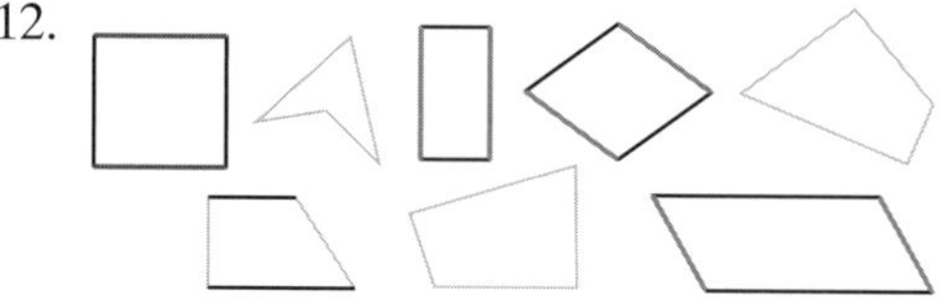

ISBN: 978-1-897164-32-7

13. trapezoid
14. square, rectangle, parallelogram, rhombus
15. 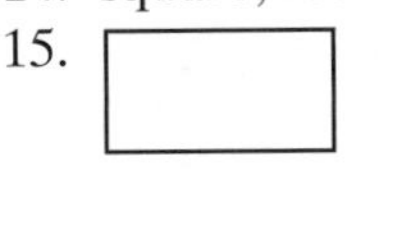
16. 
17. 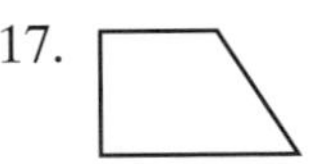
18. 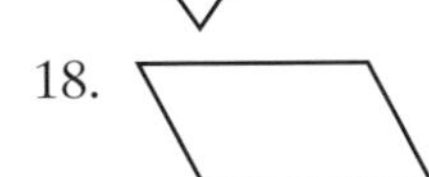

20 2-D Shapes (2)

1. straight angle
2. half of a right angle
3. right angle
4. half of a right angle
5. straight angle
6. 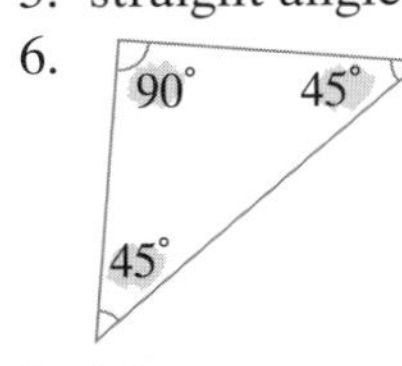

7. 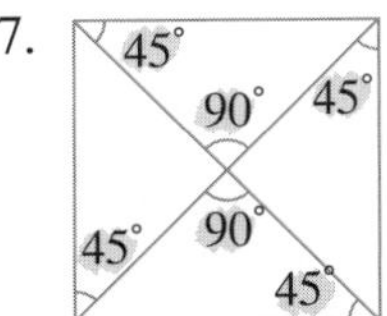

8. 90°
9. 180°
10. 180°
11. B
12. A
13. C
14. C

15-16. (Suggested answers)

15. 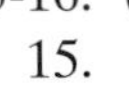 
16. 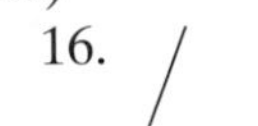
17. The angle is greater than 90° but smaller than 180°.
18. The angle is smaller than 90° but greater than 45°.
19. 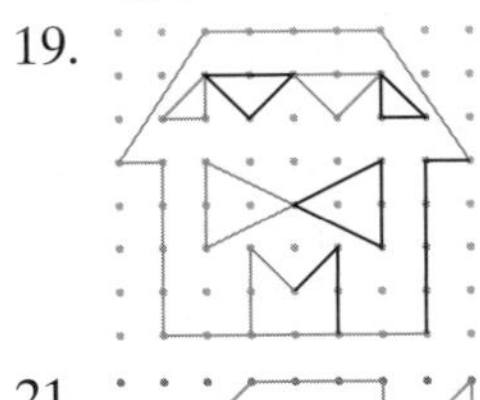
20. 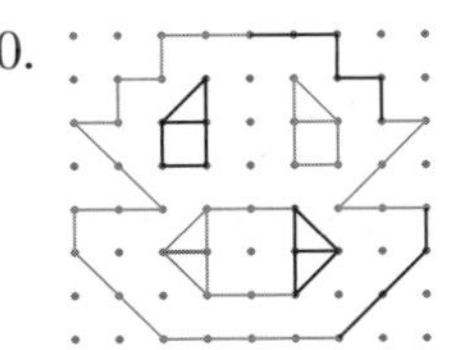
21. 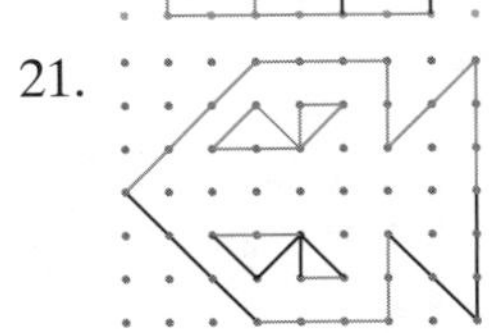
22. 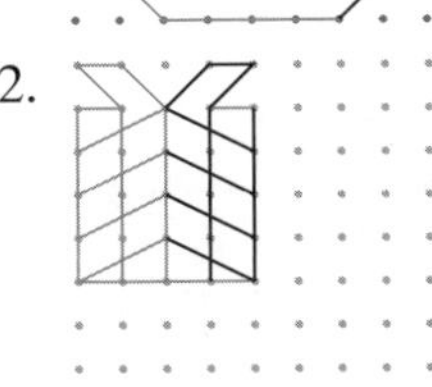

21 3-D Figures (1)

1. A: rectangular prism ; 0
   B: rectangular pyramid ; 4
   C: hexagonal prism ; 0
   D: pentagonal pyramid ; 5
   E: triangular prism ; 2
   F: triangular pyramid ; 4
   G: pentagonal prism ; 0
   H: hexagonal pyramid ; 6
2. rectangular pyramid ; 4 ; 1 ; 5 ; 8
3. rectangular prism ; 6 ; 8 ; 12 ; rectangle
4. It is a hexagonal pyramid. It has 6 triangular faces and 1 hexagonal face. It has 7 vertices and 12 edges.
5. It is a triangular prism. It has 3 rectangular faces and 2 triangular faces. It has 6 vertices and 9 edges.
6. It is a pentagonal pyramid. It has 5 triangular faces and 1 pentagonal face. It has 6 vertices and 10 edges.
7. 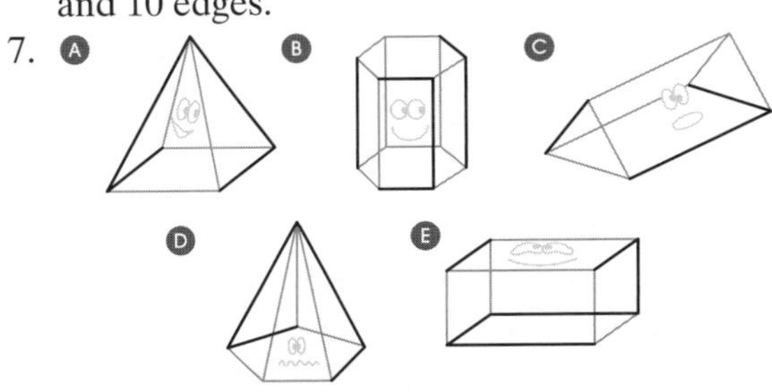

   A: rectangular pyramid ; 8 ; 5
   B: hexagonal prism ; 18 ; 12
   C: triangular prism ; 9 ; 6
   D: pentagonal pyramid ; 10 ; 6
   E: rectangular prism ; 12 ; 8
8.

	No. of Vertices	No. of Edges	No. of Faces
Triangular prism	6	9	5
Rectangular prism	8	12	6
Pentagonal prism	10	15	7
Hexagonal prism	12	18	8

9.

	No. of Vertices	No. of Edges	No. of Faces
Triangular pyramid	4	6	4
Rectangular pyramid	5	8	5
Pentagonal pyramid	6	10	6
Hexagonal pyramid	7	12	7

10. a triangular prism or a pentagonal pyramid
11. a rectangular prism or a hexagonal pyramid
12. a cube

22 3-D Figures (2)

1. A
2. A
3. B
4. A
5. A

6-7. (Suggested answers)

6. 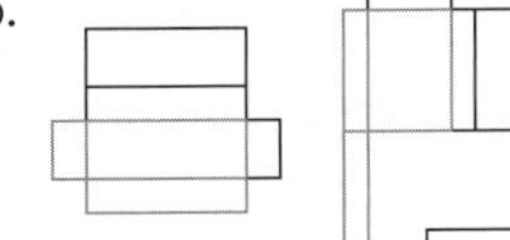 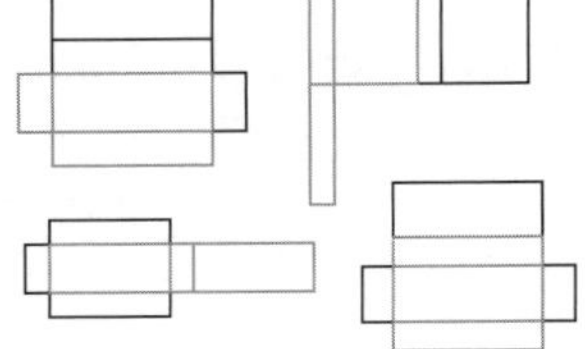

ISBN: 978-1-897164-32-7

7.

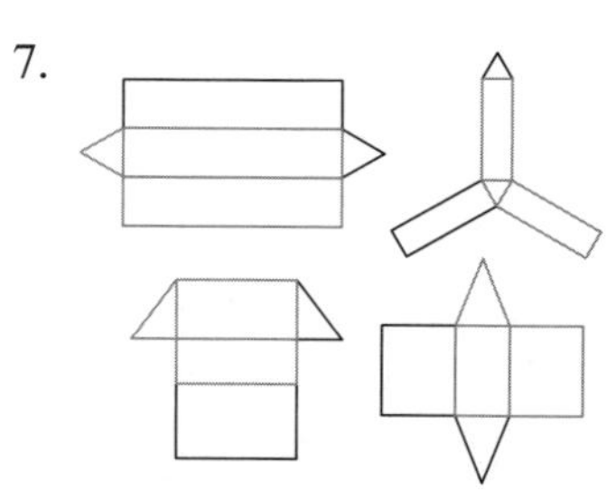

8. Colour A, B, E, H, I
9. (Suggested drawings)

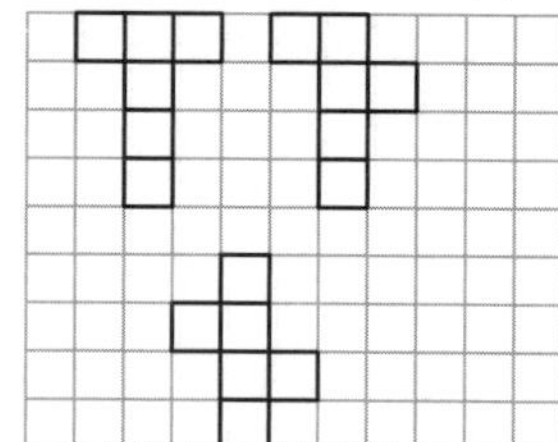

10. A, E
11. (Suggested answers)

12.

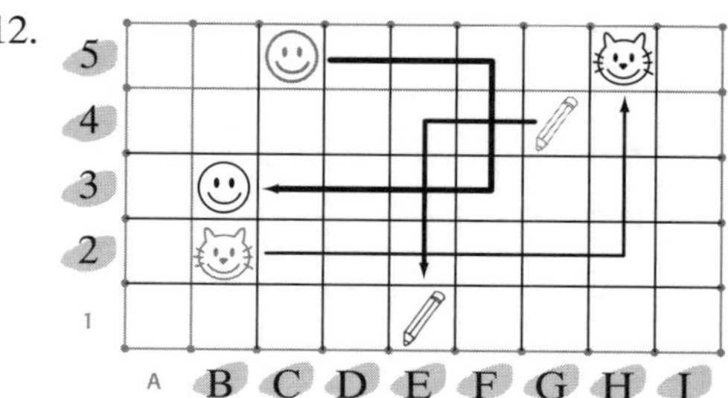

13. E1 14. H5 15. B3
16.

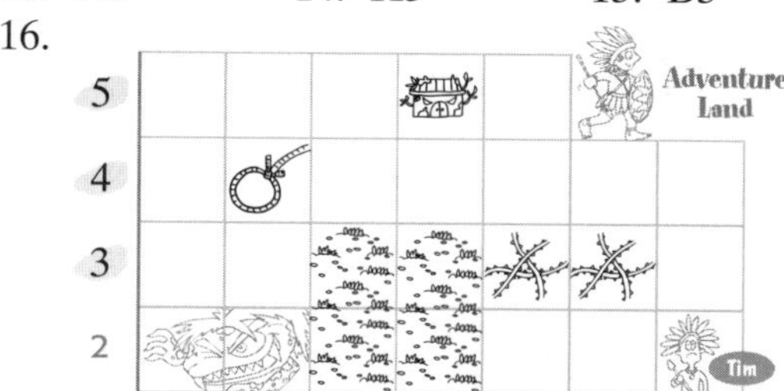

17. G2 18. A2, B2
19. 4 squares 20. 2 squares
21. He should go 2 squares up, 4 squares left, 1 square up, 2 squares left, and 3 squares down to get to the monster.

23 Grids

1. Car: A1, B3, D4, E7, F4, F6, G1
   Top: A7, C5, C6, F3, G5
   Yo-yo: A5, C1, E1, G3
2. 7 columns 3. 7 rows
4. 3 toys 5. 2 toys
6. row 1
7. a. C1, E5, G1, H1 b. B4, C3, G3
8.

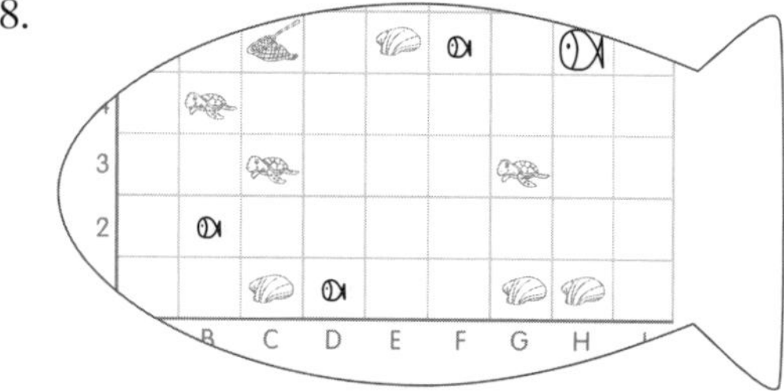

9. Its new location is E1. The path is 4 squares down.
10. The big fish should eat the one at F5 by going 2 squares left.
11. It should go 1 square up and 5 squares left.

24 Patterning (1)

1. growing ; 15 ; 17 2. shrinking ; 30 ; 20
3. repeating ; 11 ; 5 4. shrinking ; 71 ; 69
5. 6 ; 9 ; 10 ; 13 ; 14 ; growing
6. 10 ; 20 ; 40 ; 80 ; 160 ; 320 ; growing
7. 95 ; 94 ; 92 ; 91 ; 89 ; 88 ; shrinking
8. 45 ; 42 ; 43 ; 40 ; 41 ; 38 ; shrinking
9. x 2, – 1 10. – 2, – 3
11. + 2, + 1 12. x 3, +1
13. a.

Term Number	1	2	3	4	5	6	7
Term	9	13	17	21	25	29	33

b. 17 ; 29

14. a.

Term Number	1	2	3	4	5	6	7
Term	86	85	83	82	80	79	77

b. 85 ; 80

15. a.

Term Number	Term
1	7
2	14
3	13
4	26
5	25

b. 49

16. a.

Term Number	Term
1	8
2	12
3	10
4	14
5	12

b. 18

ISBN: 978-1-897164-32-7

17. 2, 6, 18, 54, 162, 486
18. 10, 12, 14, 16, 18, 20
19.

Term Number	Term
1	20¢
2	24¢
3	28¢
4	32¢
5	36¢
6	40¢
7	44¢

20.

Term Number	Term
1	48¢
2	45¢
3	42¢
4	39¢
5	36¢
6	33¢
7	30¢

21. On day 5, each girl saves 36¢.

25 Patterning (2)

1. a.
   b.

No. of Groups	1	2	3	4	5	6
No. of Squares	4	8	12	16	20	24

   c. 32
2. a.
   b.

No. of Groups	1	2	3	4	5	6
No. of Rectangles	2	4	6	8	10	12
No. of Parallelograms	1	2	3	4	5	6

   c. 18 ; 9
3. 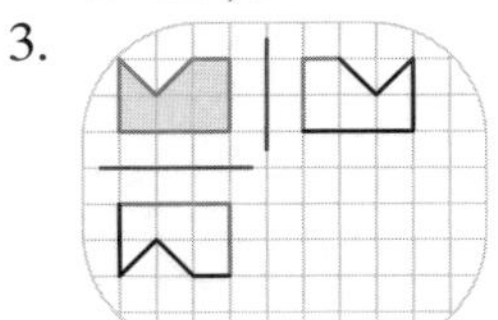
4. 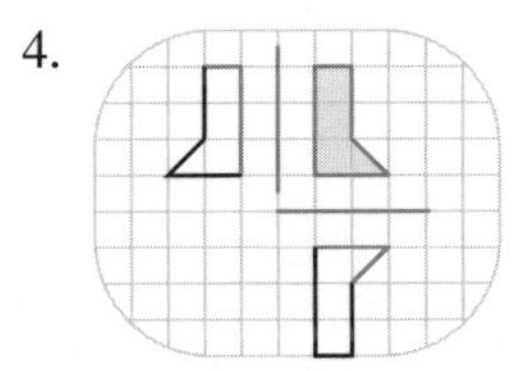
5. 6. 7. 8.
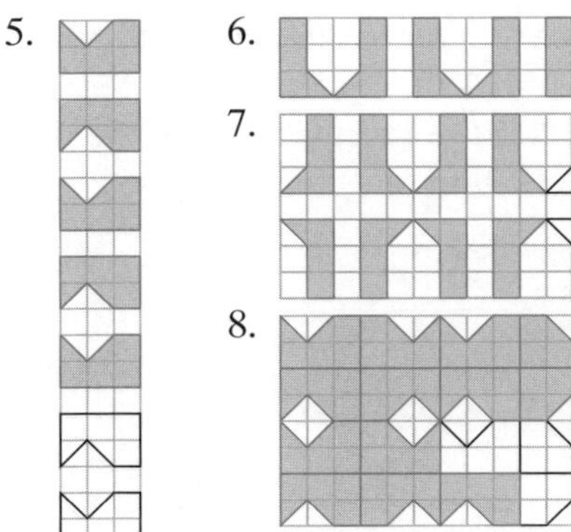

9. 20
10. 9
11. 2
12. 4
13. 13
14. 72
15. 6 ; 24 ÷ 6 = 4 or 24 ÷ 4 = 6
16. 8 ; 72 ÷ 8 = 9 or 72 ÷ 9 = 8
17. 3 ; 30 ÷ 10 = 3 or 30 ÷ 3 = 10
18. 5 ; 65 ÷ 5 = 13 or 65 ÷ 13 = 5
19. 15 ; 90 ÷ 6 = 15 or 90 ÷ 15 = 6
20. 4 ; 96 ÷ 24 = 4 or 96 ÷ 4 = 24
21. 9 ; 99 ÷ 9 = 11 or 99 ÷ 11 = 9
22. 3 ; 75 ÷ 3 = 25 or 75 ÷ 25 = 3
23. 2 ; 32 ÷ 16 = 2 or 32 ÷ 2 = 16

24-26. (Individual testing)

24. 4
25. 5
26. 3
27. 17
28. 5
29. 10
30. 8
31. 42
32. 2
33. 1000
34. 10
35. 5
36. 4

26 Graphs (1)

1. 23 children
2. 55 bounces
3. 20 bounces
4. 2 children
5. 3 children
6. 4 children
7. 54 bounces
8. Our Favourite Storybooks
9. Number of Children
10. Storybook
11. 50 boys
12. 165 girls
13. 365 children
14. Sailing, 80 boys and girls
15. 126 children
16. In order:
    128, 129, 130, 130, 130, 130, 132, 135, 135, 136, 141, 141, 142, 144, 145
    Median: 135 cm ; Mode: 130 cm
17. In order:
    2, 2, 2, 3, 3, 4, 4, 4, 5, 5, 5, 5, 6, 7, 7, 8, 9, 9, 10, 10
    Median: \$5 ; Mode: \$5
18. In order:
    23, 25, 26, 27, 29, 40, 45, 54, 54, 58, 58, 66, 66, 66, 66, 66, 70
    Median: 54 marbles ; Mode: 66 marbles
19. 23 h
20. 27 h
21. 22 years old
22. 78 g
23. 108 min

27 Graphs (2)

1. **Number of Pizzas Sold Each Day in April**

Stem	Leaves
2	9 9
3	0 4 4 5 5
4	4 4 4 4 4 4 6 8
6	0 0 0 2 2 3 3 3 5 5 8
7	0 5 5 5

ISBN: 978-1-897164-32-7

2. 4 days
3. A, C
4. 55 marbles
5. in multiples of 10
6. **Marbles Collected by the Children**

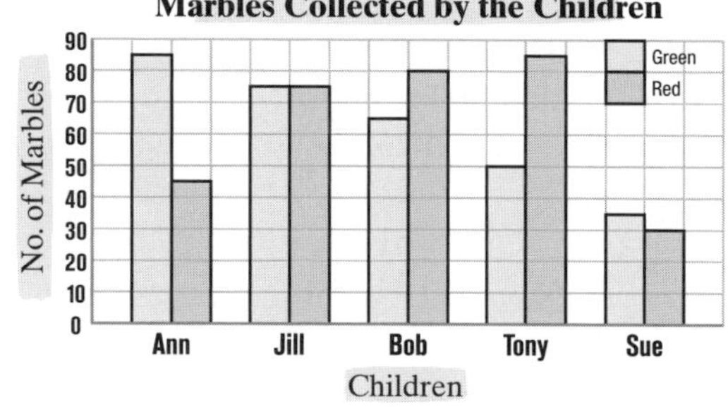

7. Jill
8. 310 green marbles
9. (Suggested answer)
The number of green marbles and the number of red marbles that the children have are about the same.
10. **Number of Apples Picked**

Stem	Leaves
3	0 0 0 0 1 1 2 2 2 3 3 4 5 6 6 6
4	2 2 3 3 5 5 5
5	4 4 5 6 6 6 8 9
6	2 2 3 7 7 8
7	0 2 3

11. 44 apples
12. 30 apples
13. 43 apples
14. 40 people
15. 9 people
16. 72 apples
17. The plot shows most people picked about 30 apples yesterday.
18. **Number of Pails of Honey Collected Each Month**

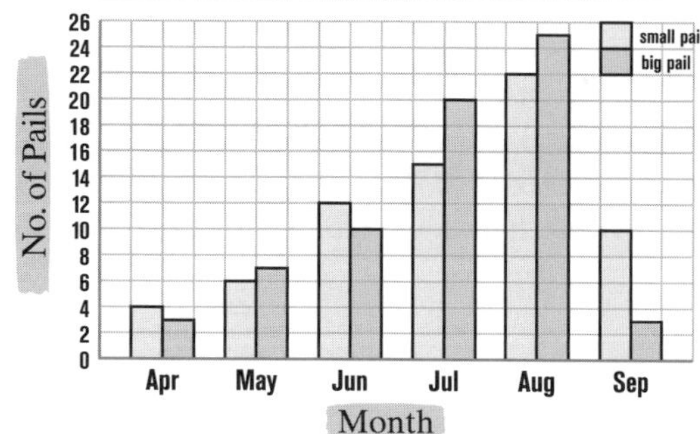

19. (Suggested answer)
The graph shows that a great amount of honey was collected in August.
20. 68 L

28 Probability

1.

2nd Cube \ 1st Cube	1	2	3	4	5	6
1	2	3	4	5	6	7
2	3	4	5	6	7	8
3	4	5	6	7	8	9
4	5	6	7	8	9	10
5	6	7	8	9	10	11
6	7	8	9	10	11	12

;

Possible outcomes: 2, 3, 4, 5, 6, 7, 8, 9, 10, 11, 12

2. a. ✘ b. ✔ c. ✘
d. ✔ e. ✔
3. Amy, Celine
4. It is more probable to get a number between 5 and 9 and less probable to get a smaller or bigger number.
5. (Suggested answers)

Outcome	No. of Times
2	3
3	6
4	8
5	11
6	14
7	16
8	14
9	11
10	8
11	6
12	3

6. A ; Since each section has the same area, the probability of landing on each section should be about the same.
7. C ; Since the star has the greatest area and the diamond has the least, the pointer will land on the star the most times and the diamond the fewest times.
8.

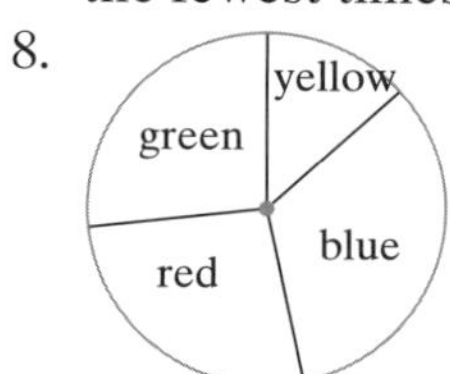

9. a.

Children	1	2	3	4	5	6
No. of Tails	3	5	6	4	7	2

b. 60 ; 27

10. a.

Children	1	2	3	4	5	6	7	8	9	10
No. of Tails	4	5	7	6	3	4	5	5	6	4

b. 100 ; 49

11. Yes

ISBN: 978-1-897164-32-7

Review 2

1. a. 4.6

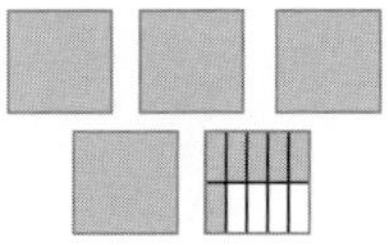

b. 3.2

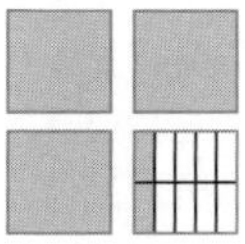

c. 3.5

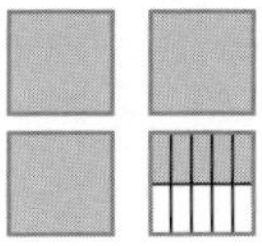

d. 4.3

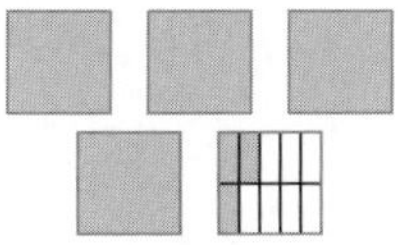

2.

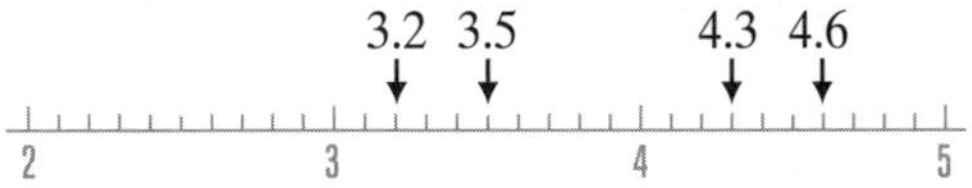

3. 3.2, 3.5, 4.3, 4.6
4.

$\frac{5}{6}$

5.

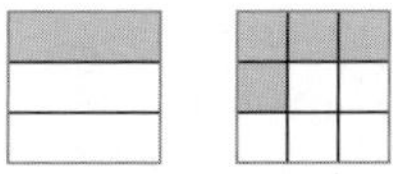

$\frac{1}{3}$

6. cat: 21.2 octopus: 38.6 seal: 56.2
fish: 38.7 crab: 38.4 cow: 47.6
snake: 15.6 turtle: 3.9 pig: 75.3
mouse: 37 rabbit: 19.4 lion: 27.3
elephant: 6.2
7. turtle 8. seal 9. fish
10. A: 73.53 B: 32.65 C: 17.37
11. $\begin{array}{r} \$73.53 \\ +\ \$17.37 \\ \hline \$90.90 \end{array}$; The total cost is $90.90.
12. $\begin{array}{r} \$32.65 \\ +\ \$17.37 \\ \hline \$50.02 \end{array}$; The total cost is $50.02.
13. $\begin{array}{r} \$32.65 \\ -\ \$17.37 \\ \hline \$15.28 \end{array}$; The price difference is $15.28.
14. $\begin{array}{r} \$73.53 \\ -\ \$17.37 \\ \hline \$56.16 \end{array}$; The price difference is $56.16.
15. 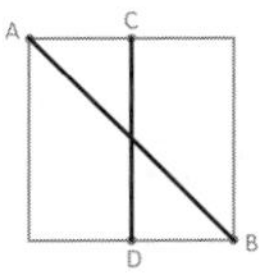

; 45° ; yes

square
16. 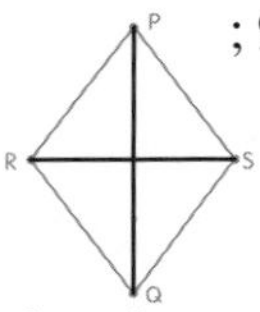

; 90° ; 2 pairs

rhombus

17. A ; 3 ; 2 ; 6 ; 9
18. B ; 1 ; 4 ; 5 ; 8
19. 7 ; 14 ; 28 ; 56 ; 112 ; 224 ; 896
20. 96 ; 93 ; 90 ; 87 ; 84 ; 81 ; 72
21. 125 22. 14 23. 7
24. 31 25. 25 26. 5
27. 9 28. 3 29. 3
30. 100 31. 7 32. 48
33. 4 34. 25 pieces 35. 96 cm
36. 42 cm 37. 35 cm
38. A ; Since the ruler has the greatest area, and the areas of the pencil and the crayon are about the same, the number of times that the pointer lands on the the ruler should be the greatest. The number of times that the pointer lands on either the pencil or the crayon should be about the same.

ISBN: 978-1-897164-32-7

1 Tim Horton

A. 1. took part in
2. start a business
3. operation
4. group of shops owned by the same company

B. 4 ; 5 ; 1 ; 2 ; 3

C. (Individual answer)

D. Common Noun: hockey ; doughnut
Proper Noun: Tim Hortons ; Stanley Cup
(Individual new nouns)

E. 1. Mr. and Mrs. Schwimmer like chatting in a coffee shop.
2. The Calgary Flames is a very strong hockey team.
3. My brother wants to be a firefighter.

F. 1. greater ; greatest
2. more talented ; most talented
3. more famous ; most famous
4. sweeter ; sweetest

G. 1. more
2. latest
3. newest
4. nearer
5. most reliable

2 The Strangest Animal on Earth

A. 1. burrows near freshwater streams and ponds
2. about the size of a cat
3. about three kilograms
4. crayfish, worms, snails, shrimp, other small water animals, and small land rodents
5. between 10 and 17 years

B. 1. a. It lays eggs.
b. It has webbed feet and a bill.
c. Its tail looks like a beaver's.
2. It is for protecting the platypus from other animals or killing small animals for food.

C. 1. swims ; I
2. have ; T
3. love ; T
4. eats ; T
5. exercises ; I
6. sleeps ; I

D. (Individual writing)

E. 1. STEADILY
2. GLADLY
3. HEAVILY
4. SPECIALLY
5. PROUDLY
6. PROBABLY

F. (Individual writing)

3 Madagascar

A. Madagascar has many species of unique animals and plants.

B. 1. unique
2. species
3. ancestors
4. unusual
5. connected

C. 1. plants ; animals
2. World Wildlife Fund
3. Dad
4. We
5. I
6. brother

D. (Individual answers)

E. 1. ✘ 2. ✘
3. ✔ 4. ✔
5. ✔

F. (Individual writing)

4 Velcro

A. 1. T 2. T
3. F 4. T
5. F 6. F
7. T 8. F

B. 1. imitation
2. stuck
3. microscope
4. designer
5. burr

ISBN: 978-1-897164-32-7

C. 1. Grandpa | invented a device that can trap mice.
2. He | had looked at various kinds of mice traps before he made his own.
3. My brother | wants to invent something too.
4. He | is thinking of inventing a device to replace the remote control for the TV.
5. He and his friend | are looking for relevant information.

D. 1. George and a French designer
2. Hooks and loops
3. My running shoes
4. I
5. Marco and Eric

E. 1. E 2. F
3. C 4. A
5. D 6. B

F. (Individual writing)

5 The Zzzzipper!

A.

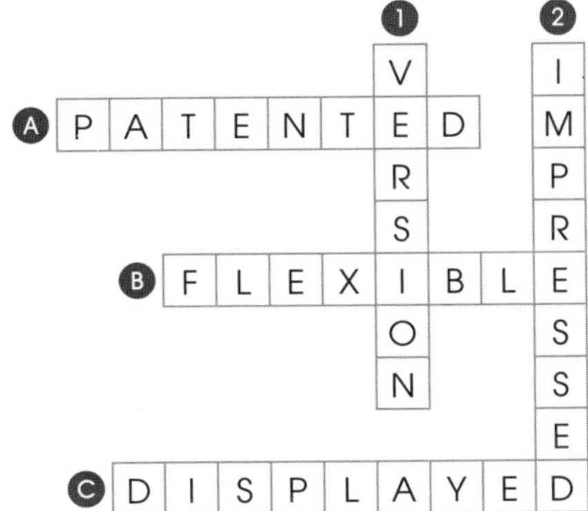

B. 1. 1893
2. Gideon Sundback produced the separable fastener with metal teeth.
3. 1923
4. Flexible coils for zippers were being made out of synthetic material.

C. 1. likes
2. need
3. has
4. were
5. Do

D. 1. ✔
2. ✔
3. takes
4. forgets
5. think

E. (Individual answers)

F. 2. A grade four student has invented this device.
3. They are very useful on rainy days.
4. This invitation card looks cute.
5. The speakers are going to demonstrate the invention.
6. Those experiments have given us some insights.

6 Third Culture Kids

A. 1. Beijing, China
2. Belgrade, Serbia
3. Nairobi, Kenya
4. 9
5. France

B. (Suggested answers)
1. The culture of origin is the culture of the parents. Emily's cultures of origin are French and American.
2. It means being familiar with many cultures. Emily is familiar with the French, Chinese, Serbian, and African cultures.

C. (Individual answers)

D. 1. she
2. It
3. He
4. They
5. I ; she ; you
6. We

E. 1. her
2. They
3. He
4. It
5. We
6. him
7. he
8. us

ISBN: 978-1-897164-32-7

F. 1. She was born in France.
2. He speaks to them in English.
3. They walk it to the park every day.
4. It is not widely spoken in France.

7 Deborah Ellis: Writing Books that Help Children

A. 1. C
2. E
3. B
4. A
5. D

B. 2 ; 3 ; 5 ; 4 ; 1 ; 6

C. (Individual answer)

D. 1. his
2. our ; yours
3. your
4. my ; hers
5. My ; its
6. their ; ours
7. their

E. 1. ✔
2. their
3. mine
4. ✔
5. her
6. ✔

F. 1. Is this kite yours?
2. These toys are theirs.
3. That is her hat.
4. This desk will be yours.
5. Will this be our hamster?

8 A Letter from the School Nurse

A.

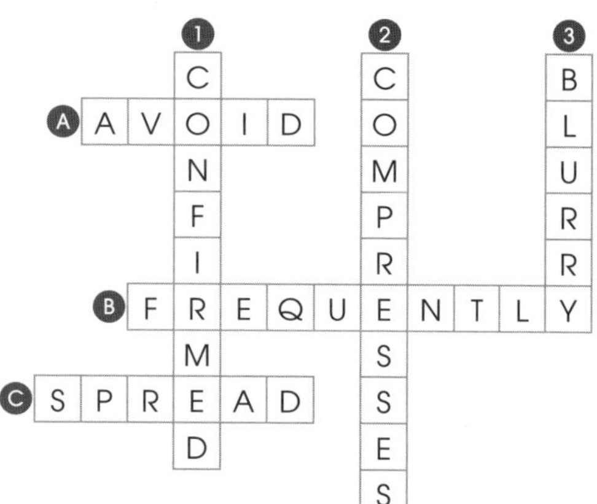

B. 1. attention
2. infection
3. symptoms
4. viruses ; bacteria
5. contagious

C. 1. on
2. at
3. by
4. on
5. from
6. at
7. in
8. to
9. from

D. 1. with
2. at
3. on
4. from
5. for

E. 1. into
2. ✔
3. for
4. ✔
5. for
6. ✔
7. about
8. from

9 English

A. 1. Turkish
2. Chinese
3. Japanese
4. Spanish
5. Greek
6. German

B.

p	F	r	e	C	z	M	a	y	F	i	n	n	T	u	r	G
o	i	S	p	z	J	a	P	o	r	t	u	g	u	e	s	e
r	n	p	G	e	r	l	G	r	e	e	k	F	r	e	C	r
t	n	a	e	c	J	a	p	a	n	e	s	e	k	k	z	m
F	i	n	i	h	e	y	a	n	c	s	C	h	i	n	e	a
e	s	h	S	p	a	n	i	s	h	c	h	e	s	i	o	n
C	h	i	n	e	s	e	E	n	g	l	i	s	h	o	n	h

ISBN: 978-1-897164-32-7

C. 1. O 2. O
3. O 4. P
5. P 6. P
7. P 8. P
9. O

D. 1. have
2. is
3. is
4. speaks
5. talk
6. run
7. serves
8. brings
9. looks
10. seems

E. 1. Jack is interested in learning Korean.
2. He wants to buy a dictionary.
3. The children play word games at home.
4. Sandy always wins the game.

10 Thailand's Floating Lantern Festival

A. 1. D 2. A
3. B 4. E
5. C

B. 1. They celebrate Loy Krathong Festival on the night of the full moon in November.
2. It is lotus-shaped.
3. They put flowers, incense, and candles on their krathongs.
4. They believe the krathongs will carry away bad luck.
5. They sing and dance.
6. The krathongs are lighted with candles and there are firework displays on this day.

C. 1. ✔ 2.
3. 4. ✔
5. ✔ 6. ✔

D. 1. celebrated
2. threw
3. cost
4. carried
5. floated

E. 1. taught
2. gave
3. brought
4. showed
5. explained
6. were
7. picked
8. cut
9. rolled
10. said

F. (Individual writing)

11 Happy "Wet" New Year

A. 1. T 2. T
3. F 4. T
5. F 6. F

B. C

C. (Individual answer)

D. 1. will visit
2. shall see
3. will stay
4. will take
5. will enjoy
6. will send
7. will be

E. 1. will
2. spend
3. take
4. will
5. be
6. will
7. record

F. 1. will make my bed
2. I will eat fewer candies.
3. I will brush my teeth twice a day.
4. I will not make Mom angry.
5. I will go running once a week.
6. I will share my toys with Johnny.

G. (Individual writing)

ISBN: 978-1-897164-32-7

12 The Lost City of Atlantis

A.

		1		2					3		
		E		S					U		
		V		H					T		
		I		A	A	L	E	G	E	N	D
		D		R					N		
		E		D					S		
		N	B	S	T	U	N	N	I	N	G
		C							L		
C	C	E	N	T	U	R	I	E	S		

B. 1. It has lowlands and beaches at one end, but steep cliffs at the other end.
   2. (Suggested answer)
      There is evidence of an ancient town on Santorini.

C. 1. A   2. I
   3. T   4. A
   5. A   6. I
   7. T

D. Have you been to the new Greek restaurant? My parents took me there for dinner last night. It was the first time I had tried Greek food. Do you know what "Horta" is? It is boiled greens. It tastes good with lemon, vinegar, and oil. Would you like to try it?

E. (Suggested answers)
   1. Is there a volcano on the island?
   2. Did the volcano explode in the last decade?
   3. Can people find evidence of explosion?
   4. Donald will go to the beach this weekend.
   5. We can go boating on the lake.

F. (Individual writing)

13 The Snake Dens of Narcisse

A. 1. dens
   2. Manitoba
   3. limestone
   4. tunnels
   5. herpetologists
   6. three

B. 1. Narcisse is known to herpetologists all over the world.
   2. The garter snake is the only reptile that can survive the cold winter in Narcisse.
   3. Many snakes are killed.

C. 1. E   2. E
   3. I   4. I
   5. I   6. E
   7. I   8. E
   9. I

D. 1. Show me your ticket.
   2. Take off the jacket.
   3. Stop running.
   4. Wait for me at the exit.

E. (Individual writing)

14 Ogopogo

A. 1. green – skin
   2. horse-like – head
   3. snake-like – body
   4. Nessie – Loch Ness Monster
   5. N'ha-a-itk – Ogopogo
   6. British Columbia – Lake Okanagan

B. 1. F   2. T
   3. F   4. F
   5. T   6. T
   7. F   8. T

C. 1. C   2. C
   3. C   4. S
   5. C   6. S
   7. S

D. (Individual answers)

E. 1. we call it Ogopogo
   2. his sister chose to be Snow White
   3. Mom wants to go shopping
   4. we will watch it tonight

Review 1

A. 1. Toronto is the capital of Ontario.
   2. School starts in September.
   3. This is the picture of Sir John A. Macdonald.
   4. The club has a meeting every Monday.

B. 1. colder
   2. fewer
   3. smallest
   4. more expensive
   5. lovely
   6. most touching

ISBN: 978-1-897164-32-7

C.

	d	r	i	a	m	f	o	r	c	e	b	
d	d	i	s	f	s	i	g	i	a	i	a	d
a	i	n	v	i	t	e	l	s	n	g	y	r
g	i	g	g	n	a	n	e	e	s	i	d	e
g	d	a	y	d	r	e	a	m	w	g	e	r
l	r	c	e	l	t	a	v	e	e	g	a	m
e	d	i	s	a	p	p	e	a	r	l	n	e
	a	f	i	m	b	c	a	n	c	e	l	

1. force ; cancel ; find ; invite
2. disappear ; rise ; giggle ; daydream
3. leave ; answer ; ring ; start

D. 1. The little girl | opened the (door) to let her dog in.
2. Aunt May and Uncle Tom | bought a big birthday (cake) for me.
3. My sister and I | have borrowed some (books) from the library.
4. Dad | took a big, colourful (lollipop) out from the bag.
5. All members | will gather at the school entrance at eight.
6. The children | tossed the empty (cans) into the bin.

E. 1. does
2. is
3. ✔
4. wants
5. are
6. doesn't
7. ✔
8. stroll

F. 1. We are going to Wonderland this Sunday.
2. That bag over there is hers.
3. She gave some stickers to them.
4. Could you pass his picture to me?

G. 1. in
2. at
3. in
4. about
5. for
6. from
7. on
8. in
9. in

H. 1. told
2. have
3. like
4. found
5. went
6. is
7. has
8. are
9. learned
10. is
11. wanted
12. was
13. came
14. asked
15. printed
16. was
17. will show
18. am
19. will like
20. do

I. 1. S
2. C
3. C
4. C
5. S

J. 1. School starts at eight in the morning.
2. Did she give you a call last night?
3. Don't ever play on the road.
4. What a great surprise for everyone!

15 Cheese Rolling

A.

B. 1. The participants chase a seven-pound round of Double Gloucester Cheese down the hillside and try to catch it.
2. The winners will get the rounds of cheese they have tried to catch as prizes.
3. (Individual answer)

ISBN: 978-1-897164-32-7

C. This year, the Warwick Cheese Festival will take place from Friday, June 16 to Sunday, June 18. This annual event is the biggest cheese festival in North America, attracting tens of thousands of Canadians and visitors from all over the world. You can sample over 100 kinds of cheese made all over Quebec at the festival. Attendees are invited to vote for the People's Choice Prize of the year.

D. 1. Vincent shouted, "I shall return next year."
   2. Bridget Carlson, last year's winner, presented the prize to Jason.
   3. The participants have to chase a big, heavy round of cheese down the hillside.
   4. The slope, the stones, and the speed have caused some cases of injuries.
   5. Mr. Douglas, their team leader, explained to them why they had lost.
   6. Unfortunately, the contest was put off because of the nasty weather.

16 Meteorites and Craters

A. 1. O 2. F
   3. F 4. F
   5. O 6. F
   7. F

B. 1. damage
   2. streak
   3. diameter
   4. hit
   5. landed

C. 1. My dad is a great fan of "Star Wars".
   2. "Dragon Rider" is a must-read for you.
   3. Wendy asked, "Do dinosaurs have feathers?"
   4. Issac has read "Harry Potter and the Goblet of Fire" three times already.
   5. The magician said, "Count one to ten with me and then you will see."
   6. "All your performances were exceptionally good," the judge commented.
   7. He added, "Everyone deserves a big round of applause here."
   8. They sang "Dancing Queen" in the singing contest.

D. 1. C 2. C
   3. P 4. P
   5. P 6. C

E. 1. Candy's uncle is a professor at the University of Toronto.
   2. The children don't want to stop the game.
   3. They're going to be late.
   4. Mr. Green's farm is near Hudson Bay.
   5. Bryan's dog doesn't like this model dinosaur.

17 The Highest Tides on Earth

A. 1. range
   2. immense
   3. coastline ; shelf
   4. extend
   5. exposed
   6. cycle

B. Paragraph One:
   The Bay of Fundy has one of the most extreme tidal ranges in the world.
   Paragraph Two:
   The main reason for the immense tides in the Bay of Fundy is the shape of the coastline and the continental shelf which makes the sea floor shallower.
   Paragraph Three:
   Wolfville in Nova Scotia attracts people from all over the world to come to see the tide and migrating birds to feast on the animals exposed at low tide in summer.
   Paragraph Four:
   The high tide rushes in and then moves out. This repeats and forms a never-ending cycle.

C. 1. If
   2. but
   3. Also
   4. Although
   5. since
   6. or

D. 1. because I did not expect they would reach that high
   2. after the waves subsided
   3. but it is a long ride to get there
   4. if Dad takes us
   5. and he will record the tidal bores

ISBN: 978-1-897164-32-7

18 The Longest Train Ride

A. 1. London – England
   2. Berlin – Germany
   3. Moscow – Russia
   4. Beijing – China
   5. Warsaw – Poland
   6. Paris – France
   7. Ulaan-Baatar – Mongolia

B. 1. It is one of the longest regularly scheduled train rides in the world.
   2. The Channel Tunnel allows people to travel from England to France by train.
   3. a. Tarskaya
      b. Ulan Ude
      c. Tayshet

C. 1. kg
   2. Mrs.
   3. Rd.
   4. P.
   5. P.E.I.
   6. Co.
   7. Jul.
   8. Lt.

D. 1. Mt.
   2. CD
   3. Bldg.
   4. cm
   5. United States
   6. Junior
   7. Tuesday
   8. Limited

E. 1. there's
   2. don't
   3. shouldn't
   4. they'll
   5. we're
   6. you've
   7. didn't
   8. I'm
   9. won't
   10. that's

F. 1. We're / I'm
   2. That's
   3. There's
   4. won't
   5. Don't
   6. didn't

19 The Great Wall of China

A. 1. B
   2. A
   3. C
   4. C
   5. C

B. (Individual answer)

C. 1. insignificant ; in
   2. defrost ; de
   3. unwise ; un
   4. prepaid ; pre
   5. disappear ; dis

D. (Individual writing)

E.

	1											
	N								3			
	O								H			4
	T		2	A	P	R	O	V	I	N	C	E
	I		U						S			A
B	C	O	N	S	T	R	U	C	T			R
	E		I						O			L
		C	T	H	I	C	K		R			Y
			E						I			
			D	A	T	T	R	A	C	T		

F. (Individual writing)

20 Tulipomania

A. 1.
   2. ✔
   3.
   4. ✔
   5. ✔
   6.
   7.
   8. ✔

ISBN: 978-1-897164-32-7

B. (Suggested answers)
1. One single tulip could be sold for 6000 florins, two horses, and a coach.
2. If the price of a tulip bulb cost 50 florins on Monday, it might cost 100 florins by Wednesday.
3. If people did not have money, they traded their jewellery, their land, and their animals to buy tulip bulbs.

C. This morning we got up early because we had to meet <u>Grandma</u> and <u>Grandpa</u> at the <u>airport</u>. They went to the Netherlands to celebrate <u>Grandma</u>'s 50th <u>birthday</u>. I saw <u>Grandma</u> coming out from the gate before <u>anybody</u> else. I was attracted by her big tulip <u>hairpin</u>. <u>Grandpa</u> said they had been <u>upgraded</u> to business class because the economy class had been <u>overbooked</u>. How lucky they were!

G	r	h	u	p	g	r	a	d	e	d	G	a
r	h	a	i	r	p	i	n	h	d	p	r	i
a	b	i	r	h	d	a	y	a	G	r	a	r
n	i	r	o	a	b	o	b	i	r	a	n	p
d	r	o	v	e	r	b	o	o	k	e	d	o
e	t	t	G	r	a	n	d	m	a	d	p	r
b	i	r	t	h	d	a	y	a	n	y	a	t

D.
1. less ; priceless
2. hopper ; grasshopper
3. storm ; thunderstorm
4. fare ; farewell
5. worth ; worthwhile
6. marsh ; marshmallows
7. table ; tablecloth

E.
1. farewell
2. marshmallows
3. tablecloth
4. grasshopper
5. thunderstorm
6. worthwhile
7. priceless

21 The Amazing Story of a Japanese Soldier

A. 3 ; 1 ; 4 ; 6 ; 2 ; 5 ; 7

B.

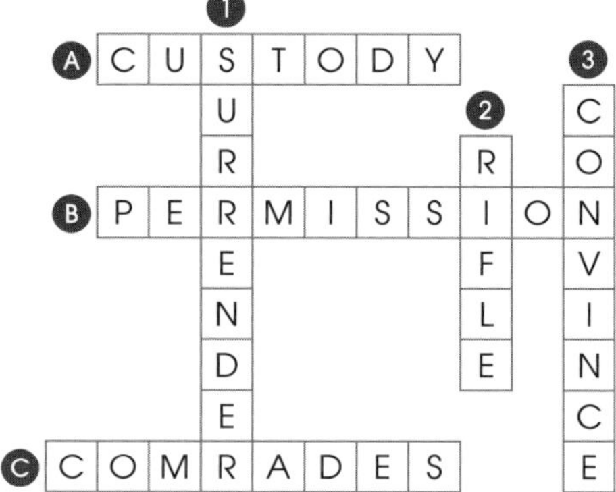

C.
1. antonyms
2. antonyms
3. synonyms
4. synonyms
5. synonyms

D.
1. pail
2. task
3. criticized
4. respected

E.
1. All
2. failed
3. destroyed
4. forbidden
5. calm
6. received

F.
1. big
2. started
3. popular
4. over
5. meaningful

ISBN: 978-1-897164-32-7

22 Ellen MacArthur

A. 1. A 2. B
3. A 4. B
5. A

B. Paragraph One:
Ellen MacArthur set the world record of sailing around the world in 71 days, 14 hours, 18 minutes and 33 seconds in 2005.
Paragraph Two:
Ellen was the fastest woman and youngest person to sail solo around the world in 2001.
Paragraph Three:
Ellen was lonely and had to fix problems all by herself during the trip.
Paragraph Four:
Ellen will continue her goal of breaking other records with the support of people around the world.

C.

d	e	c	i	m	z	o	c	b	h	o	w	r
a	b	r	e	a	k	e	r	r	a	f	e	a
i	c	u	m	b	e	d	m	a	d	e	i	s
s	d	i	f	e	m	k	e	w	a	e	p	o
u	g	s	e	i	b	l	t	e	y	m	c	t
t	t	e	a	y	h	o	u	r	s	t	e	e
f	b	i	t	e	a	m	o	z	e	m	a	a

D. 1. ceiling
2. peek
3. blue
4. night
5. roll

E. 1. It's
2. waste
3. advice
4. sight
5. loose
6. course
7. except
8. Whose
9. Maybe

23 A Mystery

A. 1. D 2. B
3. E 4. A
5. C

B. 1. Ten people had gone missing when the Mary Celeste was found.
2. a. There was half-eaten food on the table.
b. The crew left all their clothing behind.
c. Their boots were beside their beds.
3. a. The Mary Celeste left New York to sail to Italy.
b. Captain Briggs made the last entry in the captain's journal.
c. The captain of another ship found the Mary Celeste floating in the middle of the Atlantic Ocean.

C. (Individual writing)

D. 1. When / Why
2. Where
3. What
4. Who
5. How
6. Whom / Why
7. Why
8. Whose

E. (Individual writing)

24 Inukshuk

A. 1. Nunavut
2. directions
3. hunters
4. size / shape ; shape / size
5. balance
6. forbidden
7. harmony / cooperation ; cooperation / harmony
8. centuries

B. (In any order)
1. to warn others of nearby dangers
2. to mark a place of respect
3. to show travellers directions
4. to tell hunters the location of caribou herds
5. to spook caribou causing them to run to an area where hunters lie in wait

ISBN: 978-1-897164-32-7

C. 1. a. Among
b. between
2. a. lie
b. lay
3. a. rise
b. raising
4. a. bring
b. take
5. a. good
b. well
6. a. number
b. amount

25 Our Wonderful Rainforests

A. 1. the forest floor ; C
2. the understorey ; A
3. the canopy layer ; D
4. the emergent layer ; B

B. 1. The dense growth of trees there make the oxygen that we breathe with our lungs.
2. Heat and small insects break down the dead leaves and animals on the ground.
3. They want to reach the sunlight.

C. 1. A
2. A

D. (Individual writing)

26 Our Window Box Herb Garden

A. (Colour rosemary, basil, mint, and dill.)
1. dill
2. mint
3. rosemary
4. basil

B. C ; E ; B ; D ; A

C. (Individual writing)

D. (Individual writing)

27 Our Summer at the Farm

A. 1. F 2. T
3. T 4. F
5. T 6. F
7. T

B. (Suggested answers)
1. They planted different kinds of vegetables.
2. They hoed their vegetable garden.
3. They made salads and egg sandwiches with the onions they had grown.
4. They picked the potatoes.

C. (Individual answers)

D. 1. badly ; desperately
2. almost ; nearly
3. cheerily ; happily
4. really ; truly

E. (Individual answers)

F. (Individual writing)

28 The World Is Ours

A.

B. (Individual writing)

C. 1. conquer
2. dead
3. plan
4. sorry
5. poppy
6. dim

D. (Individual writing)

E. (Individual writing)

F. (Individual writing)

ISBN: 978-1-897164-32-7

Review 2

A. 1. They'll invite Dr. Hogan to the special event held next Sunday.
2. Have you seen the musical "Beauty and the Beast" before?
3. Edwin, our team leader, reminded us, "Don't forget to take a compass, a map, and enough water with you."
4. Lester's sister speaks English, French, Spanish, and Japanese.
5. The banner with the big, bright words "Come and Join Us!" has been put up since June.

B. 1. before
2. if
3. since
4. because
5. but

C. 1. lay ; lie
2. Rise ; Raise
3. amount ; number
4. lose ; loose
5. advise ; advice
6. sight ; site

D. 1. Mr. Adams doesn't live on Maple Ave.
2. Let's do a project on Mt. Alberta.
3. We're going to P.E.I. in Aug.
4. The ribbon is 60 cm long.

E. (In any order)
1. housefly
2. zookeeper
3. holdback
4. household
5. greenhouse
6. goalpost
7. backpack
8. backstage
9. housekeeper
10. goalkeeper

F. 1. indirect
2. directions
3. redirect
4. directly
5. misdirect
6. director

G. 1. What is the largest mammal on Earth?
2. Where can blue whales be found?
3. What colour is a blue whale?
4. How many blue whales are there in the world?
5. Why is the blue whale an endangered species?

H.

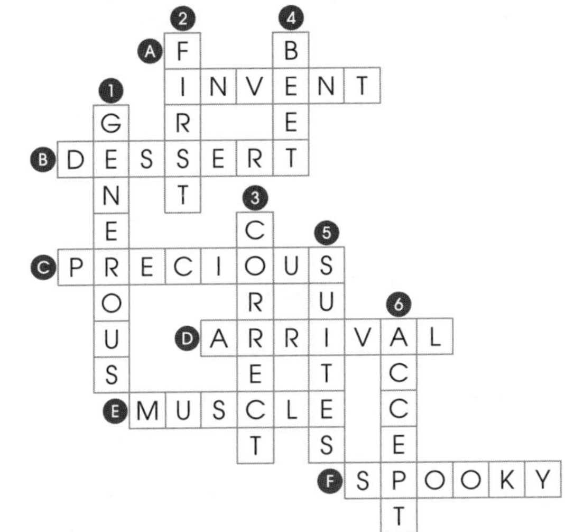

I. (Individual writing)

J. (Individual writing)

ISBN: 978-1-897164-32-7

1 The Feudal System

A. 1. knight ; king   2. vassal
   3. oath ; obey   4. manor
   5. serf ; land ; grow

B. king
   lords and nobles
   knights
   peasants and serfs

C. (Individual writing)

2 Medieval Castles

A. 1. bailey   2. curtain
   3. turret   4. moat
   5. loophole   6. gatehouse
   7. drawbridge

B. 1. portcullis   2. garderobe
   3. dungeon   4. solar

3 Knights (1)

A. 1.

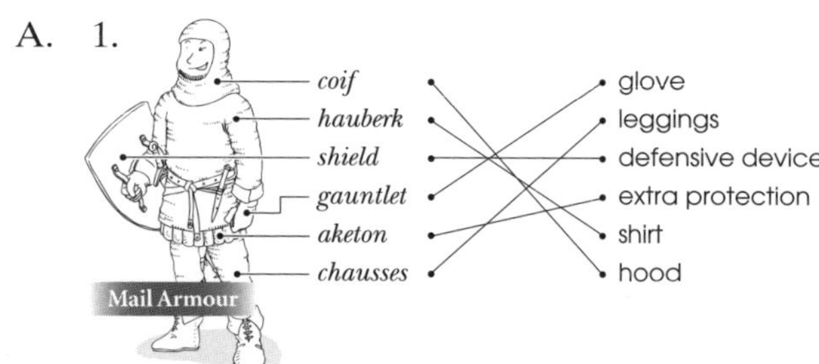

2.

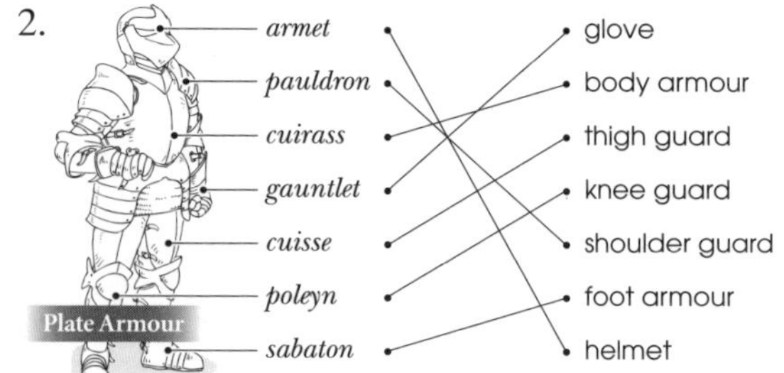

B. 1. noble   2. training
   3. horse   4. swords
   5. battlefield   6. knighthood
   7. clean   8. armour
   9. ceremony   10. vows
   11. knight   12. lord

4 Knights (2)

A. 1. dagger   2. sword
   3. club   4. flail
   5. mace   6. lance
   7. battle-axe   8. crossbow
   9. spiked club   10. pollaxe
   11. bow and arrow

B.

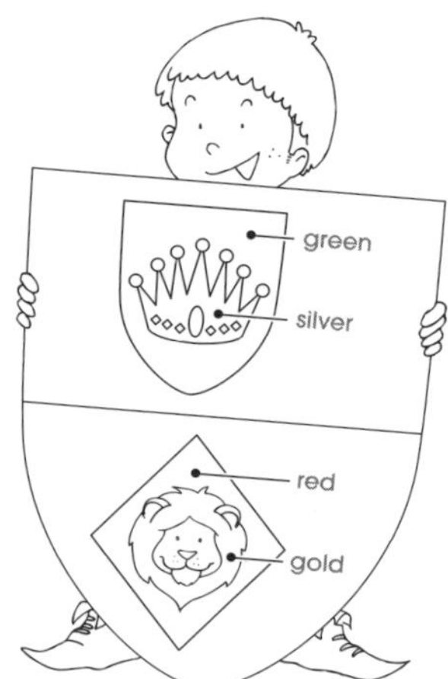

C. (Individual drawing and colouring)

5 Medieval Life

A. 1. Fall   2. Summer
   3. Spring   4. Winter

B. 1. F   2. F
   3. T   4. T
   5. F   6. T

C. 1. scythe   2. harrow
   3. flail   4. sickle

6 Medieval Food

A. 1.

Year	Field A	Field B	Field C
1200	peas in spring	wheat in fall	empty
1201	empty	peas in spring	wheat in fall
1202	wheat in fall	empty	peas in spring

ISBN: 978-1-897164-32-7

2. spring
3. fall
4. three

B. a. Peasant b. Lord

C. 1. cow's milk ; water
2. crushed nuts ; water

7 Medieval Trade Guilds

A. 1. tailor ; spinster ; shearman
2. mason ; carpenter ; tiler
3. butcher ; brewer ; baker

B. 1. blacksmith
2. scribe
3. lawyer

C.

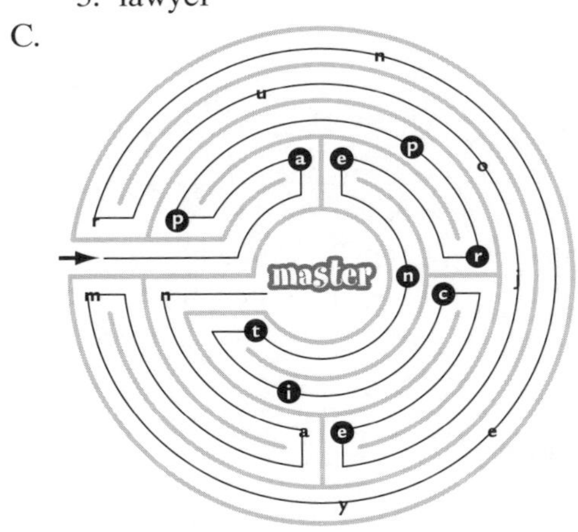

apprentice ; journeyman

8 Medieval Buildings

A. 1.

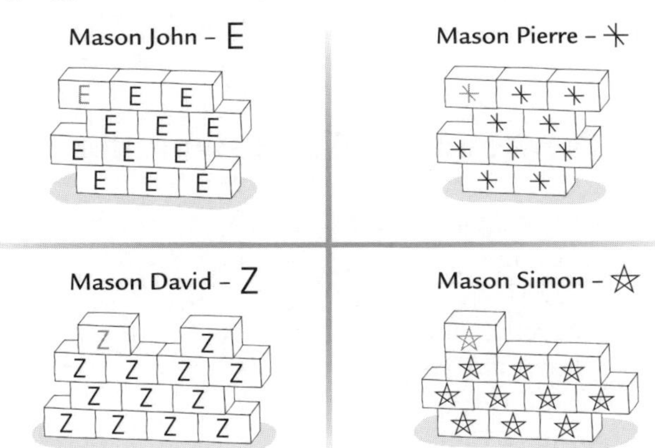

2.

Mason	John	Pierre	David	Simon
Brick Count	卌 卌 ||	卌 卌	卌 卌 |||	卌 卌 |

3. Mason David

B.

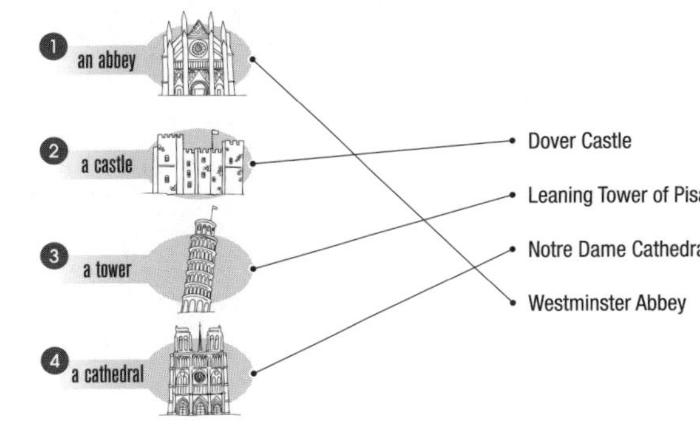

C.

9 Medieval Technology

A. 1. paper 2. mirror
3. compass 4. windmill
5. spectacles 6. wheelbarrow
7. cannon 8. printing press
9. magnet

B. 1. spectacles 2. windmill
3. paper 4. printing press
5. compass 6. mirror
7. magnet 8. wheelbarrow

10 Another Look at the Medieval Times

A. Christianity
Roman
✔
✔
China ; ✔
Black ; ✔
printing ; ✔
Canada
millennium

ISBN: 978-1-897164-32-7

B.

a	n	a	c	l	u	e	t	r	l	e	m	i	n	s	t
b	h	c	l	h	e	j	u	g	g	e	l	u	t	e	a
a	a	l	o	l	j	u	g	g	l	e	r	l	t	u	c
c	r	o	w	o	c	h	a	c	r	o	b	a	t	t	r
d	p	w	n	w	n	h	a	n	w	l	c	t	e	b	o
u	h	u	r	d	y	-	g	u	r	d	y	u	l	e	a
c	u	r	w	n	a	m	i	n	s	t	r	e	l	o	t

C.

Game:

Writing Tool:

Weapon:

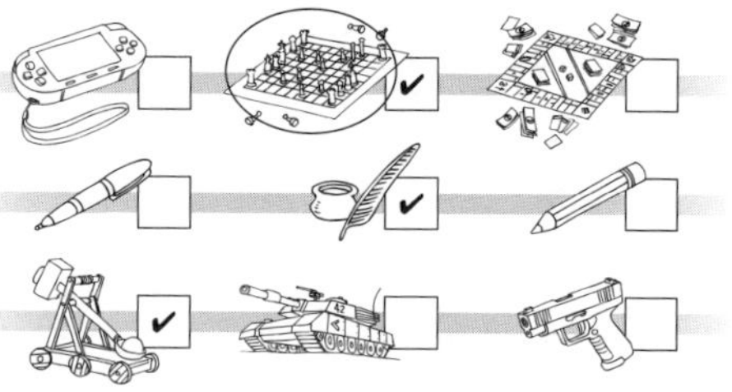

C.

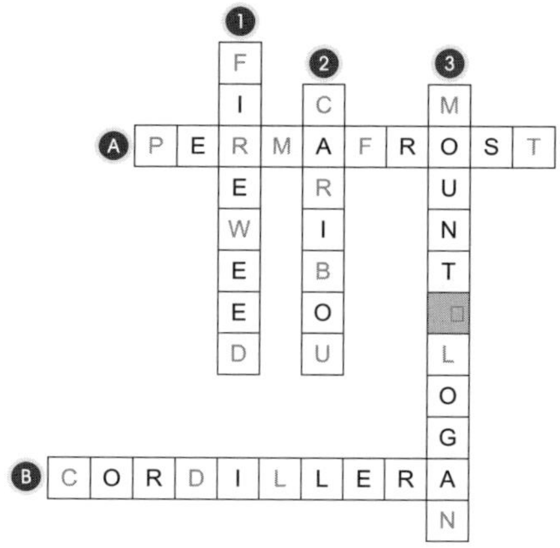

11 Canada

A. 1. Canadian Shield
Appalachians
Hudson Bay Lowlands
Arctic Lands
Great Lakes-St. Lawrence Lowlands
Interior Plains
Cordillera
2. AB ; SK ; MB ; ON ; QC ; NL ; NT ; NU
3. Great Lakes-St. Lawrence Lowlands
4. Cordillera
5. Arctic Lands
6. Appalachians
7. Interior Plains

B. a. Arctic Lands
b. Interior Plains
c. Cordillera
d. Canadian Shield

12 Yukon

A. (Colour the coat of arms accordingly)
1. gold ; husky
2. Yukon River
3. mountains ; mineral
4. explorers ; fur trade

B. N: Beaufort Sea
S: British Columbia
E: Northwest Territories
W: Alaska

13 The Northwest Territories

A. Arctic Lands
Interior Plains
Cordillera
Canadian Shield

B. (Colour the coat of arms accordingly)
Arctic Lands ; Canadian Shield

C. 1. homeland 2. frontier
3. frontier 4. homeland

14 Nunavut

A. 1. 1999 2. 30 000
3. Inuit 4. 20%
5. communities 6. purple saxifrage
7. Mt. Barbeau 8. 24

B. 1. E 2. D
3. A 4. B
5. C 6. F
7. H 8. G

15 Newfoundland and Labrador

A. 1. Beothuk 2. elk
3. Latin 4. kingdom
5. 1637

B. Churchill Falls
Churchill River
Grand Bank
Strait of Belle Isle
Port Hope Simpson
Knights Island
Long Range Mountains

ISBN: 978-1-897164-32-7

16 Prince Edward Island

A. 1. Fishing 2. Tourism
3. Agriculture 4. Manufacturing
5. Fishing 6. Agriculture
7. Tourism 8. Agriculture
9. Manufacturing

B. 1. Lawrence 2. province
3. red 4. Charlottetown
5. *Gables*

C.

17 Nova Scotia

A.

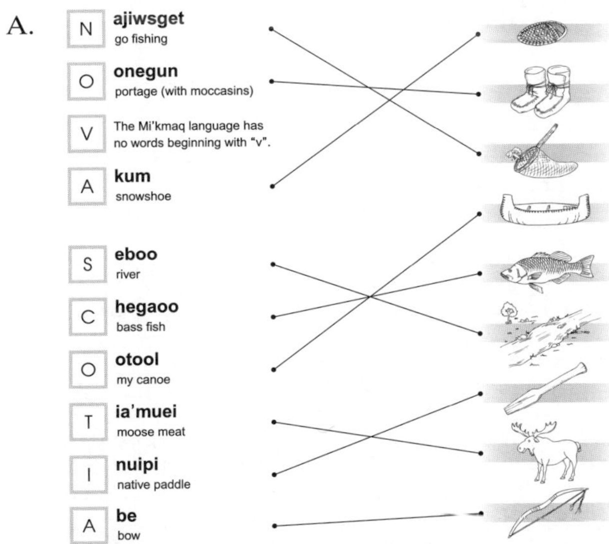

B. below ; above ; Scottish ; New Scotland

C. 1 ; 3 ; 4 ; 5 ; 2

18 New Brunswick

A.

SPEM REDUXIT

1. shipping 2. France
3. resource 4. flower

B. 1. salmon 2. lobsters
3. potatoes 4. wood

C. 1. Fredericton
2. Regina
3. Winnipeg ; Edmonton ; Regina
4. Fredericton
5. close to the sea

19 Quebec

A.

blue blue
blue blue

France ; white ; blue ; purity

B. 1. France 2. England
3. Canada 4. I remember

C. 1. capital ; city walls
2. Canadian Shield ; fertile ; agriculture

D. 1. French
2. other ; English

20 Ontario

A. 1. B
2. three
3. the Cross of St. George
4. the motto

ISBN: 978-1-897164-32-7

B.

1. Lake Huron
2. Lake Erie
3. Lake Michigan
4. the St. Lawrence River
5. Lake Ontario
6. Lake Superior

C. (Individual ranking)
1. R 2. U
3. R 4. R
5. U

21 Manitoba

A. 1. Brandon 2. Lake Winnipeg
3. Churchill 4. the Red River
5. Canadian Shield: Churchill River ; Southern Indian Lake ; Thompson
Interior Plains: Cedar Lake ; Lake Winnipeg ; Brandon ; Winnipeg ; Red River
Hudson Bay Lowlands: Churchill ; Churchill River

B. 1. Brandon ; rural
2. Winnipeg ; urban
3. Churchill ; rural
4. Thompson ; rural

C.

22 Saskatchewan

A. 1. C1 ; D2 ; D1 ; D2 ; D2 ; A2 ; B2 ; B1
2. A1: Lake Athabasca ; Cree Lake
C1: the Saskatchewan River
D1: Lake Diefenbaker
A2: Reindeer Lake
C2: the Saskatchewan River

B. 1. wheat
2. rye
3. canola
4. flax
5. oats
6. barley

C.

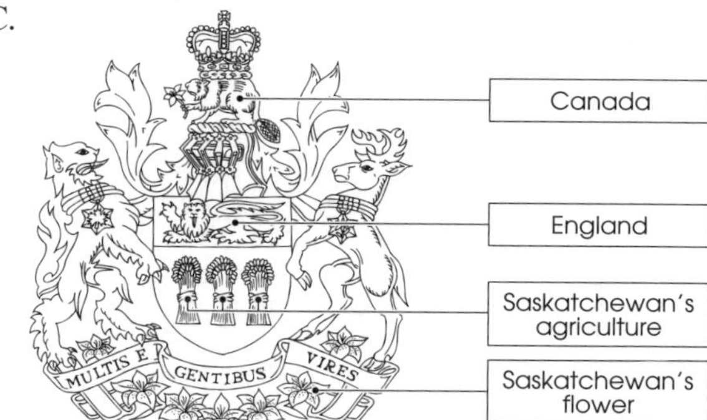

23 Alberta

A. Canadian Shield ; lakes ; ancient rock
Interior Plains ; flat ; fertile
Cordillera ; mountains

B. D ; A ; C ; B

C. plant ; ground ; plastics ; fuel

p	e	t	r	d	r	i	l	l	i	n	g	i	s	a	g
p	e	p	o	l	l	u	t	a	n	t	s	z	r	p	a
e	n		p	o	l	l	u	t	e	f	u	e	e	i	
t	o	i	l		s	a	n	d	s	p	e	r	f	p	
r	e		f	i	u	l	f	u	e	i	y	e	i	e	
o	r	w	a	e	n	e	r	g	y	p	r	t	n	u	
l	o	e	s	l	g	g	a	s	f	e	o	n	e	a	
e	i	l	s	i	n	i	p	e	r	l	r	e	r		
u	s	l	i	g	p	o	w	e	l	i	g	g	y		
m	l	r	l	g	a	s	o	l	i	n	e	e			
d	f	o	s	s	i	l		f	u	e	l	s			

ISBN: 978-1-897164-32-7

24 British Columbia

A. 1. Mackenzie
 2. Victoria
 3. Vancouver
 4. Comox
 5. Salmon Arm
 6. Barkerville

B. A ; D ; E
 B ; C ; F

C. 1. British 2. sun
 3. crowns 4. dogwood flowers

Review

A.

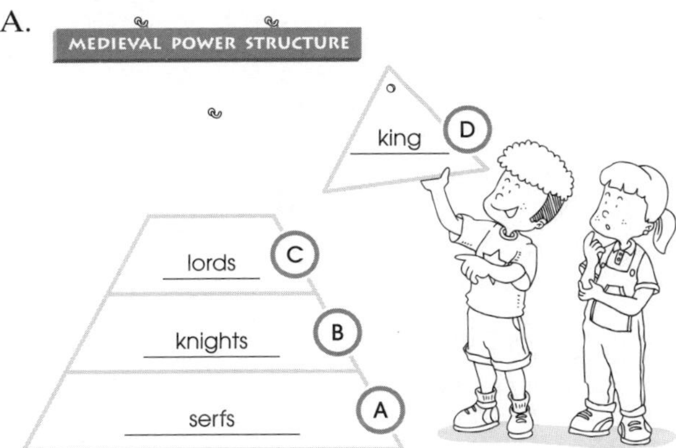

B.

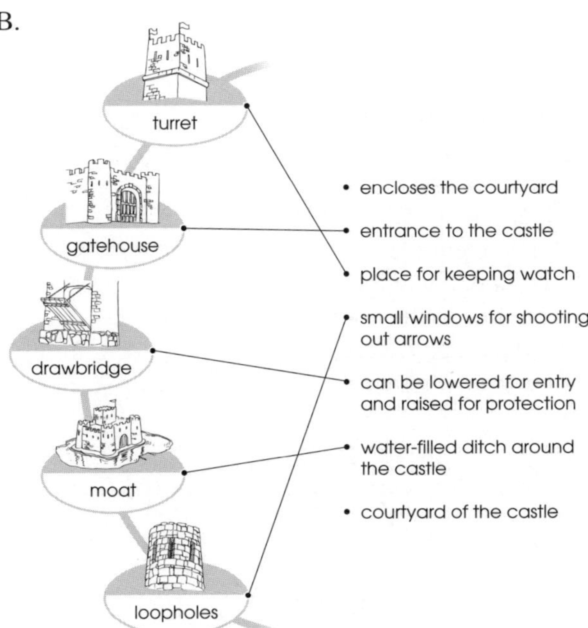

C. 1. B
 2. A
 3. B
 4. C
 5. tailor ; baker ; mason

D. flails ; flour ; fall ; grapes ; pigs ; nuts

E. 1. Yukon ; gold
 2. Northwest Territories ; gold

F. 1. BC ; AB
 2. SK ; AB
 3. PEI ; NB ; NS
 4. PEI ; NB ; NS
 5. SK ; AB
 6. NB

G. 1. Canadian Shield
 2. Arctic Lands
 3. Cordillera
 4. Hudson Bay Lowlands
 5. Great Lakes-St. Lawrence Lowlands
 6. Forests ; Canadian Shield
 7. fertile ; Quebec
 8. Alberta ; Western

ISBN: 978-1-897164-32-7

1 Habitats

A.
1. wetlands
2. carpet
3. underground
4. desert
5. savanna
6. cave

B.

	Polar Bear	Black Bear
Ice floes	✔	
Chilly water	✔	
Forest		✔
Shrubs and berries		✔
Fresh fish and seal meat	✔	
Fish streams		✔
Large space to roam	✔	✔

C.
1. estuary
2. desert
3. cave
4. rotting log
5. rainforest
6. prairie
7. woodland

2 Producers and Consumers

A. Producers: C, D, F
Consumers: A, B, E
(Individual drawings)

B. Herbivore
beaver: roots
horse: grass
Carnivore
wolf: hares
seal: squid
Omnivore
human: tomatoes
hen: worms

C. Colour the Tyrannosaurus Rex.

3 Food Chains

A. 1. 
2. 
3.
4.

B.
1. sun
2. producer
3. "provides food for"
4. consumers

C.

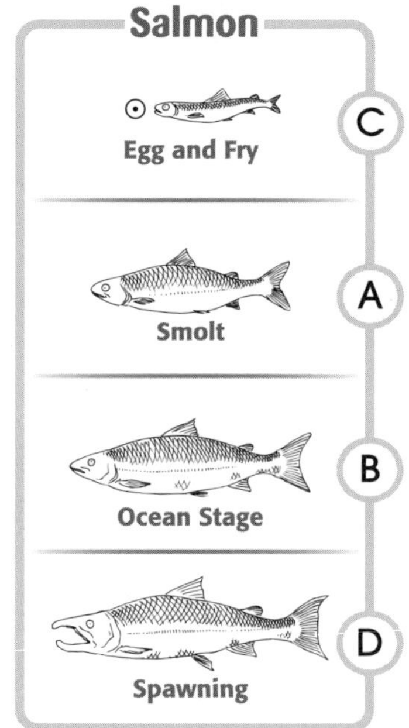

4 Adaptations

A. defence ; A, E
feeding ; B, D
movement ; C

B. 1st line: behavioural
2nd line: behavioural
3rd line: physical
4th line: physical

C.

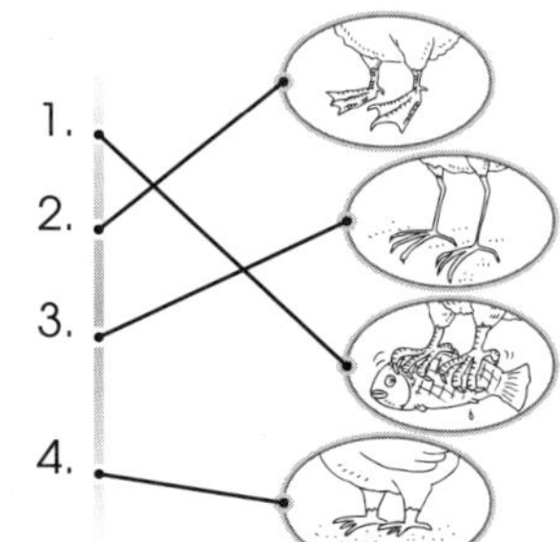

ISBN: 978-1-897164-32-7

5 Habitat Destruction

A. 1. Clothing ; cross out "plastic"
   2. Energy ; cross out "cup"
   3. Medicine ; cross out "jello"
   4. Building Material ; cross out "wheat"
   5. Recreation ; cross out "cleaning"
   6. Food ; cross out "pencil"

B. E ; C ; F ; B ; A ; D

C. From least at risk to most at risk:
Species of special concern
Threatened species
Endangered species
Extirpated species

6 The Arctic

A. 1. tundra
   2. biome
   3. permafrost
   4. community
   5. ecological niche
   6. ecosystem

B.

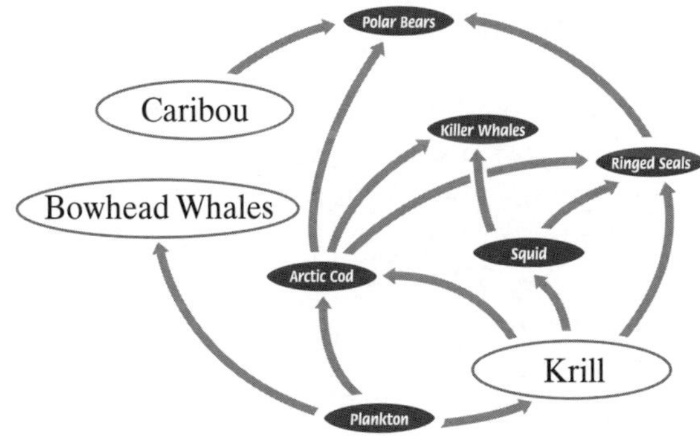

1. Arctic cod and squid
2. Arctic cod, krill, and bowhead whale

C.

1.
2.
3.
4.

7 Light

A. 1. Moon: natural ; light reflector
   Cat: natural ; light reflector
   Flashlight: artificial ; light producer
   Lightning: natural ; light producer
   2. Sun: natural ; light producer
   Water: natural ; light reflector
   Candle: artificial ; light producer
   Sunglasses: artificial ; light reflector

B.

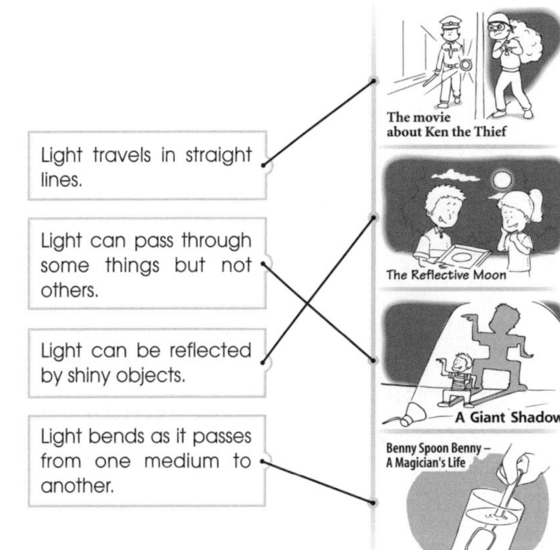

8 Light – Reflection and Refraction

A.

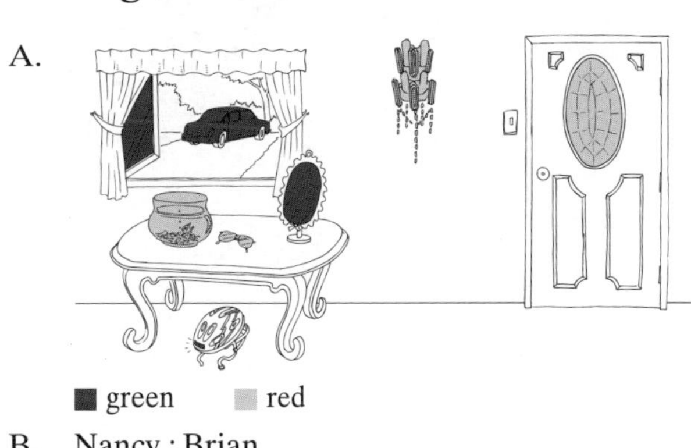

■ green ■ red

B. Nancy ; Brian

C.

1. kaleidoscope
2. telescope
3. microscope

ISBN: 978-1-897164-32-7

Experiment (Individual observation)

9 Light – Transparency

A. 1-3. (Suggested answers for the examples)
  1. opaque ; Example: rock
  2. transparent ; Example: fish bowl
  3. translucent ; Example: paper

B.

10 Light and Colour

A.

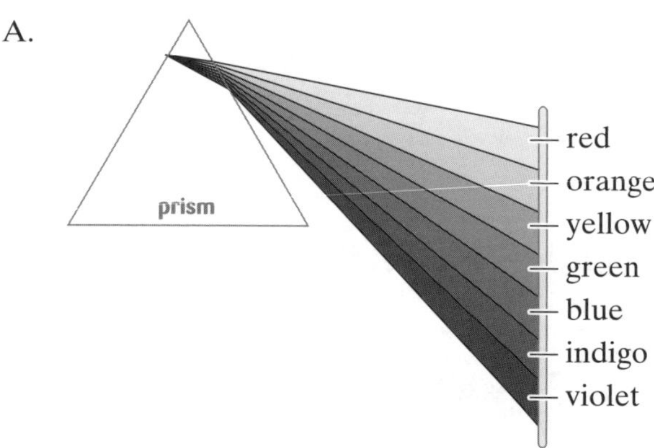

B. 1. absorbs
  2. absorbs
  3. reflects

C. orange
red
yellow
purple
green
red
blue
blue
yellow

red + yellow = orange
red + blue = purple
yellow + blue = green

11 Sound

A. 1. Saint Bernard Dog ; low
  2. Fruit Bat ; high
  3. African Elephant ; high
  4. Bottle-nosed Dolphin ; high
  5. Humpback Whale ; low

B. 1. outer ear
  2. ear drum
  3. middle ear
  4. hammer
  5. anvil
  6. stirrup
  7. inner ear
  8. cochlea
  9. nerves

12 More about Sound

A. 1. smooth and shiny ; reflect sound
  2. rough ; absorb sound
  3. rough ; absorb sound
  4. smooth and shiny ; reflect sound
  5. rough ; absorb sound

B. 1. D
  2. A
  3. F
  4. B
  5. C
  6. E

13 Special Wheels – Gears and Pulleys

A. 1. gears
  2.
  3. gears
  4. pulleys
  5.
  6. pulleys
  7. pulleys

ISBN: 978-1-897164-32-7

B. 1. ; faster than

2.  ; as fast as

3. 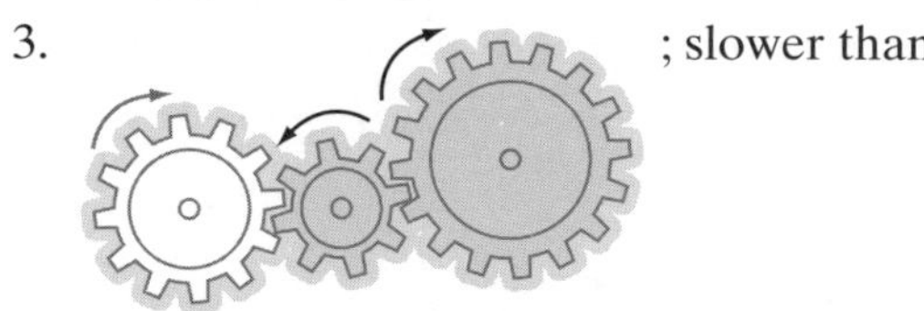 ; slower than

C. The pulleys are helping the mouse by allowing him to use his own weight to lift the heavy crate off the ground.

14 Minerals

A. 1. diamond / lead
2. lead / diamond
3. non-living
4. inorganic
5-8. (Order may vary.)
5. shapes
6. colours
7. heaviness
8. hardness
9. mineralogists
10. Minerals
11. food / tools
12. tools / food

B. (Colour the minerals as specified.)
1. diamond
2. topaz
3. emerald
4. sapphire
5. ruby

C.

2-mineral rock: DIABASE
single-mineral rock: QUARTZ
3-mineral rock: GRANITE

15 More about Minerals

A. colour: B
hardness: F
specific gravity: C
lustre: D
streak: A
transparency: E

B. 1.

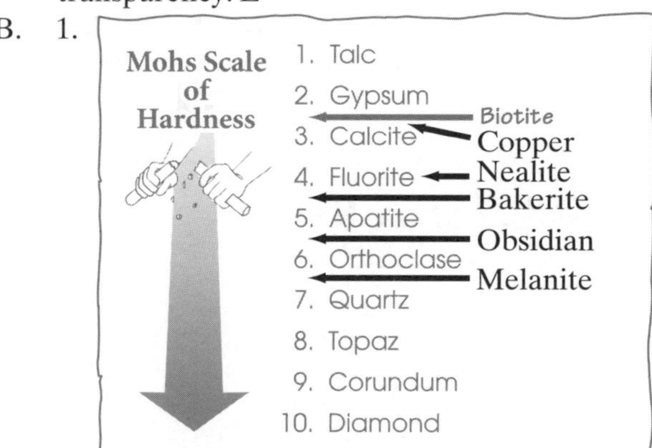

2. (Suggested answers)
a. obsidian, melanite
b. topaz, corundum
c. talc, gypsum
d. apatite, orthoclase

16 Rocks

A. 1. clay
2. mountain
3. pebbles
4. rock
5. sand
6. silt
7. bedrock
8. boulder

B. 1. This rock is from outer space.
2. When it first flows above ground, this is liquid rock.
3. Unlike most other rocks, this is made from plant matter.

C. 1. D 2. E
3. C 4. H
5. F 6. A
7. G 8. B

ISBN: 978-1-897164-32-7

17 Igneous Rocks

A. Intrusive ; in
Extrusive ; above

B. Instrusive: diabase, granite
Extrusive: obsidian, basalt

C. Colour the words:
basalt ; obsidian ; magma ; granite ; lava ; intrusive ; extrusive ; volcano ; crystals ; molten ; diabase

Experiment: (Individual observation)

18 Sedimentary Rocks

A.

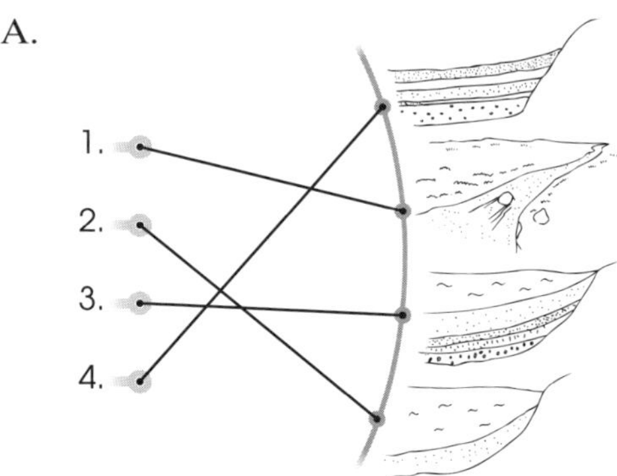

B. 1. sand
2. mud
3. shells
4. river pebbles

C. 1. ; conglomerate
2. ; shale
3. ; rock salt
4. ; limestone

19 Metamorphic Rocks

A. 1.

2.

B. 1. ; granite
2. ; gneiss

C. 1. quartzite
2. slate
3. gneiss
4. marble

D. 1. igneous rocks
2. sedimentary rocks ; igneous rocks
3. sedimentary rocks

20 How We Use Rocks and Minerals

A.

B. (Individual drawing)

C. Hematite – red
Malachite – green
Azurite – blue
Charcoal – black

ISBN: 978-1-897164-32-7

21 Erosion

A. mountain ; rock ; sand ; silt

B. 1. by moving water ; smooth river rock
   2. by wind ; sand blasting cliff
   3. by ice ; deep valley

C.

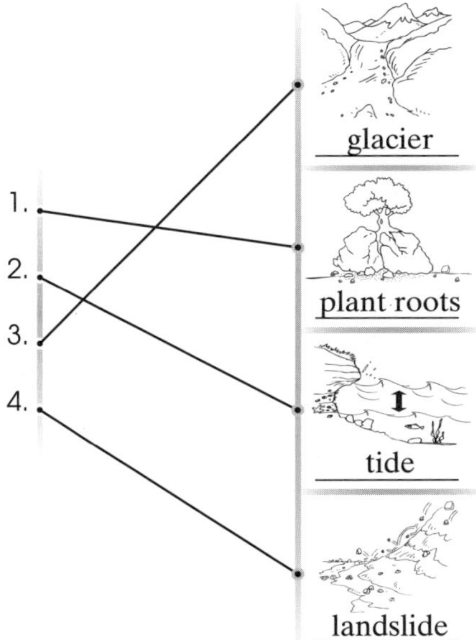

22 Fossils

A. Ammonite fossil formation: A ; B ; D ; C
   Leaf imprint fossil formation: R ; P ; Q ; S

B. 1. tracks ; egg ; dung ; bones ; teeth ; nest
   2. a. tracks, bones
      b. nest, bones
      c. dung, teeth
      d. dung, teeth
      e. tracks, bones
      f. egg, nest

23 More about Fossils

A. 1. sedimentary rocks
   2. tree resin
   3. tar pits
   4. Rocky Mountains
   5. sand

B.

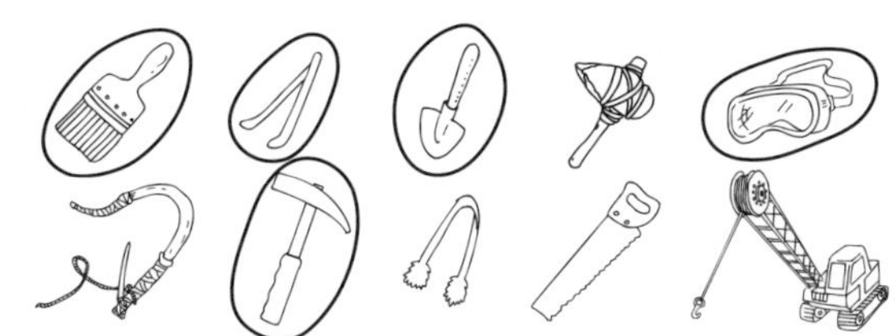

C. 1. skull
   2. back vertebrae
   3. rib
   4. tail vertebrae
   5. leg bone

24 Caves

A. 1. speleothems
   2. calcite
   3. stalactite
   4. stalagmite
   5. limestone
   6. column

B. 1. stalactite
   2. column
   3. stalagmite

Review

A. 1. Black bear – omnivore
      Food: berries, mice
      Habitat: forest
   2. Arctic hare – herbivore
      Food: grasses, shoots
      Habitat: tundra
   3. Shark – carnivore
      Food: seals, dolphins
      Habitat: ocean

B.

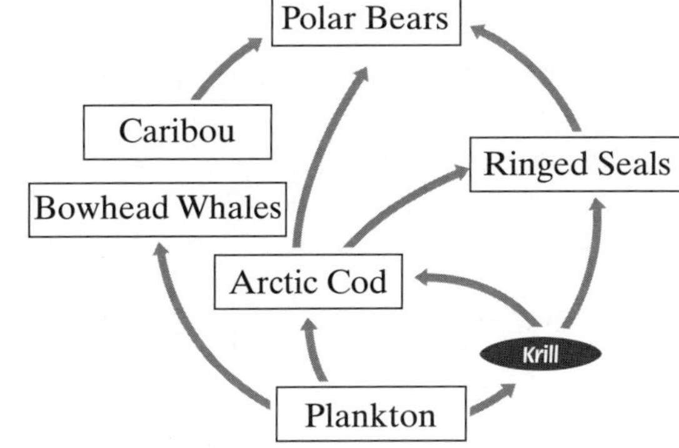

ISBN: 978-1-897164-32-7

C. 1. straight
2. some
3. shiny
4. bends

D. 1. ; transparent

2. ; opaque

3. ; translucent

E. 1. outer ear
2. middle ear
3. inner ear
A: earflap
B: eardrum
C: hammer, anvil, and stirrup
D: cochlea
E: nerves

F. 1. absorbs sound
2. reflects sound
3. reflects sound

G. 1.

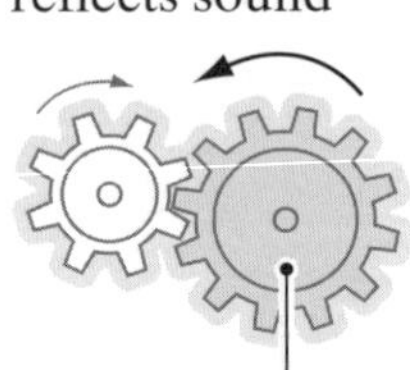

slower

2.

faster

H. Speech:
inorganic ; heaviness, colours, hardness, shapes ; diamond, salt
Mohs Scale of Hardness:
2. Gypsum
7. Quartz
8. Topaz
10. Diamond

I.

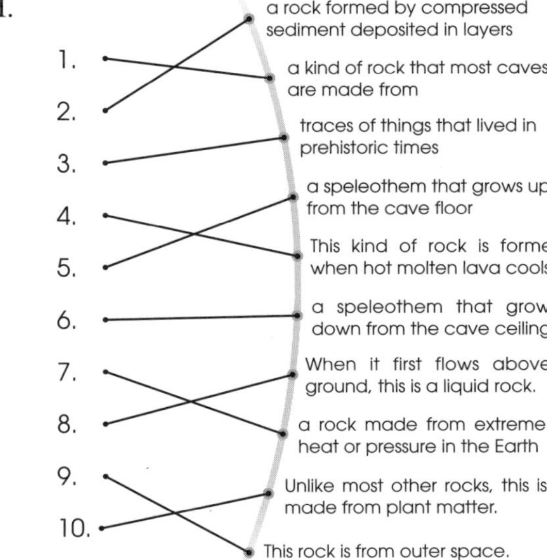
1.
2.
3.
4.
5.
6.
7.
8.
9.
10.
a rock formed by compressed sediment deposited in layers
a kind of rock that most caves are made from
traces of things that lived in prehistoric times
a speleothem that grows up from the cave floor
This kind of rock is formed when hot molten lava cools.
a speleothem that grows down from the cave ceiling
When it first flows above ground, this is a liquid rock.
a rock made from extreme heat or pressure in the Earth
Unlike most other rocks, this is made from plant matter.
This rock is from outer space.

J. 1. C
2. B
3. B
4. C
5. A

ISBN: 978-1-897164-32-7